THE ARABS

Published under the Auspices of the
Near Eastern Center
University of California, Los Angeles

THE ARABS

Their History, Culture and Place in the Modern World

ARNOLD HOTTINGER

UNIVERSITY OF CALIFORNIA PRESS

Berkeley and Los Angeles 1963

*For the English-language edition,
the original book has been revised and brought up to date*

PUBLISHED IN THE UNITED STATES OF AMERICA
BY THE UNIVERSITY OF CALIFORNIA PRESS
BERKELEY AND LOS ANGELES, CALIFORNIA
PUBLISHED IN GREAT BRITAIN BY THAMES AND HUDSON LTD LONDON
FIRST PUBLISHED IN GERMAN UNDER THE TITLE
Die Araber: Werden, Wesen, Wandel und Krise des Arabertums
PRINTED IN GREAT BRITAIN

CONTENTS

LIST OF ILLUSTRATIONS

THE MIDDLE EAST

Scale 0   100   200   300   400 Miles

THE TRANSLITERATION OF ARABIC NAMES

The representation of Arabic names in Latin characters runs up against three main diffi-culties: *a*. The Arabic alphabet has more sounds and orthographic signs than the Latin alphabet; *b*. Arabic words and names have been adopted by certain European languages in fixed forms which originate from different systems of transliteration; *c*. Arabic proper names can be transcribed in their classical Arabic form which is grammatically correct but which is never so pronounced and is occasionally unknown, or according to the sound of their dialectic form which may vary from dialect to dialect.

Orientalists overcome this confusion by employing (various!) systems of transcription in which each sign of the Arabic script is represented by one or more Latin characters. Where these are lacking use is made of diacritical dots, strokes and combinations of letters. This procedure is indispensable for the specialist who cannot print in Arabic characters or who does not wish to do so. However, it confuses the layman and raises the cost of printing and correcting.

In this book the author tries to do without it. Thereby inconsistencies and intrinsic contradictions could not be avoided. In some instances, in order to preserve the written form familiar from the world press he has refrained from consistently transliterating the phonetics of Arabic. The forms used here are as follows:

j, th, y, z—as in English (James, thing, yes, zero)
kh—as ch in German Bach, but more guttural
dh—as the English voiced th (there)
gh—as a deep guttural r
q—as a deep guttural k
all other characters are to be read as in English.

The indication of a series of specifically Arabic consonants has been dispensed with (initial 'Ain, Hamza, emphatics), nor have long and short vowels been shown. Variations in the quality of short vowels: al-, el; Khaled, Khalid; Mohammed, Muhammed, Muham-mad, correspond to Arabic linguistic usage. The only excuse the author can put forward for his failure to be systematic is that this seems to be fitting in a world in which President Sham'ūn signs himself 'Chamoun' while President 'Abd un-Nāṣir appears in the West simply as 'Nasser'.

10

FOREWORD

THIS BOOK has developed from a preoccupation with Arab nationalism. Whoever wishes to understand Arab nationalism—just like the 'national beginnings' of other states which are today aspiring to liberate themselves from European domination or dependence—continually runs up against a funda mental question: 'What is the Arab nation in whose name Arab nationalism speaks?' In simpler words: 'Who are the Arabs?'

Whoever puts this question will turn first of all to the Arabs of today for an answer. He will be amazed how vague, indefinite, general and frequently unsatisfactory is the answer which Arab nationalists themselves are ready to give. He will learn that 'all whose mother tongue is Arabic and—according to the definition of many nationalists—who are themselves willing to admit that they are Arabs, are Arabs'. The reason for the additional qualification is that there are Jews, whose mother tongue is Arabic, whom one would exclude from Arab nationalism.

One will ask: 'Is community of language the only criterion of being an Arab?' The nationalists reply: 'Certainly not! Arabs have also a common history and a common culture.' But only very rarely does one come across an analysis of what the essence of this history and of this culture comprises. Indeed, there are 'Histories of the Arabs,' detailed and descriptive like Hitti's *History of the Arabs*, and penetrating, seeking for the meaning of events, like Bernard Lewis's exemplary book *The Arabs in History*. But these are history books which ask: 'What has happened in the course of hundreds and thousands of years in the territory of the peoples who today speak Arabic?' That is a different question from ours: 'Who *are* the Arabs?' Indeed, whoever asks what is the essence of Arabism will not be able to dispense with history. But he approaches it with his eyes turned in a different direction from that of pure historians, he is not so much interested by events for their own sake, he may not be satisfied with developments and historical facts. He must try to acquire from the facts and developments a comprehensive view, a survey, a picture: 'Who were the Arabs and what were they like?'

He must take pains to pick out again and again what is characteristic from the mass of what is purely factual. He will work with comparisons in order to be able to show what strikes him as typically Arabian in Arabs, what the others, the non-Arabs, lack and what the Arabs possess as their own.

He who asks about Arab nationality will consequently work with materials different from those of a pure historian, or he will manipulate his materials in a different manner. How an historical source was composed and what its author was thinking as he wrote it can often be of more interest to him than how far the events depicted actually took place as described. For him who asks who the Arabs are, all artistic manifestations are sources of the highest order along with historical documents. Works of art are pure expressions of substance in which the role of the elements of fact and accident is reduced to a minimum.

The first part of this book attempts to survey the history of the Arabs from their beginnings up to the present time and in this the question 'Who were the Arabs?' will always indicate the road to be followed. This is therefore a some-what bold survey attempting to grasp what is at a given time typical in the several epochs of Arab history. The Arabs have naturally not remained the same in the course of their 1300-years-old history as a civilized people. The main changes which they have undergone will be indicated as far as possible.

But such a high flight through the past of the great Arab nation is not sufficient to give a clear answer to the question 'Who are the Arabs?' To be sure, every today has its roots in a yesterday and cannot really be understood without that yesterday. On the other hand, a today cannot be simply deduced from a yesterday, even less in the case of the present-day Arabs than in that of other peoples. For today the Arabs are in the midst of a tumultuous overthrow of many traditions and traditional values and are at the beginning of a fresh start of which only the fundamental features have barely become visible. The Arabs themselves call the present day the epoch of their 'Thawra', their 'Revolution'. The conscious aims of this revolution, as far as they can be understood from programmes and political manifestoes, are of a 'western' type. They have little in common with the values and aims of life, which early generations of Arabs esteemed and pursued—remarkably little in the eyes of a western observer.

The Arabs themselves are without doubt often less conscious of the change of direction in their life and aspirations than an outsider. They see their own past in the light of their present-day aspirations. Saladin drove the 'imperialist' crusaders from Palestine just as Nasser has conquered or will still conquer the 'imperialists' of modern times. The Koran is interpreted afresh, one discovers in it what it 'originally' meant and this can be brought completely into harmony with one's own 'modern' ideas and inspirations. In history precedence is given to digging up those features which seem to exemplify and prepare the way to the desired 'modern' life. Anything which contradicts modern life is widely ignored or, where it cannot be ignored, is shrugged off as 'decadence' or the result of foreign rule.

But such new interpretations of Arab history are not very tenable. The old Islamic culture was a closely knit, well formulated and articulated cultural unity,

built together according to a consistent pattern. In order to put a new interpretation on it, that is, in order to see and understand it differently from its own
way of seeing and understanding itself, in order to submit it to standards of
values different from those it itself used and measure it by ideals which are not
its own, one must, if one would remain honest, know very little of it.

This is the case with many educated men among the modern Arabs. They
acquire their view of their own past from manuals and school books of Arab
history which were written in Europe, generally a long time ago, and which
they have before them in Arabic school editions and translations. Most of these
manuals are already out of date before they are translated into Arabic. Practically
all of them were based on the intellectual premises of an age which believed in
'progress' and accepted European culture of the nineteenth or twentieth century
implicitly or explicitly as the goal and end of all historiography. The modern
concept of a distinctive culture, into which individual actions, works or types
of behaviour must be integrated in order to be understood and judged, is still
quite foreign to such manuals.

The western observer who looks at the modern intellectual life of the Arabs
and in so doing notes that the Arabs get even their view of their own past from
Europe (the Europe of a slightly out-of-date scientific 'positivism') will find
himself faced with the question: Is there any sense at all in trying to explain the
Arabs of today from their history? Have they—at least their educated and
leading men—not divested themselves of everything which not more than 150
years ago constituted the 'system' of their cultural world, the co-ordinates to
which their life and activity were related?

To this the Arabs themselves answer with an emphatic: 'The values of
"Arabism" are eternal values!' But even they find it difficult to define what
precisely are these values either in themselves or in their application to modern
daily life. In truth there is only one thing which has survived unharmed the
destruction of the last 150 years: the Arabic language. The great common
denominator of the traditional culture of the Arabs, the religion of Islam, has
been dislodged from its earlier dominant position. The intellectual life of modern
Arabs can no more be called Islamic than ours can be completely covered by
the conception of 'Christendom', indeed rather less so. (This is not to deny
that these religions constitute an important element in the systems of civilization
in both cultural areas.) Religion as the denominator and co-ordinator, embrac-
ing and valid in all spheres of life, has been giving way to a more complex
system of civilization and values since the Renaissance in the West and since
the middle of the nineteenth century in the Near East.

The breakdown was much more radical, violent and destructive in the Near
East than it was with us because it took place more quickly. Also it did not
come, as in Europe, from the internal development of the culture but occurred
to a large extent under the threatening influence of an all-powerful Europe.

Therefore it was more painful and more confusing. It was often conceived as something forced on people from outside and therefore engendered a hatred for those powers which they imagined themselves 'condemned' to imitate.

Today the breakdown has gone so far that one can assume with a fair amount of certainty that there will be no going back for the peoples of the Near East to their old system of culture. However, the breakdown is far from being completed. One can say that in the main the majority of the population in most Arab countries hardly lives differently than it has 'always' done. The peasant population of Iraq, Syria and Egypt and the Beduins of Saudi Arabia or Jordan have changed their habits of life very little. They have changed their ways of looking at life somewhat more but not yet to a radical extent.

But, at the same time, two things should not be ignored. Firstly, that today, since the end of the Second World War, mighty forces are at work whose aim it is to bring 'modern life' to the peasant masses in the villages and deserts also. In Syria and Egypt 'modern life' is planned in the form of 'national socialism' and in Iraq in the guise of 'people's democracy'. It seems that the new order is fully welcome, at least so far, in the peasant villages of the Near East, even in this garb which appears so unattractive to us; or let us be more cautious and say that it can be made very welcome by modern means of propaganda (and arms).

Secondly, those still quite extensive classes, which continue the traditional life of the Near East, have no leadership. The intellectual *élite* is as good as completely modern. In the Near East of today, much more than in Europe or America, technology, 'science', a 'modern' army and administrators wearing European dress and employing methods dressed up as European, acquire all the prestige. Even the sheikh in his mosque is a figure of fun; he is so old-fashioned in his turban and with his solemn manners. He does not command modern life but lives side by side with it without contact with it—unless the administration of the state calls on him to make propaganda declarations or to take part in public demonstrations as a decorative figure.

The majority of all those who still lead the traditional life have already accepted the verdict of the 'educated' class; they themselves believe that their life is not worth living. They only go on living in the style of bygone days because they must, because the material foundations for a change, for entry into 'modern' life, must first be gained through work. Spiritually there is a complete readiness, even among the peasants, to accomplish the breakdown.

Breakdown, change, fresh start . . . to what end? The answers are various and vague. One desires a materially better life, one wishes to live 'for the Arab nation'. In Iraq a new note can be heard; the call goes out for 'socialism' and 'peace' under the leadership of the 'democratic' peoples (by which Russia and her satellites are understood). The battle between the two tendencies, one 'Arab socialist' and the other 'international socialist' (with a Soviet stamp) has begun.

No one knows as yet how it will end. What is already clear is that people have resolutely turned their backs on the 'mediaeval Islamic' past and seek, indeed must seek, their salvation in the future, in what is new.

All this forces an observer to take seriously the break which is at present occurring in the history of the Arabs. Today less than ever can we believe that we shall get the answer to the question 'What are the Arabs?' only by studying the Arabs' past. In the Arab countries of today the sons are very different from what their fathers were. The grandsons will be doubly different.

The second part of our book is intended to deal with this second aspect of the character of the Arabs of today, their urge towards something new and to link up with an era of upheavals and revolutions. It attempts to indicate the dynamics of modern dissolution and breakdown among the Arabs. It has to go into detail, for the transformation is occurring so quickly that it is bringing about a substantial change of position every other month—particularly in the last few years. The second part attempts to provide documentation for such changes of position. But in selecting documents and describing tendencies and occurrences it must of necessity remain dependent on the subjective judgement of the author for there is still no clarified and unified judgement of modern developments in the Arab countries. Politicians and political ideologists dominate the field almost exclusively. Every one of these offers an interpretation and 'explanation' of the situation in the Near East complete with one or more scapegoats, a plan of action and 'sure' remedies for all future difficulties. The more brutal the plans of action of the political ideologists are, the more one-sidedly and fancifully they look back and attack the past, with all the more heat do they defend their way of looking at things and extol it as the only correct one.

The author could have saved himself from the criticism of politicians and the politically minded by confining himself to juxtaposing the various ideas that have been developed in recent years and are still being developed as to *who* the Arabs are or are supposed to be. However, this work has already been done. A young American-educated Arab, Nuseibeh, has written a book which gives a comprehensive view of all the ideas Arab nationalists have developed about themselves until recently (*The Ideas of Arab Nationalism*, Harvard, 1958). Moreover, it seems to me that to tackle the question of who the Arabs are in such a way would in reality mean avoiding the question. The picture which a man, and especially a politician or political ideologist, forms of himself or his nation and which he publicizes about himself or his nation does not necessarily coincide with reality.

It seems as if there is nothing else for the author to do in this second part of his book but to rely on his own judgement. He endeavours to quote as many as possible of the reasons on which he bases his judgement. But he is well aware that many reasons or assertions will be evident only to those people who know the Arab countries, that is, to those who have lived in them with so little money that they were forced to come into real contact with the Arabs. Having little money is an essential condition for this, for nowhere has money such a capacity for transforming all realities into mirages as in the Near East.

The author knows, too, that there are many people who see and judge the phenomenon of 'Arabism' from an angle that differs from his own. Faced by such people he can only give his assurance that he has done his level best to keep to facts, whether spiritual or material, and has tried to exclude political theories and myths as far as that was humanly possible.

Part One

THE HISTORY OF THE ARABS

I

The Knights of the Desert

AT THE BEGINNING of their history we find one thing that is quite individual to the Arabs. There is a rich literature of poetry that has come down to us from a time in which the Arabian peninsula lived in the twilight of prehistory. The Arabs themselves call this period the 'Age of Ignorance'. The light shed by the Prophet's mission had not then dawned over the peninsula.

Even today, the poets of that 'Age of Ignorance' are held in the highest esteem by the Arabs. Indeed, until the last century the reverence paid to these early poetic creations was so great that almost every poem written in Arabic had to be modelled on the old pagan pattern. The quality of a literary composition was measured by the extent to which it conformed to the ancient examples of Beduin poetry.

This ancient Arabic poetry on the edge of a cultured and civilized world is at the same time both primitive and refined. The ideas and range of emotions and experience which a poet could express in it are comparatively restricted. But in every respect, in its strict rules of prosody and rhyme, the subtlety of its almost unlimited vocabulary, the variety and diversity of its rhythmic and tonal nuances, its form is of such unexpected virtuosity that the clumsy European, who has taken endless trouble to learn enough Arabic to understand their rhapsodies, at least in part—with the aid of Arabic commentaries written in the course of a thousand years and voluminous dictionaries that generations of scholars have gone blind compiling—will, after all his efforts, still be left bemused. He is face to face with one of those spiritual achievements of mankind which, following laws known only unto themselves that serve no practical purpose, can only fill us with wonder.

The creative power of those Beduins, who lived their lives in a void in which there was nothing but sun, sand, rocks, and camels, was concentrated on one medium, language. This they could shape and model. There was no need for basic materials, such as marble, which the Greek sculptors knew how to fashion into statues; or for the vibrant strings of artistically fashioned musical instruments, or for the ingredients which a painter must have to make up his luminous colours. Indeed, the ancient Beduin poets used neither pen nor parchment. Their poems, hundreds of them, were committed to memory and passed on from mouth to mouth.

But if we try to answer the question 'Who were the Arabs?' just by studying the content of these poems we see that we must expect from the very beginning a false or at least a very inadequate answer. Poems are not composed to tell a story or express a thought. If their emotive content expressed in rhythms and tones could be fully rendered in another medium, in prose, in abstract ideas, as a translation into a foreign language, the poems as such would have no *raison d'être*.

To attempt to learn how the ancient Arabs lived by analysing the poems of this pagan epoch is thus to leave out right from the start a whole part of their life—and often the richer and most brilliant part. We only sketch the surface of a life which was, through its material poverty, narrowly circumscribed. We are unable to deal with the intensity, the depths and heights at which it was led. We must always bear in mind how limited our field of vision is when we attempt to draw conclusions or pass judgements.

The orientalist, Gustave von Grunebaum, outlined the 'extent of reality' which is found in Arabic poetry of these early times in his well documented book, *Die Wirklichkeitsweite der früharabischen Dichtung* (Vienna, 1937). Following his lead, we see that the ideal created by the Arabs of the desert before Muhammad was that of the Beduin Knight.

Ancient Arabic poetry is extraordinarily rich in descriptions. The Beduin poets describe, with a passionate care for detail, the landscapes, beasts and weather phenomena which they met in their everyday life. Simile was the chief tool of the ancient Arab poet. With a mere 'as if . . .' he can wander unrestrained from one description to another. But such descriptions were not composed, as a European reader, with his rather romantic conception of poetry, might expect, for the emotional value which the scene or person described, or the animal or landscape portrayed has for the poet.

Roughly, one can divide the descriptions of the early Arab poets into two categories. The first of these is where the description is undertaken from interest in the object. In these we find the 'technical' interest of a rider for his horse or camel; of a hunter in the most minute characteristics of his quarry; of a warrior in his weapons whose quality might well be a matter of life or death to him; or of a Beduin in the weather phenomena or lie of the land on whose correct interpretation the well-being, indeed the survival of his whole clan can depend.

The second large category of descriptions comprises those which basically serve to raise the poet's prestige. The ancient Arab poets are masters of the art of presenting themselves in the 'right' light by a discreet use of background descriptions. You can boast quite openly of what a fine fellow you are, but you can also use indirect means. You can tell of what terrible deserts you have crossed and on what a fine camel (what a man to be able to own such a mount!), what terrible storms and tempests, monsters and enemy attacks you have defied, what pangs of hunger and thirst you have endured, of those long seemingly endless nights spent alone in the wilderness, of how you depend on no man, though none of the tribe could possibly dispense with the poet's help and kind support, of how your beloved wept for you while you sat stoically in the saddle and said to your companions, 'Up! Enough of tears! Let us act,' and of how all the girls fall for you.

The 'art' in this sort of poetry consists of exact observation, in the choice of the correct expression and significant detail, in discovering ever new possibilities of simile, ever more artistic links between the object and the simile. The 'urge' which produces this art, the emotion inspiring the poet to plan and spin out his imagery is nearly always a desire to puff himself up, to make a good impression and to show off.

The 'super-ego' which the poet builds up with such passionate love and devotion and which he cultivates with such art and eloquence is to be equated with what he calls his 'honour'. The glorification of 'honour' comes before everything else in early Arabic poetry. Honour does not depend on wealth or power over others. True, to own thoroughbred horses, valuable weapons, many camels, beautiful women, or to have numerous kinsmen and fine clothes can redound to a man's 'honour'. He boasts of such possessions. But your 'honour' might even consist in the fact that you can manage without any of these things. There are poets who boast that they lead solitary lives, hungry and harried like wild animals, that they owe nothing to anyone in the world, save their own strong arms. To be descended from heroes and leaders of tribes redounds to a man's honour. He praises his own ancestors and mocks all who belong to a strange tribe. But one can also achieve 'honour' by founding a family that will become renowned in history, like the hero Antara who was born of a noble father and a black slave and said of himself: 'My father is of the tribe of Abs; let my arm stand surety for the rest of my lineage.'

It is 'honour', and not any feeling of friendship or relationship which bids the Beduin undertake a blood feud against the enemies of his family. It is due to 'honour' and not to any human sympathy that one shows generosity to strangers, indeed wastes one's substance on strangers caring not whether the following day will bring poverty and hunger to oneself and to the whole tribe. As 'recompense' for generosity and extravagance one expects to have one's praises sung by the guest, particularly if he happens to be a poet.

This is the typical situation of the early Beduin poet: he builds up a picture of his enhanced self and his art is put to the service of this super-ego. The whole world that is mirrored in his poem is directed towards this super-ego. The world exists only for its sake, to support it, to underline it, to enable it to express itself. Often the poet loses himself for a series of verses in some description that so arouses his interest that, for a short while, he even forgets himself. But then the ego of the poet re-emerges, not unrefreshed by his brilliance, the exactness of his description, the precision of his expertise. The world is centred round him, there to serve him and be a foil to his 'honour'. Even for deities, or God, there is hardly a place in it. The poet may often swear, 'By Lat!' or 'By Uzza!' (these were the daughters, in pagan times, of Allah who was worshipped in Mecca); but even oaths are in the end only used to show how determined and inflexible is the poet's ego.

Such is the picture we get from these poems. The reality may have been different. Perhaps not every Arab was as heroic as he liked to appear in poems. Perhaps, too, the stress which many of the early poets put on their toughness in meeting alone the terrors of the desert and how unflinchingly they spent long nights alone beneath the canopy of stars shows that 'ordinary mortals' were wont to feel afraid in the dark and alone in the desert. Perhaps we can draw the same conclusion from the many times we hear of how the poet loved to rush upon his enemy 'without hesitation, far ahead of all others, like a falcon'.

The orientalist, G. Levi della Vida, has pointed out that it is possible that (pagan) religion played a larger part in the everyday life of the early Arabs than is apparent from their poetry, for 'in poetry the heroic side of life is pushed into the forefront while other aspects which are not less important are completely overlooked' (*The Arab Heritage*, New Jersey, 1944).

Nevertheless it seems important that we accept the portrait of the Beduin Knight as it appears in early Arabic poetry. It is the earliest ideal the Arabs formed of themselves which is known to us. And such ideal portraits do show the direction which a civilization strives to follow, the way it would take and what in its culture makes life worth living. Their influence lingers on even when that civilization has turned to other goals. They are 'in the blood of the race'. The word 'honour', 'Karama', plays quite an important part and is not invoked in vain in the speeches of all modern nationalists. Even today it is able to excite the Arab masses, arouse their deepest feelings about their past, and to inflame them.

2

The Arabs in the Koran

IN THE ARABIAN TOWNS of Mecca and Medina where the new religion of the Arabs was to arise, life must have been very different from that of the Beduin tribes in the interior. One piece of evidence for this is that in the Koran the word 'Arabs' is only used with the meaning of 'Beduins'. For the inhabitants of Mecca, mankind was divided into sedentary town dwellers and nomadic 'Arabs'. Nor were the 'Arabs' always dealt with in a friendly fashion. In one verse of the Koran (Ch. 9, 97) we read: 'The (wandering) Arabs are more hard in disbelief and hypocrisy, and more likely to be ignorant of the limits which God has revealed unto His Messenger. And God is knowing, Wise.'

The Beduins obviously made every use of the freedom of the desert in order to get out of unpleasant military service. The Prophet had repeatedly to admonish them. Thus God charges him: 'Say unto those of the Arabs who remained behind: You will be called against a people of mighty prowess, to fight them until they surrender. And if you obey God will give you a fair reward. But if you turn away as you did turn away before He will punish you with a painful doom' (Ch. 48, 16). And there were doubts—quite rightly—about their honesty: 'The Arabs say: We believe. Say: You do not believe, but rather say "We submit" for the faith has not yet entered into your hearts' (Ch. 49, 14).

But the adjective 'Arabic' in the Koran is used in quite a different manner from 'Arab' as a noun. 'Arabic' means for Muhammad primarily the language and for him it is extraordinarily important that the Koran was revealed in Arabic. 'The Arabic Koran' is one of those expressions that keep on recurring. The book was revealed 'in clear Arabic speech containing no crookedness so that they may guard against evil' (Ch. 39, 28). 'And lo! it is a revelation of the Lord of the Worlds, which the True Spirit has brought down upon your heart that you may be one of the warners, in plain Arabic speech. And lo! it is in the scriptures of the men of old. Is it not a token for them that the doctors of the Children of Israel know it? And if We had revealed it unto one of any other nation than the Arabs, and he had read it to them, they would not have believed in it' (Ch. 26, 192 ff). We also find the same thought put differently: 'And if We had made it a Koran in a foreign tongue they would assuredly have said: Why are its verses not made clear? What! in a foreign tongue and for Arabs!' (Ch. 41, 44).

The fact that the text of the Koran came to him in Arabic appeared to the Prophet as something almost miraculous and as a proof of the genuineness of his mission. One short passage shows all the importance which the fact of the Koran being in Arabic had for Muhammad himself: 'We know well that they say: Only a man is teaching him. But he whom they hint at speaks a foreign tongue and this (revelation) is clear Arabic speech!' (Ch. 16, 103).

It had not escaped the notice of the people of Mecca that the message of the Prophet Muhammad contained much that derived from its two sister religions, Judaism and Christianity. 'Aha,' said his critics, 'we can see Jewish and Christian influences. Muhammad, a mere man is telling the stories which he wants to pass off as divine inspiration.' (The commentators have suggested various persons, Persian, Jewish or Christian, who may have been meant.) But God answers through the mouth of Muhammad: 'No, just see! The one you have in mind speaks a foreign tongue. But the revelation is in clear Arabic.'

At first sight the argument seems naïve. It suggests that Muhammad took the religious stories and histories in the Koran from Christian and Jewish narrators and authorities, formulated them anew in his own language and uttered them as a higher inspiration. But this all too superficial explanation avoids the heart of the matter.

If one wishes to understand it properly one must first of all take into account that the language of the Koran is not only good Arabic, but, in the opinion of nearly every Arab, it is the best Arabic that one could possibly imagine. As a model for every Arab writer it has never been equalled (nor, according to dogma, can it ever be equalled). There is one whole class of literature, the books on Ijaz, which is wholly concerned with proving this point. It analyses the prose of the Koran and compares its beauties with those of the Arab poets and thereby reaches the conclusion that the Koran is unsurpassable.

The Egyptian 'modernistic' Professor Taha Husain, who was educated in Paris and is well-known as a contemporary critic and writer says: 'There are three sorts of literary speech; poetry, prose and the Koran.' Even to his critical mind, which is inclined to consider the whole corpus of poetry attributed to heathen times as forgeries, the Koran is a work with which no other literary monument can be compared.

Considered from the point of view of its unique Arabic eloquence, the Koran is indeed a miracle. It is scarcely less so if we do not, like the orthodox Muslim, consider the holy book the Word of God but see in its Suras only the enraptured outpourings of the 'inspired' Prophet Muhammad. Whoever can appreciate the poetic and stylistic wonder of what is for the Arabs the Holy Book can easily understand that Muhammad himself could see in the inspired verses a confirmation of his mission. He was the Prophet who had been sent to the Arabs; the perfect Arabic of his revelations was obviously meant for his people!

In our speech with its rational tones which hardly express the heart of the matter one could say: For the Prophet the fact that revelation came to him in perfect Arabic was a proof that he had succeeded in conveying religion and religious sentiment of another world, of a sort that ran counter to the traditional culture of his people, in so authentic, effective and vital a manner in his own language that it could thereby be transmitted to his people.

The spiritual bases of the pagan beliefs and of the new religion, Islam, diverge widely. But one bond they have in common—the Arabic language. This, in heathen times, knew how to express life in poetry; nor did it fail when the cultural ideal changed, but reached a second and unsuspected flowering with the appearance of the Holy Book. It is not a question of inflexible traditionalism, but a creative renaissance. In both eras the Arabic language was the creative nucleus around which and from which these two opposed spiritual ideologies grew.

Islam, in theory, recognizes no other community except the Believers. All Muslims are the servants of God and their ethnic ties are of no importance. But the fact that the Koran was revealed in Arabic gave, in practice, a force and unity to the Arabs in the time of their expansion and, even in times of stagnation and decadence, an unshakeable conviction of their particular mission.

3

Muhammad in Mecca and Medina

IT IS AN EXTRAORDINARY FACT that we know more details of how the new religion of the Arabs spread in the region of Mecca, in the peasant oasis of Medina and among the tribes of Arabia than we know of events in the nineteenth and twentieth centuries which accompanied the introduction of the western secular outlook into Islamic society. Muslim historians, biographers of the Prophet and collectors of traditions concerning the acts and sayings of Muhammad and his early companions have preserved such a store of historical material that it is possible to follow the birth of Islam in all its changing phases and details, almost as if we were present.

Outstanding European scholars have studied this material, have sifted and tested it critically, endeavouring to draw a coherent picture from those individual reports that stood up to their criticism. The most up-to-date composition of this type is by W. Montgomery Watt (*Muhammed at Mecca*, Oxford, 1953 and *Muhammed at Medina*, Oxford, 1956). The chief advantage of this presentation, in contrast to earlier works, is that the approach to sources is not hypercritical. Where there is no reason for doubting the report of a Muslim scholar Watt thinks it should be accepted. Thus he builds up a mosaic of facts from which, with discernment and special regard for the social and economic factors of time and place, he has been able to draw a complete picture.

According to Watt, the world into which Muhammad was born was an age of transition from nomadic to city life. Mecca, a financial and trading centre, had won for itself a leading position among the nomads living around it. It sent caravans to Syria and Iraq, fitted out by its merchants and moneylenders, and protected by its allies on their way through the desert. The rise of Mecca as a mercantile city may be connected with the wars between the Persian Empire and Byzantium. These wars had closed the more northerly trading routes between east and west. (The Persian invasion of the Byzantine lands began in 611. In 619 the Persian army had overrun the whole of Egypt and Syria. The turning-point came when the Persians and Avars had to withdraw from Constantinople in 626 after a short siege. In the following year Heraclius invaded northern Iraq. In 630 he rebuilt Jerusalem which had been destroyed.)

But in spite of its booming trade and highly developed finance, Mecca was socially a city still organized according to Beduin principles and a nomadic way of life. There was practically no government, no state in the Greek or Roman sense. The city was ruled by a group of clans, bands of kinsmen, who were collectively responsible for the individual's security, possessions and infringements of the law. If a murder was committed the murderer's clan had to pay blood money or the clan of the dead man took vengeance on the clan of the murderer. An individual who belonged to no clan had no protection. In practice he tried to join up with a community either as a client or as an ally. The clans rivalled among themselves for the dominance of the city. The weaker communities concluded alliances in order to protect themselves against the more powerful.

Such a social system may have been suited to the desert where huge distances separate man from man or clan from clan. But in the merchant city of Mecca, or the agricultural oasis of Medina, it could only have led to perpetual friction that made life intolerable. In Mecca merchant guilds and financial groups began to exercise their power against the tribal units. Successful merchants began to insist on their rights as individuals; they no longer saw themselves as part of their clan but as persons who had acquired riches by their own talents. A money economy helped to emphasize the difference between rich and poor and thus to weaken the bonds of the tribal groupings. In Medina every clan tilled its own fields. There was perpetual strife with the neighbouring clan for possession of the land. Every family group had in the midst of their fields a fortified house to which they could withdraw in the event of an attack. Even when peace reigned a man who dared to leave the fields of his own clan and cross those of his neighbours to visit a third clan was risking his life.

Watt shows how this half-achieved transition from the Beduin way of life to a settled existence called for a re-orientation in all intellectual fields and demanded a new social order. Individuality, which as a new phenomenon was bringing about the collapse of the communal life of the clan, could not but engender a feeling of being insecure and lost. If a man could no longer be satisfied with the thought that one would live on in the memory of his descendants, then questions such as 'What happens to a person after his death?' must have taken on a new importance. The merchant morality of a commercial community cannot be the same as that of marauding Beduin tribes. The increasing distance between rich and poor must be countered by other forces if the social framework is not to fall to pieces. The Beduin ideal of 'manliness' is cast in doubt since wealth can be substituted for qualities of leadership and personal courage. City life, with its greater security, leads man to exaggerate his ability to help himself and control his own life. However, when he becomes aware of the powers that no individual can control, it also leads to a sense of insecurity and being lost.

Watt has been able to deduce from his sources that the first Meccans who went over to Muhammad's new religion fall into two categories: they were either young people of the leading families or heads of families which had not quite managed to establish themselves in the uppermost classes. The young men of good family were seeking ways and means of overcoming the tensions which were making their lives difficult for them. The heads of those families who were not quite capable of ruling hoped to advance themselves through the new religion.

It is important to realize at the very beginning that the link existing in Islam between worldly power and religion in no way smacks of hypocrisy. The Christian religion was born into a situation in which it had to separate the kingdom of Caesar from the Kingdom of God. Western thought is so used to this separation that we automatically suspect falsity, the conscious exploitation of religious motives to achieve worldly aims, as soon as we detect either in our own or in another religious tradition any co-operation between the two aspirations. In the Muslim world there is no separation between Caesar and God in Heaven. Muhammad lived in a town in which there was no government. One factor which led to the success of his mission was that he offered leadership just at that moment when the social system could no longer be contained within the narrow family and tribal system. He demanded and received this leadership in the name of God and all the sources we know of confirm that he honestly felt himself 'sent' and inspired for that purpose. What he did as Messenger of God seems to us to separate into either religious or political activities. In his eyes such a division would have been nonsense; he received messages and he acted according to these commands of God.

Both the books by Watt show us the individual steps which Muhammad took to have his inspiration accepted. Here we can only ennumerate the main stages. When he was forty years old inspiration came to him in a cave in Mount Hira, near Mecca. The first messages he received deal with the power and goodness of God, the last judgement which must be faced, the duty of man to thank and worship God and Muhammad's own position as Messenger of God. Three years after the first inspiration Muhammad begins to preach in public. Two years later a group of Muslims emigrate to Ethiopia. Shortly afterwards the 'clans' of Mecca, led by Makhzum, the foremost clan in politics, begin to boycott Muhammad's clan, Hashim. It appears that this boycott took place after the failure of an attempt to acquire a place for the local deities of Mecca in the new religion. This boycott goes on for two years and then breaks down, perhaps because the lesser clans refused to obey Makhzum. Shortly afterwards Muhammad's uncle and his most important protector against his enemies, Abu Talib, chief of Hashim, dies. The new chief of Hashim, Abu Lahab, after initial hesitation, serves notice on Muhammad that he can no longer look for protection from his own clan.

The Prophet seeks support in the neighbouring town of Ta'if, but his journey is not a success. He also makes contact with certain nomadic tribes of the region; this, too, leads to nothing. Negotiations with the inhabitants of

Medina follow and are concluded with a promise of aid by the leading tribe of that oasis. About seventy believers, the last of whom is the Prophet himself, emigrate to Medina. Watt suggests that it was the necessity of appointing an impartial judge over their internal quarrels which moved the people of Medina to invite the Prophet and his community to settle among them. Muhammad was fifty-two years old when he emigrated to Medina in 622.

The first years in Medina are taken up, as far as internal politics are concerned, with organizing the community, and externally with raids on the caravans of the merchants of Mecca and on those Beduins in alliance with them. In 624 the people of Medina and the Muslim emigrants defeat an army from Mecca in the Battle of Badr. The following year a second battle takes place at Uhud which, although it goes against the Muslims, fails to open the road to Medina for the Meccans. The people of Mecca then collect a large army, calling up levies from all the allied Beduin tribes—the sources speak of 10,000 men. Muhammad digs a ditch to ward off their attack (627) and succeeds in holding Medina.

Then the Prophet goes over to the initiative against his native town. He knows how to win friends among the nomadic tribes. He goes as a pilgrim to Mecca and is not allowed to enter. However, he concludes a treaty by which it is agreed that he may return for a second pilgrimage after one year. The Meccans vacate their city for three days to allow him to perform his rites there with the believers (Treaty of Al-Hudaybiya, 628). Further desert expeditions take place, most of them towards the north on the caravan route to Syria. Finally Mecca surrenders and is occupied almost without bloodshed in 630. A few weeks after this success the Prophet and the Meccans march against a nomad leader who has formed a strong confederation of the Beduin against Mecca. He defeats him at Hunayn. Muhammad spends his last years in bringing together the nomadic tribes in a system of alliances, in weaning them from idolatry and in preventing them from feuding. He is successful in turning their aggressive tendencies against the unconverted tribes and, later, against the settled lands outside the peninsula.

This external expansion coincides with an internal political new order. In this sphere Muhammad's reform is remarkable in that it overcomes the tribal and clan system. The Prophet substitutes the conception of a Community of Believers for the tribal principle which was the only political order acknowledged in Mecca, in Medina, and by the nomads.

This Community of Believers was later to expand enormously. Today it comprises all Muslims in every continent. But one may assume that at the beginning Muhammad envisaged it rather as a new tribe, the tribe of the converts, the believers. This new community took over the functions of the tribes. The most important of these was the protection of their members which had been ensured by the duty of vendetta. The fact that the tribe of a murdered man was in duty bound to exact vengeance from the murderer's tribe gave to every individual a minimum of security.

With the expansion of the new faith and with the manifold political ties which Muhammad forged with the various existing tribal communities in the desert, in Mecca and in Medina, the concept of the Community of Believers broadened and developed into a sort of super-tribe. Communities, nomadic tribes and sub-tribes or urban 'clans' could all join Muhammad's super-tribe. It appears that the conditions of admission were not always the same. Muhammad knew how to vary them according to the strength of the community seeking admission, the circumstances of 'joining' (whether by conquest or negotiated treaty) or the religion of the new community.

Christian and Jewish tribes could keep their religion but pagans had to forswear idolatry. All members of the Community of Believers had to under-take not to take up arms against another member. On the other hand whoever did not belong to the Community of Believers was an outlaw. There were at least two sorts of money payments to the community: the *Sadaqa* (later *Zakat*) or alms tax on Muslims. This was primarily intended for the support of needy brethren. The rules for its collection seem to have varied according to the status of the groups newly joining the community. Many of these had to pay a fixed sum of money to Muhammad and tax-collectors were appointed to these tribes. Others, doubtless more powerful, paid no alms tax. In this case, at least theoretically, the richer members had to pay alms for the support of their own poor. The second type of payment, *Jizya*, was demanded from Jewish or Christian tribes which had been subjected by force. Yet in early times there does not seem to have been any sharp distinction between this later poll tax for Unbelievers and the alms tax for Muslims. It also appears that there were Christian and Jewish tribes with which treaties were made on an equal footing. Their members became allies of the Community of Believers without having to pay *Jizya*.

Muhammad claimed one fifth of the war booty taken by the Community of Believers, whereas, before his time, tribal chieftains had required one quarter. For this Muhammad undertook the traditional obligations of a tribal chieftain: the entertainment of guests, the care of the widows and orphans of those who fell in battle, and provision for the needy.

4

A Changing Culture

BUT WHILE CONSIDERING all these political measures and manoeuvres we must not forget that under the Prophet's leadership a profoundly spiritual change was taking place along with a political one. The heart of the newly founded body politic was its religion. There is no point in our examining in detail the religious institutions of Islam introduced by Muhammad and later worked out and modified by scholars. (A competent exposition can be found in Reuben Levy's *The Social Structure of Islam*, Cambridge, 1957.) But the question 'How far did the new religion influence, alter or even determine the character of the Arabs?' is essential to our theme.

In a masterly succinct exposition the orientalist Gustave von Grunebaum outlines the cultural change which the introduction of Islam brought about in Arab history (*Vom Wandel der Kultur*, Otto Harrassowitz, Wiesbaden, 1955, *Kritik und Dichtkunst*). 'Islam', Grunebaum says, 'gives to life another worldly aim—wealth, power, courage, noble connections, fame, all are acceptable ambitions only in so far as they are acknowledged as servants in the organization of the new life and can take their proper place in it.'

The new faith—continues Grunebaum—has the effect that every action in this life is performed and viewed with a new seriousness. It may lead to damnation in the hereafter or help to achieve Paradise. In pagan times the individual was only partly raised above the community of his tribe. The new religion emphasizes his personal responsibility to the Creator.

Also Islam gives a special place to the Community of Believers. Without it certain vital ritual duties of the individual—especially the communal prayer on Friday—could not be fulfilled. The Muslim State of Believers, which was expected eventually to rule the whole world, takes the place of the tribe and tribal federation.

According to Grunebaum three fundamental questions arise from these new values which Islam proclaims. What is right thinking? What is right living? What is the right organization of the community? All three questions are bound up with the decisive question of salvation. If a wrong answer is given to them, or even to one of them, man loses hope of being admitted to Paradise. He must therefore give to all three his most earnest attention.

Education and knowledge of the teachings and actions of the Prophet help the believer to distinguish right from wrong in his daily life. The old pagan virtues which were praised for their own sakes—courage, strength, power, perseverence, etc.—give place to the overwhelming importance of religion and piety. A man's actions must accordingly be evalued anew. Islam places high above the external deeds of pagan times the inner struggles of the pious ascetic and the striving towards divine truth which is the task of the scholar. The state is not only created for the protection of its individual members, nor for its own power and glory; it is there to serve as a protection for the Faith and the believers, it is a divine institution, its norms are laid down in the religious law and it is a necessary instrument to save the believers from damnation.

In conclusion, Grunebaum says that Islam imposed new duties on the individual but also gave him new rights. Ritual duties and moral precepts must be observed and followed if the believer is to achieve salvation. He has his share of responsibility for the welfare of the whole Community of Believers, not only for that of his tribe. For this he can hope to partake of Paradise and on this earth he is sure of his superiority over those who belong to other religions. He is assured of this superiority on the physical and material plane by the organization of the 'State' and in the moral sphere by its teachings.

Islam also brings it about that the believer sees everything he experiences with a new vision quite different from that of a pagan Arab. The new religion revealed for the first time infinite realms of inward vision. 'The new discovery of his self, which Islam offered the believer by giving him a part in the regiment of a huge cosmopolitan empire, by placing the key to the hereafter in his hand, by showing him the way to the spiritual conquest of the universe and, above all, by making possible and justifying to him a more complete and more various experience in a richer and wider order of things, this new discovery compensated him for the painful sense of change, for the romantic feeling of homelessness and even for the real loss of the unfettered freedom of a past which was now rejected as being based on a wrong attitude to life. Islam gave the converted pagan more than salvation; it gave him a soul which was able to partake of that salvation.

'Thus the achievement of Islam in transforming the traditional Arabian culture can be summarized as the introduction of four basic changes: *a*. the expansion and refinement of human sensibility; *b*. the extension of the spiritual world and the means to master it through tenets which satisfied both feeling and mind; *c*. a socially justifiable and at the same time militarily powerful political organization for which there had been locally no precedent; and *d*. a new design for living, or rather a new human ideal, a pattern of minutest detail that could be realized in a model life span from conception till after the day of judgement.'

In the face of this impressive evidence of the complete change which the introduction of the new faith into the life of the early believers must have meant, one would say that the Arabs of pagan times must have been basically different from those of the Islamic epoch.

5
Conquests

HOWEVER, we must not lose sight of the fact that Grunebaum's analysis deals with 'cultural ideals'. In his description he is not so much considering the material realities as they appeared immediately after the Prophet's advent, as those new spiritual tendencies which were brought about by his teachings. These were first to be found in religious documents. They had, indeed, a decisive influence on the political events of the day, but they could not just suddenly switch off the forces of the past. A cultural ideal, almost by definition, can never be entirely realized at the level of everyday politics. It is a signpost and history tries to follow its direction.

In the case of the Arabs the process of adaptation to the new cultural ideal went on for centuries. The successive attempts of the Community of Believers to realize the cultural ideal the Prophet had created, their failures, their fresh starts, the achievement of harmonious syntheses between this cultural ideal and those counterforces which sprang from the striving for power by separate groups or individuals—these constitute in essence the history of the Arabs in the next centuries.

Here, the moments when the ideal and the political forces did find themselves in harmony are of particular importance. Later on the Arabs looked back to such historical epochs as periods of particular splendour. They see in them moments when the true genius of their race was realized. Even today when an Arab is asked about the past of his nation he recalls first and foremost, as the high spots in his nation's history, those epochs during which, for a moment, the Islamic ideal and the political life of his people were in unison: the time of the great conquests, that of the Umayyad Caliphs or the early 'Abbasid dynasty.

Yet the glories of those epochs should not prevent us admitting that times of chaos and division also form part of the historical heritage of the Arab people. We can go further and say that if we take the conception of Arabism in its Koranic sense and look upon it as the inheritance from the desert, a legacy of the conquered Beduin culture, one can only say that it is precisely these 'Arab' features which over and over again endangered and destroyed the harmony between the system laid down by the Prophet and the political development of the young Arab state. Looked at from this point of view, the history of the Arabs

33

during the first three centuries after Muhammad appears as a struggle between the spiritual legacy of the Prophet (urban in origin and theocentric in pattern) and the inheritance from the Beduin world of the pagan Arabs.

Immediately after the death of the Prophet the nomad Arab elements rose up in desperation against Muhammad's new world—and spiritual order. With his death the Beduins regarded the treaties they had made with him, as representative of the Community of Believers, as having lapsed. Later Muslim historians do not agree with this point of view. What must have appeared to them as the defection of the tribes from the Muslim system of alliances they call the '*Ridda*' (apostasy).

The Prophet's successor in his temporal office, his father-in-law Abu Bakr, had to conclude afresh all treaties with the nomadic communities. Many of the renegades had to be brought into the Community of Believers again by force. Nor would he have so easily overcome these centrifugal tendencies of the tribes had he not been able to direct the warlike passions of his allies outwards to the rich lands bordering the Arabian peninsula. News of the immense treasures which could be won by raids on Iraq and Syria must have brought back more Arab tribes to the bosom of the Community of Believers than all the weapons of the citizens of Mecca and Medina could have done.

The first raid into Iraq took place as early as 633, one year after Muhammad's death. The battle which was to decide Syria's fate was fought three years later on the banks of the River Yarmuk. Seleucia (Ctesiphon), the winter capital of the Persian Empire, was conquered in the following summer (637).

The history of the conquests has been told too often for it to be necessary to repeat it here. Nevertheless, it is important that we have some idea how these conquests took place. The methods of the first conquerors are indicative of what sort of people the Arabs must have been in the time of the great expansion. They were at home in the desert and the desert was the element they exploited in their campaigns, just as, in later times, the maritime powers used their mastery at sea to build up world-wide empires.

As soon as the dwellers in the desert took the field side by side rather than against one another, they became a formidable threat to the lands fringing the desert. Before Muhammad's time the Persian and Byzantine Empires had maintained Beduin allies and half-settled vassals on their borders to carry on desert warfare against the nomads of the interior. The most important of these were the princes of Hira and Ghassan. Once these buffer states had been overthrown by the Community of Believers, or once they had been persuaded to make common cause with their nomadic brethren, there was no other equal opponent to bar the way of the desert armies of Islam. The troops of these two empires, even after a victory, could not pursue them into the heart of the desert. Imperial generals could never know where their enemies from the desert would appear and fall upon the border lands.

A famous example of the Arabs' mastery of the desert and the way they knew how to exploit it is given by the story of how their greatest general, Khalid ibn al-Walid, marched across the desert. This march must have taken place at the beginning of the conquests. Called out by Abu Bakr, volunteers had set out for Syria. The sources speak of 7000 warriors, mostly from Southern Arabia, accompanied by their wives and children. This group of immigrants pene-trated as far as the Sea of Galilee. The superior tactics of a Byzantine general sent against them led to reverses, halted their march and finally led to their rout.

In the same year Khalid ibn al-Walid had undertaken his first plundering raid up the Euphrates. He had reached the city of Hira, near to modern Najaf, and made it pay him tribute. Here we continue with a report of Arab historians as transmitted to us in Tabari's great chronicle (year 13):

Abu Bakr wrote to Khalid while the latter was in Hira ordering him to reinforce the Army of Syria with all the men of first fighting quality he had with him. He was to march at the head of these and leave the warriors of inferior fighting quality under the command of one of their number. When the letter with Abu Bakr's command reached Khalid he said: 'This is the work of that left-handed fellow, that son of a worthless mother', meaning thereby Omar ibn al-Khattab (later to be Caliph). 'He is jealous of me and does not wish that the conquest of Iraq should be my handiwork!'

Then Khalid broke camp with those of his troops who were fit for war sending the weak and the women back to Medina, the City of the Prophets, upon whom be peace. . . .

He marched as far as Ayn Tamr where he fell upon the inhabitants and struck them down. He besieged the fort that was there and in which the Persian Emperor had put a garrison until its defenders were forced to come down. He executed these. In Ayn Tamr he captured many people and sent them to Abu Bakr. Among these was Abu 'Amra, later a freedman of the Shabban, whose full name was Abu 'Abd al-A'la ibn Abi 'Amra (and others).

Then Khalid desired to march directly from Quraqir, a well of the tribe Kalb, to Suwa, a well of the tribe Bahra. Between the two lay five days' journey. Khalid did not know the way and needed a guide. Rafi' ibn 'Amira of the tribe Tay was pointed out to him as the most suitable man and Khalid said to him: 'Go forth with the troops.' The guide answered: 'That is not possible with the horses and the baggage. By God, even a single rider is afraid of this route and dares not traverse it except in exceptional circum-stances. Five days long the horses can find no water, and there is also the danger of losing the way.'

Khalid answered: 'Woe to you! I must do it for I have strict orders from the Caliph. So tell me what to do.' The guide answered: 'Take on a lot of water and whoever can make his camel mare drink long from a water-hole must do so. This journey will be to our death unless God comes to our aid. In addition fetch me twenty first-class male camels for slaughter, fat and well-grown.' Khalid gave them to him. The guide hobbled them and let them thirst until they drank their fill. He then hobbled them again and cut off their lips. He then muzzled them so that they could not chew the cud, left them unloaded and said to Khalid: 'Let us go!' Khalid broke camp. The provisions and the baggage he carried on the horses. Each time he halted he slaughtered four of those big camels and gave the horses to drink of the fluid from their stomachs. The men drank the water they carried with them.

On the last day of the desert march Khalid was anxious about his companions. He spoke to the guide who was suffering from inflammation of the eyes: 'What ails you?' He answered: 'I hope I shall recognize the marks of this district.' When he had come to a place between two jutting hills, he said to the soldiers: 'Look and see if you can find a little Ausaj bush, as big as the space a man needs when he sits down.' They said: 'We can see nothing.' He spoke: 'Indeed we belong to God, and to Him we return! In that case you are lost, and I with you! Curse you, look!' So they sought and found the shrub. Someone had cut it down and only a little stump was left. When the Muslims saw it they praised God and the guide did likewise and said: 'Dig at its roots!' They dug and brought to light a spring, and the people drank their fill and Khalid could then march on apace. Rafi', the guide, said: 'By God, I have only once been to this spring. That was when I came here with my father. I was then still a boy.'

6

The Armed Camps

THE ARMED CAMPS established in the first years of the conquests indicate how important the part played by the desert must have been for early Islam. The camps were set up on the edge of the desert and were havens into which flowed the streams of believers coming from Central Arabia. Here they assembled and from here they organized their raids into the cultivated lands.

It was as such an armed camp that the town of Basra arose. Its foundation goes back to an order of the Caliph Omar. Ancient Basra lay nearer to the desert and farther from the sea than the present city. According to Omar's command the camp had to be set up so that there could be no obstacle between it and Medina, the centre of the state. The rivers Euphrates and Tigris (called 'seas' in Arabic) would have constituted such obstacles. Basra was founded after the Arabs had already overrun the Persian winter capital, Ctesiphon. But the Persian capital was not chosen to become an armed camp because it lay on the eastern side of the Mesopotamian plain which was, considered from Medina, the wrong side.

Kufa, too, which was near the present-day Najaf, was built on the bank of the Euphrates nearest Medina. These two armed camps were the military centres of the Arabs and Islam in the newly won subject lands in the East. All newly conquered territories, right into the heart of Persia, were subject to the commanders of one or the other of these two centres.

One must not imagine anything too grandiose about such headquarters of early times. They were not more than a huge encampment of tents, divided between the various tribal units, with open spaces between the cantonments of the various tribes. The mosque in the centre served equally for prayer, for meetings, or for parades. At first it consisted of little more than a wide fenced-in square. If the tents fell in, their fabric was replaced by the indigenous reeds such as nomads of today use when they have to settle for a long time in one place. It was only in 670, a whole generation after its foundation, that Kufa got its first stone houses and a fixed 'palace' for Ziyad, 'Son of his Father,' who was then Governor and Commandant. By then the power of the Community of Believers had spread as far as the Oxus, nearly to Constantinople and almost as far as Qairawan, which was founded in 675.

We know most about the layout of the third of the great camps, that of

Fustat whose rubbish heaps still rise above the Valley of the Nile to the East of Old Cairo. For this armed camp, too, a position was chosen on the edge of the desert. The link with Medina, running over the Isthmus of Suez then uninterruptedly through the desert to Medina was thus secured. Tribute and provisions were brought up from the Delta. Even today we can make a ground plan of Old Fustat in which the cantonment of each Beduin tribe can be traced. The Amr mosque, which was later rebuilt and enlarged, was the focal point of the camp and still stands.

The capital of Egypt, Alexandria, was left undisturbed. It paid tribute in accordance with the treaty which, after one year's siege, had been concluded with the Coptic Patriarch. In 646 it had to be taken from the Byzantines for the second time. However, it is clear that the early inhabitats of Fustat were less interested in this maritime city than in pushing on with their conquests across the Nile and the Western Desert to Tripoli, which was conquered in 644.

Not only the geographical position of these first Arab armed camps which were later to develop into large towns, but also the spread of the Arabic language right down to our own day indicate what close ties the early conquerors had with the desert. Arabic is still spoken today in the lands bordering the Arabian deserts. The valleys of the Euphrates, the Tigris, the Orontes, the Jordan and the Nile are all narrow, nor are the coastal strips of Syria and Palestine much broader. Between these cultivated regions there is always the desert. There are few Arab towns that lie more than one day's journey away from a region of the desert. It was thither, near to the desert where they were at home, that the Semitic nomad tribes, the last of which were the Arabs, immigrated in such numbers that their language became the language of the land.

Islam spread much farther afield than the Arabic language, especially towards the East. Only thirty years after the Prophet's death, Arab warriors had penetrated as far as Bactria and Afghanistan. But these immense territories on the far side of Mesopotamia did not become Arab lands. The mountain barrier, leading up to the Persian high plateau, prevented the Arabs from emigrating to Persia in sufficient numbers to dislodge the old established language.

It was the same to the north of the Muslim Empire. Although raids and occasional campaigns penetrated far into the interior of Asia Minor, nevertheless the Arabic language never crossed the Kurdish mountains nor the foothills of the Taurus. It never spread up the valleys of the Euphrates and the Tigris into the mountain hinterland of what is now Turkey.

So long as the tide of conquest poured over new lands and continents the believers had little time for introspective contemplation. One could be satisfied with a simple faith which encouraged warlike virtues and was reconcilable with the ideal of a Beduin warrior. Though this mixture of warlike virtues, lust for booty and interests of the new religion may, looked at purely intellectually and compared with the matureness of later Islamic culture, seem to us gross and clumsy, yet it has a certain grandeur. Perhaps one feels this most when reading historical sources.

Before the decisive battle of Qadisiya the Persian general, Rustam, addresses one of the Arab leaders:

'You are our neighbours and some of you were under our rule. We used to fulfil the duties of neighbourliness to them and protect them from harm. We granted them abundant aid and protected the interests of those of them who lived in the desert. We permitted them to use our pastures and provided for them from our own land. We did not prevent them from trading in any of our lands. Thus they had a means of livelihood. This they earned through their work.'

The Arab Zuhra answered:

'You are right. It is as you have said. But our desires are not their desires. We do not demand what they demand. We do not come to you seeking worldly things. What we desire and what concerns us is the other world! We Arabs were as you say. Those of us who came to you submitted to you and humbly begged for what you possess. Then God (Who is blessed and exalted) sent us a Prophet who called on us to follow his Lord, and we listened to him. God said to His Prophet (may God bless him and give him peace): "Verily I give power to this My host over those who will not follow My religion. They shall be stricken by My people to whom I shall give easy victory so long as they abide by My religion, for it is the Religion of Truth. None shall forsake it without being lost and none shall cling fast to it without becoming great".' (Tabari, year 14.)

Later on battle with the Persians is engaged:

The mill of battle revolved around the Asad tribe. The elephants (of the Persians) attacked the horsemen on the left and right flanks. Then the commander, Sa'd, sent for 'Asim ibn 'Amr and said to him: 'You of the Bani Tamim, are you not specialists in horses and camels? Do you know what we can do about the elephants?' 'Yes, by God!' He called those of his tribe who were archers and others who understood how to fight and he ordered: 'O archers! drive away the riders from the elephants, and you, the soldiers, advance upon the elephants and cut their girths.'

So they sallied forth. The battle raged around the Asad. The two wings of the phalanx were not far apart. 'Asim's men advanced on the elephants and seized their tails and the tassels of their howdahs. They cut their girths and raised their war cry. That day no elephant was left with a howdah, and all their riders were slain. The Asad got breathing space and they pressed back the Persians to their original positions. . . .

The third night of the battle came. It is called the night of Qadisiya.

The people were exhausted, not having closed an eye throughout the night. Al-Qa'qa' went among the troops and said: 'The turning-point will come in an hour's time for those who begin the attack. Hold out for an hour; attack, for victory will go to those who endure! Choose steadfastness, not faint-heartedness!'

A group of leaders gathered around him and pressed forward towards (the Persian commander-in-chief) Rustam until they were fighting hand to hand with those standing directly in front of Rustam. This happened at dawn. As the Arab tribes saw that there arose a man amongst them, called Qais and others who said: 'Those over there should not be more zealous in God's task than you, nor more willing to lay down their lives on this earth! Emulate their zeal and follow up their attack till you engage hand to hand those who oppose them!'

Then men from the tribe of Rabi'a arose and shouted: 'O Rabi'a, you are the people who have had the greatest experience of the Persians. Until today you were most courageous against them. What hinders you today from being yet more courageous than you were?'

Hormuzan and Birzan held out and stood fast to the end. The centre of the army disintegrated when the heat of mid-day broke over them and the dust made them unable to move. A mighty gust of wind arose and tore the baldachin from Rustam's throne. It blew into the ditch. It was a west wind and it bore the dust cloud in the direction of the Persians.

Qa'qa' and those with him reached Rustam's throne and uncovered it. Rustam had left his throne when the wind had carried away the baldachin and had gone to a string of mules which, laden with gold, had been sent to him that day. They were nearby and Rustam had sought shelter from the sun in the shade of one of the mules and its baggage. Hilal ibn Ullafa smote at the load under which Rustam was sitting. He cut through one of the ropes and one of the loads fell on the general without Hilal seeing him or noticing anything. The baggage fell on his spine and gave him a severe blow. A scent of musk arose (from Rustam's clothing) and the general strode to the ditch and flung himself into the water. Hilal flung himself on him and grappled with him. Rustam swam and Hilal stood up. He seized him by the foot, pulled him to the bank and struck him on the forehead with his sword till he was dead. Then he dragged him to the mules and threw him under their hooves. He ascended the throne and called out: 'I have slain Rustam! By the Lord of the Ka'ba, come to me!' The Arabs thronged round him. They could not see or touch the throne for the dust. They praised God and called to each other. The hearts of the polytheists melted within them and they fled.

The time of the great conquests was one of the great epochs of both the Arab nation and Islam. Both forces were then in harmony. Inner contradictions which existed between them were hardly expressed since the expansion, spreading out through immense spaces, offered both forces a successful field of activity. The warlike virtues of the Beduin, their lust for plunder and thirst for glory were as satisfied as Islam's intrinsic desire for world importance and world domination. For the conquerors of that time there was hardly any difference between Arabism and Islam.

7

The Rightly Guided

IN THE LATER EPOCHS OF ISLAM the age of the conquests was always looked on as ideal. The first four Caliphs, who, with the exception of Ali, reigned from Medina, were celebrated as the 'rightly guided ones' (Rashid). People have tended to trace back many of the politico-religious institutions of Islam to them. In particular Umar, the great conqueror and statesman, is extolled as the organizer of the state. Today we know that many individual institutions were introduced at a later date and that the conquered lands in the early years of their incorporation into the Community of Believers were administered by Byzantine officials in the West, or by Persian civil servants in the East. But it is certain that Umar himself did visit the western provinces and that the Caliph managed to refrain the conquerors, his own people, for the common good of the state.

The practical effect of the new religion may, indeed, be seen most clearly when it comes to questions of discipline and the curbing of the Beduin instinct to plunder. It is just possible to imagine that, without any assistance from religion, a large horde of Beduin, amalgamated by the increasing pressure of population in the Arabian peninsula, might have broken out of Arabia and overrun the Persian and Byzantine Empires, both of which had been weakened by waging war on each other. But what one cannot imagine without the new religion is the self-discipline and constancy of purpose which the invading nomads showed, going on straight away to found states on the ruins of the two empires instead of giving themselves over to mere destruction and plundering. Even though many of the characteristic Muslim political institutions were only formed during the period of development, so much is clear: The new conception of the world revealed by the Koran had penetrated deeply enough into the minds of the nomad Arabs to enable them to hold their freebooting and destructive instincts in check in the interests of a future Muslim state. Unlike the nomads under Genghis Khan six centuries later, they did not primarily burn, plunder and spread systematic terror throughout the conquered territories. They were content to establish armed camps on the edge of the occupied provinces, with forays which spread out farther and farther from the centre of the Community of Believers, and with moderate payments of tribute so that in Syria and Egypt their rule was welcomed with thankfulness in place of that of the Byzantines.

One soldier of 'Amr, the conqueror of Egypt, relates:

42

When we had conquered Babylon (present-day old Cairo) the villages of the countryside surrendered one after the other, until we came to Balhib, one of the villages in the open country. The prisoners we had taken had already arrived at Mecca, Medina and the Yemen. When we reached Balhib the Lord of Alexandria sent a message to 'Amr in which he said: 'In the past I have given tribute to conquerors that, O Arabs, were more angry with me than you are, both to the Persians and to the Greeks. If you wish that I pay tribute to you, I shall do so provided you give back to me the prisoners you have made in my land.'

'Amr replied: 'Above me is a ruler: without him I can take no decision. If you agree, I shall not get in touch with you, nor you with me, until I have announced to the Caliph what you have proposed. If he accepts it, I shall accept it. Should he order me to do otherwise, I shall obey him.' The Lord of Alexandria agreed and 'Amr wrote to the Caliph Umar—at that time no letter that was written was kept secret from us soldiers—and he explained what the Lord of Alexandria had proposed.

We kept the rest of the prisoners we had taken with us and halted at Balhib, pitched camp and waited until the answer from Umar arrived.

'Amr read it out to us. It ran: I have received your letter in which you mention what the Lord of Alexandria proposes, namely that he is willing to pay tribute on condition that you give him back our prisoners from his country. By my life, a fixed tribute to be received by us and succeeding Muslims is better to me than booty, which will be shared out and then be as though it had never been.

Propose to the Lord of Alexandria that he pay tribute on condition that the prisoners whom you hold be given the choice between Islam and the faith of their people. He amongst them who chooses Islam shall be one of the Muslims: he shall share in their riches and he shall undertake those duties which they undertake. He who chooses the religion of his people, from him shall tribute be demanded, such as befits those of his religion.

But as for those prisoners who have already been distributed in Arabia and have been sent to Mecca, Medina and the Yemen we cannot return those. Nor will we grant him peace under conditions which hold no dis-advantages for him.

'Amr sent to the Lord of Alexandria announcing what the Commander of the Believers had written and he answered: 'I agree.'

Then we gathered together all the prisoners who were in our hands. The Christians assembled. We brought forward every one of our prisoners and put before him the choice between Islam and Christianity. If he chose Islam we shouted: 'God is Greatest!' with a louder voice than we had used when their villages had been conquered. Then we led him into our ranks. If, however, he chose Christianity, then the Christians grunted loudly and led him over to their side. We laid tribute on him and were as downcast as if it had been one of our own who had defected to them. . . .

Amongst them was also one called Abu Maryam 'Abdallah ibn 'Abdur-Rahman (one of the reporters said: I know him. He is captain of the Bani Zubaid) whom we led forth and laid before him the choice of Islam or Christianity. His father, mother and brothers were among the Christians but he chose Islam. We sent him to our men but his father, mother and brothers fell upon him and kept pulling him back so that they rent his clothing. He is today, as you see, our captain. Then Alexandria was opened up to us and we marched in. (Tabari, year 20.)

8

The First Rift

THE END OF THIS FIRST EPOCH of harmony between religion and politics was to come even before the impetus of the great conquests had spent itself. Intrigues among the great families of Mecca and Medina about the succession of the Prophet brought about the first rift in the Community of Believers.

The third Caliph, Uthman, had been one of the leading early converts and had been at the same time one of the chiefs of Quraish and the Umayya clan from which the leading aristocracy of Mecca came. He was not such a strong personality as his predecessor Umar. His kinsmen, the Umayya, won enough influence over him to enable them to take over the vital governorships in the rich border lands.

A counter-intrigue formed around the Prophet's widow, A'isha, 'Amr, the conqueror of Egypt, and Talha and Zubair, two discontented Meccan aristocrats. They brought it about that in the year 656 Arab mutineers from the Egyptian army broke into the Caliph's headquarters and killed him.

Ali, the Prophet's cousin and son-in-law, was proclaimed Caliph in Medina. To be sure he had had no hand in the conspiracy which had led to the death of his predecessor but it might be held against him that he did not exert his great authority to prevent the deed.

This accusation was cast against him by Mu'awiya, the governor of Damascus and the leading member of the Umayya clan, who in his time had determined the policy of the Caliph Uthman. Also the party of the intriguing Meccans— A'isha, Talha and Zubair—repudiated the newly proclaimed Caliph, demanded vengeance for Uthman, and withdrew from Mecca to Basra. Ali and his armed forces pursued them and defeated them and their allies, soldiers from the armed camp of Basra. In that battle (which is called the Battle of the Camel in memory of the camel that A'isha rode in it) Ali won the whole of the Eastern Empire. But his power was not proportionate to the expanse of his territories. His position was weakened by the perpetual unrest and party strife which shook the great garrison towns of Kufa and Basra. He was in no position to command; he had to bargain with the various factions of his subjects and persuade and convince them in true nomadic fashion.

His only rival still surviving was Mu'awiya who had been Governor of Damascus since the days of Umar. He possessed an army which for many years he had led personally in the border wars against Byzantium. The Greek administration throughout the land had come down to him almost intact. Mu'awiya refused to give up his governorship and demanded that Ali surrender the murderers of the Caliph Uthman. Ali took the field against him and would have beaten him at Siffin, on the middle Euphrates, had the Syrians not been able to escape defeat by a trick. They raised pages of the Koran on the points of their lances and called out: 'Let God decide!' Ali saw through their wiles but the strongly religious party in his own ranks forced him to accept his enemies' proposal and appoint negotiators to try to find a compromise with the other side.

The cleavage in the eastern camp here became very apparent. A large group of Arabs broke away from Ali's camp. These have been called the *Kharijites* or seceders and they announced that a Caliph who was so uncertain of his leadership that he would negotiate with a rival Caliph could in no circum-stances be a true successor of the Prophet. They developed their own dogma and a warlike fanaticism peculiar to themselves. Down the centuries they reappear as opponents to all later Islamic order and as sectarian freebooters. Their last descendants still live as puritan sects in Southern Algeria, Oman and Zanzibar.

Ali's diplomacy also suffered from the disunity of his party. He was com-pelled by his followers to appoint a 'neutral' negotiator, while his opponent, Mu'awiya, sent plenipotentiaries to represent his own party. Later on war broke out again, but Ali had decidedly lost ground. Egypt fell away from him. Mu'awiya made raids into Mesopotamia while avoiding any decisive battle. In 661 Ali was murdered by a Kharijite. His son Hasan sold his claim to succeed his father to Mu'awiya and soon the Umayyad was acknowledged as Caliph throughout the Empire.

What, among all these chaotic events, is cognate to our question about the Arabs' past? Ali's departure from Medina and the campaigns in which Kufa, Basra, Damascus and Egypt played the decisive part show that the centre of gravity of the Empire had shifted. The Arabs had broken out from the penin-sula. Their 'Völkerwanderung' had brought them into the border lands. And from now on these border lands, with their great Arab army camps which were gradually to grow into towns, became the real home of the 'Arabs'.

The Arabian peninsula fell back into the penumbra of its own nomadic civilization and tribal feuds. Mecca and Medina remained centres for pil-grimages, and a certain amount of the wealth of the provinces flowed in. Their inhabitants devoted themselves either to the enjoyment of life or to piety. Schools of theology flourished. Singers and singing girls were trained there and exported to the border lands. The Caliph was never again to take up residence there. It was in the border lands that decisive developments and new spiritual currents were born.

At the same time that the border lands were growing in importance we can also detect a revival of the nomadic underground under the cover of 'urban' Islam. This is already apparent in the Meccan intrigues which led to Uthman's death. The charisma of the Caliph was not enough to give him authority. When he lacks a strong personality he is refused obedience, or only half obeyed. The Commander of the Believers has, like any nomadic sheikh, to create respect by his personality. We can see a nomadic heritage, too, in the wavering support given to Ali and in the tendency of his followers to split into factions or to break away.

This cleavage and the free-for-all fights that went on were, for a long time, characteristic of Mesopotamia. Kufa and Basra picked up again the tribal feuds of Arabia partly under the cover of religious topics and partly under the sign of old Arabian tribal and racial differences. Islam as a religion gained much in variety through these cleavages. Every faction, whether victorious or defeated, called upon it as a justification of its political desires. Seeds were sown for an Islamic opposition, for a religion of asceticism and turning-away from the world, for a puritanical Islam of desperate feats of war and martyrdom. Such new tendencies grew up in the shade of official Islam, in opposition to the 'state' theocracy laid down by the Prophet which sought unity between God's Law and dominion over the world.

9

The Umayyads

WITH MU'AWIYA, THE QURAISH ARISTOCRAT, Governor of Syria and founder of the Umayyad dynasty, the Community of Believers begins, also on the political level, to split into three different layers: the leading Arab aristo-cracy, the non-Arab Muslims and the non-Muslim subjects.

The Arabs of that period were primarily warriors. There was a financial organization which was supposed to distribute the national income accruing from booty and tribute amongst the Arab aristocracy. In theory Arab soldiers could not acquire land outside Arabia. Conquered land, all land, was to be left to be cultivated by the subjects. These were taxed and the state treasury of the Community of Believers was to distribute the profits arising from this co-operative undertaking of the community amongst all members who had valid claims.

Admittedly this scheme was never fully realized in practice. Under Uthman individual, powerful Arabs had already begun to purchase land. Many of the Umayyad princes were great landowners. But still the theory was influential enough to curtail the power of even the rich Arab princes. In spite of their wealth they could not arbitrarily impose their will on other Arabs. The tribes and tribal leaders in the Arab army camps laid claim to certain payments from the booty of the Community of Believers. Nor had the Umayyads the right peremptorily either to admit or disallow such claims. For important govern-mental decisions and, especially those concerning the succession to the Cali-phate, they had to obtain the agreement of the tribal chiefs. They were forced therefore to come to an understanding with their fellow Arabs. In 'consultations' both tact and gifts had to be used to get the support of the chiefs of the various communities for the views and measures put forward by the Caliph. Thus, the principles of Beduin tribal leadership remained within the Arab aristocracy even in the framework of the new giant state.

However, the antithesis between politics and theology never quite allowed the new aristocratic order to achieve tranquillity. Conversions became more numerous and the converted were quick to discover that the new religion gave them the same rights as those possessed by the Arab ruling class. The Arabs, however, did not give up their claims to precedence and to special payments from the booty belonging to the Community of Believers. They were not prepared to share their pensions with an ever increasing number of converts.

In practice newly converted Muslims had to join one of the Arab tribes as so-called *clients* (Mawali). They were considered as socially inferior. 'Three things', said the haughty Arabs, 'make a prayer invalid, should they pass by a man while he is praying: an ass, a dog and a client.' Above all there were only a very few of the new converts who succeeded in being included in the list of those favoured persons who enjoyed state pensions.

The 'clients' formed the great mass of the artisans and labourers in the large towns that had newly sprung up. They supplied the Arab aristocracy with the arts and handicrafts of the old, sedentary civilizations. They did more than the pure Arabs for the theological formulation and the general dissemination of their new religion which assured them that they counted just as much as their Arab overlords. They were, therefore, always ready to follow a leader who appealed to them to rise against the ruling class. Such appeals usually took on the form of religious sects: after the Kharijites came the various branches of partisans of Ali and his descendants and the several Shi'ite sects arose. The Beduin tribes, too, were at war one with the other. The quarrel between the so-called Northern Arab tribes and the so-called Southern Arab tribes began at that time.

The division of the Arab tribes into northerners and southerners is probably just a fiction created by the genealogists but it was a reality for the Arabs of those times. Dissension between 'southern tribes' and 'northern tribes' broke out again and again whenever the governor or caliph no longer had the power to hold the inhabitants of the army camps in check with a rod of iron. Even the Caliphate became the object of tribal conflict. Ibn al-Zubair was proclaimed Caliph in Mecca by the 'northern tribes' and the Umayyads overthrew him with the aid of the 'southern' Kalb after seven years of civil war.

It is not clear what lay behind this conflict between northern and southern Arabs. There are reasons for believing that this rift was an expression of social contrasts. Some attribute it to the conflict of interests caused by the fact that the Arabs, who had penetrated and settled in the borderlands before the conquests, were mostly of 'southern' origin, whereas the conquerors were mostly 'northern'. Some have pointed out the contrast between the puritanical 'southern' milieu of Medina which was devoted to the Prophet from the beginning and the 'northern' aristocracy of Mecca with its pagan, worldly tradition.

Yet with all these disorders and inner conflicts the Umayyads were able to maintain their state of the Arab aristocracy for 89 years. This is due to three great rulers: Mu'awiya, who founded the dynasty, 'Abd-el-Malik, who reorganized the state after the second civil war, and Hisham, who reorganized the state finances.

The Umayyads administered their empire from Damascus but themselves preferred to hold court in palaces in the desert. Many of their castles, hunting lodges and baths can still be seen on the edge of the Syrian Desert. Their ruins and remains often give a clearer picture of their way of life than the written sources. Most Arabic recording of history took place in the time of the Abbasids, an era which looked with little favour on the Umayyads.

The geographical position of these desert palaces is itself surprising. Their ruins stand in the loneliness of the desert, often so isolated that it is only in modern times that travellers have rediscovered them. More surprising than their loneliness are their mural paintings and decorations which contradict all preconceived ideas of Islam being inimical to pictures. They have a pagan Hellenistic air tinged with barbarism. Cheerful frescoes depict animals, hunting scenes and naked women bathing. Hieratic figures of kings in the style of Byzantium can also be seen. Even today the ruins betray that these palaces were once the scene of luxurious and pleasant living.

The preference of the Umayyads for the free life of the desert with all the private pleasures they could have in their palaces finds expression in many sayings about the 'unhealthiness' of town life. In Damascus they felt constricted and yellow fever lurked threateningly in the oases. Contemporary poets sang: 'Beware of the country of the tillers of the soil! It is death, swift death, to come near it.' 'What advantage is there in being near springs? Fever and mosquitoes consume us!'

Every Umayyad Caliph, the members of his family and the principal dignitaries of the state, all had their own encampments. From being originally simply camps these encampments gradually developed into permanent settlements where in the course of time permanent buildings were erected. In many cases even Roman or Byzantine frontier forts were occupied, such as Azraq which had once been part of a line of block-houses stretching from the Gulf of Aqaba to Damascus and from there to Palmyra. In this way the *Badiya* or desert was developed into a Hira, an agglomeration of partly permanent, partly movable dwellings. (K. A. C. Creswell, *A Short Account of Early Muslim Architecture*, Penguin Books, 1958.)

Many stories depict the splendid life, half Beduin, half princely which was led in these palaces. The following is a sample:

The singer Dahman was a camel driver who undertook transport to various places and at the same time carried on trade on his own account. He was also a noble and generous man.

One day, when he had hired out his camels and pocketed his money, he heard sobbing. He got up, went towards the sound and suddenly found himself face to face with a slave-girl, running along the street weeping. He asked her: 'Do you belong to anyone?' 'Yes.' 'To whom?' 'To a woman of Quraish,' and she mentioned the name. 'Would she sell you?' 'Yes.' She went back into the house and informed her mistress: 'A man is here who wants to buy me.' Her mistress said: 'Bring him in.'

Dahman came in and asked how much she wanted for the girl. They agreed on 200 dinars which Dahman paid. He then led the girl away.

Dahman himself continues the story:

She remained long enough in my house to learn my compositions from me and took lessons in singing from Ma'bad, Al-Abjar and other singers in Medina. Later on, when she had become a first-rate singer, I took her to Damascus.

Whenever we halted I bade the camel drivers go inside and remained alone with her near the baggage. I threw the camel drivers' striped cloaks over the bales and rested with her in their shade. I took out some food and we ate. Then we took the wine-skin we always had with us and drank plentifully. We sang until it was time to break camp. So we travelled on until we reached the neighbourhood of Damascus.

One day we had alighted and I was busy teaching her the following song of mine:

> If we could in pity hold back the fate of death,
> Gladly would I hold back 'Abd al-'Aziz's death.
> May God bless you who now lie in your grave,
> And whose spirit now flutters over it like a bird.

I repeated it over and over again until she had learned it and could sing it herself.

Suddenly there stopped in front of us a horseman who had approached unobserved. He greeted us and we returned his greeting. He asked: 'May I sit beside you in the shade for a while?' 'Surely.' He dismounted and I gave him food and drink which he partook of with us. Several times he asked that melody to be sung to him and then asked the singing girl: 'Can you sing melodies by Dahman?' 'Certainly.' 'Then sing me one of his compositions.' She did so, I having winked to her not to let him know I was Dahman.

He was very moved and full of joy and drank several cups while the girl sang to him. When it was time to move he leaned towards me and said: 'Will you sell me this girl?' 'Yes.' 'How much?' I said jokingly: '10,000 dinars.' 'I'll take her for that. Bring ink and parchment.'

I gave him these and he wrote: 'Pay the bearer of this document at sight ten thousand dinars. See to it that he is well treated and let me know what becomes of him.' He then asked: 'Will you give me the girl now or keep her with you until you have received the money?' 'You can have her now.' He swung her on to his steed and said: 'When you reach Bakhra, ask for so and so and give him my letter. He will pay you.' Then he went off with the girl.

I went on my way and when I reached Bakhra I asked after the man he had mentioned. I was directed to him and found him living in a palace.

I went in and gave him the letter. He kissed it and put it on his eyes then called for 10,000 dinars which he paid out to me. Then he said: 'This letter was from the Commander of the Believers' and added, 'Sit down so that I can make a report to the Commander of the Believers about you.' I said: 'I am at your service at any time.' He had provided refreshments for me but these were too meagre, so I continued on my way.

But, on the way I had lost two camels so that out of fifteen I now had thirteen. The Caliph Al-Walid wanted to see me but the steward did not know where to look for me. Al-Walid ordered him, saying: 'He has fifteen camels, seek him out and send him back to me.' But no one could find me since there was none in the caravan with fifteen camels and no one knew my name to ask for me.

The girl remained for a month with Al-Walid before he asked for her. She came to him after having been decked out and he said: 'Sing me something by Dahman.' She sang and he said: 'Sing me more.' She did so then turned to him and said: 'O Commander of the Believers! Have you not heard Dahman's songs from his own lips?' 'No.' 'Yes, you have, by God.' 'I said "no" and you say "yes" by God!' She said: 'Yes, by God, you have heard him.' 'When was that?' 'The man you bought me from was Dahman.' 'Was he?' 'Yes.' 'Why was I not informed?' 'He winked to me not to tell you.'

So the Caliph sent a letter to the Governor of Medina to send Dahman to him. He was sent to him and ever afterwards remained at court in a position of high honour. (Kitab al-Aghani.)

10

Disorders in Mesopotamia

HOWEVER, THE PICTURE OF THE ARABS in Umayyad times is incomplete if it is confined to the aristocratic idyll of the Caliphs in their desert palaces. The major part of the ruling class lived in the armed camps and the most important of these were in Mesopotamia as the course of the eastern conquests lay through broader, richer and more thickly populated lands than did the push to the west towards North Africa and Southern Spain.

The Umayyads ruled these armed camps through governors whom they themselves chose for this most difficult and important task in the state. Two of these enjoy particular renown: Ziyad, 'Son of his Father', Mu'awiya's governor in the East, and Al-Hajjaj, governor for 'Abd al-Malik. It can be seen from their way of ruling, from their careers and enemies and adversaries what cauldrons of unrest and violence the armed camps in the East must have been.

Ziyad was the son of a slave woman, Sumayya, from Ta'if, a small town in the mountains near Mecca. No one knows who his father was. Under Ali he had undertaken several diplomatic missions. Mu'awiya succeeded in winning him over by recognizing him as his half-brother. He entrusted the administration of Basra to him and later appointed him governor of the whole Eastern Empire. Ziyad's speech on the occasion of his entry into Basra as governor is famous in Arabic literature.

We read that this governor made 50,000 Beduins of Arab descent emigrate to Khorasan in the north-east of Persia in order to pacify the tribes of Mesopotamia.

Ziyad and his son 'Ubaid Allah are especially hated by the Shi'ites because it was they who quelled the first Shi'ite revolts. A certain Hujr ibn 'Adi had been a loyal partisan of Ali and had taken part in the Battle of the Camel and in the battle at Siffin against Mu'awiya. After Hasan's abdication he contacted Husain, Ali's younger son who was living in Mecca. In Kufa he organized a revolt while the governor Ziyad was absent from the city. But before the revolt spread Ziyad came back, seized the rebel and assembled a court of justice which pronounced him guilty. This agitator was then sent to Mu'awiya who had him executed. This episode would seem insignificant were it not for the fact that Hujr became the protomartyr of Shi'ism. Other attempts at revolt by followers of Ali were to ensue.

After Mu'awiya's death Husain refused to recognize his son, Yazid, as the new Caliph of the House of Umayya. Invited by the party supporting Ali in Kufa, Husain sent his cousin Muslim Ib'n 'Aqil from Mecca with a troop of partisans. The example of the Prophet's migration to Medina must have motivated such expeditions. Muslim had an enthusiastic reception in Kufa and he sent letters to Husain to follow him. But before Husain reached Kufa, 'Ubaid Allah, Ziyad's son and successor as Umayyad governor, had captured and executed Muslim. The roads connecting Mesopotamia with the desert were guarded and Husain and his retinue were intercepted and surrounded by a small Umayyad troop before they reached the bank of the Euphrates. They tried to persuade him to surrender but Husain refused. It seems that he still hoped that the soldiers in Kufa would hasten to his aid. But those in the great armed camp had been so terrified by Muslim's execution that they did not dare to stir.

The troops who were besieging Husain cut off the water supply, in the hope that thirst would compel him to surrender. After ten days of thirst and hesitation Ali's second son was massacred, along with a small number of his kinsfolk and followers, in the neighbourhood of what is today the town of Karbala, a spot sacred to his memory. 'It did not take longer than it takes to slaughter a camel' runs a report sent to the Caliph Yazid in Damascus. This was the martyrdom of Husain which is still celebrated and enacted year in and year out in Shi'ite countries. The miserable end of this grandson of the Prophet (son of his daughter Fatima, Ali's wife) stirred the imagination of the oppressed racial groups in the Islamic Empire violently.

Only those who have seen how that insignificant battle is still celebrated in the Shi'ite towns of Iraq can form an impression of what these events mean to a Shi'ite.

On the day of the Battle of Karbala you can see simultaneously three Shi'ite passion plays performed on the burnt fields on the edge of Baghdad just below the embankments. Their action is simple, monotonous in its repetition but impressive. The field is divided into two parts; on one side stand the warriors of the Caliph Yazid with their leader 'Ubaid Allah mounted on his charger, all dressed in red. They carry shields, tin swords and sticks representing lances. On the other side of the field is the camp of Husain and his companions. They are dressed in green and equipped like their opponents, save that they are all on foot since, on the day of the battle which is being represented, they were surrounded by their enemies, cut off for days from water and at the end of their strength. With a roll of drums the two armies advance towards each other. One of the Alids dressed in green, leaves his companions and rushes on his enemies. He races through their host exchanging sword blows with this one and that and cuts down many of his opponents. As the battle rages more and more violently around him the flutes shrill and the drums beat more urgently until finally the red band surround him like a swarm of bees and he falls to the ground with the last scream of the pipes. Then the instruments are stilled and a group of mourners detaches itself from the audience. Half-naked men packed tightly together run across the field towards the fallen man beating their breasts rhythmically and calling the name of the slain man: Ya 'Abbas, ya 'Abbas! They bear him on their shoulders and carry him out of the battle lamenting and beating their breasts. This action is repeated time and again. One by one Ali's friends fall victim to the partisans of the diabolical Yazid. The audience knows every part of the action. If anyone gets confused he asks his neighbour: Whose turn is it now? The nearer they come to the end, the longer the battles last. 'Abbas, Husain's half-brother, rushes about the field for a long time, striking down many of his red enemies with his sword, so many that the slain men have to get up again after the battle to reinforce their companions. When finally 'Abbas and, after him, Husain, succumb to their enemies' blows, a cry of sorrow arises not only from the chorus of half-naked mourners; the women in the audience weep aloud too and the men groan and bury their faces in their hands.

Three plays are held at the same time because each village insists on giving its own play although its inhabitants have all come to Baghdad. In almost all such performances many green-robed Alids are opposed to only a few red-robed Umayyads although, of course, it must have been the other way round at the Battle of Karbala. The reason for this is that it is difficult to find actors willing to play the part of such wicked men. 'Ubaid Allah, the Umayyad general, has his face veiled for fear lest the audience's looks of hatred might cause him harm. He has often to be paid a high fee to play the part at all.

On the evening of that same day I was present at a triumphal procession of the victorious Umayyads through the streets of Kazimain, the Persian suburb of Baghdad. One can hardly imagine a more frightful representation of absolute evil. The Umayyad warriors rode on horseback, wearing gold chains and splendid red garments. Their faces and the heads of their horses were covered by black cloth masks. The horses were spattered with blood. Thus they rode to low drum beats through the thronged streets. Behind them came a camel carrying a captured Alid in chains high above the groaning crowd, accompanied by armed guards and bespattered with blood from head to toe. Innumerable arrows were sticking in his body. Behind him came Husain's riderless horse with gaping wounds streaming blood. Then came the horrible sight of the headless corpses of the fallen borne on swaying camels. They had dressed the carcase of a freshly slaughtered ox in human clothes with boots on its feet and let the long red, fleshy stump of the neck hang out, a frightful sight.

All Kazimain was in the streets. A stillness of death fell when the drums were heard in the distance. A rain of curses, screeched out by the women and murmured by the men, fell upon the Umayyad mercenaries and their caliph as they passed. The crowd uttered a piercing cry of sorrow when their eyes caught sight of Husain's disfigured corpse.

I have never seen so many women in an oriental street as on that evening. All watched the procession pass; black veiled forms stood closely packed on the flat roofs of the one-storey buildings. Lines of veiled women stood along the streets and blocked the lanes. As their eyes fell on the headless corpse they all broke into a shrill lamentation: Ya Husain, ya Husain!

With the death of Husain there really begins the series of revolutionary attempts instigated by the Alids. A certain Mukhtar, from Ta'if, the same town from which Ziyad came, had refused to bear witness at the trial of Hujr. He had taken part in Muslim's revolt in Kufa and, when this collapsed, he was locked up. After Husain's death he was set free since the Umayyads were inclined, after the bloody deed exercised upon the Prophet's grandson, to deal more gently with his adherents. Mukhtar later went to Mecca, where the anti-caliph, Ibn Zubair, raised his standard against the Umayyads. He fought for Ibn Zubair but soon quarrelled with him and withdrew to his home town. It is probable that it was during this period of withdrawal that Mukhtar developed the peculiar religious ideas which he left behind as his contribution to Shi'ite tradition.

Mukhtar returned to Kufa where he announced that he had been sent by Muhammad ibn al-Hanafiya to help the cause of the Alids to victory. Muhammad ibn al-Hanafiya was the son of Ali by a slave and after Husain's death he had become the head of the Alid family. It seems that he was never in complete agreement with Mukhtar, nevertheless he called Mukhtar and an expeditionary force from Kufa to release him when the anti-caliph Ibn Zubair was holding him prisoner in Mecca. Mukhtar found himself several times in strong opposition to the official Alid party which was already established in Kufa before his arrival. Ali's third son neither recognized him nor denied him before the citizens of Kufa.

Mukhtar's methods were religious and military at one and the same time. He preached in a sort of rhymed prose reminiscent of the Koran and allowed people to say of him that he was inspired by the Archangel Gabriel, as he had previously inspired Muhammad! Above all, it was he who introduced the idea of a *Mahdi* into Shi'ism. He promised his adherents that a Prince of Peace would appear amongst Ali's descendants and conquer the world.

He reached the height of his military and political success when he succeeded in winning over to his cause an old general of Ali's, Malik al-Ashtar. He is said to have shown the general a letter of recommendation from Ali's third son, which he had presumably forged himself.

Together with the general Al-Ashtar he began open rebellion in 685. The official, more moderate Alids of Kufa forsook his cause but the Mawali, the less privileged clients, followed him. He defeated 'Ubaid Allah ibn Ziyad, governor of Kufa, who was held responsible for Husain's murder, and Kufa became his capital.

One of the most renowned generals of the time, Al-Muhallab, marched against Mukhtar from Basra along with Ziyad's second son. While Al-Ashtar was absent he attacked him and slew him after a four months' long siege of the citadel of Kufa.

* * *

However, the Alids were not the greatest thorn in the sides of the governors of Mesopotamia. The Kharijites caused them even greater difficulties. This is illustrated by the career of Al-Muhallab, the conqueror of Mukhtar, who had been in command of raids into Multan and Sijistan and against Kabul during Mu'awiya's reign. He had then entered the service of the anti-caliph Ibn Zubair and had been ordered by him to proceed to the East to take over the administration of Khorasan. But at that time a band of Kharijites had become so dangerous that they threatened Basra and Al-Muhallab was despatched against them. He defeated them at Sillabra in 686 and rid Basra of them. He then marched against Mukhtar whom he defeated in the following year. Then came campaigns against the Umayyads and their Syrian troops but the Kharijites raised their heads again and the general had once more to turn his attention to them. In the meantime the Umayyads overwhelmed the supporters of the anti-caliph Ibn Zubair in Mecca and Al-Muhallab put his services at the disposal of the Umayyad 'Abd al-Malik. The first Umayyad governor of Mesopotamia felt that he could do without his services but the Kharijites inflicted a series of defeats on him. A section of them, known as the Azariqa (plural of Azraqi), constituted a permanent threat to Basra. They massacred everyone who did not belong to their way of thinking and even declared as unbelievers other Kharijites who did not join them, the Azariqa, in their campaigns.

Pressed by Al-Muhallab's attacks the Azariqa had made an exceedingly capable man, Qatari ibn al-Fuja'a, their 'caliph'. This latter led his followers over the mountains of Southern Persia into Fars and Kirman and in those distant parts, protected by immense mountain chains and deserts, he re-organized his warriors. Then he attacked once again the lower regions of the Euphrates and the Tigris, took Ahwaz and threatened Basra.

A new governor was appointed in Kufa, the renowned Al-Hajjaj. He called Al-Muhallab back into service although he had supported the Umayyads' enemy, Ibn Zubair. Al-Muhallab pushed Qatari and his followers back into Central Persia in battles which went on for several years and the Kharijites held out for a long time in Kirman. But, finally, a breach in their ranks brought about a quarrel between the Mawali, the clients, and the pure Arabs. The clients remained in Kirman where they were beaten by Al-Muhallab while the Arabs under Qatari withdrew to Tabaristan, the wild mountain region on the southern shore of the Caspian Sea. Qatari was killed there in an ambush laid for him by the Arab governor of Rayy (close to present-day Teheran) and his followers were exterminated in subsequent battles. This Kharijite leader was the prototype of an Arab chief of pre-Islamic times, eloquent, an excellent poet, brave and inordinately proud of his descent and of his independence from the whole world.

Al-Muhallab, who had finally extirpated the Azariqa, in his last days achieved the governorship of Khorasan which had been promised him a decade earlier by Ibn Zubair.

It is said that the governor, Al-Hajjaj, had been a school teacher in Ta'if. In the service of the Umayyad 'Abd al-Malik he defeated the anti-caliph Ibn Zubair and had him put to death before the sacred Ka'ba in Mecca in 692. After serving as Governor of Medina and Southern Arabia where he restored law and order, 'Abd al-Malik sent him to Mesopotamia. We also have a description of his entry into Kufa and of his inaugural speech.

He required the support of Syrian troops in the wars he had to wage against the Kharijites. Along with Qatari, another Kharijite leader, Shabib, gave him a lot of trouble. This latter was from the desert in the region of Mosul and had good relations with the Syriac and Kurdish Christians of Northern Iraq. A shrewd guerilla warrior, he defeated several generals whom Al-Hajjaj sent against him. Twice it happened that the Governor lost patience with cautious generals who, in his opinion, were not showing enough energy against the Kharijites and replaced them. Both newly appointed commanders were beaten and slain by Shabib, who even occupied Kufa for a time. In the end he was beaten by the Syrian troops of the Umayyads towards the beginning of 697.

These Syrian troops received a higher wage and a larger share of the booty than did the 'regulars' in the army camps. The bitterest war Al-Hajjaj had to wage was an army revolt of these 'regulars' led by a certain 'Abd al-Rahman. He had been sent at the head of Mesopotamian tribes to Sijistan but turned back with his troops and attacked the Governor. He conquered both army camps, Kufa and Basra but finally Al-Hajjaj succeeded in overcoming him in the murderous battles of Dair Jamajim and Maskin in 701.

A precarious peace reigned in the exhausted province after all these campaigns and the governor Al-Hajjaj was in a position to dig canals, introduce Arabic as the only language used in the administration, and turn his interest towards the state finances and the striking of a coinage. He forced the new converts, the Mawali, to leave the army camps and return to the villages to till the soil which had lain fallow for so long. It is said that he even branded the name of his village on the palm of each one so that he might not run away. He built a new city, called Wasit, half-way between Kufa and Basra and from there kept an eye on the two army camps with his Syrian garrison.

After his death every trace of his grave was erased so that his enemies could not avenge themselves on his corpse. This measure shows how insecure the eastern provinces must have remained in spite of his iron hand.

II

The Abbasids

THE UMAYYAD DYNASTY collapsed a generation after the death of the great governor Al-Hajjaj when at length one of the Alid revolts succeeded, the Arab aristocrats being no longer able to withstand the concerted attacks of the under-privileged Arabs and the Islamized clients. The afore-mentioned son of Ali, Muhammad ibn al-Hanafiya, for whom Mukhtar had fought, had sons, the last of whom, being childless, is said to have bequeathed his claim to the leadership of the Community of Believers to a descendant of 'Abbas, the Prophet's uncle. The new dynasty of Islam was called the Abbasids after him.

The heirs of the house of Abbas sent propagandists for their claims to spiritual and temporal power to the far East of the Empire, to Khorasan where the governors of Mesopotamia had usually settled the most unruly Arab tribes. After initial failures one of these propagandists was successful with the inhabi-tants of the province and the troops stationed there. He was Abu Muslim, off-spring of a Persian client. What he preached must have been anything but orthodox doctrine. There on the borders of Central Asia the Abbasids living far away in Mecca and Kufa appeared as long prophesied God-kings and princes of peace. Their coming would rid the world of all injustice and assure for their supporters power, riches and glory in both this world and the next.

The black banners which the Abbasids raised against the Umayyads in 746 were a sign that a new kingdom of God was about to spread over the world. Having firmly established their power in the East, thanks to divisions among the Arab tribes, the rebellious armies advanced quickly westwards and broke the power of the Umayyads in battle on the Greater Zab in Central Mesopotamia. The Abassid Abu-l-'Abbas was proclaimed Caliph with the ambiguous title Al-Saffah (shedder of blood or of gifts).

Abu Muslim remained in the East and held the office of Governor of Khorasan for the Abbasids for the next five years. In 751 his general, Ziyad ibn Salih, defeated a Chinese army at Talas in Transoxiania thus opening up the way for the Muslims into Central Asia. Four years later the Caliph, Al-Saffah, managed to lure Abu Muslim, to whom his house owed its power, to Mesopo-tamia where he had him murdered. Persian and Turkish folk romances are still told from which one can see how strongly his fate must have affected those peoples subject to the Arabs.

The Abbasids' treatment of Abu Muslim is characteristic of the methods employed by this new dynasty of Arabs. They used him and with him the discontented and underprivileged in the Empire in order to bring about the downfall of the Umayyads. At the height of his power Abu Muslim had welded together a great coalition consisting of not only the Persian clients and the Persian landed gentry, the Dehqans, whom he himself had won over to his own kind of Islam, but also Arab elements, mainly from the South of the peninsula, who were not full partners in the power of the ruling class, partisans of Ali and his house, and, in general terms, all the enemies of the House of Umayya.

But no sooner had the Abbasids come to power than they cast the mantle of orthodoxy over all the alliances they had concluded with the heterodox and extremists. With the murder of Abu Muslim they broke their ties with the Shi'a, Ali's party. Henceforth they were to appear as champions of orthodoxy. Quite early they set on foot religious propaganda which began to depict 'Abbas, Muhammad's uncle, as one of his principal supporters, although he had fought at Badr *against* the young Community of Believers. This then went on to denounce the Umayyads and their forefathers as enemies of the Prophet and unworthy successors of the first four Caliphs. And the Abbasids appear as restorers of the true religion of the Prophet as practised in the early period in Mecca and Medina.

A poet of the time exclaims: 'Would that the "tyranny" of the sons of Umayya came back to this earth and the "righteousness" of the sons of 'Abbas descended to Hell!'

The rise of the Abbasids can be called a 'corrected' revolution. It was a revolution because it stripped the existing ruling class of their power. It was 'corrected' because the new caliphs dropped to a great extent the revolutionary forces on which they had at first relied. In their efforts to make their power permanent the Abbasids relied neither on Persian support from Khorasan nor on the old Arab ruling class of the days of the conquests but, rather, they developed a *mélange* of both parties on which they put their own stamp.

They went back to the old oriental idea of a divine ruler. To be sure, in Islam they could no longer appear as 'Gods' but they did the next best thing: they surrounded themselves with the Nimbus of His vicar on earth. Unapproachable in their palace cities in Hashimiya, Baghdad, Samarra, Raqqa and all the rest, they delegated the powers of government through a ramified hierarchy of officials whom they arbitrarily appointed, dismissed or executed. Even the greatest of these officials had to prostrate themselves before them. The executioner stood by their throne with drawn sword. These servants in mundane matters were appointed by the Abbasids without consideration for any inherited privileges. Even Jews and Christians could achieve high positions if it pleased their almighty master, the Caliph, that they should do so.

The Abbasids sought to win over the orthodox as their allies. They, the representatives of the Prophet on Earth, wished to use the respect enjoyed by scholars and masters of the religious sciences in order to strengthen their position. Just as the Umayyads had known how to win the 'free approval' of those Arabs who had shared power with them, so did the Abbasids cultivate with care the approval of the religious authorities in their empire. These, in their turn, were able to obtain and keep alive the respect of the people for their unapproachable rulers.

The Arab aristocracy lost its place to a large extent as mainstay of the Empire as a result of this preference for scholars, and the Abbasid Empire became 'Arab' in a different sense from the Umayyad Empire. To be sure, many of its great men were still of Arab descent while others, from snobbery, invented their own Arab genealogies. The Caliph himself belonged to a great Arab family, although, for generations, the mothers of the Abbasid Caliphs were Persians. The Persian, Syrian and Iraqi dignitaries of the state stood side by side with the Arabs on an equal footing and were, like them, completely dependent on the favour of their master. In later centuries these were joined more and more by emancipated slaves who were raised to high office, having been bought by traders as youths in the border lands and brought to court. That this happened shows most clearly that it was the ruler's favour alone that decided who the dignitaries of the state were to be and how high they rose. The proud Arab was just as much a slave in the presence of the Caliph as prisoners of war and bought slaves from Turkistan and Russia.

On the other hand, knowledge, and especially learning in religious matters, gave a Muslim a modicum of independence from his ruler. Strictly speaking, a scholar was not the slave of the Caliph like his officials and dignitaries. Thanks to his spiritual power and the respect in which he was held by the masses who, without him, could not be held in check, he was accepted by the ruler as a sort of weak ally. This or that scholar might be suppressed, removed or silenced but the Caliph had to retain the good will of the scholarly caste as a whole.

Thus in the Abbasid Empire the pen gained supremacy over the sword and hereditary nobility. Clients and Arabs contended with each other in the lists of science, poetry, philosophy and theology.

Along with the scholar we have the merchant, who, also, was not the absolute slave of the Caliph. To be sure, the government was given to sequestrating his wealth at the time of his death but as long as he lived he was permitted to travel, trade and amass profits. It was recognized that his enterprise, experience and shrewdness were essential for the maintenance and welfare of the state.

Scholars and merchants were the real citizens of the Islamic Empire. It seemed created just for them and it was they who developed and worked out its charac⁄teristic way of life and culture. It was they who created, along with their lesser fellows the shopkeepers and artisans of the bazaars, those cities of the Thousand and One Nights which we still imagine typical of the Arab Orient.

The sources have nothing to say about the peasants who were certainly the great majority of the population. Only now and then do we come across the Beduins in later history but only as plunderers of caravans and, in times of trouble, as armed bands.

So, to what extent was this new Islamic Empire, which began with the Abbasids, an Arab empire? Certainly its language was Arabic, which pre-vailed both as a colloquial and literary language in the 'Arab lands' as far as North Africa and as the language of letters far beyond Persia and deep into India and Central Asia. It was only in the tenth and eleventh centuries that Persian was reborn as a literary language and Turkish only became one in the fifteenth century. But, apart from the language, what about the race or races? A greater mixture of races can hardly be imagined than the one existing in the Abbasid Empire, all sharing in the power. Religion? To be sure, Islam had come out of Arabia and we have seen how indissolubly it is tied to the Arabic language and we have recognized how opposed this religion was to the Beduin Arab life of the desert tribes. The later development of Islam was due in the main to Greek influences and the work of scholars of those great cities whose civilization we would hesitate to describe as 'Arab'.

Of course, there is no reason for not calling a civilization after the language which is its principal medium. But when we say that the civilization beginning with the Abbasids was an Arab civilization we must be conscious of the fact that we are using the word 'Arab' in a sense essentially different from that of the aristocratic racial Arabism of Umayyad times. Indeed, in a sense diametrically opposed in many respects to that of the ancient Beduin Arabs. . . .

Of one thing we can be certain when we talk about the bearers of the torch of civilization in this classical Arab epoch of the Abbasids, that class of merchants and scholars who were the fertile soil out of which grew the advanced civilization of the Middle East in the Middle Ages: they were all *Muslims*. The Muslim Empire comprised them all: Indians, Turkomans, Afghans, Persians, Kurds, Armenians, Berbers and Negroes. Similar social and administrative institutions existed in all parts of the Muslim Empire. A Muslim pilgrim felt 'at home' even in regions whose local tongue was foreign to him. The same mosques gave him shelter in which the same type of scholar dealt with the same problems using the very same methods. Near the mosque there was the same type of market, the Suqor Bazaar, and from Fez to Samarkand trade and life were carried on according to the same principles.

All Muslims who were wealthy enough made the pilgrimage to Mecca at least once in a lifetime and merchants travelled over the whole breadth of the Empire from Spain to India. Scholars travelled in search of knowledge, poets and singers in search of princely favour, officials and soldiers at the behest of their master the Caliph, merchants for profit, pilgrims for the edification they sought at the holy places and the propagandists of religious and political ideas on the service of their new ideas and their concealed prophets.

According to the Spanish historian, Américo Castro, the principal characteristic of classical Islamic civilization was its fluidity, the infinite variation and juxtaposition of similar things. The pleasure the spirit of a Muslim derived from the spectacle of the infinite variety of the world and its component parts within the wide framework of the Empire:

When the Moors gave expression to their consciousness of life it could clearly be seen that they saw themselves as floating along, as if they were being carried away through a world, which, too, was floating along with no fixed purpose. Here is an example from many. A man hears a song which moves him; he stops to listen and then expresses what has happened as follows:

'Do not reproach me with being inconstant because my heart is moved by a voice singing.

'At times one should remain serious, at others give way to emotion, just as, from wood, two things can be made: the warrior's bow and the singer's lute.' (*El libro de las Banderas*, translated E. García Gómez.)

According to these verses the life of a Muslim was as varied and 'inconsistent' as that of matter itself. In the poem quoted the word 'taqallub', 'change', 'inconstancy' denotes a person's change of direction or of interest. This word is connected with the word 'qalaba', 'to overturn, change' and again with the noun 'qualb' which, according to the dictionaries, means 'heart, soul, spirit, inner thought'. In the language one feels the rhythm of variety and changeableness which exists in the driving forces of an Arab's life. He neither feels compelled nor is he accustomed to contemplate things quietly as essential facts. The Arab flows along, a part of a transitory world on which he has built his life. Rather like a river which only achieves a sense of self-realization through the sea into which it runs and the course it follows, existing simultaneously and completely as river and sea.

No wonder that the Moors were interested in alchemy, that is, in the transmutation of metals, in the influence of the stars on men's lives, in the succession of Neoplatonic ideas or in the flow of clear, repetitive designs and ornaments which we call Arabesques. It was not only the satisfaction in achieving a goal an Arab felt as he let the water flow along the ditches and irrigation channels and toiled in the eternal circle of sowing, reaping and sowing again. The water flowed through aqueducts and pipelines just as the spirit of the wine passed through the tubes of the distillation apparatus. Did not Ibn Battuta, the great traveller, play on the words of the Koran saying '(Praise be to God) who has made Earth a wide expanse for His Servants that they may go along therein on wide paths' (Sura 71, vv. 19, 20), and again, 'Who established the three events of human life on this earth: creation from dust, return into the earth and resurrection' (Sura 20, v. 57).

The translators of the afore-mentioned Ibn Battuta (1304–1377) say: 'Few peoples have carried the love of travel so far as the Arabs' (*Voyages d'Ibn Batouta*, trans. Defrémery et Sanguinetti, Paris, 1893). 'And this same traveller describes Cairo as follows: "There you can find everything you desire: wise men and fools, industrious men and good-for-nothings, tame and wild, high-born and low-born, unknown and famous. The inhabitants of Cairo are so many that their surge makes the city a raging sea. . . . Although it was founded a long time ago the city enjoys youth which is ever renewed" (I. 67f.). Thus one feels one's own life flowing away like a river: this is what I have tried to bring out. They did not travel to 'see the sights' as Herodotus did but, rather, so that the course of their own lives might be in harmony with this wandering and change of scenery.' (*Ensayo de Historiología*, New York, 1950.)

12

The Zenith of Islamic Civilization

FOR THE SAKE OF CLARITY we prefer to describe the civilization of the Middle East which began with the Abbasids, as a Muslim civilization rather than an Arab one. Nevertheless it is necessary to describe this civilization in order to arrive at an answer to our question 'Who were the Arabs?' This civilization did not comprise only Arabs nor were Arabs the only people who built it up, but it had a decisive influence on the character of the Arabs.

How can anything so complex as a civilization be described in a few pages? One way leads to the artistic achievements of such a civilization, for works of art are creations which express freely the character of their creators.

If we pass the spectrum of the Muslim arts before our eyes we see that it lacks certain art forms which we in the West count among the most important. He who has acquired some familiarity with their traditions and conventions will also see that other arts which we in the West count among the 'minor' or 'applied' arts hold a more central position in the Muslim world. Muslim literature has no drama in the tradition of Greek tragedy (although certain beginnings are visible in popular literature) and only Persian has an epic. The novel is a modern development which arose by imitating Western models, with the exception of a few popular romances. There is practically no monumental sculpture or painting.

But, on the other hand, if one studies classic Muslim vases and vessels for a time one realizes that these marvels of harmony can no more be brushed aside as a 'minor art' than any other great work of art. The same goes for really good carpets compared to which hybrid forms like European Gobelin tapestries are seen as compromises between the art of the carpet weaver and that of painting. Persian miniatures also can be treated on the same level as western painting. In later times calligraphy developed into a fine art in its own right.

The fields in which works of art of the classic Muslim Empire can be compared with those of the western world are restricted; but the epic (if the Persian epic can be allowed to speak for the whole cultural area), architecture, narrative prose, essay prose, lyric poetry, and painting all provide parallels between Western and classic Muslim works of art.

If we compare works like Firdausi's *Shahnama* and Dante's *Divina Commedia* it becomes evident that the differences between Eastern and Western life are enormous even in works of art of the same 'genre'. In the *Divina Commedia* the strict rules of composition (three parts each of which contains thirty-three cantos) are combined with a highly dramatic and passionate treatment of the individual episodes; the great poem is given unity by the person of the poet himself as he wanders through Heaven and Hell. Firdausi's great work is, on the other hand, a loose series of episodes held together by the thread of Iranian history. 'The poet refrains from trying to see any specific "meaning" in the history he narrates. Firdausi is alone among the major contemporary students of history in that he seems to be utterly unable to extract any general ideas from the developments which he presents in such masterly fashion.' (G. E. von Grunebaum, *Islam, Essays in the Nature and Growth of a Cultural Tradition.*) The author of this sentence contrasts the attitude of the Persian poet to that of Virgil. Firdausi has no framework of philosophy into which he would force the events of his history. As a result he can see no real tragedy since a tragic situation arises from man's will coming into conflict with a closely knit, superhuman obstacle, 'fate'. Instead of 'fate' all Firdausi sees is chance and transitoriness.

Yet, this lack of the dramatic and colossal does not indicate any defect. That brilliant kaleidoscopic vision of people being born, living their lives and dying, on which the beauty of Firdausi's poem rests, would not have come about had he been constrained by any definite philosophical frame such as alone makes tragedy possible. Perhaps something of this can be perceived through the grey veil of a prose translation:

Such a dragon came out of the River Kashaf that the world lay before him like a flat hand. His length stretched over the land from city to city and his breadth from mountain to mountain. The heart of everyone was filled with fear of him and every man was on his guard night and day. His foam burnt up even the feathers of the vultures and the earth heaved under his poison. He pulled the furious crocodile from the water and plucked the winged eagle from the sky. He emptied the earth of all human beings and four-footed creatures, who surrendered the world to him to live in. When I saw that there was no one on the face of the earth who dared to challenge him I banished all fear and anguish from my heart, strengthened by the Ruler of the World, the pure God. I girded my loins in the Name of the One on high and mounted my light-coloured elephant. I went out like a furious crocodile, ready for battle. His breath was sharp.

'Farewell!' said I to all who saw me raise my club against the dragon. I advanced towards him. He looked like a mountain, every hair on him thick as a rope, his eyes like two lakes of fire. He saw me and roared and rushed on me full of fury. I had planned, O King, to approach close to him not-withstanding the fire he breathed. His tongue licked across the ground, which became like the Chinese Sea with his poison. I roared at him like a lion as befits a courageous man. When he had hemmed me in I raised my club to strike, the one shaped like a cow's head. With the strength of God, Lord of the World, I spurred the elephant forward. I brought my club down on the dragon's head. You would say that the vault of heaven had fallen upon a mountain. I smashed his skull like the head of a mad elephant and out of it flowed a river of poison like the Nile. *One* wound was enough; he needed no other. His brain lay like a mountain on the ground. The River Kashaf became a river of gall. The earth became a place for rest and sleep. An enormous crowd looked on at this fight for that dragon was bitterly hated. They called me 'Sam, who makes only *one* wound.' The whole world poured precious stones over me.

Let us compare Firdausi's description with Dante's description of a dragon: 'Behold the wild beast with the pointed tail who strides over mountains and breaks through walls and weapons. Here he is who makes the whole world stink!' Thus said my guide to me and signed to him to come on shore near to the end of our stony road. That unclean image of deceit came up and thrust its head and breast ashore but did not drag its tail on land. Its face was the face of a just man and its hairiness appeared outwardly so friendly. The rest of its body was that of a serpent. It had two paws, hairy up to the armpits, its back, and breast and both its sides were studded with knots and rings. Never have Turks or Tartars woven fabrics with such colours and embroidery; nor did Arachne ever lay such tissues. As sometimes barks lie upon the shore, half in water, half on land, and as among the greedy Germans the beaver plants himself to catch his fish, so lay that foul monster on the bank which was of stone, surrounded by sand dunes. Its whole tail was threshing in the air, the venomous point turned upwards, like a scorpion armed with its sting.

My guide said: 'It is now time to wend our way a little to that evil beast, lying yonder.' So we went down to the right and took ten paces on the shore, avoiding the sand and flames. As we came closer I saw not far off on the slope of the sand some people sitting. The Master then said to me: 'So that you may have full experience of this on all sides, go round and see what their condition is. Let your conversation be short and, until you return I shall speak with him yonder that he may lend us his strong shoulders. . . .' (*Inferno*, Canto XVIII, beginning.)

There is something naïve about Firdausi as compared with Dante. His dragon slayer narrates what he sees, step by step, in imagery interspersed with neat, short comparisons. The narrator expresses his own horror in not a single word, as he observes how the brain of the slain dragon flows out, how the monster's tongue licks over the ground. The beast which pulls crocodiles from the river and snatches eagles from the air is described with a visual delight.

Dante, on the other hand, begins in his very first words to create an atmosphere. He does not merely describe his monster objectively but also notes and evaluates the impression it made on the describer. Dante uses adjectives which pass judgement on the beast 'sozza immagine di frode', 'la fera pessima', and his dialogue introduces a dramatic element into the narrative. He increases the tension by interrupting the action. Detailed comparisons, whole sentences and verses, draw the narrative out and transform it from being purely descriptive into a dramatic encounter between the reader and the beast. The reader's attention is diverted to the barks and to the beaver only to be brought back again suddenly to the dragon.

It is not easy for us, to whose traditional art world Dante belongs, to discern the motives for Firdausi's refraining from involving his reader in any way in his poem. The reader has only to 'look on'; he is not expected to 'experience' or 'participate'; in no way has he to identify himself with the narrative or make up his mind about it. The world is a *fait accompli*. Man did not create it and so he should not presume to change anything in it.

If the reader accepts this 'proviso' of Firdausi's, if he keeps himself and his feelings outside, the Persian poet is prepared to show him the world as it *is*, as a garden, verdant and blooming, with the most marvellous and rare plants. To keep at a distance and forget oneself is a prerequisite for seeing the picture in all its variety and colourfulness. The dragon is a grotesque, even disgusting, beast; the hero, Sam, on his light-coloured elephant may be handsome, but both are there as equal creatures in this diverse world.

Dante's beast is disgusting from the point of view of the human being who sees it and must approach it. This 'sozza immagine di frode' does not exist in its own right as does the 'Dragon from the River Kashaf'. Dante's beast has an *effect* both on the describer and the reader. Thus Dante's poem is 'humanistic' composed for and from the point of view of men. Firdausi, on the other hand, looks at things from a superhuman point of view. His poem follows the contortions and ramifications, the growth and decay of this world in all its branches and parts; men are only parts in this involved game. The game itself, not just man's part in it, is the theme of the poem. Firdausi might well have said: 'Only the game as a whole is an object worthy of a poem. . . .'

The illustrators of the great Persian epic have, with their means, reproduced the spirit of the poem in an incomparable manner. If we compare one of their works with a Renaissance painting dealing with the drama of human life, such as the frescoes by Signorelli in Orvieto, we see the contrast between the above-mentioned poetic works reproduced in painting.

Signorelli depicts in a moving way the attitudes of men rising from the grave or judged and on their way to Hell. The frescoes are full of movement which carries the viewer along with it: it has to be followed with the eye and with the spirit. To be sure, Signorelli was a 'classic' painter, that is to say, every one of his characters lives in itself and exists by virtue of its own being and importance; but at the same time he was a humanistic painter and his persons alone are important to him. Their passion, their 'soul', had to be expressed in the picture, too.

A painter of Persian miniatures knows nothing of this high evaluation of what is human. Monsters, trees, rocks, the hero, plants and sky, all have the same value to him. One could call his way of painting 'idyllic', but be careful not to underrate him. We can say his work is 'decorative', but that is not enough if by decorative we mean something superficially and pleasantly inconsequential. The Persian, too, sees some 'inner' meaning. However pretty his picture is, it is not devoid of 'content'. But the Persian refuses to let his human figures say more about what he is trying to convey than the rest of the picture. The whole is intended to be a picture, a polished mirror of the inner harmony which is or should be fundamental to this world. No doubt, Signorelli and his art would appear 'superficial' to the Persians for it gives transitory things, men with their torments and conditions, emotions of the moment, 'undeserved' importance, instead of striving for the basic superhuman harmonies underlying them.

Poetry is *the* art of the Arabs; they hold poets in much higher esteem than other artists who are considered mere artisans. The mass of poetry we possess is enormous. In Abbasid times not only Arabs, but also Persians, devoted themselves to composing Arabic verse. Arab and European scholars have dealt with this poetry *in extenso*. The Arabs collected and commented on the works of their great poets. Philologists in Baghdad in classical and post-classical times put together anthologies of the most renowned pieces and debated the accomplishments of this or that poet. Since the eighteenth century Europeans have produced critical editions of one Diwan after the other (a Diwan is the collected works of one poet). They have tried to make a historical survey of the development of Arabic poetry, as is done with the literature of Europe. They have produced translations and poetical renderings in which, unfortunately, they often paid more attention to their own versification than to translation. They have compiled biographies of poets and written monographs on poets and their works.

In spite of all these efforts in both East and West it is not easy to obtain access to the Arabic poetry of the Middle Ages. For one thing there is the difficulty of the language used in classical verse. The Arab poets, who grew up in towns, usually went for the perfection of their talents to the desert, to some Beduin tribe or other which still spoke the old Arabic language with its wealth of synonyms, its innumerable words for animals and plants and its traditional pictures and hyperboles for the simple things and events of Beduin life. Arab schoolboys of today read their classical poets in glossed editions. Every verse contains three or four words which have to be explained in notes. After having given the meaning of the individual words in the verse the commentary very often adds: 'In this verse the poet means . . .', since the verse as a whole requires further clarification.

People with a good memory and the requisite industry can overcome this language barrier. But can such scholars derive from the huge treasure-house of Arabic poetry that aesthetic pleasure which they richly deserve as reward for their industry? It appears at least questionable. Many European scholars have edited and published Arab poets; only one of them, Theodor Nöldeke, collected an anthology which he entitled *Delectus Veterum Carminum Arabicorum* (Berlin, 1890; 2nd ed. Wiesbaden, 1961). Innumerable Oriental scholars have collected, annotated, taken extracts from and made comparisons of poems, as well as composing their own. Few of these poets can give the European an indication of what is of artistic value therein. A modern author who is fully at home in both cultures, Amin al-Rihani, confesses frankly that he knows no Arab poet who for majesty and power of expression can be compared with Shakespeare and that there are only three Arab poets who really move him: the mystics Al-Ma'arri and Ibn al-Farid, and the most famous of all later poets, Al-Mutanabbi.

Behind the barrier of language difficulties there is a second and much more difficult one to be overcome. That of artistic traditions, conventions and associations in which Arabic verse lives and which are completely foreign to us.

To mention only one of these: the principal form for lyric poetry is called the *Qasida*, but this 'form' does not only prescribe such things as the rhyme and the metre. Its authority extends even to the content of the poem. A Qasida must always contain the same episodes in the same order. The only freedom the poet has is to vary the length of these episodes and the rhetoric means he uses in them. The poem begins with the description of the effaced traces of a Beduin encampment in the desert sands. The poet sees these before him and recalls the time when a camp stood on that spot. His beloved had lived there and he describes her and their meetings nostalgically. He then sets off on a journey across the desert, describing and praising his horse or camel and often interweaving his own and his horse's past achievements. His description of his journey may be more or less detailed, and here he can deal with desert animals, hunting scenes and battles. The goal of the journey is without fail a great man, the prince or potentate to whom the poem is dedicated. Finally there follows an often long panegyric of this man and of his ancestors, for it is from this patron that the poet hopes to get a reward for his Qasida.

Of course, this convention has its origins in ancient Beduin times, but has been retained throughout all the centuries. A large part of all Arabic poetry has been forced into this scheme, although some poets revolted against its restrictions. Among these we naturally find poets of Persian origin. But the Qasida with its great tradition was victorious again and again over such rebellions, and it was only in the last century that it was defeated by the attitudes of modern times, namely 'modernism' in Arabic literature.

In view of an artistic tradition so foreign to us should we refrain from trying to penetrate to the heart of this poetry, to catch its 'message'? Has it any message at all? And, if so, is it accessible to us? There are certain hidden ways to it, back doors through which a European can manage to get a glimpse into the inner chambers of this labyrinth of words. Although he can hardly succeed in understanding or mastering it as a whole, nevertheless he can get some idea of the 'purpose', the mainspring of that extensive, complicated and debilitating effort of the human mind. He can guess the direction in which such 'purpose' must be sought and thus get a handle which permits him to arrange the whole complex of classical Arabic poetry as an artistic phenomenon and assign to it a temporary and tentative place in the world of art.

One of these ways has been opened up to us by G. E. von Grunebaum by translating a part of Al-Baqillani into English (*A Tenth-Century Document of Arabic Literary Criticism*, Chicago, 1950). This Baqillani, who died in Baghdad in 1013, was a renowned theologian of his time. He wrote a book on the inimitability of the language of the Koran and in order to prove his thesis he gives detailed analyses of two famous Arabic Qasidas, dealing with them verse by verse and pointing out their weaknesses and beauties. His statements show the effect 'poetry' must have had on him better than most works of philologists and literary theoreticians. He says:

The most original verse in the field of eulogy is by Al-Nabigha:

'For thou art like the night which overtakes me even when I imagine the distance from thee is great.'

He means thereby that the power of the King he is praising is like the night which extends over everything.

Al-Farazdaq, a famous poet who died in 728, imitated him and said:

'Were the wind to carry me off and were thou to try to follow me, I would be like a thing overtaken by fate. . . .'

But neither in the words he used nor in his ideas did he reach the level reached by Al-Nabigha before him—Then Al-Akhtal, who died in 710, took up the same idea and said:

'Indeed the Commander of the Believers and his actions are like fate. There can be no shame where fate ordains.'

Similar to this is a saying of the Prophet:

'Terror has supported me and my sustenance has been given to me under the shadow of my spear. For sure this religion shall penetrate wherever night penetrates.'

Ali ibn Jabala, who died in 828, took up this idea and said:

'The man thou contendest with has no escape from thee even were he raised up among the stars in heaven.

'Nay, even a fugitive, he whose refuge neither darkness nor bright sunlight penetrates, could escape thee.'

Similar to this is the verse by Salm al-Khasir, who died in 802:

'Thou art like fate whose tentacles are spread and there is no refuge and no escape from fate. Even were I to hold the reins of the wind turning it in every direction thou wouldst not fail to catch me.'

Al-Buhturi, who died in 897, also took up this idea:

'Even were they to ride the stars, no refuge would save them from fear of thy might.'

Thus does the observer of Arabic poetry, the 'expert', deal with the images and pictures contained in the individual verses one by one. Where the 'motif' is dictated by the choice of a certain form or the 'ideas' to a great extent determined by the 'motif', interest must be concentrated on the method of representation alone. The thing to be admired in a poem is the mastery of the poet, who contrives to find new images, comparisons and rhetoric figures for all the traditional motifs and emotions. The poet's creative imagination is not directed towards inventing new situations, to beginning from one individual position or to creating individual figures, characters and human types. The task of an Arab poet is solely to discover new ways of expressing a given situation.

The 'message' we asked about in the beginning cannot lie in the always more or less hackneyed poetic situation, which is conventional. The feelings the poet attributes to himself are conventional, as are the objects he describes. All this is merely a pretext, material by which the art proves itself and this art lies in the individual expression or picture. And in this field it performs wonders. It is inexhaustible in finding new comparisons, infinite in its ability always to see the same motifs with new eyes, from new angles. It is these very angles, the manifold aspects and the new and surprising sides of what is familiar that inform it. They are its message.

The European convention of the lyric deals with men. It seeks to give life to a 'person', that of the poet or of his beloved. Its interest is concentrated on creating such a human figure. Exceptionally, the poet's efforts are concentrated on a landscape. It must be created and come to life through the poem. Arabic poetry, on the other hand, does not concentrate its efforts on one focus. No single person, no definite landscape is conjured up in it. It is a rain of single illuminating sparks which light up the objects fixed by ancient conventions.

The focus around which a poet in the European tradition concentrates his poem is directly connected with the idea of individuality. An Arab poet illuminates the whole species, not one individual, not one definite sword but all swords. Comparisons like the following throw light on what a sword, all swords, can do:

The swiftly advancing (riders) drew their swords in Najd after the first quarter of the night; the people of the Hijaz prepared for a storm. (Because they took the flashing of the swords for lightning.) (Al-Mutanabbi, quoted by Al-Baqillani.)

The Arab poet is not interested in what is individual, a situation, a person, a special occasion and so on. He smoothes them out with conventions until they

Courtyard of the Umayyad Mosque in Damascus, originally the Church of St John Baptist, rebuilt in the eighth century.

2 *The Great Mosque in Cordova, Spain, begun in 785 in the reign of 'Abd al-Rahman.*

3 The Great Mosque of Qairawan, built over the grave of Sidi' Uqba in the ninth century. Roman columns were incorporated in the structure.

4 *The Shahzade Mosque, one of the most outstanding of the domed buildings built by the master architect, Sinan, for Sulayman the Magnificent in Istanbul between 1543 and 1548.*

lose all importance. His whole attention is concentrated on what covers the whole species. His verses illuminate what is common to one species, horses, roses, the desert, power, maidenhood and heroism. The wondering listener sees these through ever new similes and new paraphrases; but no grouping is made, no one person or specific situation is singled out. One by one each part receives its spark of poetic illumination, side by side and equal one to another.

The Spanish orientalist E. García Gómez has provided us with another approach to Arabic poetry. While he was in Egypt in his youth he was referred to a small manuscript entitled 'The Book of Banners of the Famous and Standards of the Eminent.' This was an anthology of selected verses by poets from the Arab Orient and the Arab West which a famous Spanish Arab man of letters, Ibn Sa'id al-Maghribi (1208 or 1213–1274 or 1286) had collected according to his own taste and for the use of a patron in Cairo. This small and very strict selection is distinguished by the fact that it was compiled according to criteria of taste, not according to the demands of scholarship or tradition or literary preciosity. García Gómez proved an ideal editor and translator. Ibn Sa'id was so selective that he collected only single verses or series of verses which specially moved him and left out the rest of the poems. García Gómez translated many of these separate poetic fragments into a Spanish so vivid that the reader could easily take them for original short poems.

We shall try here to give a translation of a few of these with our eye fixed above all on the poetic technique employed by the originators of these verses to achieve their specific beauty.

Almost every verse of Ibn Sa'id's collection contains a simile. They are nearly all of them descriptions effectuated by perceiving in the object described aspects which are hidden to a non-poetic eye. This is done by emphasizing unexpected but striking 'similarities'. Oranges on the tree:

The orange tree shows us its fruits; they look like tears coloured red by the chagrin of love.

Balls of coral on topaze branches; the zephyr holds clubs in its hand to play with them.

At times we kiss them, at others smell them so that now they are the cheeks of maidens and then perfumed apples.

The poet is not satisfied with one simile. To the first (tears made red by sorrow) he immediately adds a second (balls of coral), which has nothing to do with the first which leads on to an image conjured up by the latter simile (the wind driving the balls). To pass on to a third and fourth simile the poet has to mention himself—for the first time in the lines quoted. According to their effect on him the fruits are compared first to maidens' cheeks and then to perfumed apples. The whole poem consists of a net of imaginative similes which is woven around the concept of an 'orange'. These similes serve to illustrate what an orange is by revealing secret and hitherto unknown relationships between the object described, the world around and the poet himself. New and surprising relationships and harmonies show an 'orange' in a light which gives it a new and deeper significance than everyday light. Our matter-of-fact way of looking at oranges gives way to a new and extraordinary one; these new, poetic relationships make the object described fresh to the eyes and 'new' to the understanding.

Such similes easily become artificial:

Darkness is a fleeing army of Ethiopians to pursue whom the dawn has sent out Copts (128).

Presumably the Arab listener accustomed to the technique of such similes feels less their extravagance than the aesthetic pleasure in discovering and interpreting an unexpected similarity. A maximum of effect is achieved when the simile is unexpected and new, and can yet be felt to be justified.

The Sword whose two edges are covered with blood is like a brook on whose banks anemones bloom (242).

In order to provoke an element of surprise the poet compares that which strikes horror with what is dear. He finds a relationship between opposites. The artistic result of the verse is not so much the image of a sword stained with blood nor of a brook decked with anemones as the basic harmony common to both images, an almost abstract combination: blood-red, brilliantly white, blood-red. This abstract combination is emphasized and rendered effective by being distilled from two quite different, indeed contradictory pictures. What is horrible and what is delightful both arise to illuminate the abstract basic harmony common to both.

Another refinement of the technique of similes is that the simile is spun out into an action which itself returns to the point of departure of the verse:

The river is like a sheet of paper on which the zephyr writes its lines. When its beautiful script appears the branches droop to read it (172).

The picture of a boat on a river is drawn with the same technique:

A swimmer broke the surface, coming forward without moving his feet, quick like a falcon pouncing on a heron.

It looked like an eye scanning the heaven, the lids furrowed by the eye-lashes of the oars (278).

Two corresponding ideas (dawn and dusk) can also be coupled and thereby link two verses together.

I stirred up the dust of the earth with my smooth-haired, golden coloured horse as soon as the dawn had cast a girdle around the body of night.

My horse astounds me; it is like the dusk. It has night in its mane and twilight in its eyes (189).

The parallelism between dawn and dusk indicates that the coupling of the two verses is a purely 'formal' one. More importance is given to 'surprising' parallelisms, the chance likeness, the 'astounding' and for this reason revealing similarity of a girdle to the dawn and of a horse to the night, than to more hackneyed relationships, such as causal connections. That is not to say that the relationships that we consider hackneyed would necessarily appear so to an Arab poet. He 'thinks' to a large extent in 'harmonies' while our 'thinking' is almost exclusively directed towards categories such as 'cause and effect', 'origin and consequence'.

Not only objects like oranges, boats, swords and horses can be described with the aid of such similes revealing 'harmonies of form'. The same method can also be applied when it comes to the describing or influencing of human beings.

Leave riches to the rich; they are the field on which all cares struggle with each other.

Divest thyself of desire and hope; the sword cuts only when it is naked (262).

The end of the second verse has a most poetic effect. It draws its power from the comparison of a man stripped (of desire and hope) with a naked sword. A man can be compared to 'other' things in this world just as can the oranges or the boats in the preceding fragments. He is not considered something funda-mentally different from a sword.

The poet aligns himself with 'things':

I breathed deep in the wind for I desired to still my longing, hoping that it would bring me a breath of thee.

But, on the contrary, it fanned the hidden fire of my love and uncovered my secret sorrow, for always when the wind blows over smouldering ashes it fans these to renewed flames (292).

He feels himself and his love as something comparable to the—for us—inanimate process of smouldering ashes bursting into flame when the wind blows on them. Because he does this and is prepared to depict himself and his 'chagrin d'amour' not as something happening only once, not as something extraordinary which has never existed and never been heard of before, but puts it on the same level as the everyday, soulless effect of fire and hydrogen on each other, for this reason our Arab poet can achieve no dramatic tragic effect. He shows clearly enough that he is burning with love but at the same time he stresses the fact that burning is a phenomenon of this everyday world. Indeed, he describes how his burning follows the same laws as 'other' fires: when the wind blows on it it blazes up. By this simile the burning of the poet loses its dramatic effect but, on the other hand, it becomes more real by being set in relationship to other fires. Whatever dramatic hyperbole is lost is replaced by a special kind of 'realism' which is founded on the belief in the community of all creation, on a feeling of solidarity which embraces the poet and all creatures and gives each one of them his proper place and function in an organic whole.

Turning to architecture we find in classic Arab mosques a method of con-struction related to that of the poems. An outer courtyard is surrounded by a hall of columns whose pointed or horseshoe arches are also the main element of the inner prayer-hall. The whole complex of buildings of a classic Arab mosque is composed of uniform arches. The inner prayer-hall is a forest of pillars which stands in contrast to the shimmering, sun-lit expanse of the outer courtyard.

The history of their growth shows how easily such mosques with their uniform pillars could be added to. Many of the renowned early mosques, for example that of Amr in Cairo, the one in Cordova and that of the Aghlabids in Qairawan, became what they are today by adding extensions to the original hall. When such extensions were made the old mosque was not left as the central building; it generally became a corner of the new hall of pillars. The old construction knew no specially emphasized central nave of higher pillars, as we find in churches. For this reason it could be used as a mere corner of the enlarged new mosque.

When it was desired to give special emphasis to a central line in the expanded halls this was done most discreetly. The central arch was simply constructed a little wider and a little higher than the neighbouring arches. Looking into the inner part of the hall one gets the impression of a regular forest of columns in a polyvalent roofed hall. To be sure, every mosque has its Mihrab or prayer niche in front of which the Imam stands in the communal Friday prayer. Though it is often richly decorated the Mihrab remains essentially a direction indicator. The space inside the mosque is not directed towards it, as churches are towards the choir, but remains 'unorientated', polyvalent. This is a direct result of adding one structure to another. All the elements are the same, or almost the same so that none of them has preponderance over the others.

The contrast to a Gothic church is obvious. In the latter all the elements of construction serve to enhance and lead to the central point of worship. Thus when one enters a mosque one gets a completely different impression from that on entering a church. In a church one feels 'lifted up', often 'thrust up', the eyes *fly* forwards and upwards to the intersection. In a mosque one is 'safe'. You get a feeling of space, of undemanding openness, and achieve peace no matter in which part of the hall or forecourt you happen to be.

Surprisingly this contrast continued even in Turkish times. The great Turkish architects, especially Sinan, derived the motif of a domed mosque from Byzantine traditions. Nevertheless, they preserved the restfulness and pure unorientation which are characteristic of a mosque. This has been illustrated in a memorable essay by Ulya Vogt-Göknil in *Atlantis* of December 1957: the domed mosque, with its tiled walls smooth as a mirror, with no side chapels and no shadows to create a special frame of mind, strives to become pure 'space crystal'. The domes of Hagia Sofia with their interrupted mosaic surfaces, their dull glitter of gold and their dark aisles, try to give the impression of floating in the air, the *Illusion* of open sky: they invite upwards and outwards. . . .

The courtyard of a Persian mosque with its four niches or liwans opening inwards is like a compass. One finds one's direction in it and its four great niches keep the world back from the visitor; they create an opening for him.

This character of 'pure opening', of the abstract and crystalline which is possessed by the great works of Islamic architecture, goes along with the co-ordination of different objects in the miniatures, as in a garden, with the spontaneous sequences of individual illuminations in the poems and with Firdausi's nimble and luminous figures refusing to be confined within one system. We find it again in the infinite, free flow of the tales in the 'Thousand and One Nights', with their mixture of humans, animals, demons, common-ness and beauty which Hofmannsthal has described like no other:

Here is a poem on which doubtless more than one poet worked but which is as if it had emanated from one soul. It is a whole, a complete world. And what a world! Compared with it Homer might often appear colourless and unnaïve. Here we have colourfulness and thoughtfulness, superabundance of phantasy and incisive worldly wisdom; here we have infinite adventures, dreams, wise speeches, pranks, indecencies, mysteries; here we have the boldest spirituality and the most complete sensuality woven into one. There is no sense of ours which is not moved, from the highest to the lowest; everything in us is here animated and invited to satisfy itself.

There are tales after tales, some of them even fantastic and absurd; there are adventures and pranks some of them grotesque and vulgar; there are dialogues consisting of riddles and parables and unending comparisons: but in the air of this whole the fantastic is not fantastic, the dissolute is not vulgar, the prolix is not tedious, and the whole is nothing less than wonder-ful: an incomparable, a perfect, a noble sensuality holds the whole together.

In this poem, sensuality is what light is in Rembrandt's pictures and colour in Titian's paintings. Were it anywhere confined or were it to break through these barriers in some places, it could be insulting. But since it flows untrammelled through this whole, this world, it is a revelation.

We move from the highest to the lowest of worlds, from Caliph to barber, from poor fishermen to princely merchants and all the time we are sur-rounded by a humanity which lifts and carries us along on broad, light waves. We are among spirits, magicians and demons and again we feel at home. A never-failing objectivity depicts to us the hall gorgeously paved with flagstones, the fountain, the head of the old mother of a robber, swarming with vermin. It puts the table before us, covers it with fine dishes and deep vessels; it lets us smell the foods, the fatty ones, the spiced ones and the sweet ones, and the drinks of pomegranate seeds and shelled almonds, prepared with much sugar and aromatic herbs and cooled in snow. With the same joy it shows us the hunchback's hump and the horror of wicked old men with slavering mouths and squint eyes; it makes the donkey driver speak and also his donkey, the enchanted dog and the brass statue of a dead king, each full of wisdom and truth. It depicts with the same composure, nay, with the same enormous pleasure the load borne by a donkey, the glittering procession of an emir and, gesture by gesture, without inhibition, the erotic pantomime of the lovers united at last after a thousand adventures in a brilliantly lit, strongly perfumed chamber.

The more we read, with the more pleasure do we surrender to that world and lose ourselves in the medium of the most incomprehensible, naïve poetry and only then do we really possess ourselves, as when a man, bathing in a beautiful brook, loses his weight and only then gains a feeling for his body, a feeling which is both voluptuous and enchanting. This leads us into the inner nature of oriental poetry, indeed into the secret weave of the language, for this mysterious thing, which unburdens us of every anxiety and all meanness in the presence of the supreme semblance of life, is at the same time the deepest element of oriental language and poetry. In it every-thing is a figure of speech, everything a derivation from ancient roots, conceived in many ways, floating in the air. The first root is sensual, primitive, concise and powerful; gradually it passes over to new, related, then hardly at all related meanings. But even the most distant of these still contains a ring of the original sound of the word and there is still a shadow of the image of the first sense as in a dull mirror.

If we thus look at this boundless sensuality lighting up from inside with its own light we see that this whole is interwoven with poetic spirituality in which we progress with lively ecstasy from the first perception to complete understanding. All these sensual things are covered by a presentiment, a presence of God which is indescribable. Over this maze of what is human, animal and demonic there is always stretched the shining canopy of the sun or the sacred starry heavens. And like a gentle, pure and strong wind eternal, simple, holy sentiments blow through the whole: hospitality, piety, constancy in love. (*Tausendundeine Nacht*, in the second volume of the collected prose, S. Fischer-Verlag.)

But this 'pure opening' is also to be found in those oriental arts which we consider artistic handicrafts. The sublime peace of a Persian dish, the abstract harmony of a nomad's Kelim, the infinitely measured, black marks on the broad white page of Turkish calligraphy, all these tell of an art which is not concerned in the first place with what is human, with the expression of tensions, with 'greatness'—which is surely nothing but standing fast against tensions—or even with 'tragic greatness'. So much is it marked by harmony, balance and reconciliation that it turns away from the individual to the general, to the mathematical law, to the generic and regular. It traces the growth and harmony of the whole; its works seek to present small images of cosmic harmony and to catch reflections of the great harmony of the universe. For this reason individu-ality has only a subordinate position in it. Harmony can often be more truly represented in the picture of an animal or a flower or in an abstract ornament than in the human shape where the will of man so often comes into conflict with the consonance of the whole.

This is what one means when one says that the art, indeed the whole essence of classic Islamic culture, is *unhumanistic*. Expressing this in positive terms one should say that classic Islamic civilization is interested in something more than merely man. In it man stands side by side with the innumerable number of other creatures of God. He is not the centre to which everything points, for whom everything happens and whose reason measures and presents other things so that only then do they really begin to exist.

The disadvantages of such an attitude are clear at once to a European because his culture is opposed to it. Measured by European concepts man is neglected in Islamic art; little attention is paid to his personality and he is scarcely recognized as the crowning creation. He is not taken seriously enough for tragedies to be written about him and his capabilities are not believed in sufficiently for sciences to be constructed on the judgement of his reason.

We of the West must learn to understand its advantages. These are to be found in the field of the harmony of the individual with creation as a whole. The gift of orientals (of classic times) to enjoy simple things like running water, an orchard, the blossoming of spring in the desert, a noble horse, fine clothes and handsome male and female servants, without needing or even desiring more, has to be understood in connection with this.

Certain sciences are compatible with this unhumanistic attitude, those which require observation and registration such as descriptive geography, botany, anatomy, descriptive zoology, geometry and other branches of mathe-matics. To these should be added all the other sciences which arrange, register, collect and classify. The Muslims had quite a list of these which we no longer recognize: the enormous science built up on the Traditions of the Prophet, that of Arab tribes and genealogies, that of Arabic lexicography, that of historical traditions so long as they were merely collected and classified by orthodox historians who dared not criticize them. In late times mysticism was counted one of the sciences because it developed a systematic doctrine of classified stages of the soul. Philosophy and the natural or mental sciences which are investi-gated in a philosophic manner remained foreign to this unhumanistic attitude because they cannot be practised without reference to man, his reason and his power of judgement. There are two kinds of theology—philosophic, which is built upon human reason and speculates from these premises, and revelatory, which mistrusts man's power of judgement and is inclined to confine itself con-sistently to the mysteries of revelation and to rely on them. After bitter struggles it was this second type which finally prevailed in Islamic civilization.

13

The Heritage of Greece

IT IS NOW TIME for us to leave the consideration of what is purely phenomenal in works of art and trends of civilization and turn to historical perspectives. For a cosmic 'eternal Orient' was not always throughout the centuries in irreconcilable opposition to a humanistic 'eternal West', above all not in the field of *Islamic* civilization. From earliest times the civilizations of the Near East have grown up on the land bridge between East and West and they have received influences from both sides. Those arts which we consider full arts in Islam, such as carpet weaving, miniature painting, calligraphy and pottery, and which Europe only considers applied arts, are Asiatic arts. In all probability they were first developed in China but they have made themselves at home on the Near Eastern land bridge. In classic Arab civilization these were met by the heritage of Greece and Greek attitudes of mind which also, if only for a short time, found their own ways of expression within the framework of Islamic civilization.

Damascus and Alexandria were Greek cities when the Muslims conquered them. It was Greek craftsmen, architects and artists who built and decorated the Mosque of Damascus and the palaces of the Umayyads. In those early times there was no really fruitful cultural contact between the Greeks and the Arabs. The Arab overlords were all too devoted to their own desert life and were too convinced of their own superiority to become actively interested in the arts and sciences of their subjects.

The social and psychological conditions for a fruitful contact with the heritage of Greece were only created in Abbasid times. A fusing process set in in which the diverse elements of the Empire were amalgamated with each other. The new cultured class of scholars and merchants was no longer proud of their blood, but of their learning; people were curious and anxious to learn. The aspect of the Greek mind which was primarily taken up was the one which satisfied curiosity, thirst for knowledge, desire to recognize the manifoldness of things and the urge to discover the laws governing such variety. Greek art and Greek literature were ignored and only traces of these trickle through the substratum of popular culture, the techniques of craftsmen and school traditions, into Islamic intellectual life. They were never consciously studied as they were during the Italian Renaissance or even as they were in Europe in the Middle Ages.

But with the sciences it was another story. Greek books on medicine, astronomy and astrology, mathematics, geography, botany, zoology and, finally, also philosophy, were studied by the Arabs, incorporated in their culture and further developed by them. A routine method of transmission came into being. There was in Baghdad during the reign of the Abbasid Caliph Al-Ma'mun, a 'House of Translation' in which scholars, often of Christian descent, translated Greek scientific texts into Arabic. Their work was often based on earlier translations from Greek into Syriac or Aramaic.

The Muslims soon began to divide the sciences into Arabic and Greek sciences. All those branches of learning which deal with the Koran, the Arabic language, law based on the Koran, Islamic history and religious history, the past of the Arab tribes and the life and activities of the Prophet and his early companions were *Arabic* sciences. The *Greek* sciences dealt primarily with the external world around, the body, countries, the world, the stars and the laws underlying these things.

In external matters these two systems can be clearly demarcated but if one looks for the principles underlying each of them one recognizes that they are opposed to each other. The Arabic sciences rest primarily on authority, prophecy and the transmission of 'facts' which have been recognized as correct. The objects being transmitted, the 'facts and data', were not subjected to criticism and the Arabic sciences were confined to collecting these facts and data, to reducing them to systems and to seeing to it that they were handed down correctly from generation to generation.

The way in which errors, which had crept in in the course of transmission, were recognized and cut out shows clearly the nature of the Arabic sciences. The sayings and actions of the Prophet can in no way be criticized even when they do not agree with other sayings and actions of his. There are even verses in the Koran which seem to contradict other verses. Some of these were revealed by God but later abrogated and others perhaps only seem to be contradictory. Who are we humans to presume to find fault with the Word of God and the sayings and actions of His Prophet with our limited understanding?

The same goes for historical traditions. The fact that an event is improbable or even, according to our limited experience, impossible, is not sufficient reason for declaring it false. For does not God occasionally bring about miracles?

In view of the fact, founded in theology, that a historical tradition cannot be accepted or rejected because of its inner consistency or inconsistency the Arab sciences developed a special system which nevertheless permitted them to subject 'factual material' transmitted from the past to a certain amount of criticism. A chain of authorities had to be cited along with every tradition. The first of these should have witnessed the fact with his own eyes and personally reported it to the second authority and this latter to the third. Really strict critics accept only reports which have been handed down from man to man by word of mouth, so that each reporter knew the preceding one personally and could vouch for his honesty. It is easier to lie on paper. . . .

This method is used most strictly for the transmission of juridical and theological rules. But even historians or collectors of anecdotes cite before each one of their individual reports the list of reporters who can vouch for the authenticity of the report.

There are also some Greek sciences which primarily 'catalogue' by presenting and enumerating the given facts. It is surely not chance that the Arabs achieved great things in just these sciences. Geographers quenched their thirst for know-ledge by describing and drawing maps of the infinitely rich surface of the earth. Arabic travel books and geographical works are among the best sources for the history of classic Islamic civilization. There are Arab botanists and zoologists who described new species extending far beyond anything known to the Greeks. The most important advance made by Arab physicians on Greek medicine was doubtless in diagnosis, in recognizing and describing the course and symptoms of specific illnesses. Arab astronomers made observations which were far more exact than those of the Greeks.

But the Greek sciences did not consist merely of observing, presenting, enumerating, cataloguing and measuring facts. They enquired after the causes of the phenomena which were observed. Indeed, many of them maintained that a thing was only recognized when its cause could be stated. This is the field in which the two scientific systems could not avoid coming into conflict.

Fired by the spirit of Greece there arose a theology which endeavoured to put the divine truths stated by revelation upon logical foundations. Greek philosophy awoke the interest of select minds which strove to lay aside God's revelations, at least as a working hypothesis, in order to explore whether it was possible according to the laws of logic to construct a picture of the world in conformity with the Prophet's revelations, or whether one could even understand the Prophet's revelations as being symbolic in order to make them conform to the picture of the world demanded by philosophy.

In the field of theology it was the Mu'tazilite school which was the principal vessel into which Greek thought was poured. This was the predominant theology at the Abbasid court in Baghdad for twenty-five years, just at that time when the activities of translators from Greek reached their height. The struggles of the Mu'tazilites with those theologians whose way of thinking was later to carry the field and become the 'orthodox' one lasted for more than 200 years and contributed decisively to the final formulation of Islam.

Today it is assumed that the Mu'tazila began as a puritanical movement in the first century of Islam. It stood midway between the extreme doctrines of the Kharijites, who strove to prove their faith only by 'deeds', and those of the so-called Murji'ites who held that the Omnipotence and Omniscience of God, and the resulting predestination, relieved believers of all 'deeds' and imposed nothing upon them but belief. In the second century the intermediate school of the Mu'tazila was especially active in the struggle with the Manichaeans and Dualists who had been widespread in Iraq from ancient times. It was then that their theology must have come into close contact for the first time with Greek logic and they began to use logical arguments to support their theses. Their disputes turned primarily, on the one hand, on the problem of God's Justice and the connected question of predestination and, on the other, on God's Attributes (such as hearing, seeing, speech, will, etc.).

In both fields they represented the views which appear as the more 'logical' to the European educated in the Greek tradition. For them God was Just and so man himself had to bear the guilt of his own shortcomings and his freedom of will was a logical necessity. But for their opponents it was a limitation, a restriction of God to try to force upon Him the attribute, the title of the Just One as conceived by the human mind. They considered God far beyond human conception as a pure manifestation which no man could conceive.

This discussion about God's Attributes developed into a dispute as to whether the Koran was created or not created. The 'logical' Mu'tazilites refused to consider God's attributes as being co-eternal with Him. They maintained that His Speech, His Hearing, etc., could not be co-eternal with Him otherwise God would no longer be a Unity but a Plurality. For this reason they attacked the traditional view according to which the uncreated original text of the Koran had existed with God or in God from the beginning of time.

For our purposes it is not necessary to follow in detail the highly intricate arguments which both sides worked out to defend their points of view. It is enough to recognize that the Mu'tazila applied criteria of reason, that is to say criteria derived from human experience, to the revelation of the Koran while traditional theology which later was accepted as the orthodox one defended the 'abstract', 'non-human', traditionally Semitic concept of God with which human experience has nothing to do.

However, the later orthodoxy was to change materially its defence technique in the course of the two-hundred years' long stuggle with the Mu'tazila. It gradually took over the methods of logical arguing of its opponents and itself used premises and conclusions to defend its view of God. Al-Ash'ari worked out a logical formulation of the orthodox articles of faith which was given general recognition about 1065. Certain theologians of the old school, however, considered the whole complex of 'Greek' argumentation as superfluous, clinging fast to the revealed truth they had received from the Koran and the Tradition, and saw all reasoning around this truth not only as superfluous, but even as sinful.

Al-Ash'ari solved the problem of man's free will and God's Almightiness by a subtle doctrine. According to this, man 'acquires' the responsibility for his actions even though these actions are willed, indeed created, by God. According to Al-Ash'ari there is no such thing as cause and effect; every happening is brought about directly by God, all existence is continually being re-created by Him and what appears to men as cause and effect are simply the 'habits' of God which He can break as He wills.

Thus the technique of the Mu'tazilites was preserved while the spirit moving that technique was rejected. The instrument of logic, worked out in the belief that the human mind is capable of penetrating into the mysteries of the meta-physical, was used to support, explain and defend the revealed truth but not to investigate or in any way modify it. This was perhaps necessary for the preserva-tion of the religion of Islam. As Gibb says in his *Mohammedanism, A Historical Survey*: 'Anthroposophism is more fatal to a religion than anthropomorphism.' In other words: whoever makes his reason rule his religion can very soon do without religion.

The philosophers of Islam seem to have passed through this last stage. At any rate they were all suspected of heresy, and not without some cause. The Muslim philosophers continued the philosophy of the Ancient World. For them there was only one philosophy, that which began with Socrates and Plato and reached its height with Aristotle. This they continued to work out, explain and adapt to the experiences of their times. Their works, from Al-Farabi, who died in 950, to Averroës or Ibn Rushd, who died in 1198, have much to say about the Prophet and the Revealed Truth. In many places they say that this revealed truth is above any truth which can be opened up by logic, but one suspects that they did not really mean what they were saying.

On the basis of careful analyses of Al-Farabi and other mediaeval philosophers of the same and related civilizations, L. Strauss has shown convincingly that the Muslim philosophers used a double style (*Persecution and the Art of Writing*). In their writings they keep one meaning uppermost for the mass of their readers while concealing a second meaning in these same works for the chosen few who can read between the lines. From time to time they throw out hints about the inner, deeper meaning of their writings by logical breaks in the line of thought; their true meaning is concealed by 'repetition' of the views which were severally held. In secret the philosophers esteem truths arrived at by abstract trains of thought higher than those revealed by the Koran. This latter is only the popular, symbolic and disguised manifestation but to pass beyond that to the 'World of Ideas' would be harmful only for one not schooled in philosophy. Therefore the philosophers of Islam confined themselves to handing on their teachings to their pupils or to compiling them in a form which was both concealing and revealing.

However, the people were never completely deceived by them. Suspicion of impiety and heresy accompanied a philosopher everywhere. In later, more narrow-minded times, he found, like Ibn Rushd and Ibn Sina, no refuge except at princely courts and even the princes had to give way to the people's rage and the suspicion of orthodox divines in unruly times. His patron, Ya'qub al-Mansur, banished Ibn Rushd under pressure from the Andalusian jurists and divines and his works were burned in 1195. When the danger of a popular revolt was over Al-Mansur helped to restore the philosopher to honour.

'Islamic philosophy' very probably manifests a hidden Greek Platonic under-current beneath the surface of Islamic orthodoxy. This is not the only under-current, for, with the strengthening of the orthodox system and its becoming rigid and making greater and greater claim to universality and infallibility, a large part of the Greek heritage was either eliminated or diverted into such undercurrents.

Islam has been able to take over and appropriate much, very much, of the spirit of Greece, Greek thought and Greek sciences. But in the end the spirit of Islam which is concentrated on God and the Greek heritage which is centred on man found themselves in opposition. This opposition was to blame when, after three hundred years of arguing with the spirit of Islam, the essence of the Greek heritage was finally rejected. Those three hundred years were extra-ordinarily fruitful. They led to what the great orientalist, A. Mez, called the 'Renaissance of Islam' and which he depicted in an unforgettable book (Heidelberg, 1922). But it was not a complete Renaissance. It did not represent, like the Italian Renaissance, a successful intellectual revolution, but, in the end, a spiritual revolution which came to an armistice and in which the 'reactionary' forces were to gain the victory.

No judgement on values should be inferred from this. Islam could only remain what it had been by protecting itself against the onrush of the virus of Greek humanism. It succeeded in neutralizing this virus, in isolating it in a few non-essential branches of its body and in killing it in others which were more vital. Islam did not die through this crisis in its life, nor was its progress halted as has often been suggested. It continued to flourish and to bear rich, wonderful fruits. But after the Greek foreign body was excluded it no longer developed in the same manner as did its European younger sister civilization. The latter received the Greek virus five hundred years later. It did not eliminate or isolate it but rather entered thereby into a period of hybrid growth which has resulted today in its spanning and endangering the whole globe.

After overcoming the Greek crisis Islam and its civilization turned away more and more from the world or, rather, from the world as seen with Greek eyes, from the world of the laws of Nature, that world which at all costs must be conquered and ruled. Islam went back more and more into that 'oriental' world in which one simply strolls along, which one suffers and feels, with which one vibrates in harmony and in which one feels safe. . . .

14

Unsuccessful Attempts at Revolution

WHILE THIS INNER STRUGGLE for the acceptance or exclusion of the spirit of Greece in Islamic civilization was going on revolts were also taking place against orthodoxy in the external political sphere. As in the spiritual field these revolts were put down after they had been on the point of succeeding, and each episode contributed to a consolidation but also to a stiffening of the position of orthodoxy.

Political revolts took place under religious banners throughout the period of the Abbasid Empire. There was *Sonpadh*, a former companion of Abu Muslim, who led an uprising of Persian peasants, Zoroastrians as well as Muslim heretics, in 755. For centuries there had existed a 'communist' opposition against the landowning aristocracy which is generally called by the comprehensive name of *Mazdaism*. Mazdak was a revolutionary who almost brought about the downfall of the Sasanid Empire in the fourth century but whose revolts were finally drowned in blood by the Emperor Chosroes Anushirvan. His doctrines which were tinged with communism continued to live on among the peasants and the discontented middle classes of the cities, resulting in uprising after uprising. Sonpadh was followed by *Ishaq the Turk* in 757, Ustadhsis in 767 and Al-Muqanna' (776–789). Most of these revolts were centred in Khorasan and Transoxiania. In Adharbaijan, another frontier province which has been a centre of unrest and innovations throughout the centuries, *Babak* raised his standard. From 816 to 837 the northern trade route of the Muslim Empire leading from the southern shore of the Caspian Sea to Baghdad and Aleppo was virtually closed.

The revolts of *Zanj* were uprisings of negro slaves who worked for the great landowners of Southern Iraq in the marshes between Baghdad and Basra. The leader of this movement was a Persian, *Ali ibn Muhammad*, who called himself an Alid, but whose religious tendencies were more in the direction of Kharijism. The negro slaves overcame one army of the Caliph after the other, taking Ubulla, Ahwaz and finally Basra (871) and Wasit (878). Their capital Al-Mukhtara was in the midst of the marshes. After a long siege it was finally taken by a large army from Baghdad and destroyed (883).

However many such revolts failed they left behind them a continuously increasing social malaise. All that was needed was a rallying point around which the opponents of the existing order could gather to pass from uprising to the foundation of a new empire. The Ismaili branch of Ali's descendants proved to be just such a rallying point.

The fifth Imam of the Shi'ites, Ja'far, who died in 765, had had several sons. His community split into two main branches one of which recognized *Musa*, the other *Isma'il* as the divinely inspired head of the Alid school of thought. Musa's community followed more moderate articles of faith; they were to recognize the descendants of Musa up to the twelfth Imam after Ali and so are called the Twelver Shi'a. Their faith is today the state religion of Persia. According to this faith the twelfth Imam did not die but went into hiding. His return, which is expected to take place in Meshhad, is expected to usher in the reign of peace of the Mahdi. . . .

Isma'il's community inherited the extreme tendencies of earlier Shi'ism. Their opponents, whose writings are almost the only source of information about their faith, say that they believed in the communal ownership of property and even of wives. Such propaganda reports are certainly exaggerations and conscious slander, but it seems established that the Ismailis knew how to exploit the social unrest and tensions in the country in order to spread their religious ideas.

The *Qarmatian* bands, which burnt and pillaged in Syria, Palestine and Northern Iraq between 901 and 906, were in alliance with the Ismailis. These latter succeeded in founding a state in the distant province of Ahsa in the east of the Arabian peninsula where Aramco is today extracting the oil. All we know about their life in that province is that they formed an oligarchic republic under a ruler and council in the capital Al-Ahsa. This republic is said to have been rich and flourished for more than a hundred years.

The Ismailis were successful in the Yemen too, another border province of the Empire. From there they penetrated to India and North Africa. Their missions moved along the periphery of the Empire and set up their own authority in lands where the control of the central power, the Caliphate, was only weak. Their most decisive success was to be in North Africa. The Ismaili dynasty which came to power there called itself the Fatimids, emphasizing their descent from Fatima, the Prophet's daughter and Ali's wife. Coming from the West they conquered Egypt in 969 and established themselves in the Valley of the Nile. Cairo, Al-Qahira, founded by the Fatimid conqueror Al-Mu'izz, was built a little to the north of the old Arab army camp Al-Fustat.

The Fatimid Caliphate was soon to become more powerful than the orthodox one in Baghdad, and extended its authority to Syria and Arabia. The renowned Al-Azhar Mosque which is today the doctrinal centre of Islamic orthodoxy, was founded by the Fatimids and made the central seat of their teaching.

We still have no full description of what this teaching was, how it developed and what it represented. There is still perhaps too little material available on certain sectors of this field to permit a general view of the subject. Certain general tendencies can be recognized. The dilemma of revelation and the postulates of logic, from which the orthodox of the period suffered, was overcome by the Ismailis by introducing the idea of a 'hidden meaning', the *Batin*. The Koran was something 'external' whose inner meaning could only be recognized by the initiated. The essence of the initiate was the Imam, who sent 'callers' (Da'i) throughout the Muslim countries. They put questions to the Muslims, like the one on the problem of predestination and free will, problems whose insolubility was to persuade their hearers to recognize certain parts of the revelation as symbolic and requiring interpretation. The adept had to promise not to reveal the doctrines which were imparted to him. There were many degrees of initiation and even the Da'is were not all of the highest degree.

In the doctrinal system thus revealed ideas derived from the philosophers played a decisive part. God in Himself cannot be understood. Reason, *Logos*, which rules the world, was created by an act of His will. The goal of man is to unite with Him and dissolve into Him. This is 'Paradise'. 'Hell' is to be banished from universal understanding. It cannot last for ever and whoever cannot unite in this life with the Logos will be reborn. . . .

Only the Imam along with the Prophet can grant admission to the Truth. The Prophet gave the truth to the world in its symbolic outward form but only the Imam can recognize and interpret its inner content. The believer must strive after this truth step by step. Thus his faith becomes a dynamic one and his life a life of search. This seeking after God can be recognized in many Ismaili biographies (cf. M. Hodgson, *The Order of Assassins*, p. 17, note *et passim*).

The dramatic nature of the Ismaili faith stands in sharp contrast to the attitude of orthodoxy. It was enough for the Sunnis to follow the commandments of the Prophet. The process of salvation happened only once and in the historic past; all one had to do was to recognize it and follow its rules. But for the Ismailis the truth had to be won by a struggle and conquered step by step. They had to seek out the Imam who remained hidden and to strive to be worthy of and to understand his revelation.

Both elements, the central position given to rationalism and the activist character of their doctrine, exercised a great power of attraction on the educated men of the period. Al-Mutanabbi and Al-Ma'arri, the two greatest poets of the time, both show, and not by chance, certain Ismaili features. The *Batinist* conspiracy spread in secret throughout the whole Muslim Empire and we can read the account of his travels by one of its 'callers' Nasir-i-Khusraw. This conspiracy broke out in the most diverse parts of the Empire: in the Hindu-Kush, in India, in the Caspian provinces, in Ispahan and in Syria. In the meantime it was established in Egypt and North Africa.

The downfall of the Fatimid dynasty of Egypt followed the same pattern as that of the Abbasids in Baghdad. The military generals of mercenary troops seized the real power in the state and kept the caliph on mere sufferance as their puppet. Saladin broke the power of the Fatimids in Cairo in 1169 and Hulagu the Mongol that of their Abbasid rivals in Baghdad in 1258.

The Ismailis made one last grandiose attempt to conquer the Community of Believers from the inside before they finally had to abandon their hopes of conquering the whole world of Islam. Wherever they saw the slightest prospects of success they rebelled against the ruling orthodox politico-religious system. It soon became their tactics to attempt to take cities or fortresses by guile or by force and in this their principal weapon was assassination. The most famous of them and also those who held out the longest were the followers of Hasan-i-Sabbah in the fortress of Alamut in the mountain province of Daylam to the south of the Caspian Sea. Risings of Ismailis took place all over the Empire and a map by Hodgson (*op. cit.*) shows more than twenty places between Syria and Sistan where revolutions were attempted. They managed to establish them-selves in four districts. These Ismailis who were attempting to bring about the final downfall of the Empire are known to western readers of history as the Assassins of the Crusades.

They were a serious danger to the Muslim state towards the end of the eleventh century and, for a time, it looked as if they would really succeed in overthrowing the orthodox order. Later, in the twelfth century, they withdrew into certain districts. One of these was the land around the fortress of Alamut and another was the region between Homs and Tripoli. To be sure they con-tinued to struggle against orthodoxy but those struggles had now only local importance. For the rest all they lived for was the often rather peculiar develop-ment of their religion. The 'Resurrection' was proclaimed in Alamut in 1164 and from then on the faithful considered themselves living as 'resurrected' in 'Paradise'. Disbelievers were in 'reality' dead!

Alamut was finally destroyed by the Mongols but there are still small Ismaili communities in Syria and Persia. The majority of them live in India, Oman and Zanzibar and their numbers have increased greatly in East Africa in modern times. Some sections of the Indian, Syrian and African Ismailis recognize the *Aga Khan* as their Imam.

For the main current of the history of Muslim civilization the importance of this unsuccessful religio-political revolution, like that of the unsuccessful intellectual revolution or struggle with the heritage of Greece, lay in the way it affected the spirit of the victorious 'orthodox' Community of Believers even after it had been put down. The fixation of the Muslim faith and civilization took place to a large extent under pressure from these two revolutionary tendencies. This fixation is to be understood as an answer to this pressure and the narrownesses and rigidity that characterize it, just as any other closed and final system of faith, are to be attributed to the necessity of protecting itself against being led astray by revolutionaries.

15

Sufism

THE PRINCIPAL OPPONENTS against whom the Ismailis directed their last great attacks were not the Caliphs of Baghdad who now played only a subordinate part. They were the rulers and wazirs of a great new state, that of the Seljuks. The Seljuks were not Arabs but the ruling warrior family of the Turkish Oghuz tribe which had been driven westwards out of Central Asia by the consolidation of the Sung dynasty in China.

These Turkish nomads had penetrated into the Islamic Empire about the year 970. Persian was their literary language and Persian civilization, Persian methods of administration and Persian court officials set the tone for their rich men. For a long time the centre of the Empire of the Seljuks was in the East, in Khwarezm and Khorasan and for these Turko-Persian Seljuks who now ruled the largest Islamic state Palestine and Syria, which were being attacked by the Crusaders, were considered no more than a distant frontier province.

The fact that the rising power of the Turkish dynasties turned to orthodoxy and not to one of the many forms of Shi'ism was to be decisive for all later development of Islam. The conversion of the Turkish tribes to Sunni Islam from paganism is connected with the appearance at that time of a new type of 'missionary' on the borders of the Islamic Empire. If 'callers' to Shi'ite beliefs were the most active in spreading Islam at the time of Abu Muslim, at the end of the Abbasid period Sunni *Sufis* had reached the limits of Muslim territory and were playing the decisive part in converting to Islam those foreigners who had just come within the circle of Islamic civilization.

The Sufi or mystic movement originated in the asceticism of the early believers. Hasan al-Basri (died 728), one of the greatest of the early ascetics, is considered the ancestor of both mysticism and the Mu'tazilite movement. Contrary to Shi'ism mysticism never entered the field of politics and for a long time remained the concern of only a few pious men. It had in common with Shi'ism its function of a door through which entered many ideas emanating from the religious currents of the Near East. Christianity, Gnosticism and Manichaeism played the main part but more primitive religious remnants of animism, shamanism and fetishism were to acquire acceptance of sufferance in Islam by way of mysticism.

That does not mean that mysticism was a 'primitive', 'reactionary' and frivolous type of religion. Exactly the contrary was the case. Through mysticism Islam succeeded in acquiring a dimension which it would otherwise never have had. The element of personal piety, of 'experience', wins its rights in it as against the colder, more formalist element of the 'Law' as laid down in the Sunni rules and ordinances for living and acting. A mystic seeks to gain a personal, intuitive knowledge of God. The message of the Prophet is the model that shows him which road to take. However, at bottom there is always the tendency to override the law and seek direct communion with God. Once this is achieved all theological 'learning' becomes much less important than mystic 'knowledge' and the theological sciences become many empty formalities. The mystic Al-Hallaj (858–922) said: 'I am the Truth', and was executed for this heresy.

The tendency of the individual to seek direct contact with his God made mysticism almost impossible within the framework of Shi'ism for the Imam was always the most essential thing to the Shi'a. If there is a mystic 'way' of avoiding this figure and rendering its role as intermediary unnecessary and superfluous then there is no place for an Imam and consequently for Shi'ism. It was rather Sunnism, orthodoxy relying on the Law and the Sacred Texts, which needed the personal, passionately devoted features of mysticism to complete it. For the Shi'ites there was always the Imam.

For these reasons it was not fortuitous that Sunnism and mysticism should be compatible and one can indeed say that orthodoxy owed a great part of its final victory over 'philosophy' and 'Ismailism' to its alliance with mysticism. In the political sphere this is clear from the fact that the mystic Sheiks led the newly immigrated Turkish element, which was soon to assume the leading political role, to orthodoxy. Our sources tell how the new Turkish rulers respected the orthodox divines but venerated the mystic Sheikhs.

In the field of the spiritual development of Islam it was Al-Ghazali (died 1111), the greatest Muslim theologian, whose life's work brought about this alliance between mysticism and Sunni theology. Al-Ghazali not only demanded this alliance in abstract terms and made it theologically possible; he was also a living expression of it.

He relates in the autobiography of his spiritual life (Al-Munqidh min al-Dalal):

> The thirst to understand things as they really are was from early on natural and customary to me. It was inborn, part of the nature God gave me, a matter of temperament, not of my own will and decision. As a result the bonds of authority and tradition ceased to hold me as soon as I drew near to man's estate. Inherited articles of faith lost their hold on me for I saw Christian young men grew up to be Christians, Jews to be Jews and Muslims to be Muslims.

His search for the truth at first led him into the deepest scepticism:

My belief in the Tradition is lost and I cannot trust my senses. Do intellectual truths, which are axiomatic (or derived from axioms) perhaps offer something to rely on? Something like the statement that 10 is more than 3 or that the same thing cannot be both affirmed and denied or that a thing cannot be both created and yet eternal, nor still existent and non-existent, nor at the same time necessary and impossible. But then the observations of my senses answer, saying: 'Are you not afraid that, if you wish to rely on intellectual truths, the same thing will happen to you as to the observations of your senses? Before you trusted us; thence came the judge of intellect and proved that we were wrong. Were there no judge of the intellect you would have continued to believe in us. Perhaps behind intellectual understanding there is another judge who, when he becomes visible, will explain how the intellect also gives a wrong judgement, just as the intellect, when it appears, reveals the falsity of judgements founded on the observations of the senses. The fact that such a super-intellectual observation has not yet appeared is no proof that it is impossible. . . .'

When these thoughts had come to me and penetrated my being I sought a way of curing my evil condition. This was, however, not easy. Such thoughts can only be overcome by proofs but proofs demand the knowledge of axioms. If axioms are no longer valid it is impossible to pass on to proofs. My sickness was too much for me. It lasted for almost two months during which I was a sceptic although I kept myself away from sceptical theories and the outward expression of my confusion.

In the end God cured me of my sickness. My being became healthy and balanced again. The necessary basic axioms of the intellect once again became acceptable to me and I recovered confidence in their certain and firmly established nature.

But this did not happen through systematic processes of proof or through the weight of arguments but through a light which God (to Whom be Praise) cast into my breast. This light is the key to the greatest part of all knowledge. Whoever believes that the understanding of divine things rests only on logical proofs narrows in his mind the breadth of Divine Grace. . . .

After he had received this light Al-Ghazali determined to make a thorough study of all the branches of knowledge of his time in order to find out which of these could help his progress in understanding divine things. He found four classes of seekers: the (orthodox) theologians, the Ismailis (Batiniya) who were in pursuit of symbolic explanations, the philosophers and the mystics.

The theologians could not help him since they used their science primarily as a definition and apology for a faith which was already accepted as true. They were compelled to rest their arguments on premises which were based only on transmitted belief, the consensus of the community and simple acceptance of the Koran and the Tradition. Some of them, however, busied themselves with:

'studying substances and accidents, their nature and their properties but, since this was not the real task of their science, without thinking very deeply about the question and therefore without achieving results sufficient to dispel the darkness and confusion everywhere which had arisen owing to man's many points of view. I do not wish to exclude the possibility of their results satisfying others than myself, indeed, I do not doubt that this was the case with quite a number of people. But these results are mixed with traditional belief in certain respects which cannot be counted axiomatic.'

Al-Ghazali studied philosophy for two years and for a year pondered on what he had learnt in these two years.

> I had to pursue this goal during my free time after having given and written my lectures on the religious sciences, for at that time I was burdened with the teaching and training of three hundred students in Baghdad.

In the end he admitted that even philosophy could not help him for philosophers are basically unbelievers. They deny the resurrection of the body; they assert that God alone knows the universal matters but does not concern Himself with individual happenings and they imagine that the World is eternal, without beginning and without end. All three propositions are in the light of the Koran sheer disbelief. Al-Ghazali dealt with their views in his 'Incoherence of the Philosophers' which has been preserved for us. (Later on the Andalusian philosopher Ibn Rushd (Averroës) answered him in a rejoinder which he entitled 'The Incoherence of the Incoherence'.)

Al-Ghazali reproached the Ismailis with recognizing a false Imam. He admitted that, as they argued, an authoritative interpretation of the Divine Truths was necessary. But the interpreter sent by God was not the Imam but Muhammad himself. Moreover, says Al-Ghazali, the followers of the Imams derived no science from their infallible doctrines.

> We went a long stretch of the road and always agreed that they were right. We accepted their assertion that 'doctrine' and hence an infallible 'teacher' was necessary; we even admitted that he could be he whom they mention. But then, when we asked them what sort of knowledge they had derived from that infallible person, and when we put forward counter-arguments, they did not understand our counter-arguments and in their confusion took refuge in their 'hidden Imam' and said that one had to set out and travel to him. Yet many of them say they have a special knowledge but this knowledge, when it is described, comes to nothing more than a few unimportant details from Pythagoras's philosophy. He was one of the earliest of the ancient philosophers and his system is the weakest of all. Aristotle not only criticized him but also pointed out how weak and corrupt his thinking was.

In his search for God Al-Ghazali finally turned to the writings of the mystics:

I easily understood their basic teachings about what was intellectual and made such progress in the knowledge of mysticism as is possible by study and oral instruction. But I soon understood that the most characteristic quality of mysticism cannot be comprehended by study but only by direct ecstatic experience and after a spiritual rebirth. . . . What a difference there is between the knowledge of the scientific definition of intoxication (that is to say that the word denotes a condition in which the seat of the intellect is shrouded in fumes from the stomach) and actual intoxication.

I understood that mystics are men who have actual experiences not just theories and I realized that, as far as it was possible, I had made some progress along the road of intellectual understanding. What was left could not be achieved by studying books and by oral instruction but only by direct experience and by following the mystic faith.

But it was not easy for him to give up his duties in Baghdad and his honourable post as Professor of Theology. He hesitated and doubted for six months and finally fell sick. He found himself unable to deliver his lectures and went to Damascus. From there he later went to Mecca and lived the life of an ascetic and mystic for ten years:

I realized with certainty that it is the mystics above all others who are on God's Path. Their life is the best life, their methods the best methods and their character the purest character. Were the intelligence of all intellectuals, the wisdom of all scholars and the scholarship of all professors who are experienced in the profundities of the Revealed Truth brought together in an effort to improve the mystics' conduct and character they would achieve nothing, for all movement and all rest, both external and internal, illuminate the mystic with light from the Lamp of Prophetic Revelation and there is no light on the face of this earth which illuminates more than this Light of Prophetic Revelation.

How must one follow this mystic path? Purity, the first condition, means complete purification of the heart from everything but God (to Whom be praise). The key thereto, and also the password of the ritual prayer, is to sink one's heart in the contemplation of God; its goal is complete identification with God.

With this first stretch of the mystic path there begin the revelations and visions. In a state of waking the mystics see angels and the spirits of prophets, they hear them speak to them and learn from them. Later they reach a higher stage. Instead of seeing forms and figures they come to steps along their path which it is difficult to describe in words. As soon as one tries to express them one inevitably says things which are incorrect.

In short, what they are able to achieve is nearness to God. Many speak of this as 'inherence', 'union' or 'communication' although these are all wrong expressions.

Certainty acquired by proofs is called knowledge and familiarity with the mystical state is direct experience (literally 'tasting'), acceptance of the Truth as probable by hearsay and experience is Belief.

His mystic experience permitted Al-Ghazali to construct his new system of theology on certain belief communicated to him by his direct experience of the Divine Truth. In his system scholastic conclusions and premises count less than the texts of the Koran and the Tradition along with living piety which springs from personal experience of God. Al-Ghazali appositely called his main work 'The Revival of the Religious Sciences'. This revival was brought about by uniting the sciences of the Holy Book, of the Traditions of the Prophet and of the Substance and Attributes of God with the personal piety and personal experience of God of the mystics.

16

Mystic Piety

AFTER THE MOVEMENT of Islamic mysticism had established itself in the orthodox system it began to penetrate the whole of Islamic civilization. What was to remain in other civilizations an activity confined to outsiders, ascetics, monks, nuns and divines struck deep roots into the daily lives of the masses of ordinary Muslims and indeed became the most important social link holding Muslim society together for centuries.

It may at first seem surprising that such an unworldly force as mysticism should play a decisive leading role in all later Muslim civilization. This has to be understood from the history of the development of Islamic culture. Erected on the foundation of a law which was intended to control the life and religion of a small desert town on the fringe of civilization, Islamic culture saw itself faced with the necessity of adapting itself to the requirements of a world power holding sway over the great cities and empires of the Near East.

In order to bring about an expansion of the relatively narrow horizon of Mecca and Medina recourse was naturally had to the earlier civilizations which had predominated in the various regions of the Empire. In this the Greek-Hellenistic civilization was to prove the most fruitful. Much of it was assimilated and it was only after a three hundred years' struggle that Islam finally rejected the spirit underlying that civilization. The Greek element, so far as it had succeeded in penetrating, was again banished from those sciences, philosophy, theology and the sacred law, which held together the structure of Islamic civilization.

Under the sense of spiritual loss consequent on renouncing Greek ways of thinking, mysticism was accepted into the orthodox system of Islamic civilization. From this moment on the mystics found themselves in the position of holding a monopoly of culture. The orthodox view of life and legislation which rested on tradition and prophecy began to become more established and more rigid. Only quite unimportant details remained for discussion, the main truths were fixed and laid down once and for all in an imposing structure. Mysticism was the only 'open' branch of culture which was still tolerated in that closed system. Since it sought and found direct communion with God it was not subject to the universal suzerainty of the Sacred Law. Only in it was the creative urge of the individual allowed to live and flourish, only here were spiritual

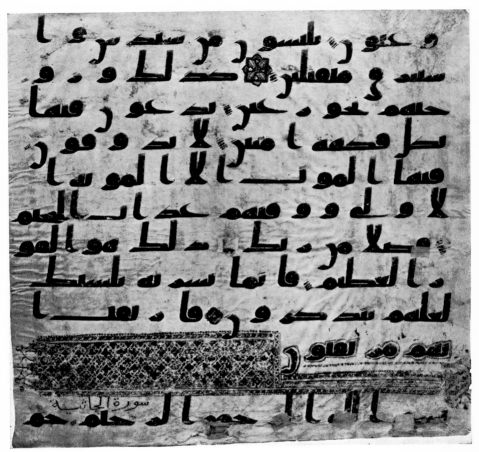

5 Arabic calligraphy:
A page from a Kufic Koran, Egypt, eighth century.

An example of Thuluth writing, sixteenth century.

6 A page from a manuscript by the calligrapher, Sultan 'Ali of Meshed, Persia, end of the fifteenth century.

adventures possible. Activities in all other fields of intellectual life could only be imitative since binding models and obligatory results already existed. At the most these could be collected and presented in a new form, arranged in detail or compiled in encyclopaedias. . . .

It is easy to see how, in these circumstances, mysticism must have exercised an irresistible attraction for creative spirits. These saw themselves essentially faced with the choice of either putting themselves, secretly or openly, beyond the pale of the orthodox system, as the philosophers did, or turning to mysticism.

Even the arts did not escape the attraction of mysticism. These were times in which lyric poems were either purely philological performances or mystical poems. Where Persian was spoken there appeared the mystic epic, and the 'Asiatic' arts of pottery, miniature painting, carpet weaving and calligraphy received a new lease of life. These were anonymous arts of harmony. They were in direct association with the mystic goal of 'Fana' in which the individual loses his identity in something greater than himself.

The mystics knew how to exploit their cultural monopoly. They knew how to change later Islamic civilization into one which was permeated through and through with expressions of the mystic's outlook on life and which widely adapted itself to his conceptions. In their own field, that of personal religion, they brought about an enormous deepening and intensification of religious experience and they exercised an effective civilizing power in other fields, too.

In the politico-social sphere the mystics took over the role of link between the masses of the people and their autocratic rulers. The mystic sheikhs became, more than the orthodox scholars could ever be, the mouthpiece of the people and their aspirations which very few rulers could afford to ignore. They also became the bearers of a new, peaceful movement of expansion of Islam. They carried their message eastwards into the heart of India and into Indonesia. In later centuries they penetrated into Africa where, in both East and West, they are succeeding in overtaking the efforts of Christian missions with an incom-parably smaller expenditure of time and money.

It is difficult for an outsider to appraise the devotion with which religion is experienced and lived. However, the orientalist, Hellmut Ritter, has found a way of demonstrating the degree of intensity at which mystics live and for this he had recourse to a poet. The Persian poet Attar (died *c.* 1220) wrote religious tales in verse permeated through and through with anecdotes, stories, fables and rhetorical amplifications, all with one goal in view: to give an objective picture of the poet's religious experience and make it outwardly visible, not only its doctrines but also the force of its influence on him and his fellow believers.

Ritter uses Attar's stories to throw light on the inner life of Sufis. From his great book *Das Meer der Seele* ('The Sea of the Soul') (E. J. Brill, Leiden, 1956), we take a number of stories which deal with one of the main problems of Islamic theology, the question of God's Almightiness and with the problem whether and how this Almightiness of God can be reconciled with man's freedom and responsibility.

In early centuries this antithesis had been the cause of quarrels between Mu'tazilites and those who were later accepted as orthodox. In the later Sunni system a solution was found which in practice laid emphasis above all on God's almightiness. Al-Ash'ari held that man 'acquires' responsibility for his actions although these are 'willed', hence caused, by God.

In practice the great masses avoided the dreadfulness of such an inhuman doctrine by saying: 'Believers cannot be completely cast out by God even if they have committed sins.' A widespread idea was that the Prophet would intercede for them on the Day of Judgement. Ritter quotes a question which he overheard being directed to his Greek barber by an old Turkish gentleman: 'When we die we go straight to Paradise but what will happen to you (unbelievers)?'

But the religious *élite* could not take the matter so lightly, for they fully recognized the absurdity of that dogma in all its horror:

A polo player strikes the ball from East to West and says to it: Take care in your course not to fall into a ditch! For if you go astray you will remain for all eternity in fire and prison! But since the course of the ball is determined by the strike given it is not the ball's fault if it goes off course. Even if the sin is not committed by you you still have it hanging around your neck!

I know not, I know not! O God, Thou Knowest, Thou Knowest what Thou willst! The one Thou hast called to Thee with a hundred signs of kindness, the other Thou hast driven away from Thee with a hundred pains. Neither has the former given proof of obedience nor the latter sinned. None has access to Thy Secret!

Even Satan did not become accursed because of his sin:

A great man hears Satan say: It is not willed that I be obedient and yet my sin is hung around my neck.

In one half hour God threw Satan's thousands of years of obedient service in his face. God is cunning! He loves to lull His creature into security and then suddenly He casts him into perdition.

When Satan was cursed Gabriel and Michael began to weep and wept for a long time. God said: 'Why are you weeping?' They said: 'We do not feel safe from Thy cunning.' Then God said, 'That is right. Do not feel safe from My cunning!'

The drowning Pharaoh wishes in his last moments to pronounce the Declaration of Faith but God fills his mouth with wind from the sea so that he cannot finish uttering it and dies an unbeliever. . . .

Reason found no way out of this dilemma but only became more confused:

Bal'ami worshipped God for four hundred years and wrote four hundred books proving the Unity of God but one night he got up, found a hundred proofs for denying God and began to worship the sun. That is the result when reason oversteps its bounds.

Even God's kindness is capricious and unfathomable:

A pious ascetic met the funeral procession of a sinner and turned aside so as not to have to say the funeral prayer over him. That night he saw in a dream the dead man strolling around in Paradise and asked how it came about that he was thus honoured. The sinner answered: 'God had mercy on me because you had been so unmerciful.'

Gabriel heard the Lord say: 'Here I am!' He thought that God was answering someone's prayer and flew through the whole world looking for this man but could not find him. Returning to Heaven he again heard God's Voice answering someone's prayer and again he flew through the world in vain. Finally he asked God to whom He was speaking. The Lord said: 'Go to Asia Minor to such and such a monastery!' Gabriel went there and found a man praying to an idol (a crucifix). In amazement he asked God how He could answer an idolater. God said: 'He is gone astray and I wish to open up the way for him to Me. Thus wills My Kindness.' Thereupon He opened up the man's heart to the True Faith.

That is why even Satan still cherishes hope:

The mystic Shibli met Satan among the pilgrims to Mecca at 'Arafat and in amazement asked what he, the accursed one, was doing among the servants of God. Did he still hope for God's Grace? The accursed one answered: 'For 100,000 years I worshipped God in fear and hope. I showed the angels the way to His Presence and opened the gate for everyone who had lost his way to God. My heart was full of His Majesty and I confessed His Unity. If, in spite of all these deeds of obedience, He can drive me from His Door—and no one can ask why He does what He does—then He can take me up again for no reason. As there is no Why and Wherefore in what concerns God's actions one should never give up hope in God. His Severity drove me out and His Kindness can take me back.'

But how can a man live at all if he has to keep this cruel capriciousness of his Creator before his eyes every day? The answer which the pious Muslims of later times found to this seemingly insoluble dilemma was love, mysticism. Precisely because of their Lord's capricious rule they desired with ever renewed ardour to come near to Him. It was precisely His Incalculability, His cunning, that compelled them to surrender completely to Him and to desire nothing other than to lose their identity in Him.

Ritter's book is full of pictures of this burning longing of the soul for God. Often they are derived from worldly love tales:

Zulaikha was sitting by the roadside as Joseph was riding to visit his father. He saw her and struck at her with his whip. She uttered a cry of sorrow with such fiery breath that the whip began to burn and Joseph had to throw it away. Then Zulaikha said: 'This fire has been in my soul for years. You cannot bear even the breath of it on your hand.'

Examples of worldly love serve to illustrate directly how one should behave in spiritual love.

A lover is on the point of going on the pilgrimage and before departing asks his beloved if he can perform a commission for him. In reply the latter drops a tile on his head. The other silently picks up the tile, kisses it, makes a hole in it and hangs it around his neck with a cord as a souvenir.

If the beloved behaves cruelly towards the lover he welcomes that for he nevertheless achieves the undivided attention of his beloved if only for a moment.

How should such a bond of relationship not satisfy you? Has he not thereby preferred you to all others?

Pull an arrow with my name on it from your quiver and draw it on your strong bow! Do you seek a target? Here is my heart! It is for you to hit hard and for me to cry 'woe!'

This is also why Satan is proud of the curse God hurls against him:

Satan bore the pain his Divine Friend caused him. He did not flinch from the blows of his Beloved but turned them into hundredfold balm.

The blow dealt by the Beloved God is so precious that it is not bought too dearly with a thousand years of obedient service. Satan does not see the bitterness of the dregs offered to him; he sees only the pourer. He does not see whether the curse that falls on him is good or bad; he only sees that it comes from Him.

In the end this true love causes the person of the lover and that of the beloved to dissolve into each other:

A lover knocks at the door of his beloved and when the latter asks: 'Who is there?' says: 'It is I.' Whereupon his beloved considers him still immature and sends him away. After a long time he becomes mature and knocks again at his beloved's door. This time he answers the question: 'Who's there?' with: 'It is you.' He is then admitted.

A stone and a clod of earth go together on a journey. Unexpectedly both fall into the sea. The stone says: 'I am drowned. Now I can tell the bottom of the sea of my experiences.' But the clod of earth disappears and loses its identity. He says in a silent language which is nevertheless audible to the initiated: 'Nothing remains of my body in either world. Neither my body nor my soul can be seen. If you dissolve and disappear in this sea you will become a shining pearl in it. If you wish to keep your substance you will achieve neither life nor wisdom. So that this may happen to you you must leave your self.'

When the mystic has reached the end of this path, when he finally loses his identity (*Fana'*), he realizes that it was not he who had been wandering along the mystic path but God who made him wander along it.

In the beginning I was wrong about four things. I had thought that I was mindful of Him, could recognize, love and seek Him. In the end I realized that His mindfulness, His love, His recognition and His seeking preceded mine.

What is visible in such tales is the ability of Islamic mystics to derive life from a hopeless, hard, unfruitful and inhuman dogma. Dogma did not make them despair or turn away from all religion but rather drove them to erect a mystical superstructure around and above life. In spite of dogma a whole religious dimension was won by what we can call the creative power of mysticism. An experience was of value to a mystic even when no words could describe it. But when a poetic expression is found, as by the poet 'Attar, even outsiders get some insight into the lively, absorbing inner world of the mystics.

This power, which was able to erect such inner worlds over the void of a deadly dogma, also decisively changed the shape of the outer world. The Sufis began in the thirteenth century to group themselves into loose 'orders' (Tariqa) and in the course of the centuries these orders spread over the whole territory of the Empire. New ones appeared right up to the end of the nineteenth century, and the older ones developed and split into branches and sub-branches. The net of these mystic orders covered the whole Muslim world. They were of all sorts, rural ones and urban ones, some tending towards orthodoxy, others heterodox, some that went in for spectacular shows and miracles and others which avoided every outward sign of belonging to them; some were military and some missionizing, some political and others quietist. Each had its own technique to achieve ecstasies and visions of God. Certain basic forms were common to all, such as the 'mentioning of God', the *Dhikr*, which consists of repeating the Name of God or a formula like: 'there is no god but God,' over and over again, aloud or inaudibly, alone, in seclusion or in an assembly of persons similarly disposed. One prepares for ecstasies by mortification of the body, by fasting and by surrendering one's will completely, *so as to be in the hand of one's mystic master and teacher like a corpse in the hands of the corpse washer*. Practically all the orders had teaching periods and induction ceremonies for young members. In many orders the 'dervishes' lived a communal life in a sort of monastery community; others were organized as 'lay orders', the members going about their work during the day and meeting in the evenings or on festival days for Dhikr sessions and ceremonies.

The guild system, which earlier had been associated with Ismailism and Shi'ism in general, was woven into the mystic orders. Mystic sheikhs wandered around the countryside with their followers, being revered as living saints and consulted and given hospitality by the peasants. On the frontiers of the Empire military bands of seekers after God, the Ghazis, were formed who succeeded in converting the nomadic Turkish tribes to their form of Islam and in taking the place of the 'holy men' (Kam Ozan) of their earlier pagan religion. The

Janissaries maintained mystic dervishes to act more or less as spiritual fathers for the whole period of their existence; these were the famous Bektashis. The Maulawis (Mevlevis), their rivals, enjoyed the favours of the Sultan since the Bektashis often had concentrated too much power in their hands.

The leadership of the individual orders was often hereditary with sons and descendants of the founder exercising it although a fixed line of succession was not always followed. The founder himself was in many cases revered as a saint and festivals and prayer meetings were held at his grave or supposed grave. Birthdays, or 'Maulids' of revered sheikhs then often developed into public festivals and fairs. It was easy for residual local cults peculiar to one place and often inherited from ancient or Christian times, to be transferred to the order celebrating there or to its holy founder.

Naturally, much that was not compatible with strict orthodoxy penetrated the movement of Sufis, sheikhs and dervishes by way of the mystic orders and their popular customs and ceremonies. Such foreign elements came either from the popular sphere of 'superstition' and 'superstitious practices', remainders of old forms of religion, or from half overgrown strata of ancient magic and sorcery which can hardly be differentiated from the practices of primitive religions.

Naturally there had always been such relics of earlier religions and religious feeling in the life of the common people. The mystic movement drew them out of their shadowy existence as forbidden and pagan and clothed them in Islamic garments. Mysticism cannot be held responsible for the existence of such 'superstitious customs', nevertheless it provided a framework within which such relics of pre-Islamic religion acquired the right to establish themselves in Islam and admittance to the orthodoxy, unseen and uncontrolled.

The second cultural current, which reached mysticism and was developed in it, achieving in this way acceptance as a part of orthodoxy, was not popular but scholarly and artistic. This was the 'philosophy' of mysticism, its way of thought being concerned with the Unity of God and the world, with God's immanence, even if it concealed the last consequences of its teaching so as not to contradict the official faith too openly. The Andalusian mystic Ibn al-'Arabi (1165-1240), whose grave can still be visited in Damascus by anyone, even by a Christian, gave this teaching its classic theological philosophy. The great mystic poets in Arabic, Persian and Turkish have expressed the same basic thoughts in lyric and epic form with constantly new similes, phrases, illustrations and ideas, taking over and in certain cases developing ideas from Islamic philosophy and Ismailism.

This 'high type' of mysticism remained active much longer than one would at first suspect. Many of its main works date from the high or late Middle Ages but we know, too, that original mystic thinkers lived later than that. The writings of many of these still await investigation and it can be assumed with certainty that valuable works from more modern times and even from the last centuries would come to light if the infinite treasures of manuscripts lying unexplored in the provincial towns of Turkey were examined by interested and understanding hands.

The penetrating and cementing power which mysticism exercised in spiritual matters extended to the social field as well. Just as it had been able to act as a great, creatively rich bracket holding together all previously irreconcilable spiritual elements and incorporating them in Islam, so also did it bring the various groups and social classes within the Islamic peoples closer together and in contact with each other. Indeed, intermixed them more thoroughly than orthodoxy alone had been able to do in the early centuries of Islam.

Until the time when mysticism concluded its alliance with orthodoxy we saw how the socially underprivileged classes tended to express their antagonism to the prevailing system in the form of a current of politico-religious opposition to the predominant Community of Believers. We have seen the Alids, the Kharijites, the early Shi'a, the Qarmatians and the Ismailis, to mention only the most important of these movements. When Sufism penetrated the Community of Believers opposition gradually decreased and finally ceased altogether. The Shi'a, which had wandered over the whole Empire and become at home in certain classes and social strata, now became concentrated in particular areas, like the Twelver Shi'a in Persia since the reign of Shah Isma'il (1497–1524) where it has become the faith of all classes of the people. Similarly orthodoxy, in its own territory, penetrated more and more all classes of the people, peasants, artisans, merchants, landowners and the ruling class of the military and civil hierarchy. The instrument of this penetration was mysticism. It gave the 'primitive' faith of the peasants a place beside the different one of a man who had spent his whole life pondering on God's law. It brought both these into touch with the ruling class which was constantly being changed by the fortunes of war and which could be counselled and influenced by the mystics at all stages of intellectual development, from that of a half-pagan animist of nomad origin to that of a philosopher king tired of life.

A social balance arose which lasted for five hundred years, a fact that should be sufficient to show us that the achievements of the mystics in the politico-social field were considerable. From the point of view of the mystics this contri-bution of mysticism was merely a by-product. Their interest was completely concentrated on spiritual things and the last thing they would have thought of was to lay down rules for the life of the Community of Believers as was con-sidered its duty by orthodox religion. Rather did they preach abstention from all worldly life, the power of government being in itself evil since whoever exercised it was caught up in the injustices of this world. The quietism of the mystics and their doctrine of the uselessness of all effort in this world no doubt contributed to the lowering of social tensions and to making people satisfied with what they had. The Sufis have often been reproached for being the principal agents of the spread of oriental 'fatalism' which made such a deep and disagreeable impression on European travellers in all countries of the Near East in recent centuries.

But one only needs to read descriptions of the traditional oriental cultural life, such as the classic one by Lane (*Manners and Customs of the Modern Egyptians*), to realize how the Sufis created, incidentally and unintentionally, a whole civilization within which the activities of the great intellectual *élite* of the Islamic countries were carried on.

In the beginning of the month of Rabi'al-Awwal preparations are commenced (in Cairo) for celebrating the Birth of the Prophet which is called 'Maulid al-Nabi'. The principal scene of this festival is the south-west quarter of the large open space called Birket-al-Ezbekiyeh, almost the whole of which, during the season of the inundation, becomes a lake: this is the case for several years together at the time of the festival of the Prophet, which is then celebrated on the margin of the lake; but at present, the dry bed of the lake is the chief scene of the festival. In the quarter above mentioned, several large tents (called 'siwans') are pitched, mostly for dervishes, who, every night, while the festival lasts, assemble in them to perform dhikrs. Among these is erected a mast ('sari'), firmly secured by ropes, and with a dozen or more lamps hung to it. Around it numerous dervishes, generally about fifty or sixty, form a ring, and repeat dhikrs. Near the same spot is erected what is termed a 'Qa'im', which consists of four masts erected in a line, a few yards apart, with numerous ropes stretched from one to the other and to the ground: upon these ropes are hung many lamps, sometimes in the form of flowers, lions, etc., sometimes of words, such as the names of God and Mohammad, the profession of the faith, etc., and sometimes arranged in a merely fanciful ornamental manner. . . .

I write these notes during the Maulid and shall describe the festival of this year (1250 A.H., A.D. 1834), mentioning some particulars in which it differs from former years.

During the day time, the people assembled at the principal scene of the festival are entertained by reciters of the romance of Abu Zaid, conjurers, buffoons, etc. The Ghazawi have lately been compelled to vow repentance, and to relinquish their profession of dancing, etc.: consequently there are now none of them at the festival. These girls used to be among the most attractive of all performers. In some parts of the neighbouring streets, a few swings and whirligigs are erected, and numerous stalls for the sale of sweetmeats, etc. Sometimes rope-dancers, who are Gipsies, perform at this festival, but there are none this year.

At night, the streets above-mentioned are lighted with many lamps, which are mostly hung in lanterns of wood. Numbers of shops and stalls, stocked with eatables, chiefly sweetmeats, are open during almost the whole of the night, and so too are the coffee-shops, at some of which, as well as in other places, reciters and story-tellers amuse the persons who choose to stop and listen to their recitations. Every night, an hour or more after midnight, processions of dervishes pass through this quarter. Instead of bearing flags, as they do in the day, they carry long staves with a number of lamps attached to them. The procession of a company of dervishes, whether by day with flags, or by night with lamps, is called the procession of the 'Ishara' of the sect; that is, of the 'banner', or, rather, the term 'Ishara' is applied to the procession itself. These dervishes are mostly persons of the lower orders and have no distinguishing dress: the greater number wear an ordinary turban and some of them merely a tarboosh, or a padded or felt cap. Most of them wear the common blue linen or cotton, or brown woollen shirt, the dress which they wear on other occasions at their daily work or at their shops.

On the last two nights the festival is more numerously attended than on the preceding nights and the attractions are greater. I shall describe what I have just witnessed on the former of these nights.

This being the eleventh night of the lunar month, the moon was high and enlivened the scenes of festivity. I passed on to a street called Suq al-Bekri, on the south of the Birket al-Ezbekiyeh, to witness what I was informed would be the best of the dhikrs that were to be performed. The streets through which I passed were crowded and persons were here allowed, on this occasion, to go about without lanterns. As is usually the case at night, there were scarcely any women among the passengers. At the scene of the dhikr in Suq-al-Bekri, which was more crowded than any other place, was suspended a very large 'Negefeh' (a chandelier, or, rather a number of chandeliers, chiefly of glass, one below the other, placed in such a manner that they all appeared but one) containing about two or three hundred 'qandils' (or small glass lamps). Around this were many lanterns of wood, each having several qandils hanging through the bottom. These lights were not hung merely in honour of the Prophet: they were near a 'zawiye' (or small mosque) in which is buried the Sheikh Darweesh al-'Ashmawi, and this night was his Maulid. A dhikr is performed here every Friday night (or what we call Thursday night) but not with so much display as on the present occasion. I observed many Christian black turbans here and having scarcely seen any elsewhere this night, and heard the frequent cry 'A grain of salt in the eye of him who doth not bless the Prophet!' ejaculated by the sellers of sweetmeats, etc., which seemed to show that Christians and Jews were at least in danger of being insulted, at a time when the zeal of the Muslims was unusually excited, I asked the reason why so many Copts should be congregated at the scene of this dhikr. I was answered that a Copt, who had become a Muslim, voluntarily, paid all the expenses of this Maulid of the Sheikh Darweesh. This sheikh was very much revered: he was disordered in mind, or imitated the acts of a madman, often taking bread and other eatables, and stamping upon them, or throwing them in the dirt, and doing many other things directly forbidden by his religion. Yet he was esteemed an eminent saint, for such acts, as I have remarked on a former occasion, are considered the results of the soul's being absorbed in devotion. He died about eight years ago.

The 'dhikkirs' (or the performers of the dhikr), who were about thirty in number, sat cross legged, upon matting extended close to the houses on one side of the street, in the form of an oblong ring. Within this ring, about the middle of the matting, were placed three very large wax-candles, each about four feet high, and stuck in a low candlestick. Most of the dhikkirs were Ahmadi darweeshes, persons of the lower orders, and meanly dressed: many wore green turbans. At one end of the ring were four 'Munshids' (or singers of poetry) and with them was a player on the kind of flute called 'nay'. I procured a small seat of palm-sticks from a coffee-shop close by, and, by means of a little pushing, and the assistance of my servant, obtained a place with the Munshids and sat there to hear a complete act, or 'meglis', of the dhikr, which I shall describe as completely as I can, to convey a notion of the kind of dhikr most common and most approved in Cairo. It commenced at about three o'clock (or three hours after sunset) and continued for two hours.

The performers began by reciting the Fatiha altogether, their sheikh (or chief) first exclaiming: 'Al-Fatiha!' They then chanted the following words: 'O God! Bless our lord Mohammad among the former generations; and bless our lord Mohammad among the latter generations; and bless our lord Mohammad in every time and period; and bless our lord Mohammad among the most exalted princes (the angels), unto the day of judgement; and bless all the prophets and apostles among the inhabitants of the heavens and of the earth: and may God (whose name be blessed and exalted) be well pleased with our lords and our masters, those persons of illustrious estimation, Abu Bakr and 'Omar and 'Uthman and 'Ali, and with all the other favourites of God. God is our sufficiency and excellent is the Guardian. And there is no strength nor power but in God, the High, the Great. O God, O our Lord, O Thou liberal of pardon, O Thou most bountiful of the most bountiful. O God. Amen.' They were then silent for three or four minutes, and again recited the Fatiha, but silently. This form of prefacing the dhikr is commonly used by almost all orders of dervishes in Egypt.

After this preface, the performers began the dhikr. Sitting in the manner above described, they chanted in slow measure 'La ilaha illa-llah' (There is no deity but God), to the following air:

(Lane, Everyman's edition, reprint 1944, p. 452, gives the notation of the melody.)

bowing the head and body twice in each repetition at 'La ilaha illa-llah'. Thus they continued about a quarter of an hour, and then, for about the same space of time, they repeated the same words to the same air, but in a quicker measure, and with correspondingly quicker motions. In the mean-time the munshids frequently sang, to the same, or to a variation of the same air, portions of a 'qasida', or of a 'Muwashshah', an ode of a similar nature to the Song of Solomon, generally alluding to the Prophet as the object of love and praise. . . .

At frequent intervals (as is customary in other dhikrs), one of the mun-shids sang out the word: 'Meded', accentuating each syllable. 'Meded' signifies, when thus used, spiritual or supernatural aid, and implies an invocation for such aid.

The dhikkirs, after having performed as above described, next repeated the same words to a different air, for about the same length of time, first very slowly, then quickly. The air was as follows: . . . .

Then they repeated these words again, to the following air, in the same manner: . . . .

They next rose and, standing in the same order in which they had been sitting, repeated the same words to another air. During this stage of their performance, they were joined by a tall, well-dressed, black slave, whose appearance induced me to inquire who he was. I was informed that he was a eunuch, belonging to the Basha. The dhikkirs, still standing, next repeated the same words in a very deep and hoarse tone, laying the principal emphasis upon the word 'La' and the last syllable but one of the words following, and uttering apparently with a considerable effort: the sound much resembled that which is produced by beating the rim of a tambourine. Each dhikkir turned his head alternately to the right and left at each repetition of 'La ilaha illa-llah'. The eunuch above-mentioned, during this part of the dhikr, became what is termed 'melbus', or possessed. Throwing his arms about, and looking up, with a very wild expression of countenance, he exclaimed, in a very high tone, and with great vehemence and rapidity, 'Allah, Allah, Allah, Allah, la la lala lah. . . .' His voice gradually became faint and when he had uttered these words, though he was held by a dar-weesh who was near him, he fell on the ground, foaming at the mouth, his eyes closed, his limbs convulsed, and his fingers clenched over his thumbs. It was an epileptic fit: no one could see it and believe it to be the effect of feigned emotions. It was undoubtedly the result of a high state of religious excitement.

Nobody seemed surprised at it, for occurrences of this kind at dhikrs are not uncommon. All the performers now appeared much excited, repeating their ejaculations with greater rapidity, violently turning their heads, and sinking the whole body at the same time, some of them jumping. The eunuch became 'melbus' again several times and I generally remarked that his fits happened after one of the munshids had sung a line or two, and exerted himself more than usually to excite his hearers. The singing was, indeed, to my taste, very pleasing. Towards the close of the dhikr, a private soldier, who had joined throughout the whole performance, also seemed, several times, to be 'melbus', growling in a horrible manner, and violently shaking his head from side to side.

The contrast presented by the vehemence and distressing exertions of the performers at the close of the dhikr, and their calm gravity and solemnity of manner at the commencement, was particularly striking. Money was collected during the performance for the Munshids. The dhikkirs receive no pay.

In the pages immediately following Lane describes in the same detail the ceremony of the 'Dose' in which the sheikh of the Sa'diya dervishes rides on horseback over the bodies of his dervishes without their being harmed by the hooves.

17

New Cultures and Ruling Classes

DURING THE LONG PERIOD—from about 1100 to 1800 on—which we have described as that of co-operation between orthodox Islam and mysticism, the position of Arabic in the linguistic and allied politico-social field underwent a considerable change. To begin with, Persian arose as a new language of civilization in the Islamic world side by side with Arabic. It was the great poet Firdausi (died shortly after 1020) who raised Modern Persian to a literary language. From his time on songs and poems in Persian became more and more popular in the Persian part of the Empire. Arabic remained for centuries the language not only of the 'scientists', that is, the scholars who busied themselves with the Koran and Tradition, but also of the theologians, historians, natural scientists and philosophers. Al-Ghazali, who was by birth a Persian, compiled some Persian writings and letters but his main works are in Arabic. The same was the case with the great philosophers and natural scientists of the Persian half of the Empire in that epoch.

Under the Seljuks Persian prose began to appear. Those Turks, who were the ruling class of that state, learned Persian as the first literary language they came in contact with as they penetrated into the Islamic Empire. Arabic was their 'second foreign language' and one can understand why prose writers who wanted to be read by the rulers, like the famous Wazir Nizam al-Mulk, wrote their works in Persian. Persian kept its place as the language of education and literature not only with the Seljuks but also with the early Ottomans. In modern Turkish there is a large number of Arabic words but many of these were not taken directly from Arabic but from Persian which itself is full of Arabic loan words. About the time of the conquest of Constantinople (1453) Turkish, too, came more and more into the forefront as the third literary language of the Islamic Empire.

Arabic continued to be studied in the non-Arab territories of the Empire because a knowledge of it was essential for all Koranic sciences. Thus it had a position in Turkey and Persia not unlike that of Latin in our Middle Ages. Much is owed to Turkish philologists for editing and commenting on Arabic texts and to Turkish princes for collecting Arabic manuscripts.

But also inside the Arabic-speaking territory there were tendencies which gradually turned 'Written Arabic' into a sort of 'Church Arabic'. The Arabic dialects developed farther and farther apart from each other and Written Arabic followed, not the language spoken by Arabs, but the great models of Arabic literature and the grammatical norms of the Koran. With the increasing political importance of Turkish rulers and the rise of the Porte, Turkish became the language of government and had to be used even by an Arab author if he wanted to be understood by the Government and not only by his colleagues, the religious dignitaries and sheikhs. The educated upper classes, who did not belong to the class of religious scholars, cultivated Persian as the language of the great mystic poets and of a new rising mystical literature.

In the political field there were for long Arab splinter states within the Muslim world as a whole. This latter gradually fell apart into certain individual regions: Persia, Afghanistan, the Mogul Empire in India, the new Turkish Empire in Anatolia and Eastern Europe and an Arab territory which was ruled from Egypt.

The onslaught of Genghiz Khan and his Mongols caused more damage to Persia than to the Arab provinces of the Empire. Practically the whole of Persia was laid waste and came under Mongol domination. Of the Arab provinces only Iraq came under direct Mongol control, although they destroyed Damascus. But in the end the Persians were able to assimilate their Mongol conquerors and so, in the long run, the Mongol attack left few traces in Persia.

From Egypt the Arabs resisted the Mongols and Iraq fell to the rank of a frontier province. After the Mongols the Jala'ir ruled in Baghdad for seventy years then, for about one hundred years, the Turcoman dynasties of the Black and White Sheep and finally the province of Baghdad was incorporated in the rising Persian Safavid Kingdom in 1508. Throughout this period Arab Iraq shared the fate of the eastern, 'Persian' half of the Empire. The desert between Syria and Mesopotamia became once more a frontier desert after having been for long an Arabian inner desert.

So the main body of Arab civilization moved away from the central desert, to Cairo. Aleppo and Damascus, having lost their 'counter-weight' in Meso-potamia, became provincial towns of an Egyptian Kingdom. This Egyptian Kingdom, the Empire of the Bahri and Burji Mamelukes, was not devoid of brilliance. European travellers and pilgrims, coming from Jerusalem on the traditional road across Sinai to Cairo and Alexandria, praised the wealth of the Egyptian capitals and Cairo seemed to them the greatest and richest city in the world. Goods from the Orient came up the Red Sea coast to Qusseir, from there to the Valley of the Nile, then down to Cairo and through the Delta to Alexandria where they were shipped in the Venetian spice fleet.

Sultan Baibars, in many respects the founder of the dynasty, pushed the Mongols back out of Palestine and drove the Crusaders out of the Holy Land in which only a last small group remained. He invited a descendant of the Abbasids of Baghdad to his court in Cairo where he whiled away his life as a purely decorative figure among the other officials of the Mameluke court. New editions of a popular romance on the life and heroic deeds of Sultan Baibars in several volumes are still being printed and sold in the villages of Syria and Egypt.

The Mamelukes take their name from the word 'mamluk', meaning 'possession', that is to say they were slaves, who were bought by the Sultan when they were still boys. They mostly came from the Caucasian and Turcoman border lands to the north of the Empire, but they also included Europeans, Greeks, and prisoners of war from the Balkans and even captives from Western Europe taken by pirates. The sultan gave them a careful education and a thorough military training in the use of weapons and riding. They passed through several stages of instruction and, on reaching man's estate, were nominally emancipated, at the same time pledging themselves to the service of the sultan.

They were granted lands from the produce of which they had to maintain themselves, their horses and weapons and, in certain circumstances, their followers. They generally lived in the capital or in garrison towns and the most energetic among them rose to high military commands and important offices in the civil administration. The higher they rose in rank the more land they acquired but, contrary to western custom, only very few of them succeeded in acquiring the hereditary possession of their lands. The sultan could take them back at any time and he used this right when he thought fit. They were also forbidden to give away their lands as subfiefs.

Who should enjoy the office of sultan was decided among themselves by the great Mamelukes, and here arms often had their say. There was no fixed line of inheritance and after an inevitable period of insecurity and unrest the strongest of the nobles in the state was chosen. In times of decadence, however, someone was chosen who it was hoped could easily be led and influenced.

In all this the Egyptians had no right to open their mouths. The government was carried on by foreigners of whom the most that could be expected was that they would not demand exhorbitant tribute. Intercourse between these and their subjects was provided for by a class of scribes and tax collectors, often of Coptic origin, who were organized in the main according to the system of the Byzantine Empire. When irregularities went too far, the religious dignitaries, the orthodox sheikhs, jurists and heads of the Sufi orders 'intervened'. These religious dignitaries belonged to the ruled class of Egyptians. Their offices were often hereditary, yet it was easy, perhaps easier than was the case with the mediaeval clergy of Europe, for any gifted peasant son to go to school and, if he possessed outstanding intellectual gifts, to raise himself to the ranks of the religious dignitaries. There was a large number of schools with stipends and with their own income from land. In these the traditional Koranic sciences were taught and they were the citadels of Sunni orthodoxy. At the same time the religious houses of the mystics, often richly furnished, came more and more to the fore. In these the Sufis lived together and strove for direct knowledge of God.

The greatest achievement of the Mamelukes, so far as we can survey their epoch today, seems to have been in the field of architecture. Innumerable mosques, domed schools, hospitals and fortifications in Cairo, Damascus and Aleppo are eloquent testimony to their joy in building and the superiority of their architects. Seen from the outside, Mameluke mosques are heavy, square blocks with high walls and towers. Their inner courtyards are narrow and dark. They lack the openness and expanse of the early mosques. They often have something of the air of fortresses reminiscent of the heavy stone masses of Florentine palaces. Their interior shows a wealth of stone-work of which earlier epochs knew nothing. The dome structure with squinches reaches a new refinement. The stone-masons of the Mamelukes were unsurpassed in mortising and chamfering, in the decoration of archways and domes and in the invention of new patterns and ornaments. In spite of all this magnificence one cannot walk through the streets of Old Cairo without feeling that the domes and walls of Mameluke buildings have something overwhelmingly oppressive and repul-sively blocklike about them. They are not, like the contemporary buildings of the Persians, the centre of the world, microcosms in harmony with the macro-cosm around them, but citadels and refuges of the spirit, richly decorated cells of ascetics and places of segregation. As such they are signs of a narrowing world. Life is approached defensively, a feeling of uncertainty and suspicion prevails; confronted with it, people tend to withdraw to a circumscribed realm which they adorn and furnish for themselves.

We do not know enough about the literary life of that epoch to allow our-selves a final judgement, especially not on the rich, flourishing mysticism of the time. We also lack comprehensive biographical works and books on history and cultural history. But, in spite of these lacunae, it is improbable that we would obtain a general picture different from the one conveyed by the archi-tecture of Mameluke times. With all its magnificence there was something stagnant about the Mameluke Empire. This can be linked to the geographical position of Egypt. Egypt is one of the best isolated areas of the world. Even when it has subordinated territories stretching out towards Syria, even when it succeeds in drawing a considerable part of the trade of the Orient to the Red Sea and along its own shores, the Valley of the Nile is and remains a side-track, a sort of deviation leading away from the great land bridge between Asia and the Mediterranean. The great current of civilization between India and Europe, between China and the Mediterranean flows past the Nile Valley, hardly touching it.

While the Mamelukes were setting up their Empire on that siding of world history, there occurred, on the main line in Transoxiania, Persia and Anatolia a new and fruitful encounter between the Far East and the Near East as a

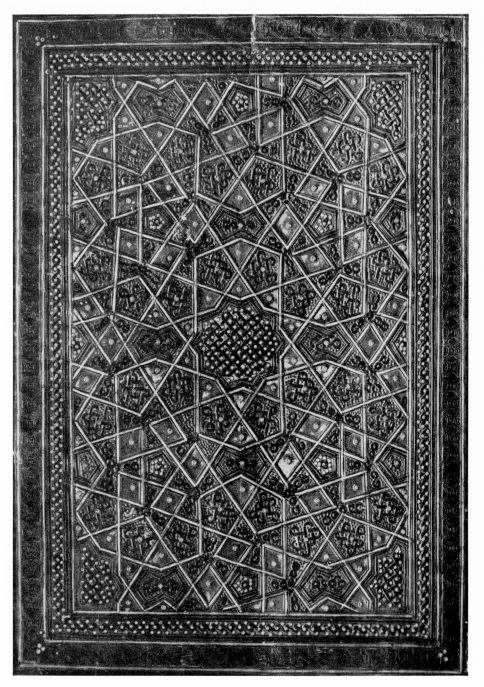

7 *Book binding with a geometrical pattern in gold, Egypt, fourteenth century.*

8 *Prayer carpet from Asia Minor in the Ottoman Museum, Istanbul,
sixteenth century.*

consequence of the Mongol conquest. The Mongols linked Central Asia, deep into China, with Persia. It was possible for Marco Polo to travel under their rule from Anatolia through Central Asia to China and from China to India. In the following centuries Persian miniature painting influenced Chinese miniatures and Chinese pottery influenced Persian. The Turcomans penetrated into Anatolia and southern Russia and in the opposite direction Tamerlane (Timur) dragged the artisans of Damascus to his distant capital Samarkand to adorn it.

From these contacts there developed two new Islamic states, one Persian which was finally formed by the Safavids, the other Turkish which was subsequently much influenced by Byzantium. In both states Central Asian elements mixed with those of the Near East on whose territory they had settled. Persian and Central Asian Mongol illustrations are to be found side by side in the sketch book of the court artists of Mehmed, the conqueror of Constantinople. The city of Isfahan blossomed on Persian soil as the symbol of a state that only needed a period of peace to make the seeds of Persian cultural traditions burst into new flower.

18

Decadence?

SO MUCH HAS BEEN SAID, especially in the Near East itself, about the decadence of the Arabs under Turkish rule that one has to be very careful when one uses that term. 'Turkish tyranny' is often given by moden Arabs as an excuse for the Arab countries not being 'more modern', 'more progressive' than they are today. The sentence one hears so often: 'We have to make up the cultural arrears of 500 years!' is so popular partly because one thinks primarily of the centuries of 'Turkish rule' and believes that they can be held responsible for these 'arrears'.

It should be clear enough from our historical references how injudicious it is to try to measure the 'development' of Arab society by that of European society as if there were *one* compulsory and correct sort of 'development' (the European one) and as if all societies which have not experienced this development and have gone other ways could simply be characterized as 'retarded' or 'under-developed'.

The values set itself by the Islamic world and the aims it strove after and which it kept until late into the last century were in fact different from those pursued in Europe since the Renaissance and later in America. No one can presume to decide with certainty whether the traditional Muslim aims or those of European civilization are in themselves more worthy of being pursued. Even the fact that the Arabs of today are very strongly inclined to make the western attitude their own and thus turn away from the tradition of their own civilization does not really decide which of the two systems of civilization is superior or inferior. Every observer will come to the conclusion that the 'modern' Arabs who are trying to take over the ideals of the West do not know exactly what they really want, nor, indeed, can they know since these ideals stem from a foreign world. They have hardly the slightest idea of the internal problems and dangers western civilization itself has to face today.

So that when one speaks of the Arabs degenerating under Turkish rule one must take one's standards from Islamic civilization itself, avoiding comparisons with other, unrelated, systems. But was there not also a noticeable decline in the development of Arab civilization, already begun in the time of the Mameluke Empire and hastened after the conquest of that Empire by the Turks in 1517? Such a decline is perhaps most noticeable in the political field; the Arab

Empire shrinks and in the end disappears completely. But immediately doubts arise. Had not an Arab empire already ceased to exist ever since Turkish leaders of mercenaries came to power at the Caliph's court (*c.* 842)? And should the Abbasid Empire not be called an Islamic empire rather than an Arab one? In which case we go back to before 751 to find a really Arab empire!

It is the same story in the cultural field when we try to establish exact criteria for the concept 'degeneration'. To be sure, fewer and fewer important works are written in Arabic—or does this only seem to be the case because Islamics and orientalists have concentrated their studies above all on the early centuries? We know far less about the intellectual life of the Arab world in the sixteenth and seventeenth centuries than about that in the ninth or tenth century. More-over, mysticism was never especially interested in writing books. Perhaps the lack of documents which we would consider important is partly to be ascribed to the increasing concentration on mysticism and the dervish system? Should one say that an epoch is degenerate because of such a concentration of energies?

It cannot be denied that in the course of the centuries two new literary lan-guages developed in addition to Arabic—Persian and Turkish; add to this that Turkish became, with the advent of Turkish rule, the language of govern-ment, while Arabic became the special language of theology. In this way everything which shone, glittered and pleased was considered, under Turkish rule, as part and parcel of 'Turkish' civilization even if it had been created by the hand of an Arab artisan or the brain of an Arab scholar.

We do not get very far when we try to differentiate 'Arabic' from 'Turkish'. The Ottoman Empire was not a national state but a great, successful and brilliant common enterprise of the Islamic peoples of the West. In it, apart from Anatolia, Turkish was not the language of a people but of a class, the ruling aristocracy. Whoever belonged to that aristocracy, and many Arabs did, spoke Turkish, just as a Turk had to learn Arabic in order to study religious writings. Does the rise of a new language of culture and government justify one speaking of the degeneration of the old one? It is remarkable that in this 'period of degeneration' the whole social structure survived the rise of the new language of government without any break worth mentioning and people seemed to have acquired a certain balance between their daily life and their ideals, desires and aspirations. This picture of a well-ordered life, which in spite of its wretched-ness (measured by present-day American or West-European 'living standards') satisfied those who lived it, is the main impression one gets from contemporary sources. Even European observers, who knew the language of the country perfectly and who took it upon themselves to live for some time among its inhabitants, are agreed in this. Lane's book, *Manners and Customs of the Modern Egyptians*, is eloquent testimony of it.

To be sure, other European travellers did not take the trouble to familiarize themselves with the world of late Islam which was so foreign to that of their own times. They simply measured the oriental world by the standards of their own cultural ideals and found it wanting. They summed up all that wide sector of the later Islamic spirit, which they with their ideas of enlightenment, could not penetrate, under two catch-words: superstition and fatalism. But even today it is well to remind people who speak inconsiderately of superstition that there is no objective frontier between 'religion' and 'superstition'. Where 'religion' ceases and 'superstition' begins depends entirely on the speaker's point of view. For a Muslim 'religious truths', like the Incarnation and the trans-formation of wine into blood, etc., are the grossest superstition. Dervish practices which are decried by practically all present-day Muslims as 'super-stition' were accepted by their fathers and grandfathers as legitimate religious exercises and even orthodox theologians took part in them.

The word 'fatalism' is just as much a confession of not understanding as the word 'superstition'. By it one civilized community expresses its impatience with another civilized community which is pursuing its own particular aims. The indifference towards religious matters prevalent in Europe since the Enlighten-ment could just as well seem 'abominable fatalism' to a Muslim of the tradi-tional school as the Oriental's 'lack of provision for the next day and the next hour' which is considered so 'decadent' in Europe. A Muslim might reproach a European: 'You are a fatalist for you concern yourself with non-essential matters such as the question of who governs or should govern in your country. But in the much more important question of what will happen to you after death you simply give up.' Muslims of the 'period of degeneration' certainly did not prove themselves fatalists as far as religious questions are concerned for they were constantly and vitally interested in the basic problems of the world and Eternity. They continued to cultivate their religious sciences and in the last years of the old Muslim civilization there were still scholars whose 'knowledge', purely as a feat of memory, may have been several times greater than the 'knowledge' stored up in the brains of most European scholars. Moreover, and apart from this there was a method which strove to acquire direct knowledge of 'essential matters', mysticism which followed its own laws and paths no matter how strange these may seem to us.

A historian finds again and again that, the more intensively he studies a supposedly decadent civilization, the more difficult it is to use the term 'decadence'. Where did the 'decadence' of ancient civilization begin? With Justinian? Constantine? Marcus Aurelius? Cicero? With Socrates, as Nietzsche believed?

I, personally, am inclined to support Nietzsche. In most civilizations one can clearly discern an *Edad de Oro*, to use the Spanish term, a sort of culminating period. It is always short and there leads up to it a longer, preparatory, 'young' period which bears all the marks of freshness. What follows the peak period, often for centuries, can from one point of view certainly be called 'decadence';

but it can also be a period of consolidation, a period when the civilization spreads for the first time over its whole geographic area and penetrates from the *élite* down into the 'people', a period in which the achievements of the peak period are first examined, organized and stated. 'Decadence' in the sense of a monotonous, progressive decline lasting centuries is scarcely in accordance with the biological laws of the history of humanity. Post-classic periods reach new heights of civilization and new periods of decline. There has certainly never yet been a period of 'decline' which lasted for centuries.

How differently specialist scholars deal with the question of the 'decadence' of Islamic civilization can be seen from a French book entitled *Classicisme et Déclin Culturel dans l'Histoire de l'Islam*, edited by R. Brunschvig and G. E. von Grunebaum (Paris, 1957). On the one hand one finds the traditional view of the 'decadence' of Islamic civilization, not unmixed, it would seem, with racial theories, for example in a sentence such as this: 'The brilliance which the Arabs spread about them in the Golden Age of their borrowed civilization had merely been a chance occurrence in their history and it was natural that a balance should be struck on a lower level more in keeping with their abilities' (p. 85). Less prejudiced is the attitude of a specialist in Islamic theology and philosophy (L. Gardet) who confines himself to speaking about the 'ankylosis' (stiffening) of religious thought and trying to find its causes, concluding his essay with the words: 'There is still hope of a revival for nothing in the historical conditions of ankylosis justifies the assertion that it entails an irrevocable decline' (p. 105). A quite positive attitude is taken by the well-known orientalist Ritter to certain aspects of later Islamic civilization and he does not shrink from asking the counter-question: Where are we ourselves going? '. . . towards the mastery of Nature, a mastery which reaches its zenith in the benefits of the atom bomb; towards such an inflation of knowledge that no one will be able to acquire more than the tiniest part of the culture of his times, towards an excessive expansion of European American civilization by radio and press, spreading its hodge-podge of culture into the farthest corners of the Orient at every hour of the day and night' (p. 179).

In view of such differences of opinion about the concept of 'decadence' it is safer to confine oneself to establishing the growth, culmination, stagnation and decay of individual disciplines, without presuming to judge whether a certain type of human behaviour is superior to another or not.

The decay of the Muslim arts and handicrafts set in much later than would seem to fit into the scheme of the decay of Muslim civilization. It became noticeable in every place where European articles, architectural styles, ways of life or methods of manufacture appeared: at the Court of Istanbul in the seventeenth and eighteenth centuries, in Cairo at the beginning of the nineteenth and in Damascus in the main only after 1860. Wherever the influence of the West made itself felt, a general and irresistible confusion of taste began which led within one generation to the reduction of the old handicrafts and building techniques to a pitiable state. Today one can still encounter traces of this confusion in the 'sitting-room' of an upper-middle-class or rich oriental family with its accumulation of tasteless objects.

The irruption of western objects into the world of Islam has never been systematically studied but we believe, on the basis of our personal and casual experiences, that the real collapse of the Muslim arts and handicrafts is to be put much later than the beginning of the 'decadence of Islamic civilization', as historians are inclined to see it, and that this practically total collapse has hardly yet ended.

Until a few decades ago Lebanon had its own particular architectural style which was a Mediterranean style in which Italian influence was discernable and which had close ties with Venice. It was a unified style and one met it in both peasant houses and palaces. Its principal feature was the great pointed arch window in palaces and the pointed arch entrances and terraces of the peasant houses. Its monuments are decaying today unheeded and disregarded in the peasant villages and in Beirut.

When the Americans Bliss and Dodge built their American university in Beirut two generations ago they tried to adapt it to the local style. The result of their efforts was a somewhat artificial, but not unattractive 'missionary Orient' in warm, yellow natural stone with loggias and clock-towers. Similar efforts were made by the French architects of town-planning in Damascus. They laid out suburbs in the Syrian capital distinguished by 'oriental' features. The French Jesuits have attempted the same thing in building their university in Beirut. Their style in imitation of the East united European 'utility' with oriental 'decoration' but met with little sympathy from the orientals even when the result was harmonious.

Away with that old-fashioned, 'oriental' stuff, say the constructors of the modern block of flats and sky-scrapers in the East. If they are talented the result is a superficial imitation of the international modern style of architecture, at best a house which could just as well stand in Argentina or Texas. At worst they are buildings put together according to their own ideas by local architects who have not studied the technique of the masters of modern architecture. Then they produce horrors of casinos, mountain hotels, holiday chalets and 'villas' in mechanically cut natural stone or in concrete painted white, red, yellow and blue with gigantic flights of steps, bright red iron banisters, neon lighting in green, pink and sky-blue, gravel paths and entrances for the Cadillacs, monstrosities which are well on the way to transforming the splendid old villages on the western slope of the Lebanon into accumulations of pretention and false splendour.

It is not a very different picture when one turns to sacral architecture. The last great architectural innovation in the building of mosques was the introduction of domes. The idea of building mosques completely vaulted over by one great dome was without doubt taken by the Turkish architects from the St Sophia Church in Istanbul. Ulya Vogt-Goknil has shown convincingly in her essay referred to earlier that they nevertheless constructed something spiritually quite different from the work of the classic builders of Hagia Sofia. Instead of a transcendental, floating space they created a static 'space crystal'.

The greatest architect of this style and in fact the creator of the domed mosque was Sinan (1498–1578), whose masterpieces in Istanbul belong to the great architectural monuments of the world. Under his successors the domed mosque passed through a 'romantic' phase and a 'baroque' period. Both periods produced masterpieces like the Ahmed Jami (1610) and the Yeni Jami (1643) in Istanbul.

The new style spread from Istanbul all over the Turkish Empire. The possibilities of the domed mosque were exhausted, varied and presented in different ways which proved alive enough to produce as late as the last century mosques which can be accepted without reserve as noteworthy works of art. This also happened in the Arab parts of the Empire. The Sinaniya Mosque in Bulaq, Cairo (built by Sinan in 1573) is a genuine work of art whose qualities become all the more noticeable when they are compared with the mosque built by King Faruq in what is now the Midan al-Tahrir in the 'forties.

Arabic literature seems to have begun to stagnate considerably earlier than the plastic arts. The last Arab poets of modern times, recognized as classic poets, are Al-Ma'arri (973–1058) and Ibn al-Farid (died 1235) whose works are closely bound up with mysticism. The last great historian, whom orientalists hail as an outstanding genius, was Ibn Khaldun (1332–1400) who, as Muhsin Mahdi has demonstrated, was influenced by Islamic Greek philosophy (Ibn Khaldun's *Philosophy of History*, London, 1957).

However, one should be wary of accepting as final the remarkable panorama of Arabic literature which western orientalists have constructed, for a great literature of later centuries still lies mouldering and unread in the libraries and archives of Cairo, Damascus, Istanbul and the Turkish provincial capitals and also in the libraries and mosques of the Maghrib. In those centuries of 'decay' not a little was written but an enormous amount and the natural process of elimination which, with the passing of the centuries, separates the inferior from the valuable has not been able to produce its effect. The authors of the later periods were decided polygraphs. Their works can often not be conceived as books in the modern sense; they do not claim to add anything new to the storehouse of known knowledge and can to a great extent be compared to very well kept college note books in which the subject matter available is arranged in the most expedient manner possible.

The 'manuals' and encyclopaedias of the late Middle Ages read like handbooks which scholars had prepared for their own use. In the later centuries every Islamic academy, the Azhar in Cairo, the schools in Mecca and those in Istanbul, Damascus, Fez, Tunis and Qairawan, had its own favourite manuals. Just as today in our universities, 'handbooks' are not always the most brilliant products.

Not only scientific literature, but also 'belles-lettres' was organized into surveys, encyclopaedias and anthologies. We know the names of a few scholars whose works extended beyond the requirements of school teaching but in most cases these works still await study. Other names would doubtless turn up if Arabists with sufficient patience and knowledge of the language would only set about separating the school books from the productive works.

One field of work which is still almost untouched is that of popular literature. The collection of tales, 'The Thousand and One Nights', is in its present form a product of the 'period of decay' but its beginnings go back to classical Islamic times. Its Arabic with its limited vocabulary is close to the spoken language and differs considerably from classic models. This collection which is so well-known in Europe is still dismissed by Arab men of letters as 'back-stairs literature'. In addition there are a large number of works of the same style, popular romances, known to every Arab. They were told to him by his grand-mother in his childhood and have been collected in editions of several volumes. Until very recently the readers and tellers of stories in the oriental coffee-shops derived their subject matter from them and they are still sold in the villages and read by the peasants. No doubt the cinema, radio and television will soon cause them to disappear completely.

They show all the signs of the 'period of decay', especially its loquacity and prolixity but taken as a whole they form a very noteworthy achievement of the 'poetic imagination' of the Arabs of the late Middle Ages. A collection of popular romances still being printed in Cairo from old plates would fill a bookcase and there is still probably some material in manuscript form which has not yet been explored.

What we have said about literature also applies to religious works. Their being so abundant and on the average of little quality and originality has been the cause of the whole ocean of religious writings of the 'later period' being neglected and ignored by orientalists trained in the sciences of literature and religion. It is probable that no great new ideas and developments can be dis-cerned in that ocean. Apparently the final balance of Islam was reached with Al-Ghazali and tendencies and personalities, unable to reconcile their belief with that of the orthodox, from then on found plenty of scope in mysticism.

A reaction was to come only towards the end of the so-called period of decay. A teacher appeared in Arabia in 1744, preaching the return to 'original' Islam. He was called *Muhammad ibn Abdul Wahhab* and had studied under the influence of the 'Puritans' of Islam, the Hanbali school. Rather like Muhammad himself a thousand years before him he concluded, after initial failures in his home town, an agreement with one of the emirs of Arabia, Sa'ud who was lord of Dar'iya. Emir and teacher in co-operation were able to spread their faith and rule over the whole Arabian peninsula. Their followers, the *Wahhabis*, appeared to the 'Muslims' of those times as barbarous fanatics and cut-throats. Muhammad Ali and his son Ibrahim drowned their religious movement in blood in 1818 after two hard-fought campaigns but their state and their faith were both resurrected in the twentieth century by the great Abdul Aziz ibn Sa'ud and their fundamentalist articles of faith have had great influence on modern Islam.

Wahhabism is by no means the only expression of religious life and the creative power of religion in the later period. Those fascinating social organizations which one calls *Tariqas*, or 'paths' were in full bloom at that time. These 'paths' are to be understood as 'ways' of seeking for God. Mystics who set out on the same 'path' formed one 'order'. It is no exaggeration to say that the inhabitants of the Muslim countries lived in the main in and for these orders during the later centuries. It was only when they, as a result of europeanization and 'enlightenment', disappeared from the life of the people that the spiritual impoverishment and loss of bearing set in which today make the masses of the Near East an easy prey to any kind of demagogy and tastelessness.

The destruction of the 'orders' has not yet been finally completed in any Muslim country. They were about to be permitted again in Turkey, a consciously lay country, in 1957. But nowhere can they still be counted among the socially effective and active religious forces; they vegetate away in the lowest classes of the population where europeanization has not yet penetrated very deeply and they no longer have any leadership or contact with the active *élite* of the state. The only exception is the Sudan for there the Mahdiya 'order', whose founder, the Mahdi, conquered and murdered General Gordon in 1886, is still one of the decisive political forces in the country. Libya, too, owes its existence as a state to the Sanusiya 'order' whose leaders are the Idris family.

Problems of social organization can only be understood in connection with the life of the Tariqas. Modern Arab historians like to point out the 'terrible' social conditions under 'Turkish rule'. To be sure, measured by the European ideal of personal freedom and the rights of man, the capriciousness and egoism of the great men of the Ottoman Empire do not always paint a pretty picture. But if one compares conditions in the Ottoman Empire not with things as they are today in the privileged modern nations of the West but with the social set-up in the Near East today one can pass a considerably more favourable judgement. The differences in wealth and the power money gives the rich are rather greater today than formerly. Governmental authority is perhaps used a little less capriciously but on the other hand it interferes much more with the life of the individual.

Today the little man has no defence against the privileged, the big landowner or army officer for his 'organization', the Tariqa, which formerly looked after him, has now either completely disappeared or has, at least, been rendered powerless. The Tariqa also provided the common man with his spiritual sustenance, society, an aim in life and a place inside his own community. The 'proletarian' or peasant of today has nothing of the same value which can replace all that, neither the cinema nor the political organizations nor the third-rate newspapers, and even orthodoxy with its impersonal abstract manner cannot satisfy him without the Tariqa. But, instead, there is another organization in the modern world which is capable and willing to take the place of the organized orders which have disappeared, the communist cell. With its common action, driven by a quasi-religious spirit, its comradeship, which also strives for something 'higher', and its spirit of mutual aid it revives many of the decisive values of the old Tariqa. Other parties, too, can profit by the vacuum left by the collapse of the orders. As long as they are in opposition to a ruling power they flourish, because they are forced to use methods similar to those of the communist cell. The Muslim Brotherhood, the PPS, the Baath are such parties. They evince an astounding ability to survive as long as they are 'fighting communities'.

19

The End of 'Muslim Civilization'

WHAT WE TERMED 'MUSLIM CIVILIZATION', that civilization composed of Islamic religion and Arabic language on the bridge between East and West, has today come to an end in the Arab countries. For a long time the new literary languages, Persian and Turkish, did not break the unity of Islamic civilization. The formation of states in the fifteenth and sixteenth centuries did, it is true, bring about the first split into Shi'ite Persian and Ottoman-Arab-Sunnism but, nevertheless, one can still consider the Islamic Near East as one cultural community right up to the beginning of the eighteenth century.

The seed which was in the end to disrupt this cultural community was sown by 'europeanization'. The centres in which western 'reform movements' began in the eighteenth century are today focal points of Turkish, Arab and Persian nationalism. A Pakistani nationalism will no doubt develop, too.

As we are dealing with the Arabs this is the point where our eyes must turn away from Turkey and Persia. The detachment of Arabs from Turks will continue to occupy us for some time but the detachment of the Arabs from the Persians took place unnoticed since it did not require a war. It can be measured by the decay of the knowledge of Persian in the Arab Near East which is almost total. Among the thousands of educated Arabs who speak French and English, and even German, Italian or Spanish, and who are striving to adopt the cultural standards of the European civilizations, you will scarcely be able to find one who cultivates Persian or who is even conscious of the role played by the spirit of Persia in his grandfather's or great-grandfather's cultural world.

The detachment of the Arabs from the Persians also finds it expression in the decay of the arts among the Arabs. Persia had been from early times the centre of that tendency which we have claimed was characteristic of 'Muslim civilization', the tendency towards a 'decorative' art with an unhumanistic, cosmic outlook aiming towards harmony. The separation from Persia brought with it an immediate decline in Arab handicrafts, indeed of Arab artistic taste. Today you have to explain to an Arab the beauties of an Oriental carpet, a classic Mosque, a miniature or a classic melody with at least as many words as to a European; perhaps it is more difficult to awaken an appreciation of art in him. Many an Arab of today shows at first an instinctive distaste for 'old-fashioned' oriental things, whereas a man from the West, because of a certain romantic interest in the 'East', can be more easily induced to make a serious attempt to understand an oriental *objet d'art*.

In order to answer our question 'Who are the Arabs?' we must at this point of our investigation also change the tempo of our study. A broad survey of the Arab people's past was sufficient for our secondary question 'Who were the Arabs?' The dissolution of Muslim civilization, however, took place at that very moment in which what we now call 'Arabism' emerged. It is a long 'moment'; its early beginnings become apparent about the middle of the nineteenth century, its roots even go back into the eighteenth century, and it is still not ended. The concept of an 'Arabism' is now as ever fluid. It will be the task of the second part of this book to investigate the various interwoven features of the end of the old 'Muslim' civilization and of the beginning of a new, still half-veiled phenomenon which has itself taken the name of 'Arab nationalism'.

We are faced with a change of civilization like the one brought about by Muhammad when he preached a new religion to the Beduins. But it is much more difficult to understand this change of civilization because it is not concentrated in a great personality like a prophet. It stretches over several generations and is expressed in an ever fragmentary, often very clumsy manner. It has created no symbol, has found no single figure to express it nor has it worked out a unified doctrine by which its significance could be made comprehensible. Nasser is no more an adequate expression of it than Al-Afghani was; they are both only contributory forces in a complicated process which is composed of innumerable forces and influences.

The change is not less real, not less radical because of this; it is only less apparent because it is taking place gradually and because it has found no outstanding single creative personality symbolic of all its deeds or utterances. We must be satisfied with seeking it step by step through the penumbra of modern Near Eastern history if we wish to come to a conclusion as to who the Arabs are today.

Part Two

THE ARABS IN MODERN TIMES

THE TURNING-POINT OF AN EPOCH

I

Al-Jabarti

THE SIGNS OF THE APPROACH OF THE FRENCH increased day by day. People discussed which side they might come from; many said they would come from the Western Desert, others said they would come from the Eastern Desert and still others said they would attack from both sides. But none of the military leaders took the trouble to send out scouts or to order the rearguard to begin to attack them before they reached Cairo. All Ibrahim Bey and Murad Bey did was to muster their soldiers and remain motionless where they were, awaiting their fate. That was very bad organiza-tion and negligence in the face of the enemy.

On Friday, the 6th, the French reached Al-Jisr al-Aswad and on the Saturday morning Umm Dinar, where there was gathered a large number of soldiers from the countryside, subjects and peasants whose villages were in the vicinity of Cairo. But the soldiers had divided hearts, weak wills and conflicting opinions and their only care was to remain alive and enjoy life. They were proud of their finery, and quarrelsome in their assemblies, had a poor opinion of their enemy, thinking only of their own affairs and sunk in their heedlessness. All this helped to bring about the destruction that was to befall them. They believed the French would come from both sides whereas they were to come from the west only.

When the midday heat of that day had come the soldiers who were in the Western Desert advanced towards Bashtil, a village not far from Imbaba. They clashed with the French vanguard and attacked them with cavalry. Both sides fought well.

When the soldiers on the eastern bank of the Nile saw the fighting they determined to cross over to the other bank in boats. They withdrew to Ma'adi so that the ferrying-over could be concentrated in one place but there were only a very few boats available. All the troops could not reach the battlefield before the soldiers on the western bank were put to flight. In addition, the wind was blowing from the wrong direction and the river was very rough. The wind whipped up the dust and blew it in the soldiers' faces so that not one of them could keep his eyes open.

Then the French unit, which was fighting Murad Bey, split into two, a manoeuvre they were well trained in, and advanced on the barricades from two sides. They beat their drums and fired their muskets and cannons in continuous salvoes. The wind blew harder and harder and the dust became thicker; everything was dark with the smoke of powder, the dust and the wind. Because of the noise of the continuous firing one no longer knew what was going on so that one felt that the earth was quaking and the heavens were falling on it. The fighting lasted about three-quarters of an hour then the soldiers on the west bank turned and fled. Many cavalrymen drowned in the river because they were surrounded by the enemy and because it was dark; others were taken prisoner.

The French conquered the barricades and Murad Bey and those with him fled to Guizeh. Murad Bey went to his palace, did what he had to do in about a quarter of an hour, then mounted and made for the south. The dead, clothing, baggage and weapons were left lying in the desert of Imbaba.

Having routed the troops on the west bank the French turned their cannon and their muskets on the east bank. A great cry went up in Bulaq. Ibrahim Bey and the Pasha mounted with their officers and the cavalry. They left all the baggage and the tents where they were, taking nothing with them. Ibrahim Bey, the Pasha and his officers proceeded toward Al-Adiliya while the panic-stricken subjects fled into the city and awaited their end in terror. They sobbed and howled, imploring God to save them from destruction on that evil day and in the houses the women screamed at the top of their voices. All this happened before sunset.

When Ibrahim Bey reached Al-Adiliya he sent messengers to fetch his wives and so did the officers who were with him. They mounted the women on horses, mules, donkeys and camels while the slave girls and servants went on foot. The flight of the majority of the inhabitants from the city went on all night long, many with their wives while others tried to save themselves alone. Some went to Upper Egypt and others, the majority, to the East. Those who remained in Cairo and braved the danger did so only because they were unable to leave and escape their fate. Those who were not strong enough to flee or who had no one to help them save their families or who had no money to support them in the villages surrendered themselves to their fate and to God Who decrees the end of all things.

What terrified and drove the people to flight most of all was the rumour that went around that night that the Franks had crossed over to Bulaq and burned it down as well as Guizeh and that the first of them had already reached the Gate (Bab al-Hadid) where they were killing and raping the women. The cause of this rumour was that one of Murad Bey's soldiers had set fire to the galleon he was in in Imbaba anchorage when he saw that their soldiers had been defeated. Likewise Murad Bey had ordered the great galley to be towed away from his palace so that he might flee southwards in it. However, it could only be towed a little way before it was grounded on the mud because of the shallow water. It was loaded with a great quantity of war material and cannon shells and Murad ordered it to be set on fire. A great tongue of fire arose in Guizeh and Bulaq and when the people in the city saw it they thought, nay they were sure, the enemy had set fire to these villages. They became excited and the fear, terror and panic, which had already broken out, was increased. The dignitaries and well-to-do citizens fled and along with them everyone of any position and also some of the sheikhs who were in a position to do so. When the common people saw that they became even more terror-stricken and decided to flee also. No one knew which way to take nor where to make for. They followed each other, keeping close together, crowding and pushing each other. Lame donkeys or broken-down mules were bought for many times their value, but most went out on foot, with their belongings on their heads and followed by their wives carrying the children. Whoever had a riding beast put his wife or daughter on it and walked beside it. But most women went on foot carrying their children on their shoulders and weeping in the darkness of the night. So it went on all night long before Sunday and all the next morning. Everyone took with him what money and household goods he could carry.

In the desert they had to pass through they were met by Beduins and Fellaheen who robbed them of their possessions, clothing and baggage and whoever met this fate was left with nothing to cover his nakedness or still his hunger.

When the Sunday morning came all those remaining behind could do was to await the arrival of the French and the calamity they were bringing with them. Many refugees returned in a terrible state, naked and terrified. Then it became clear that the French had not attacked the eastern bank and that the fire had come from the afore-mentioned boats. Several scholars and sheikhs collected and took counsel in the Azhar Mosque. They agreed to send messengers to the Franks to see what answer they would give. They did so sending a delegation consisting of a man from the Maghrib who knew their language and a companion. Both went and came back to report that they had been received by the supreme commander of the army. They had delivered their message to him and he had had his interpreter translate it to him. Its content was that they wished to be informed of the intentions of the intruders. He said to them through the interpreter: 'Where are your great men and sheikhs? Why have they not come to us so that we can take the necessary measures with them to ensure peace and quiet?' and he treated them affably. They said: 'We desire peace from you.' He answered: 'I have already offered it to you.' Then he wrote for them a message which read: 'From the camp in Guizeh a letter to the people of Cairo. We have already sent you letters in which everything was clearly expressed. In them we informed you that we have only come to put an end to the rule of the Mamelukes because the Mamelukes treat the French with haughtiness and contempt. And because they have appropriated the wealth of the merchants and the property of the state. While we were in the Western Desert they came out against us and we received them with what they deserved. We have killed some of them and taken others prisoner. Still others have fled but we shall seek them out until not one of them is left in Egypt. But as for the sheikhs, the scholars, the wage-earners and the subjects they can rest assured that they will remain unmolested in their homes, etc.'

Then he said to the messengers: 'The sheikhs and the chiefs must come to us so that we may appoint from them a Diwan of seven intelligent men to take over the administration.'

When this answer was received the people were reassured and Sheikhs Mustafa al-Sawi and Sulaiman al Faiyumi and others rode to Guizeh. He received them in a friendly manner and said: 'Are you the great sheikhs?' They informed him that the great sheikhs had fled in fear and he asked: 'What were they afraid of? Write to them to come and we shall set up a Diwan so that everything may be quiet.' They wrote several letters from him to them that they should appear under safe-conduct. Then they left the camp after the evening prayer.

The writer of this report of Napoleon's conquest of Cairo was himself a sheikh and we know that he was a member of that 'Diwan' which the conqueror set up to administer Cairo. When he wrote the book from which this report is taken he nevertheless preferred not to say anything about his 'collaboration with the enemy', for at that time the Mamelukes had come back to Cairo.

Sheikh Al-Jabarti (1754–1822) belonged to one of the most respected sheikhly families in Cairo. Before him his father and grandfather had been 'professors' at the Azhar University. Their family owned several houses in Cairo and rich landed property outside the city. Azhar 'Sheikhs' were not simply just professors. The 'Government' accepted them as representing at one and the same time, the people, morality, Divine Law and the Islamic tradition. They acted as link between the Turkish Mamelukes with the soldiers and the inhabitants of the country. Napoleon tried to continue using them in this function. He accepted them as the leaders of the people and it was they who put the complaints of the people before the Government, if the latter departed too much from justice and tradition. They enjoyed enormous respect from the citizens of Cairo and to their religious power were linked political influence and economic precedence.

The *Jabartis* were originally from Ethiopia. Today there is still a 'student-hostel' in the Azhar reserved for students from Jabart. Our sheikh, Abd al-Rahman al-Jabarti was well-known as a mathematician and astronomer and it was his duty to calculate the dates and times for the religious calendar. His son was also learned in this science. Al-Jabarti had acquired a taste for history by contact with the Damascene historian Al-Muradi and he corresponded with this sheikh of Dasmascus until the latter's death. He collected for him biographies of Cairene scholars.

There is no doubt that the great events he witnessed gave him the idea of writing his own chronicle. The subject matter of his first book from which we have quoted the description of the battle was later altered and included in a large-scale chronicle which he entitled 'Wondrous Remains of Biographies and Reports'. It is a gigantic work which presents the events of each year in chronicle style and includes biographies of great men and scholars in the years of their death. There is a French translation of this chronicle entitled *Merveilles Biographiques et Historiques ou Chroniques* (Cairo, 1888–94).

The work is an incomparably rich mine of information. Every detail of that period in which Egypt was still leading her own life undisturbed is recorded in it along with a detailed description of the first military and organizing penetration of Egypt by the 'Western World'. (It sticks in the throat of anyone who has looked at this great chronicle to say 'civilizing' penetration.) The West has the opportunity to see itself in this work as in the mirror of another world. Napoleon's attack only released the first shock and it was only Muhammad Ali's 'western-ization' and 'modernizing' of Egypt by force that changed her from top to bottom. It is a privilege, that no historian should miss, to see this change through the eyes of a highly educated representative of traditional Egyptian civilization.

We can learn from Al-Jabarti that the 'Spirit of the West', the 'Spirit of the Modern World', did not break into a sort of vacuum but that it itself created this vacuum by leading to the destruction of old Egypt. Anyone wishing to know in detail how this process developed must follow this for himself in the chronicle; here we must confine ourselves to extracting a few typical pages in the hope that a well-considered selection may soon be published in translation, for no book could make a better contribution to an understanding of the effects of the western spirit on Arab civilization.

The technical superiority of the French, of which we are still so proud, impressed a man like Al-Jabarti but little.

On the 20th (of the Second Jumada) they printed a number of papers and posted them up in the market-places. They read: 'On Friday the 21st, we intend to make a ship fly through the air at Lake Ezbekiyeh by a French trick.' As usual people gossiped a lot about it.

When the day came many people and many Frenchmen assembled in the early afternoon to see this miracle. I was there, too, and saw a piece of cloth round in shape and resting on props. It was coloured white, red and blue and the props were arranged in a circle. In the centre was a bucket with a wick standing in some kind of fat. This bucket was tied to the circular cloth with wires. The cloth itself was extended with ropes and pulleys and the ends of the ropes were held by men standing on the roofs of the surrounding houses. About one hour after the afternoon prayer they lit the wick and the fumes arose into the cloth and filled it. It swelled up and became a sphere. The fumes wanted to rise inside it and, finding no way out, carried it up in the air. They pulled it together with the ropes until it rose above the ground and when they cut the ropes the wind carried the cloth up into the air. It moved quite prettily for a while then the bucket with the wick fell off and down came the cloth. When it fell one could see what it was and it was clear that what they had asserted was not correct, namely that people could travel with it to distant lands to discover new things and such fantastic illusions. Moreover, it was clear that the balloon was something like the kites the carpenters make at the time of festivals.

Nevertheless, in spite of the historian's reservation, one can see from his interest and his exact description that he was not completely averse to the infidels. His description of the British landing in Alexandria in 1807 is significant. He recognizes that the existing order was not harmed by the infidels' invasion.

On the 9th of Muharram 1222 (1807) runners brought letters from Alexandria; this was on a Thursday afternoon. They said that English ships had arrived at Alexandria. They were 42 of which 20 were big and the others small. The English requested to speak with the Governor and the Consul and discussed with them. They demanded admission to the city and the answer was: 'You cannot be allowed in without the written authority of the Sultan!' They replied: 'We have no document from the Sultan but we have come to protect Alexandria from the French. There is a danger that they may land secretly in a moment of relaxed vigilance. Therefore we have brought five thousand soldiers in friendship whom we wish to station in the fortress towers to guard the country, the fortress and Alexandria.' The reply was: 'We have no authority to do that. On the contrary we have written orders to prevent anyone coming from landing, whatever his nationality may be.' They said: 'Impossible! Either you let us land and everything will be all right or it will be done by force and arms. You have 24 hours within which to reply. Afterwards you will regret having refused us permission to land.'

This was transmitted to Cairo and when the letters arrived Katkhoda Bey, Hasan Pasha and Bonaparte (a nickname), that is, the Master of the Treasury, the Keeper of the Taxation Records and the Chief of Protocol, met along with other notables. This happened after sunset. They took counsel and decided to report all this to Muhammad Ali Pasha and ask him to intervene with his troops and take what measures he saw fit since he had the greatest authority and knew best what to do. They did this and departed for their homes late at night. They sent him those letters by mounted messenger on the Friday morning. The news spread and the people began to talk excitedly about it.

When the 24 hours were up, which was the respite the English had given to the inhabitants of Alexandria, and since the latter continued to refuse, the English bombarded the fortifications from the sea with frightful grenades and cannons, destroying one side of the great tower and also the small towers and the walls. Thereupon the people of Alexandria sued for peace and the English ended their bombardment. They entered the city on the Friday. Letters reporting this were sent to Cairo from Rosetta but only in very general terms without giving much information about the exact situation. It was learned that they had landed in Alexandria and penetrated inland but no one knew what the situation was nor how it was developing. The whole affair was not clear.

The French Consul came to Cairo. He had been in Alexandria and on the arrival of the English ships had gone to Rosetta and when he learned that they had landed he went to Cairo. He said he wanted to leave for Damascus along with the other Frenchmen who were living in Cairo.

On the night before Thursday, the 16th, a letter came from the Pasha saying that he had taken the field against the (upper) Egyptians and triumphed over them. He had taken Assiut from them, captured some of them and killed many of their scouts and Mamalukes in a battle. Thereupon a festival was held and many shots were fired from the cannons in the Ezbekiyeh fortress. This went on for three days and at five different times, for the last time on the Saturday. They also spread the report that Alexandria had not let the English in but that those had landed in Ras al-Tin and Al-Agami, that the inhabitants had gone out against them, fought them and driven them back from the mainland. It was even said that the ships had been boarded in order to destroy them and had in fact been burned. Many of the English had been killed and only a few had remained alive. This was the condition for some days with confusion in the south and in the north with no messengers and no certain news coming from Alexandria.

In the same month it was correctly reported that the English had occupied Alexandria. They had taken possession of it from the fortification towers early one Sunday morning. They lodged their commander-in-chief in the Consulate and concluded an agreement with the inhabitants of the land which stipulated among other conditions, that they would occupy no houses by force but would only rent them by agreement with their owners. They profaned no mosques and did not prevent people from following the rites of Islam. They granted peace to the ruling Agha and his troops and permitted them to go wherever they wanted. He who was owed money by the Diwan could receive a half immediately and the rest later. Traders and others who wanted to embark were permitted to travel under their protection wherever they wanted, but not to Istanbul. As for the West or Damascus or Tunis or Tripoli and the vicinity people were free to travel backwards and forwards without let or hindrance. The agreement also stipulated that the English would not make impositions on the people of Alexandria when they required money and also that the Islamic courts would remain open and continue to pronounce the law according to the Shari'a, also that the Muslims would not have to listen to any religious propaganda without their consent. They would be protected against all troops admitted by the English into Alexandria and that these would conduct themselves peaceably under the supervision of the people of Alexandria, that no one there would suffer injury, not even the French and that the duty on goods of every provenance would be $2\frac{1}{2}$ per cent. So ended the compacts.

It should be known that this crowd of Englishmen and others—it is said that they were 6000—had not come to Alexandria with any desire to conquer Egypt, but rather they had come to support and help Alfi (one of the great Mamelukes) against his enemies. He had asked them to come to his aid some time before they actually arrived. The reason for their coming so late was that they were at peace with the Ottomans and so could not take the field against Mamelukes of the Porte without its permission if they were to observe the laws. But when the aforementioned quarrel broke out between the English and the Porte they seized the opportunity and sent that squadron. Alfi awaited their arrival in Buhaira Province but when he got tired of waiting and thought that he was being hemmed in in Buhaira he marched south with his army and God decreed his death in the vicinity of Guizeh.

It was only after this event that the English arrived in Alexandria. They found that he was dead but were in no hurry to return. They sent messengers to the commanders in the south and proposed to them that they would help them against their enemies. They said: 'We have come to your country at the request of Alfi to come to his and your aid but we find that Alfi is dead. He was one of you and you all belonged together. Do not keep us waiting but come so that your matter may be cleared up. You will never again have an opportunity like this one.'

When the commanders in the south received the English letter they were of divided opinion:

Othman Bey, who was called the pious and had a large army with him, had separated from them. They sent a message to him, too, and summoned him but he answered: 'I am a Muslim and have performed the pilgrimage. I fought the French earnestly. Shall I now conclude my career by seeking refuge with Franks and helping them to gain a victory over Muslims? That I shall never do!' . . . On Friday, the 14th, a message came from Rosetta to the effect that a group of Englishmen had penetrated the interior of the land. The people of the little town and the soldiers were, however, on their guard and prepared to fight by the houses and under their arcades. When the English reached the centre of the little town they were attacked simultaneously from all sides. The English threw their weapons down and sued for peace, but the people of Rosetta seized them, without paying attention to their plea, and slaughtered many of them and took the rest prisoners. They sent runners to Cairo with the good news and there guns were fired and the Katkhoda Bey gave the runners robes of honour. The retinue of the Ottomans, that is, the Turkish Kavasses, hastened with the good news to the houses of the notables and congratulated them, receiving in return bakshish and robes of honour. The people did not know whether to believe it or not, but on Sunday, the 16th, it became known that the heads of the slain and with them the prisoners were arriving in Bulaq. The people thronged to see the show and many of them went to the bank of the Nile at Bulaq. Many high officers with their detachments of soldiers were there to receive them.

They were brought on land and with them were all the soldiers who had travelled with them and those who had followed them from outside Cairo. They were brought in by Bab al-Nasr and led through the city. Among them was an old sergeant and another old man; these were riding on donkeys, the others going on foot surrounded by soldiers and the heads of the slain stuck on stakes. The heads were already decayed and smelt unpleasant. There were 14 of these and 25 survivors. They took them on to Lake Ezbekiyeh and on their arrival the guns were fired and they entered the fortress with the survivors and with their sergeants.

While recounting how the British later withdrew, how the struggles for power among the beys and their mercenary troops became more and more confused, how the troops treated the peasants in the open country worse than animals our sheikh and historian often permits himself a sigh which clearly reveals his view:

The situation in the south and in the north of the country became so bad that the people reached a point where they would have been satisfied with Government by the French. . . . The soldiers laid their hands on the women, old men and children; they seized them and sold them to each other. Their conduct was so bad and their deeds so shameful that the people longed for the Franks to come back of whatever kind they might be (French or English) and put down those destructive bands, those troops who belonged to no nation, who recognized no law and no path which they followed.

Then Muhammad Ali gradually came to power. The 'people', led by a 'politician', Saiyid Omar Makram, whom the Egyptians of today like to celebrate as the first revolutionary leader of the Egyptian people, finally 'elected' Muhammad Ali as Pasha because they were tired of the perpetual fighting. From our view of the Egyptians' 'revival' under Muhammad Ali as described by European historians, we should expect our sheikh and historian to support enthusiastically the Pasha's rising power. To be sure, it at last guaranteed him peace, an efficient administration and glorious campaigns! But it is not so. Al-Jabarti determinedly opposed Muhammad Ali's claim to rule.

The historian reports that the sheikhs assembled in the Azhar called out: 'We elected him to rule us with justice, not to practice tyranny and the rule of violence.'

Muhammad Ali saw himself, rather like the European absolute monarchs, as the master of his country and his subjects. He decided to 'modernize' his country probably, in the first place, because he needed a 'modern' army with which he could compel the Porte to give him his own hereditary state. Sheikh Al-Jabarti strictly denies him the right to rule absolutely and to introduce 'reforms' according to his own lights.

Financial reform was to be the foundation for the erection of the Pasha's modern power apparatus. He had all land holdings surveyed anew and later made himself the sole proprietor of land. There was in all Islamic countries from olden times much land set aside as pious foundations (Waqf, Habus). Pieces of land were reserved for the maintenance of mosques, schools, hospitals, tekkes and so on, and their produce went to those institutions. A part of the produce could also be reserved for the family of the founder. The state had no power over these institutions which were administered by sheikhs and whose administration was only loosely controlled by the state. In the course of the centuries large territories had been set aside as such foundations. Muhammad Ali stretched his hand towards these and also levied other taxes to set up his armies and construct the modern Egyptian state. The sheikhs denied him the right to do so, for, in Islamic Law, it is laid down exactly which taxes the state may collect. Anything over and above that, said the sheikhs, is 'tyranny'.

The Azhar sheikhs came as usual to deliver their lectures but there also attended many women, common people and relatives of persons in gaol, all shouting and raging so that they made the lectures impossible. Then the sheikhs assembled in the prayer niche and sent for Sayyid Omar, the chief of the Sharifs (i.e. the Sayyids, descendants of Ali), who came and sat down beside them. Later they got up and went home. The next day they met again and drew up a letter of protest to the Pasha. In it they told what had happened: tyranny, illegal innovations, stamp taxes on goods, the confiscation of property and incomes which belonged to pious foundations, inheritance taxes and in addition also the arrest and imprisonment of a relative of Baqali who was innocent. This was done after they had held a secret meeting, praised each other and affirmed that they would hold together and forget mutual rivalries for the moment.

Thereupon the Diwan Effendi appeared and announced to them: 'The Pasha sends you his greetings and asks you what you want.' They told him, what they had written, in chosen words and explained it to him in every detail. He answered: 'You must go to him and discuss your point of view with him in conference. He will not go against your commands and will not reject your protest. But it is necessary to speak to him politely for he is a young man who has gone astray, ignorant, tyrannical and capricious. His heart will not allow him to be led by anyone else and perhaps his aberration may even lead him to do you harm and not to do what you recommend.'

The sheikhs answered as one man: 'We shall never go to him as long as he continues to act as he does. If he desists and puts an end to these illegal innovations and tyranny over God's creatures then we shall come back to him and account to him as we used to. We appointed him Sultan so that he might exercise justice, not the rule of violence and tyranny.'

The Diwan Effendi replied: 'It is exactly my intention that you should speak with him in an assembly and induce him to carry out your wishes.' They answered: 'We shall never go to him but we do not want to stir up a civil war; we would rather retire to our houses and remain there alone and be patient and see what fate God has in store for us and the other citizens.'

Then the Diwan Effendi took the letter of protest and promised to bring them an answer. After his return they released Sayyid Hasan al-Baqali who had been imprisoned without anyone knowing about it. The sheikhs waited for the Diwan Effendi to return but he did not come before five days had passed. Sheikh Al-Mahdi and Sheikh Al-Dawakhili met Muhammad Effendi, the supervisor of the War Depot, all three bearing a grudge against Sayyid Omar (the Chief of the Sayyids). They conferred together and in the afternoon separated. Al-Mahdi and Al-Dawakhili went to Saiyid Omar and told him: Muhammad Effendi has told us that the Pasha does not covet the moneys of the foundations nor their incomes. Whoever had reported this had lied. Moreover, he had told them that the Pasha had said he would fall in with the wishes of the sheikhs. If they went to him and explained themselves to him he would fulfil all their wishes. Sayyid Omar answered: 'As for his denying the fact that he covets the moneys and incomes of the foundations I have papers made out to certain tax farmers empowering them to collect one half of the legacies and moneys of the foundations and their interest. As for going to him, I shall never do so. If you wish to keep the oath and compact we swore together, well and good. If not then do as you wish.' Thus ended their meeting. However, the Pasha did all he could to sow dissension among them and to bring it about that they would desert Sayyid Omar, for he was badly disposed towards him because of his opposition and because he had refused to carry out his intentions. He was afraid of his power, for he knew that the subjects and the people listened to him. If he wanted he could unite them and if he wanted he could keep them apart. It had been Sayyid Omar who had helped the Pasha to win his victory; he had brought the people and the notables together and had handed the country over to the Pasha to be governed. Muhammad Ali realized that he could also do the opposite if he wanted. Then Al-Mahdi and Al-Dawakhili went with the Diwan Effendi and the interpreter to the palace where they met the Pasha and where they had an interview with him.

The Pasha in his speech said: 'I shall not stand in the way of your arrangements, neither shall I turn down your requests nor refuse to give you what you need. If you see me go astray advise me and guide me!' Then he began to blame Sayyid Omar for having opposed and criticized him, but the others praised him. 'He opposes me continuously and makes my arrangements come to nothing and threatens me that he will stir up the people against me.'

Sheikh Al-Mahdi answered: 'Sayyid Omar has no power save when he is with us: if we desert him he will be nothing. He is only a simple employee or official who has begun to collect voluntary donations and distribute them among those who deserve them.' At that time they understood what the Pasha's intentions towards Sayyid Omar were and these intentions coincided with their own envy of him.

Thereby Muhammad Ali achieved what he had been aiming at first and foremost, namely to split the united front of the sheikhs. Sayyid Omar's fall from power and banishment from Cairo was the result (1809). Muhammad Ali had thus taken a considerable step nearer towards his conquest of absolute power.

All our historian does is to set down the events and only here and there does he express his disapproval in marginal notes:

An incident also happened in the street of the Ka'ak bakers. Two men of the Dalmatian troops were chasing after a Beduin youth who had been a soldier with the troops trained in the western manner. One of the two Dalmatians called to him that he owed him some money and he fled from them into the above-mentioned street. The two galloped after him with drawn swords. The young man fled to the street with the bath and the western troops, who had their cantonments there, rose against the attackers and fired on them with their muskets. The horse of one of the Dalmatians fell and its rider was hit. The other ran off to the Katkhoda Bey and told him what had happened. The Katkhoda ordered the officers of the western troops to be summoned and asked them why the shots had been fired. However, he could not get to the bottom of the matter. They arrested the young man who had fled and put him in gaol. The citizens were full of terror and the shops on the market of the cookshop keepers, roasters and charcoal merchants were shut up; the young man remained locked-up and the Dalmatian who had been hit died in the night before Saturday. Then they brought that youth to the Zuwaila Gate and beheaded him. They had no right to do so for it was not he who had fired.

Many a modern historian feels he must defend Al-Jabarti's unfriendly attitude to Muhammad Ali. An Egyptian biographer of the historian, Khalil Shaibub, says: 'He did not know what Muhammad Ali's real intentions were and he did not understand his plans. But what we moderns cannot understand at all is how it was possible for the historian to prefer the English to Muhammad Ali.'

It appears to us that he knew all too well what was at stake. The landings of the French and the British were in the eyes of the Sheikhs only an episode. The foreigners were infidels and nothing better was to be expected of them than 'tyranny' for they knew nothing of the traditional laws which God Himself had given and which had ruled the Muslim world for centuries. It was another story with Muhammad Ali. He was a Muslim ruler under the supreme authority of the Turkish Sultan. When he systematically began to undo the old order and to despise and alter the laws under which the life of the metropolis Cairo had developed and over which Al-Jabarti felt himself a guardian, that was 'tyranny' of the worst sort. Thereby he was attacking the roots of what Al-Jabarti recognized as the Muslim order of things, the only right order of things.

To be sure, men of Al-Jabarti's class had been very comfortable in that old order of things. 'You complain of my tyranny,' Muhammad Ali is said to have said on one occasion to the sheikhs, 'but you are even worse tyrants over the people than I am over you.' Nevertheless, one feels inclined to consider Al-Jabarti right. Muhammad Ali's 'progress' smashed more than the privileges of a class. With him there began the process of the dissolution of all the values of Islamic civilization.

What one might claim as the greatness and strength of the Islamic world view has proved since Muhammad Ali's time a disadvantage which cannot be overcome: the close intertwining, indeed unity, of 'world' and 'religion'. Islam is a 'religion' and a 'social order' at one and the same time. You cannot upset the social order without harming the 'religion' and endangering the whole structure of the Islamic world. With Muhammad Ali a process set in which aims at changing the traditional world, through will to power, through 'social necessity' and through 'political necessity'; in this Al-Jabarti knew what modern Muslims do not know or do not want to know, namely that Islam is tied to that world one wants to get rid of, that it is perishing along with it.

Must it perish? Not necessarily; 'Islam' can change, adapt itself, revive itself and its view of the world. But what is significant of Muhammad Ali's procedure and what has fundamentally not changed since his time is the fact that the world is outstripping the spirit. Innovations are forced, 'tyrannically' in the interest of material development, the power of a prince or the might of the motherland. The re-formulation of Islam, its 'revival' limps after material 'revival'. Objects are taken over from the west; they must be taken over, people say to themselves, if the state, or the Arab nation is to continue to exist. At best an attempt is made to adapt oneself to transformations and changes which have

already taken place; often not even this is attempted and all one does is deny that
'real' changes have taken place and are taking place. Refined methods of self-
deception are worked out: 'There is nothing in modern life contradictory to
religion; on the contrary . . .', and they forget that a spiritual force must lead and
cannot remain passive as long as it wishes to make any claim at all to remain a
spiritual force.

But we are going too far ahead. Al-Jabarti still knows that 'progress', which
does not stem from an inner change, is 'tyranny'. He is not prepared to justify
the means (tyranny) with the end (power politics, the strengthening of the
nation). Nor did Al-Jabarti succumb to the brilliance of this 'progress' which
the West, often in good faith and, indeed, often to silence its own bad conscience,
wished to recommend to the East.

Egyptian intellectuals of later generations have pushed aside Al-Jabarti's
objections. They followed the West, its ideas and arrangements blindly without
ever wanting or being able to give up their old civilization entirely. Where that
will lead no one can foretell with certainty; but it often seems as if they are
unable to escape from the circle of 'tyranny' which began with Muhammad Ali
and which Al-Jabarti resisted in vain.

A 'modern' state was founded at that time or, rather, imposed from the
outside. It must develop and advance for purely biological reasons. Where in
Al-Jabarti's time $2\frac{1}{2}$ million Egyptians lived, nowadays 26 million must
subsist. But society is not in a position to develop itself organically, from the
inside. It borrows ideas and procedures from outside in an ever increasing
quantity and it needs a tyrant to impose these ideas and procedures on it.

In the last analysis it is a battle between the modernizing tyrant and the
creative forces in the Egyptian people. It would be their task to recognize the
problems of their society and find their own solutions in order to dominate
the modern world, instead of being dominated by it. The tyranny appears in
the most diverse forms. 'Circumstances' call for it: the Khedive's debts, the mis-
management of the Wafd and the King. It may make use of different instruments; cunning, strength of will and a sword as under Muhammad Ali,
paternalism and soldiers as under Cromer and demagoguery, police and military
power as with Nasser. It is a necessity because the Egyptians cannot manage
their modernized surroundings without its iron control.

For this reason the true history of the Arabs (what goes for Egypt one can say
cum grano salis for the other Arab countries, too) is the history of its intellectuals.
Intellectual power slipped out of the hands of Al-Jabarti's generation; they
turned away outraged and desperate and left the tyrant to seek his intellectual
apparatus from elsewhere, in another world which they wanted to ignore,
because it bore no relationship to their own.

To be sure, Muhammad Ali created his own 'intellectuals' from the bottom
up. He ordered young men to go to school in Paris. Lane, writing in 1833,

says: 'With regard to the more recent innovations I have made only a few short notes because I found the lights of European science almost exclusively confined to those government officials who had been *forced* to study under Frankish instructors. European customs I found hardly anywhere except among a few Turks. Certain Egyptians who had studied a few years in France explained to me that they were not even able to convey the ideas and knowledge that they had acquired there to the minds of their best friends.' Is it not the same with many of today's intellectuals? Have they not also been compelled? Certainly by more 'subtle' methods, doctrinary schoolmasters and doctrinary school books with propagandist newspapers as the only leisure reading and the radio.

Has the number increased or decreased of those, who not only do more or less creditably what the tyrant wants of them but who seriously ask themselves the questions 'Who are we? Where are we going?' In the last analysis the future of the Arabs depends on this.

Al-Jabarti summed up his opinion of Muhammad Ali in a famous sentence:
If God had given him (the Pasha) only a little justice along with the determination He gave him, his gift for leadership, his outstanding talent, his power of organization, his ability to wait for the right moment, he would indeed have been the wonder of his age and the pearl of his time.

What is justice? Al-Jabarti still had a clear standard for it, anchored for him in the Koran and the Divine Law of the Shari'a. Are the Arabs of today as sure of their cause? Few of the intellectuals who are the spiritual leaders would refer to the Koran or only to the Koran. Many of them would, to be sure, speak vaguely of the 'nation', others of the rights of the people. He who actually and in practice exercises 'justice' is frequently still someone like Muhammad Ali who obtained his standards from outside, from the West and latterly also from the East.

2

Dependence on the West

THE MODERNIZATION OF HIS STATE achieved by Muhammad Ali brought him many external successes. As 'modern' soldiers on a French pattern the Egyptian fellaheen fought successfully in Arabia against the Wahhabis, in the Sudan against the native dynastics and in Syria against the troops of the Porte; in Greece along with the troops of the Porte they were less successful against the Greek insurgents and along with the Turkish army they suffered a defeat on the Russian frontier. Muhammad Ali's troops occupied and held an enormous area stretching from the Sudan to Crete and, for a time, deep into the interior of present-day Turkey.

The fellaheen who had to serve as soldiers hated military service. Clearly they had reason for this for self-mutilation was frequent in order to avoid conscription. Anyone falling into the hands of the conscripting troop had to reckon with being a soldier for the rest of his life. Muhammad Ali collected the money for his wars from the state monopolies which he set up all over the country. All land and all the produce of the land belonged to him and he conducted all trade with foreign countries. A peasant was simply a day-labourer in the service of the state. Today it seems to us most dubious when we hear the European historians of that period, among them humanists and outstanding scholars, say that 'after all oriental methods were necessary if the great ruler was to do anything with his people'. They clearly did not suspect that roughly a hundred years later 'oriental methods' would threaten their own country; otherwise they would have exerted their power of imagination a bit more and tried to see themselves in the skin of the Egyptian fellah.

Muhammad Ali's successes had of necessity to remain partial successes. The efficiency of his army and of his 'modern' administration depended on his importing a limited number of European techniques. These techniques allowed him to show his superiority to his Ottoman overlord who used these techniques either not at all or only a very little. But towards the West on which he was dependent for the acquisition and replacement of his techniques Muhammad Ali submitted to a kind of dependence which no oriental ruler had known before him.

Since the time of Frederick the Great western weapons and military techniques had undoubtedly been superior to the oriental ones. As the first oriental ruler consistently bent on imitation Muhammad Ali recognized the intellectual leadership of the West and thus became completely dependent on western specialists and their methods.

It was the man's political greatness that he recognized this. In spite of his intoxicating successes, in spite of the enormous territories he was able to conquer and although he could have, at the height of his career, marched his armies right up to Constantinople without any resistance from the Turks, Muhammad Ali over and over again followed the dictates of the West. It must have made his blood boil when Britain robbed him of the fruits of his conquests and when the European diplomats compelled his son, Ibrahim, to halt at Konya, withdraw from Greece and give up Syria but Muhammad Ali knew how to conceal his rage every time. He hardly ever let it come to warlike measures with those powers who provided him with the means of exercising his local superiority. In his old age he reaped the political reward for his realistic appraisal of the power ratio between himself and the West: the assurance of the governments of Egypt as a hereditary right of his family.

*   *   *

It was not only Muhammad Ali who made a correct estimate of the new power ratio between East and West (which he himself had brought about). The clear-sighted Englishman, Kinglake, who travelled through Syria at the time of Egyptian rule there (1834) gives us a description of the unnaturally exalted position assumed by an English 'lord' in Syria at that time:

> Successive political convulsions had at length fairly loosed the people of Syria from their former rules of conduct, and from all their old habits of reliance. The violence and success, with which Mehemet Ali crushed the insurrection of the Mahometan population, had utterly beaten down the head of Islam, and extinguished for the time at least, those virtues and vices which had sprung from the Mahometan Faith. Success so complete as Mehemet Ali's, if it had been attained by an ordinary Asiatic potentate, would have induced a notion of stability. The readily bowing mind of the Oriental would have bowed low and long under the feet of a conqueror whom God had thus strengthened. But Syria was no field for conquests strictly Asiatic—Europe was involved and though the heavy masses of Egyptian troops clinging with strong grip to the land might seem to hold it fast, yet every peasant practically felt and knew that in Vienna, or Petersburg, or London, there were four or five pale looking men who could pull down the star of the Pasha with shreds of paper and ink. The people of the country knew, too, that Mehemet Ali was strong with the strength of the Europeans—strong by his French General, his French tactics, and his English engines. Moreover, they saw that the person, the property and even

the dignity of the humblest European was guarded with the most careful solicitude. The consequence of all this was that the people of Syria looked vaguely, but confidently, to Europe for fresh changes; many would fix upon some nation, France or England, and steadfastly regard it as the arriving sovereign of Syria; those, whose minds remained in doubt, equally con- tributed to this new state of public opinion, which no longer depended upon Religion and ancient habits, but on bare hopes and fears. Every man wanted to know—not who was his neighbour, but who was to be his ruler; whose feet he was to kiss and by whom *his* feet were ultimately to be beaten. Treat your friend, says the proverb, as though he were one day to become your enemy, and your enemy as though he were one day to become your friend. The Syrians went farther and seemed inclined to treat every stranger as though he might one day become their Pasha. Such was the state of circumstances and of feeling which now for the first time had thoroughly opened the mind of Western Asia for the reception of Europeans and European ideas (*Eothen*, Ch. xxv).

Thereby the first foundation was laid for what was in later decades to become clearer and clearer as the inferiority complex of the 'Oriental' and so of the 'Arab.' The common man found himself surrounded by a double hierarchy.

On the one hand there is the traditional one of the oriental government; it is authority, but one knows it and knows how to treat it. Centuries of bitter experience, of worldly wisdom or grim humour taught one to kiss the foot of him who kicked one; if possible to kiss it before being kicked; and to apply one's kisses in such a way that the kicking foot could gradually no longer do without them. One understands the mechanics of an outwardly despotic régime which was tempered internally by an infinite number of nuances and cross connections. The tempering influences range from protests of the religious authorities to 'interventions' in which pieces of gold play a part.

But then side by side with it a second hierarchy grows. It is protected by the government, but it is clear that it is in reality stronger than the government. Its methods, the men representing it and their spirit is foreign. One does not know what attitude to adopt towards it. One would prefer to have nothing to do with it but at the same time one understands that it is precisely this second hierarchy which is really powerful and on which one must lean if one wants to get on.

One sees how native Christians, not so long ago still despised, get on because they seem to have access to that second mysterious power; the language and confidence of the 'Lords' allow them to disregard the old hierarchy of govern- mental quarters. Meanwhile simultaneously the pressure of these same govern- ment quarters on their faithful subordinates and brothers in Islam increases constantly. It becomes intolerable and finally leads to their impoverishment and distress.

I was lounging one day, I remember, along 'the paths of the faithful', when a Christian Rayah (subject) from the bridle path below saluted me with such earnestness and craved so anxiously to speak and be spoken to that he soon brought me to a halt; he had nothing to tell, except only the glory and exultation with which he saw a fellow Christian stand level with the imperious Mussulmans: Perhaps he had been absent from the place for some time, for otherwise I hardly know how it could have happened that my exaltation was the first instance he had seen. His joy was great; so strong and strenuous was England (Lord Palmerston reigned in those days), that it was a pride and delight for a Syrian Christian to look up and say that the Englishman's faith was his too; if I was vexed at all that I could not give the man a lift, and shake hands with him on level ground, there was no alloy to *his* pleasure; he followed me on, not looking to his own path, but keeping his eyes on me; he saw, as he thought and said (for he came with me on to my quarters), the period of the Mahometan's absolute ascendancy —the beginning of the Christian's. He had so closely associated the insulting privilege of the path with actual dominion that, seeing it now in one instance abandoned, he looked for the quick coming of European troops. His lips only whispered and that tremulously, but his fiery eyes spoke out their triumph in long and loud hurrahs! 'I, too, am a Christian. My foes are the foes of the English. We are all one people, and Christ is our King.' (Kinglake, *Eothen*, Ch. XXVII.)

From Muhammad Ali's times on, the leading strata in the Arab countries began to turn to Europe, that is, to a world previously foreign to them. To begin with they have to, later on they also want to learn from it. This new direction of their gaze estranges them from the lower classes who up to now do not possess either the horizon nor fulfil the requisite conditions (knowledge of languages, travels, a minimum of historical knowledge) in order to understand what the *effendis* are newly concerned about. The effendis for their part are for a long time restricted to absorbing only; they themselves have nothing to contribute to the building up of the new ideas, techniques and methods. The traditional habits of thought and action of their society are closer and more familiar to them and appear to them more 'human' than the ones they are forced to learn. For they themselves, their ancestors and their environment have all contributed to build up and preserve the traditional values.

Thus there arises a leaderless under layer which does not understand what is going on in the 'higher ranks', and an upper layer, which, in order to be able to continue to exist at all, is forced to imitate the foreigner. Muhammad Ali *wants* a modern army just as most modern young Arabs would like a Thunderbird racing car. The material means are provided and the 'toy' can be acquired.

Muhammad Ali sends slave raiders into the Sudan, sets up a barracks in Aswan and has the slaves drilled by a French officer until they are soldiers.

The attempt fails as most Sudanese would rather die than become French soldiers. Later on the fellaheen were to prove themselves tougher.

The young Arab of today manages to get the money from papa. When at last the new toy is owned both Muhammad Ali and the car owner learn that it imposes its own laws on them. Not only does one have to maintain it; spare parts and supplies are also necessary; and one feels the urge to do something with it. The army must be despatched on conquests, the car must be driven, along an asphalt road, to a western cabaret, a big hotel or an elegant excursion spot.

An oil sheikh sends his son, who is studying in Beirut, a luxury car, painted white, with the arms of the ruling family on the number plate. The next day the owner of the apartment he is renting comes to the young man and says: 'No one who has such an elegant car can live like you in a two-roomed flat. I have a penthouse in this same building which will go much better with your car.' It is not difficult to persuade the young student from the Persian Gulf but in his heart of hearts he is sorry to lose his pleasant two-roomed flat; now he needs a maid, and he *has* to give parties, because he has such a large flat.

In the case above it is not much different from tying a horse up by its tail. The origin is not an idea from which the object gradually develops; one begins by importing the ready-made object which by its presence cries for the material, intellectual and psychological foundations. Crisis follows after crisis while the substructure for the foreign object hanging in the air (it can just as well be a method or a technique) has to be laid down feverishly, layer by layer.

So far the substructure has made remarkably little progress: Muhammad Ali imported methods, experts and ready-made products along with a small number of machines. Today methods, machinery specialists and ready-made products are still being imported. The 'revolution' of the nationalists includes the *attempt* to import, instead of ready-made products, more and more machinery to produce these same ready-made products in the country, by foreign methods and under the guidance of foreign experts. The Arabs of today like to blame imperialists for this 'lack of progress'. 'It was in their interest', they reason, 'to sell us their methods, experts and ready-made products. At times they have backed up their sales with guns. They have intentionally kept us at the level on which Muhammad Ali began to do business with them.' It cannot be denied that the colonial powers knew how to make their profits and perhaps, too, these profits were inflated by present-day standards. (European industrialists themselves felt that high profits were quite justified morally by whatever methods they were made.) But in spite of everything the truth is that no one can get the successors of Muhammad Ali out of the vicious circle they are in, except themselves. They must begin to develop their own methods, ideas and products if they are to free themselves from continuing to remain to a certain extent dependent.

Until this happens, the inferiority is real. The complex sets in when one tries to dismiss one's inferior position, instead of overcoming it by one's own deeds, by persuading oneself that this subordination is not 'real'. For this reason critical observers have remarked over and over again that it is not at all a question of an 'inferiority complex' but of a 'superiority complex', in which people are inclined to think themselves worth more than they really are.

3

Emancipation

HOWEVER, AT THE BEGINNING of the conflict between East and West there was still little to be found of complexes. Curiosity outweighed everything else. Post-revolutionary France to which Muhammad Ali sent his student missions was also less foreign to the spirit of traditional Egypt than the industrial society to come later. France itself was still a land of peasants, the new nobility and the bourgeois; it was still comparatively easy to get a general view of human relationships, knowledge and civilization. The Egyptian travellers viewed the life of Paris with pleasure and from their descriptions one can see how the spirit of enlightenment was winning them over.

The Imam who accompanied the first large student mission to Paris as a sort of spiritual father, Rifa'a al-Tahtawi, has bequeathed to us a lively description of the French capital:

The clothes of the French women are pretty, although they are, in their fashion, a bit immoral especially when they put on the prettiest dresses they possess. They use only few adornments, their jewelry consisting of only a gold ring in their ears and a sort of bracelet of gold which they wear on their wrists, outside their sleeves, in addition a light chain around their necks, but they never wear anklets.

Their dresses are generally of some thin material, silk or gaily coloured cotton or light taffeta. For the cold they have a sort of strip of fur they put around their necks so that both ends fall by their sides like a coat, long enough almost to touch their feet. One of their customs is that they wind a high scarf around themselves over their dresses so that their waist may appear small and so that their bust sticks out. A peculiar thing about the women is that they encase themselves in a scarf fitted from belly to the lower part of the breast with metal strips so that their form may be always smooth, with no padding showing. They have many such tricks. One of their peculiarities which no one could ask to be done better than by them, is that they do not let their hair hang freely like Arab women; French women pile their hair on top of their heads and always have a comb or something similar stuck in it.

It is one of their customs that they leave all the external parts of their bodies uncovered on hot days. They go about uncovered from head to just above the nipples of their breasts and it is even possible to see their backs. At night, when they dance, they leave their arms bare and this while in company. The people of that country do not consider this sinful but they may not show even the smallest part of their legs. They always wear skirts covering their legs, especially on the streets and, to tell the truth, their legs are anything but pretty.

As for the wineshops in France, they are innumerable; there is not a street which is not disfigured by these wineshops. Only the meanest and lowest men go there with their wives. They make a lot of noise there and when they come out they shout a word of theirs which means: Drink, drink! But in spite of their drunkenness they seldom cause any damage.

One day it happened that, as I was walking along the streets of Paris, a drunk man called after me 'Turk, Turk!' and caught hold of my clothes. I was near a shop selling sugar and such like so I went in and made the drunk man sit down on a chair. Then I said to the shop-keeper jokingly: 'Will you give me as much sugar or confectionery as that man there is worth?' The shop-keeper answered: 'We cannot do here as you do in your country. You cannot dispose of a human being here like some article of merchandise.' But all I said was: 'This drunkard cannot be reckoned a human being in his present condition!' All the while the man was sitting on his chair and did not realize what we were talking about. I left him there and went away.

Curiosity is evinced even more clearly than by this Egyptian sheikh by the traveller and writer who has been called the Arab Voltaire, *Ahmad Faris al-Shidyaq* (1804–1887). Not only does he have something of Voltaire but also something of Montaigne. In addition to travel books he left us his auto-biography in which he speaks of himself as the 'Faryaq' and of his wife as the 'Faryaqiya'. The word means just as little in Arabic as in English, being merely the first and last syllables of his two names. So strongly did he feel himself *sui generis* and with such intense individualism did he express himself that only a word that he himself had formed and which no one before had heard, seemed to him to be a fitting designation for his own person. At the same time he was not lacking in humour and self-criticism.

Faryaq was born a Maronite in a Lebanese village. His brother had come into conflict with the Lebanese Patriarch and had died in the dungeon of this spiritual prince. Shidyaq himself had joined the American missionaries in Beirut as teacher of Arabic. For this purpose he had even become a Protestant for a time. He was not at all a man of religion but remained a man of letters all his life. In him we find the mentality of an ancient Arab poet side by side with that of a modern journalist. The poet praises him who pays him, the journalist writes what will be read and pleases. Faryaq earned his living with his pen, his sharp mind and his perfect knowledge of ancient Arabic vocabulary for which he had the true love of a philologist. The Americans found employment for him in Malta where they had their mission school and sent him to England and Paris. Faryaq had intercourse with scholars in Paris and Cambridge and was proud of being the first Arab to have a panegyric of his in praise of Paris published in a Parisian newspaper. Finally the Bey of Tunis got to know him and had him brought to his capital in a warship. There he became a Muslim and editor of the first newspaper to appear in Tunis. In 1856 the Sultan Abdul Majid invited him to Istanbul where he died after having edited a newspaper for twenty years. The scope of his personal intellectual development may be compared with that which Europe saw between Montaigne and Voltaire. This naturally also implies a judgement on values. The discovery of his 'ego' cannot have been such a profound process with him as it was with Montaigne; his brilliance does not have as much fire as that of the champion of French enlightenment. If nothing else, he does not have enough time. The atmosphere of haste, 'We must catch up with 500 years,' is first apparent in him. It is visible in Faryaq's travels and restlessness as he went from one patron to another, from religion to religion and from one editorial office to another.

His writings give us an exhilarating feeling of being set free. 'I am me,' speaks from every page and he was intelligent enough to grant his fellow men the right to be themselves. It is the contact with the spirit of emancipation prevailing in Europe which made Faryaq's individuality flourish. The fetters of a narrow social order, controlled by religion and a rigid social structure, fell from him and the Faryaq skipped free all round the Mediterranean, learning and observing. He refrained from passing judgement and only occasionally does he allow a slight derision to appear: 'Travel, take a look at the world,' he recommends his compatriots with subtle irony:

You, sir, who are rich, the first thing you have to do is to travel, away from this city in which you live, so that you can see with your own eyes what you can never see in your own country and hear with your own ears what you have never before heard; and in order to learn in what conditions peoples, other than your own people, live, their habits and behaviour; so that you may learn what their character is, and what their faith and their politics are. After this you can compare what is good with us and what is not good with us.

When you reach their country and do not know their language, do not seek at first to learn from them all their words of abuse and do not confuse the euphony of a name with lovableness of the thing named. Every language in the world has something beautiful and something ugly about it, for language is nothing more than the expression of the activities, thoughts and actions of human beings. There is naturally always something to blame and something to praise.

I also warn you: do not behave like so many travellers who learn nothing of the languages of foreigners but a few expressions and words. No, you should rather, once arrived safely on land, go first of all to schools and printing-presses, libraries, hospitals and lecture-rooms. These are places where scholars lecture on all sorts of sciences and arts. There are some in which there is nothing but a table for the speaker and others which contain all the instruments and chemicals required for the science in question.

And when you come back to your country—with His help, He is exalted—bestir yourself to write a description of your journey and distribute it among your compatriots so that they may profit by it; but not with the intention of making money from selling it. Who knows, perhaps a few friends who are rich will help you to set up a printing-press and then you can print other books in it which will benefit men, women and children, each according to his ability, so that they may learn what rights are due to them and what duties are owed by them, no matter whether such books be Arabic books or translated works. But be careful when you bring something from abroad not to confuse the good with the shameful and the sound with the corrupt. In the cities of the rich there is much that is disgraceful, and also much that is excellent.

Yes, among these people you will find men who refuse to receive anyone while they are at dinner and when they are obliged to receive someone while they are at dinner they offer him nothing of what is before them. But there are also men among them who will invite you to their mansions in the country and there you can stay for a week or even two and order what your heart desires. There are some who are too miserly even to return your greeting. If you go to the house of such a man and find he has a company of friends who already know you not one of them will deign to rise, no one will pay any attention to you. But there are also people who, if they know you, will be solicitous for your wishes, whether you are present or absent, and if you tell them a secret they will keep it as long as they live.

Many of them will address you by nicknames from the very first time their eyes fall on your moustache and beard or on your turban or perhaps they will tug you from behind by the skirts of your garments. But among them there are some who are anxious to become acquainted with a foreigner and who are glad to keep his company and do him a kindness. They consider it their duty to help and protect him. Some will laugh at you when they hear you speaking their language incorrectly but others are anxious to teach you their language for no reward, perhaps they themselves or with the help of their wives or daughters. They are anxious to lend you books which will help you and guide you to success.

You will meet people who think you have come to their country to compete with them and rob them of their profits; these look at you surlily and askance. But you will also find men who receive you in their country like a guest to whom honour and respect are due and who must be so closely protected that when you leave them you find them closer to you than your own family. There are some who ostentatiously order you to translate something for them or to teach them something and when you have done it do not even say: 'Thank you, teacher,' or 'Thank you, translator,' but you will also find others who do not hold a conversation with you without rewarding you for just opening your mouth and moving your lips. . . .

So hear how Faryaq fared. When he wanted to travel from the island (of Malta) to England many people used to say to him: You want to go to a land in which neither cereals nor vegetables grow, where there is nothing to eat but meat and potatoes! Others said: I fear for you that you will lose your lungs for lack of air. Others again said: Your stomach for lack of food, or your chest or other parts of the body. When Faryaq arrived there he saw that the sun was the sun, air air, water water, men men and women women, the buildings inhabited and the cities well built; the countryside was broad and tilled, full of strength, landmarks, green bushes, huge trees and forests, well-kept meadows with bright fields and rich fruits. If Faryaq had listened to those people his eyes would never have fallen on all this.

If you are afraid you will not have the enjoyment of the narguileh there or the luxury of a foot-massage before going to sleep, know that the wonders you will see there will make you forget that sort of pleasure and make you forget what you used to do in your dear native land. How can you be satisfied with yourself if you leave this world without having seen it although you were in a position to see it. Has not Al-Mutanabbi said: I consider nothing more shameful for a man than to give up when he is capable of running the course.

How can you be satisfied with knowing only a quarter of a language; do you not wish to learn what another man is thinking; does he not have under his hat thoughts and ideas which have never penetrated under your tarbush?

Faryaq's humanity, irony and gaiety are more apparent when he talks of himself. We take the following extract from his autobiography which is a chaotic book, descriptions of foreign lands and people, philosophic aperçus in which 'the women' always fare badly, lexicographical reflections and essays:

Faryaq began to walk around the streets of the city with his wife. She was wearing Egyptian dress and he the baggy Turkish trousers which completely concealed his legs and fluttered all around him when he walked. She was wrapped in a burnous, the sleeves of which were so long that they swept the ground. The passers-by and shopkeepers never knew whether the person with Faryaq was a man or a woman. Many asked: 'Is that a man or a woman?', others followed them and still others tugged at their clothes and gazed into their faces saying: 'We have never seen the like of this, something which is neither man nor woman!'

A well-known English lawyer, called Stephen, met them. He looked into their faces and realized that Faryaq was a man and Faraqiya a woman. He approached them and said: 'Will both of you, husband and wife, take lunch with me next Sunday?' They answered: 'With pleasure!' He said: 'My house is at the seaside, near such and such a place; visit us in the morning.'

When Sunday came they took a cab and drove to his house. There they found him getting ready to go out and it seemed he was going to fetch a few acquaintances to introduce them to his guests. However, it is probable he got drunk on the way for he never came back. On greeting them he said: 'I have to go out on business. My wife and my daughters here will keep you company until I get back, then we'll all have lunch.' They said: 'Make yourselves at home,' and sat down with his wife.

In the company there was a young Englishman who flirted with one of the lawyer's daughters. To begin with he held her hand then began to kiss her in the presence of her mother and the visitors. Faryaq went pale, his wife blushed and the face of the girl's mother began to twitch. Faryaqiya said to her husband: 'How can the girl kiss that young man without shame?' He replied: 'The Franks don't consider a kiss anything to be ashamed of. Often when someone visits his friend's house he kisses the latter's wife and daughter, too, especially if it is his birthday.' She replied: 'But aren't they ashamed in front of us who are strangers to them?' He said: 'When something is permitted it doesn't matter whether it happens before strangers or relations. Perhaps the man thinks we don't know what it is to kiss in our country.' She answered: 'How stupid he is who could think such a thing!'

Then they talked until it was mid-day. One of the lawyer's daughters came in with some bread and cheese and began to eat it in our presence. She went away and another got up and did the same. The lawyer had seven daughters and a number of sons! At two o'clock the mother said to the guests: 'I am afraid you are hungry; it is past lunch-time but my husband is not back yet!' They replied: 'Let us wait until he comes!'

At five o'clock the bell rang for the various servants in the house to go to dinner, as happens in great English houses. An hour passed and the bells rang again. The hours passed until it was eleven o'clock and all the while the mother kept running backwards and forwards to the kitchen and whispering angrily to her daughters as if the misfortune of the Barmecides had broken over her.

Then Faryaq said to his wife: 'If we don't leave now we won't find a cab and there is no suitable night lodging on this seashore.' So they got up, wished the lady of the house good evening and took a cab back into the city where they arrived at midnight. Then they had supper in a restaurant and it was their lunch too!'

What makes such descriptions attractive is at bottom the pleasure Faryaq takes in finding out the customs of foreigners. It seems to give him an inner satisfaction to note that: 'They are quite different from us and yet they are human beings! They have their customs and we have ours. Each side thinks his are the only right ones.' You can feel Faryaq silently drawing the conclusion that: 'These customs are not so important after all. It seems that the rules of life a society sets up for itself cannot be the last criterion of "good" and "bad", "beneficial" and "harmful". But must there nevertheless be an absolute standard of values behind the relative values of customs?' Since in his oriental experience customs were closely bound up with the different religions this consideration of the mani/foldness of customs and the realization that neither set of rules of the game was 'right' or 'wrong' led Faryaq to relativity in matters of religion. He proved this in his own life by changing his religion twice. Religion seems to have been a garment for him, to be changed according to one's environment.

What absolute values remain are an indefinite ideal of 'usefulness' and 'humanity' which is close to the ideals of the Age of Enlightenment. Experience, knowledge for its own sake, and the full exploitation of all the capabilities of the human mind were in Faryaq's opinion things worth striving after. He had stepped beyond the bounds which his own social order had set upon itself during its 'Middle Ages' and he felt himself thereby 'liberated' and the old bounds appeared to him now as fetters. With one blow his horizon broadened by all the dimensions which the West had won materially and spiritually ever since the Crusaders. However, it can be seen that Faryaq was most interested in the spiritual. You can see how he always feels for the main spring driving that foreign society he is investigating. Although his work tools are insufficient to completely grasp the historical growth of the foreign society his psychological perception is so sharp that he again and again sees through the people of this western, to him foreign, society. He feels quite equal to them although he clearly recognizes that their 'sciences' and 'social organization' are much more effective than those of his compatriots. 'You can easily catch up,' is his message to his compatriots, 'if you only wish: if you only study, print books, open schools (for girls, too), if you import the things of value from the West, not the trifles and articles of fashion.'

However, one can see very clearly today that the principal impetus Faryaq and the 'men of enlightenment' gave to their generation was the tendency towards 'liberation'. What they consciously wished to achieve: to do like the West by one's own achievements, has for a long time been less effective than the psychological spring from which they derived their enthusiasm, perhaps unconsciously: the wish to be free of the 'fetters' of old customs which all of a sudden appeared old/fashioned, free from social subordination to people one could no longer recognize as superior, and from a religion which appeared in the modern view all too formal or all too undisciplined and irrational. No doubt it is the curse of 'men of enlightenment' that they pay so much attention to explainable, logical reasons and incentives and that the more concealed, irrational causes of a course of action, their own or that of others, escape them. Perhaps Faryaq did not know at all that he went on his travels not only through a thirst for knowledge and to be 'of use to his compatriots', but also, and above all, to free himself, to break away from the narrow Maronite village in which he was born. He wanted to rid himself of the pressure of ancient prejudices and religious institutions, in order to become one of those who have the world at their feet instead of being one of those who let themselves be constricted and harnessed by it. Presumably he did not realize that by his writings he awakened this same urge to sit on 'top' in his readers in much greater measure than the need to benefit society and acquire 'insight'.

Most strange of all is the fact that the deep driving forces which make the West 'tick' have remained hidden not only to Faryaq in the nineteenth century but even today to almost all educated men in the East who have not themselves visited the West. Such concepts as 'duty', especially as elaborated by early Protestantism, 'work ethos' and 'proving oneself through success in one's work' are recognized by very few Arabs as the real driving forces which have set the wheels of 'industrial society' in motion.

Perhaps most of them find it so difficult to see that because it is a question of psychological stresses which appear in a less acute form in their society. Their prime interest is still in 'liberation', emancipation; they want at long last to have control of their own fate. But this control of one's own life, which the individualist Faryaq was able to achieve already in the nineteenth century thanks to his travels, his lively pen and his ready conversions, has continued to escape the majority of Arabs. Again and again it escapes them. Why? Not so much because, as they themselves often say, the West is so wicked and they are 'exploited by imperialists', but because they themselves as a society lack those psychological driving forces to which the West and, indeed, Russia too, owe the construction of their scientific ethos and industrial society.

4

Reform in the Ottoman Empire

AT ABOUT THE SAME TIME as enforced modernization was spreading in Egypt a reform movement also began in Istanbul. The two great reforming sultans were Mahmud II (1808–39) and Abdul Majid (1839–61). Turkish reform was, however, to assume a quite different character from that of Muhammad Ali's. It was less successful and attracted the derision of the West whereas Muhammad Ali earned the admiration of his teachers. Whoever studies in greater detail the attempts at reform made by the 'Sick man on the Bosphorus' will nevertheless have to revise his judgement. Just because it was not so successful the sultan's new order laid the foundations for a real reform. Just because they were too successful Muhammad Ali's efforts perhaps nipped much in the bud which in later decades might have led to a real reform movement in Egypt.

The Turkish Empire was the opposite of Egypt in everything. It was a conglomeration of wild provinces of a quite different type, with many peoples, religions, tribes, laws and states within the state. It was exposed to pressure from the great powers on almost all its frontiers and coasts. Compared with it, Egypt is the ideal country for centralization and isolation where it is enough to seize the nerve centre, Cairo, to put through a new order.

So the new order in Turkey was to lead at first more to chaos than to re/organization. Towards the end of Mahmud's reign the young officer, Hellmuth von Moltke, was in Turkey as a 'military expert' and in his *Briefen aus dem Orient* (Letters from the Orient) he describes, not without sympathy, the con/fused mixture of old and new, honest efforts to achieve a better administration, ambition of individuals, intrigues and conservatism.

Mehmet Khosrev is, next to the sovereign, the most powerful man in the country. In his appearance there is hardly his like in the whole world. Imagine an old man of about 80 years who has preserved all the vitality, nimbleness and temperament of a youth. The ruddy face with a snow/white beard, large hooked nose and remarkably small but flashing eyes presents a striking physiognomy which is not improved by the red cap pulled down over his ears. The large head rests on a small, stocky body with short, bandy legs. This general's uniform consists of a blue blouse with no badges of rank, white pantaloons and leather stockings (Terlik).

Khosrev Pasha has been able to maintain himself in the highest offices for 35 years, which is a tribute to his cleverness; but if one is asked to name the deeds of his long public life one is amazed to find that in fact almost all his working efforts have been directed against rivals for the favour of the sovereign.

When Khosrev Pasha was sent to Egypt there was in his following a Tüfenkji-Bashi (Master musketeer) called Mehmet Ali, who, to his great chagrin, later became Viceroy. If Khosrev had had an inkling of this at that time he would not have worried very much whether there should be one Arnaut more or less in the world. He took part in the conquest of Missolunghi as Kapudam-Pasha (Grand Admiral) and since then carried favour with the sultan and made himself indispensable in two functions, as Police Chief in the capital and patron of reform.

In the first capacity Khosrev Pasha rendered undoubted service; doubly important in Turkey where a sovereign may lose battles and provinces, but cannot bear an uproar in Constantinople. The Ser-Asker (Minister of War) nearly always speaks in a joking tone but the mighty tremble at his smile. He knows everything that goes on in the capital, has his spies everywhere and spares none who oppose the new order of things.

Khosrev Pasha was the first to parade before the sovereign troops trained in the European fashion and the first among the nobility who gave up the beautiful, old Turkish mode of dress for the tasteless and uncomfortable imitation of European uniforms. For this reason he is considered one of the main patrons of reform.

The Ser-Asker has hundreds of Aghas, Kavasses and Seymens in his personal service, not one of which receives a single para of regular pay. But everyone is zealous in giving presents to the followers of the Grand Pasha. Enormous sums flow into his pockets from those who wish to have something done for them in Constantinople. No sacrifice seems to be too high for the Governor of a province to win over such a patron in the capital; no major trade agreement can be concluded and no delivery take place without his assent. He must draw up the Firman when a Christian church is to be built or only repaired. On him depend all promotions in the army and his all-powerful influence is felt in things which seem to lie quite outside the province of a generalissimo. But in Turkey the office is less important than the man filling it and so it is on a small scale with all the Pashas of the Empire.

Mehmet Khosrev is said to have amassed enormous sums in cash and at the same time he is the most sober, moderate man in the world. He drinks champagne with any foreigner of importance travelling through in order to show how completely he has sloughed off the old Turkish prejudices knowing well that this will result in an article in the newspapers, but he prefers to drink water from the renowned springs of Chamlija. Many dishes are served at his meals but he touches only one or two of these.

It often seems to me that the Ser-Asker Mehmet Khosrev is managing the reform in his heart of hearts most ironically, but it is one of his means to power, his one true, ungovernable passion. Let him who challenges him in this respect be on his guard. Anyone who occupies a high position without having reached it through him he already considers his enemy. . . .

I was having breakfast with the Ser-Asker when Ahmet Pasha was announced. Old Khosrev immediately got up on the sofa and looked with infinite attention out of the window into the street with his back to the door while the Mushir of the Guards stood waiting, his heart boiling with indignation and annoyance at this reception. 'Effendim!' he said once or twice but the old man did not hear him. This scene lasted for at least five minutes until Khosrev decided he had humbled the proud Mushir enough in the presence of an unbeliever. Then he turned around quite unconcerned and called out: *Mashallah Ahmet Pasha! Hosh geldin! Sefa geldin! buyurun!* (Welcome!), *Sen buradami?* (Are you here?), and embraced him tenderly. He clapped his hands and a swarm of servants rushed in whose heads he was going to cut off because they had not announced the dear *Musafir* (guest) to him. (*Briefe aus der Türkei*, No. 7.)

As in Egypt, the reform began with an effort to create a modern army. As in Egypt, the government had soon to carry out a 'coup' against the traditional 'army' in order to free their hands for reform. Muhammad Ali had the Mamelukes massacred in the citadel of Cairo and Mahmud, for his part, had the Janissaries either massacred or dispersed in 1826. In both countries new troops had to be raised. The process of conscription—practically for life—of troops from the population which had not been accustomed to any sort of military service for centuries became in both countries the symbol of the 'tyranny' of the modern state—but here the parallels between the Empire of the Porte and its 'vassal' Egypt end. Muhammad Ali was successful in enforcing his tyranny on the fellaheen but for the Porte, on the other hand, there began a long period of only half effective tyranny. Its soldiers desert, die, mutiny, go over to the enemy, let themselves be massacred and themselves massacre. Moltke was one of the first to realize that the new army, the 'militia', entailed the necessity of reforming the system of administration and especially the tax system. In retrospect one can see how an army, which was supposed to function according to western principles, was reconstituted again and again after it had collapsed in disorder, how it became more and more 'western' in command and structure and dragged the country after it, not only with regard to administration but also in its whole mentality, until it turned it into a 'modern' national state. Turkey went from sacrifice to sacrifice and from defeat to defeat until it was ready for Atatürk to make it a modern national state.

Egypt was spared many of these defeats but to offset this the country was never able to get rid of its rulers. It was changed by commands from the top; even Egypt's 'revolutions' were ordered. It did not experience the long fermentation such as spread in the later years of the Ottoman Empire. Egypt had very few men who thought, who studied of their own accord the strange western conception of the liberty of the individual and his 'human rights' and wanted to apply it to the East. Egypt may have been militarily stronger than the Turkey of the Ottomans but the latter was intellectually 'more modern', more versatile and more inquisitive than Muhammad Ali and his successors.

Near Eastern *Liberalism* grew up in this climate of reform on the soil of the Turkish Empire which began but never quite succeeded. Stirred by the doctrine of European liberals, the two tendencies we have dealt with in the preceding paragraphs were lumped together in a doctrine of 'Liberty'. If we were free like the citizens of the modern European states, it was proclaimed, if we were allowed to print what we want, if we could fight against the 'superstition' and 'prejudices' of the masses, if human life and human worth were guaranteed here as they are in Europe and if the property of the rich were insured against the state laying hands on it, then progress could come to us just as it came to Europe.

It is clear that this doctrine which caught on and quickly spread among the upper-class intellectuals in the Ottoman Empire had to come into conflict with the government sooner or later. To be sure, the Porte itself had initiated the reform because the Sultan wanted a 'modern' army at his disposal, but the reform overtook the government after a very short time and it was now the subjects who were putting forward demands and seeking a new order of things. The liberals were sons of well-to-do citizens and senior civil servants and it was they who formulated the new ideas. They spoke to all their compatriots in the name of Liberty. Young 'Arabs' took just as much part in this movement as young 'Turks', 'Armenians' or members of other nations of which the Turkish Empire was composed.

This doctrine of the Ottoman Liberals was most clearly expressed by Mustafa Fazil (1830–75), a prince of the Egyptian ruling house, who had come while still young to Istanbul. There he held several high political offices but because of his liberal views he fell from favour and went into exile in Paris in 1866. From Paris he directed an open letter in French to the then Sultan 'Abdul 'Aziz (1861–76). It was published in the French newspaper *Liberté* on 24 March 1867 under the title 'Manifeste de la Jeune Turquie'. It has been translated and printed several times in the East and was recently republished in *Orient* No. 5, 1958:

Sire! The rebellions which are breaking out among the peoples of Christian faith in your Empire are in the first place the work of our external enemies. But they are also a symptom of the general situation into which

your peoples of all races and religions have been cast by a system of government which today—although its existence was at one time justified—
produces nothing but tyranny, ignorance, misery and corruption. In Europe
people imagine that it is only the Christians in Turkey who are exposed to
capriciousness and persecution and who suffer humiliations of every kind.
But this is not so. The Muslims, just because no foreign power interests
itself in their fate, are plundered and robbed even more ruthlessly and are
bowed under the yoke even more deeply than those who do not recognize
the Prophet. So far they have suffered patiently because they bear in their
hearts a secret of proud resignation and patient waiting which men in the
West do not understand. But they are of the same blood as the noble family
which controls the fate of the Empire and the respect with which they view
the throne is mixed in their thoughts with that they cherish for the Koran.
But allow me, your loyal servant, to say: The Muslims, Sire, have reached
the end of their readiness to suffer and to make sacrifices. Scarcely concealed
protests can already be heard everywhere. It would be dangerous for your
noble dynasty and for you yourself were they to be driven to desperation.

In addition to the moral decline of the Turkish and Christian peoples in
the Empire I feel I must speak to your majesty not only of their ignorance
but also of their intellectual degeneration.

Ah, intelligence dies for want of nourishment under a machinery of
government which leaves nothing to the initiative of the citizen. . . . Do not
be deceived, Sire: to spread education in your Empire it is not sufficient to
set up schools everywhere; they will remain empty or be attended only by
humiliated and feeble-minded children.

The first teacher of nations, the one who produces all the others and whom
all the others cannot produce is Liberty!

A nation of slaves despises science as useless. Only when nations have
their rights assured do they try to educate themselves so that they can make
good use of them.

. . . Yes, Sire, Save the Empire! Time is short! This empire that has cost
so much blood and fear! Its history is glorious but its present condition is
sad. What an enormous weight this present situation must be on Your
Majesty's soul! Everything threatens you from outside and everything
threatens to collapse and dissolve internally. For a mind as clear as Your
Majesty's there can be no more illusions. Your brave troops will put down
all rebellions which our enemies may stir up from abroad, but can they grant
those they have conquered bread, education and the assurance of not being
oppressed?

By concession after concession to the Powers, who hope to inherit your
Empire, you can postpone the hour of the decisive battle but what shall we
gain thereby if, at the moment of the last crisis, we stand still weaker, still

more disunited, still more hopelessly ruined than we are today? So let us seize the initiative, Sire; let us seize it not with weapons in our hands but accompanied by all kinds of progress; let us improve our situation morally and intellectually, let us become rich, and so we shall already have won half the battle!

The cure this eloquent prince and grandson of Muhammad Ali proposes to his sovereign seems to us today strangely naïve:

Set up in each one of your provinces a freely elected assembly to advise you and to help you to realize your fatherly purposes. Permit the delegates of these assemblies, summoned by your high initiative, to place their requests and an exact description of the state of affairs in your provinces and of your peoples at the feet of your throne periodically in Constantinople.

But one must take into consideration that this open letter was written during the time of Napoleon III. Only experience could teach that 'freely elected assemblies' just could not be elected freely in practice, that the interests of long-established aristocracies proved themselves far too powerful to permit a real liberalization. The pressure from Europe was to lead in the course of a cruel war to the occupation of almost all the subject territories and many parts of the Turkish homeland. This occupation released nationalist counter-forces of anything but a liberal type. The pressure of the underprivileged classes was thereby increased, at first in harmony with the nationalist counter-forces, later in competition with them and still later . . .? In short, it is only ninety years after this open letter was written that the possibility arises of a 'moral' and 'intellectual' climate in which in a few privileged countries of the former Empire the tender plant of liberty promises to take root.

The struggle for freedom was the main theme of the intellectual life of the second half of the nineteenth century. It was fought in all developed provinces of the Turkish Empire, from the Balkan countries right down to the Arab Levant and Palestine. The demands of the liberals concentrated more and more on the question of a constitution. Sultan Abdul Hamid (1876–1908) was forced by Midhat Pasha to grant this long-hoped-for constitution in 1879. A transport of joy broke out, the intellectuals and progressives, both Arabs and Turks, believing that they had reached the goal of their desires.

All the greater was the disappointment and depression of the liberals when the Sultan took back his promise just one and half months after granting the constitution. He was determined to follow a path opposed to that of the liberals whereby he sought to gain support from the conservatives and pious elements in his Empire. His government became an autarchy with a system of informers and secret police notorious in the Empire, and at the same time he tried to use the religious currents of Islam for his own purposes.

The constitution remained suspended for thirty years. The intellectuals who saw themselves robbed of a victory they thought they had already won, struggled steadfastly throughout this period to recover their civil liberties. The minds of the liberals were so exclusively preoccupied by the 'tyranny' of Abdul Hamid that they hardly had the time to think seriously about constituting a new order of things. A few liberal writers of that time read rather like the more popular authors of the Risorgimento when they fulminate against Metternich. But it seems there were no Mazzinis and no Cavours at hand. There was no realistic self-evaluation. In general the view prevailed that first of all abuses and tyranny must be ended and freedom introduced; the rest, so one thought, would then come of its own accord.

This fixation, which originated in Turkey in the nineteenth century, became in later times only more radical. People became accustomed to hold an external 'enemy' responsible for all grievances. To begin with he was Abdul Hamid, then 'the Turks', later 'the French' and 'the British', 'imperialism' with its economic system and policy of alliances, then the 'reactionary Pashas', in the future perhaps 'the reactionary dictators and army officers'. To be sure, the grievances are by no means only imaginary in the case of all the political forces enumerated above; but the illusion consists in imagining that with these once removed the gateway to a political paradise is there to enter. So long as one does not see that the actual grievances have deeper causes than the political systems of any given time, the removal of one régime will only bring forth a second which in the long run will prove at least as 'tyrannical', insufferable and cruel as the one which has just been dislodged.

5

Particular Developments on the Fringes of the Empire

INDIVIDUAL PROVINCES DEVELOPED separately inside the far-flung Ottoman Empire. Certain countries, especially provinces on the fringe of the Empire, which were to come into specially close contact with Europe, began to go their own ways, more than the central lands in Turkey. We must devote special attention to these for their fate had a decisive influence on the rise of the modern Arab states.

There was Egypt which had been separated from the Porte *de facto* ever since the Napoleonic invasion; there was Lebanon with its Christian and Druse elements which for many centuries had managed to maintain a semi-independence from the Ottoman Empire; and lastly there was North Africa and especially Algeria, an exceedingly stagnant, tradition-bound, impoverished Muslim land which was the first to be conquered, occupied and colonized by the army of a European power. It has also been the last Arab country to gain its freedom from colonial power.

We have already dealt with the modernization of Egypt ordered by Muhammad Ali. This was at first interrupted by the immediate successors of the energetic Albanian, the system of state monopolies and state-directed agriculture breaking down even before Muhammad Ali's death. Of the schools, printing-presses, factories and workshops set up by him only the Ecole des Langues in Cairo was to survive. It was enough that the Khedives no longer took an active interest in these institutions for them to go into a decline. A second push towards modernization and europeanization did not take place until the reign of the Khedive Ismail (1863–79). This was no longer a process of modernization, centring around the Army, which was ordered by a potentate but a reorganization introduced and borne by private enterprise. The 'Levantine' communities of Cairo and Alexandria now came into being. This class of merchants, technicians, scholars, artisans, etc., which was required to modernize the country grew up between the Turkish-Egyptian upper class of great land-owners and rulers and the Arab-Egyptian lower class of *petits bourgeois* and *fellaheen*. It was primarily a question of immigrants; along with the wholesale merchants, adventurers, bankers and technicians from Northern Europe came

Greek, Italian, Maltese and Cypriot traders, contractors, artisans, mechanics and labourers. All these immigrants grouped themselves around the consulates; French or British nationality (for use in Egypt) could be acquired and brought the new citizens weighty privileges of a social, economic and judicial kind. French was to become the language of the bourgeois quarters of Cairo and Alexandria and has remained so up to now. The native Christians, the Copts, attached themselves to a great extent to the foreign colonies. They received their education in French religious schools and they found work and subsistence as the indispensable agents and assistants of the European powers. This was the period during which the Suez Canal was constructed (1862–9).

A clearer light has only recently been thrown on the banking operations carried out by the bankers of Paris and London at that time. The American economist, David S. Landes, dug up the correspondence between a French private banking-house of international standing, André Marcuard et Co., and a banker of the Viceroy Ismail, Dervieu. Dervieu served André as his 'correspondent' and agent on the Alexandria market. A glimpse into the special nature of the Alexandria money market and the mentality of the Europeans operating on it can be gained from this correspondence. Indeed, one can sense something of the motives that drove the Viceroy Ismail to his financial policy which ended so badly. With great skill the economic historian has been able to correlate the correspondence of the two bankers with the whole business situation in Alexandria and he has succeeded by quoting concrete examples in showing how the business climate of Alexandria differed from that of Europe.

It is not only a question of rates of interest; the 10, 12 or even 15 per cent could perhaps be justified on the ground of the greater risk attached to business ventures in Egypt. The real difference was primarily that, in the event of a speculation failing, it was not the European speculator or the bankers financing the business who paid, but practically always the Viceroy and the Egyptian Treasury. It was the consulates who gave judgement when it was a question of claims by their nationals against Egyptians. These 'claims' might be quite imaginary but a foreigner nevertheless always had good prospects of being supported by the representatives of one of the Western Powers. The consulates called in their foreign ministries when it was a question of business engaged in by the Viceroy or the Egyptian state with one of their compatriots. A European had only to have gambled away or speculated large enough sums and he could count on 'France' or 'Britain' intervening in the end and forcing the Khedive to pay.

Ismail seems to have seen through the system completely, but it is strange that he nevertheless could not refrain from getting involved with European business-men and usurers. He needed money and piled debts upon debts, on conditions which became increasingly difficult for him and with the result that he gave the consulates and foreign ministries more and more cause to intervene and give more and more scope to extortionary enterprises. Landes indicates that it is probable that Ismail also took some pleasure in annoying his creditors in certain business transactions. He despised European businessmen and to a certain extent he enjoyed the struggle with them. However, again and again he had to give way when confronted with Europe's superior power and he almost always paid, and paid heavily, at the end of each financial dog-fight. In spite of this he could not give up fighting right to the bitter end.

Landes makes it clear that a great number of the claims which were constantly made on the Egyptian state, indemnity for promised or allegedly promised agreements and other damages of all sorts, would have had no possibility of being admitted in a normal business and judicial climate. Dervieu, the Viceroy's French private banker, was not by any means one of the great, overt usurers but belonged to respectable Alexandrian society and was a pillar of the French colony there.

But when, after the end of the American Civil War, the great cotton boom came to an end for Egypt, when the banks collapsed and even Dervieu's business was forced to go into liquidation, Ismail's private banker turned to the same means which the finance hyenas at the Khedival court always employed, to extortion. He brought a complaint against the Khedive through the Consular Court and wrote to his friend in Paris that he knew so much about the Viceroy's shady financial dealings (in which he himself had been partly engaged) that he was in a position to demand from the Viceroy the tenfold of what he was actually demanding. What he was in fact demanding, and in the end did receive after long negotiations, was the exact sum equal to Ismail's share in his liquidated company. In this way Dervieu was able to buy up his other partners (apart from the Viceroy) after the Egyptian economic boom collapsed and still rescue for himself a pretty fortune of five million francs.

However fascinating it is to follow step by step the complicated affairs of international bankers in Egypt as recounted in Landes's well-informed book, what interests us above all here is the general foundations underlying the special business situation of Egypt at the time when the Suez Canal was constructed. Landes has described this in a masterly manner in his concluding chapter. He shows how the large-scale extortioners of Alexandria thought of themselves as completely upright, honourable, indeed virtuous and patriotic businessmen of honourable principles. He remarks that men like Dervieu moreover develop a certain ability to 'live with their consciences'. Their partners in London and Paris, men of André's stamp, do not even need to do that; they keep their hands as white as snow. André granted Dervieu advances as long as the cotton boom in Alexandria lasted and thereby received his own share of the dazzling profits. (Dervieu's company recouped as profit 35 per cent of its capital within thirteen months of being constituted.) Great and well-established bankers like André were not interested in *how* high profits were made. Their art consisted simply of conjecturing how long they would continue and then of cutting off and demanding the return of their credits and capital at the right time. In order to be able to do this they had to be kept in the know by their 'correspondents', who were present at all transactions as observers. If a transaction proved to be 'absolutely safe' they themselves took an active part in it through the agency of their correspondents. But they left it to the local banking houses in Egypt and to the consular authorities of the Great Powers to do the work of thinking up more and more operations and tricks and of proposing them and making them palatable to the Viceroy, as well as the dirty work of practising extortion on him if one of their operations went wrong or threatened to go wrong.

The fact that with all this going on the local business people and consular authorities still could consider themselves honourable and virtuous 'entre-preneurs' and civil servants is ascribed by Landes not only to the elasticity of their consciences. He attributes it rather to what he calls a *double standard*:

> While most Europeans in Egypt lived according to principles, they had two sets of principles: the same rules did not apply in dealing with the in-group of Westerners and the out-group of natives. . . . All were agreed that Egyptian society was backward and that the European could not afford to submit to the customs of the country, but that the Egyptian would have to learn the ways and accept the justice of the European; that the stan-dards of behaviour accepted in Europe, the values of honesty, fair play, reasonableness, and so on, that shaped—at least in principle—the social and business relations of the West, had to be modified to fit the circumstances of a strange environment.

> In litigation, for example, justice as dispensed in the consular courts of Alexandria or as extorted in negotiations with the Egyptian Government was a caricature of the Western ideal. The forms were generally observed in that the European was expected to prove his case; but the double standard was reflected in the different weights accorded European and native testi-mony and interest; one man's word was worth more than another's, his limbs were more precious, his property more valuable. Only too often, the assertion of the Westerner was equivalent to proof, the presence of the Egyptian was evidence of responsibility. It was as though all the meticulous safeguards, all the precautions, caveats and complicated defences of modern law had been swept away, and only the shell remained to cloak the sham of predetermined justice.

> Yet litigation was only one aspect of relations between Westerner and native in Egypt; the double standard, with its corollary sentiment of superiority, shaped every action and reaction of the European colony. It could be seen in the forms of address, in the courtesies extended and with-held, in the pride and arrogance the Westerner offered and the humility and deference he expected. The diplomatic archives and pamphlet literature of

the period are full of stories and statements that reflect this relationship; a book could be written around them.

More than anything, more even than the enormous material costs of Imperialism, it was the imposition of inferior social and moral status that shaped the reaction of the Egyptian to the European. Actually, the one implies the other: material exploitation is difficult if not impossible without the sanction of a double code of behaviour; if they were not there to begin with, the exploiter would have to create them. The fact remains, however, that in the many-sided impact of imperialism, it is the injury to self-respect that hurts most. It is the resentment aroused by spiritual humiliation that gives rise to an irrational response to rational exploitation. The apparently unreasonable, and certainly unprofitable, resistance of many of the world's underdeveloped countries today to Western business enterprise makes sense only in this context. (David S. Landes, *Bankers and Pashas—International Finance and Economic Imperialism in Egypt*, Heinemann, London, 1958.)

These banking operations and debts of the Khedive led to the control of all Egyptian finances by Britain and France. An attempted rebellion by Urabi (Arabi) Pasha against the Khedive Taufiq, Ismail's successor, resulted in the bombardment of Alexandria by the British Navy and the occupation of Egypt by British troops in 1882. Thus ended in Egypt what one can describe as an early capitalist epoch and the colonialist epoch begins.

Present-day Egyptians see in Urabi Pasha's insurrection a forerunner of Nasser's *coup d'état* of 1952. Urabi was an officer of Arab descent and the friction with the Khedive had begun because Urabi and his colleagues felt themselves subordinated to the Turkish aristocracy. The highest ranks in the army were reserved for the ruling Turkish families. At first, in 1881, the quarrel was about the appointment of a Minister of War who should enjoy the confidence of the Arab officers. When the Khedive resisted, the Arab officers for their part intensified their demands and they succeeded in forcing the Khedive to summon a parliament, to dismiss the ministers who were loyal to him and to increase the army.

The British Consul-General, Sir Auckland Colvin, had an interview at that time with Urabi who was in power if only for a short time:

Arabi described the government of the Mamelukes and of the present dynasty as oppressive for the Arab population. He endeavoured to show that up to today the Egyptians enjoy no security of life and property. They were thrown into gaols, banished, strangled, thrown into the Nile, starved and robbed just as it pleased their masters. He thought a freed slave was freer than a free-born Arab. Turks, who were completely ignorant, were preferred to the best Egyptians. He then explained at length that all men have a common origin and had the same rights to personal freedom and security.

He took some time to develop this theme and it was strange to hear it as expressed by a native; but it could clearly be recognized as the general line of the speaker's slow train of thought, the expression not of rhetorical phrases but of real conviction.

He and the Army stood for right and justice. In the clearest words possible he rejected the reproach that he wanted to be rid of the Europeans. He spoke of them as of the necessary teachers of the Egyptian people. He himself, he said, and the other two officers—he pointed to them—had never gone to school. Intercourse with Europeans had been their school.

Another Englishman, Wilfred Blunt, was even more friendly disposed towards Urabi than the Consul-General. His history of the intervention and the political manoeuvre preceding it, entitled *The Secret History of the English Occupation of Egypt; being a personal narrative of events*, was translated into Arabic and is still accepted by the Arab world as the authoritative source for the events which were to ensue. Attacks on Europeans took place in Alexandria, about fifty Europeans being murdered and about 200 injured. Blunt maintains that the Khedive's party instigated these troubles but Cromer, who sees the intervention from the British point of view, is in doubt whether it was Urabi or the Khedive who had a finger in the pie. The outcome was to destroy Urabi and save the Khedive and his dynasty. Alexandria was bombarded by a British fleet, troops landed and occupied the Canal Zone, Urabi was defeated and captured at Tell el-Kebir (1882) and Cairo fell. Muhammad Ali's dynasty was saved but henceforth it was to live always in the shade of the British Consul-General. The temporary occupation of Egypt by British troops 'for the protection of British subjects' was to last seventy-four years.

Britain would not have had a free hand in Egypt had France not been engaged in North Africa at the same time. The occupation of Algeria had taken place a generation before these events in Egypt which we have tried to sketch.

The famous blow with the fly-switch, which the Bey of Algiers gave the French consul, had been the cause of the war. But what is not so well known as the blow itself is the dispute which led up to it. The Frenchman had spoken most insultingly when the Bey reminded him that payment was still due for large deliveries of corn made many years before to the Directorate.

We have no adequate description of life in Algeria before the French invasion of 1830. Reports of travellers which speak of the decay of the country, of anarchy, superstition, etc., have to be accepted with reserve. Not every European merchant imbued by the spirit of the enlightenment was in a position to survey a civilization and society so different from his own, let alone pass judgement on their values. That life on the Pirate Coast did not conform to the ideals of enlightened absolutism can hardly be expected to be otherwise. If one wanted to get a true idea of its advantages and disadvantages, of the Turkish government and its rule over the nomads and town-dwellers of the interior one would also have to consult the Muslim sources. Perhaps Algeria did not produce a Jabarti; nevertheless, a vivid picture of Muslim life on the North African coast as seen by Muslim eyes should be obtainable from the documents which have survived.

Until this is done we shall have to be satisfied with an indirect testimony. The French invasion met with resistance from an indisputably eminent man: *Abd al-Qadir* (1807–88). A country that could raise such a personality against the invaders cannot have been quite so 'bankrupt' as the European sources would like to have it. The following is an extract from the biography of Abd al-Qadir by *Jurgi Zaidan* who was one of the representatives of the Arab literary 'renaissance'. This biography is not only interesting for its content; it is at the same time the most important document through which the Arabs of the East learned of Abd al-Qadir's deeds.

His father was one of the most important scholars of his time and was respected in Algeria for his generosity, his noble manners and his quiet bearing. He spared himself no pains to teach and educate his son because he saw he was intelligent and eager to learn. Abd al-Qadir was able to master many of the (traditional) sciences in a short time and he learned the Koran by heart and mastered it. He was outstanding in his seventeenth year for his great strength, courage and horsemanship. He was well-known for his skill on horseback and in games played on horseback. He used to hunt and kill wild swine in the woods without such sport diverting him from his religious duties.

In November 1825 he accompanied his father on the pilgrimage, passing through Alexandria and visiting Cairo. That was during the time of Muhammad Ali who received them and their companions with honour. They reached the Hijaz by way of Suez and after the pilgrimage visited Damascus where they stayed for some time. They then made their way to Baghdad and visited the grave of Abd al-Qadir al-Gilani. There they were received with honour and respect. From there they returned once more to Mecca and Medina and then to their homeland which they reached towards the end of 1828.

That journey increased Abd al-Qadir's thirst for knowledge and he went into seclusion to devote himself entirely to the study of books on the (Arabian) sciences and philosophy. He studied writings of Plato, Pythagoras and Aristotle and made a deep study of the law and the traditions, of geography, astronomy, history and medicinal plants. He collected a library which was one of the most valuable of his time.

In 1830 the French seized the city of Algiers and proclaimed that they also intended to take possession of the country and that it was no longer under Ottoman rule. The tribes living in those regions rose up against the French.

At that time Emir Abd al-Qadir was fighting the French in a place they now call Fort Philippe; the Algerians sent for him and appointed him their Sultan. He was then 25 years old. As soon as he had been chosen he went to the Great Mosque where he prayed with the people and delivered an address, enjoining them to obey him: they were to act in accordance with the Holy Law of the Koran and live as the rightly guided caliphs had lived. He then assembled the spokesmen of the tribes around him and reconciled them to each other so that they might become strong enough to rise against the foreign enemy and throw him out of the country. He fought a series of battles with the French in which he was successful, especially the battle of Wahran where he had a brilliant victory.

In 1834 peace was concluded between him and the French and when quiet had returned the Emir set about putting the internal affairs of his country in order. At the same time he was preparing everything required for war for he knew that further battles would have to be faced. He set up arms workshops, cast cannons and produced gunpowder and also organized his army. As he was forced to pay out large sums he demanded of the tribes that they should pay him the alms tax from their flocks. Many refused but by his skill he was able to bend them to his will without driving them into rebellion. His authority spread and his influence increased.

This did not please the French commander-in-chief and he called upon Emir Abd al-Qadir to remain within his boundaries and not extend his authority beyond the town of Wahran. The Emir answered that his territory had not been fixed in the treaty which had been concluded between the two parties. . . .

When in November 1835 the French forces advanced on Wahran he prepared for battle but many of his men did not stay by him and left him. So he saw himself forced to return to Maskara which he had chosen as his capital. It was occupied by French troops and to begin with he could not enter there. He encamped in a village not far off, almost in despair. Then he received news that the French had left the town. He entered and the upright citizens swore him fealty and so his situation improved and he began to punish those who had opposed him.

In 1837 a new agreement was reached between the two parties. It provided for the exchange of consuls and laid down that the Emir should not surrender any part of his territory to a foreign power, without previously consulting the French. Then the Emir again turned his energies to setting the interior affairs of his country in order. He also devoted himself to military preparations, as was his custom, in order to be ready for all calamities. At that time certain tribes rebelled against him, especially the Azraq, but he succeeded in subduing them by the sword and skilful politics. He built a commercial city which he called Taqadduma. He also built many fortresses and employed European officers to organize his army. He set up in and around Tilimsan (Tlemcen) workshops to make guns and all sorts of weapons. He carried on mining and furthered agriculture, industry and trade. He saw to it that education spread by increasing the number of schools and it was his intention to establish a great university in Taqadduma, which would teach both the traditional Muslim sciences and modern ones. He struck silver and copper coins on one side of which was written: 'This is the Way of God; on Him I rely.' On the other side: 'Struck in Taqadduma. Sultan Abd al-Qadir.'

It was soon to come to further fighting with the French:

When the Emir saw that the whole land had again become a theatre of war, he constructed a transportable town. It was composed of tents which could be set up in streets and it followed the army on its moves. In it arms were manufactured and the prisoners quartered; the soldiers found refuge in it when they were sick and the women and children lived in it and prepared the meals for the soldiers and the workers. This organization was very useful for the Emir and the French exerted all their strength to rob him of this town. They succeeded, by treachery, in reaching the town of tents and burnt it down as they had already laid in ashes the city of Taqadduma which the Emir had built. They plundered everything they found in the town of tents and killed a large number of its inhabitants.

The Emir was absent when the town of tents was burnt down and when he heard of that he took it very much to heart. But he remained impassive and said to his followers: 'Do not weep and do not grieve for God is with us. Our brothers whom they have killed are alive now with God their Lord who is sustaining them.' Then he mustered a new army and built a second town of tents. He had asked the governments of England and Morocco for help but they sent him none.

This struggle was to last until 1847 and on 21 December of that year the Emir was compelled to surrender to the French. An agreement was drawn up according to which Abdul Qadir and his followers were to be granted safe conduct to Bursa or Alexandria. In Paris he had an enthusiastic reception although later on he got to know what the inside of a French prison was like. Napoleon III at last let him go free and Abd al-Qadir chose to reside in Dasmascus.

He and his people reached Beirut on 24 June 1856 and from there he proceeded to Damascus where he was given a great popular reception. He lived in a building they called the 'Imara' and divided his time between religious worship, teaching, writing books and meeting scholars and pious men.

The country of Algeria came under French rule and was exposed to the pressure of French administration and French immigration much longer than any other Arab country. It was also subjected to French culture, language, education and modes of thought longer than was to be the case with any other Arabic-speaking country. In Algeria Arabic almost became a dialect and when the members of the 'Provisional Algerian Government' in Cairo had to converse with Egyptians they did so in French. Their Algerian dialect was too different from the Egyptian and they had not learned classical Arabic well enough to be able to express themselves adequately in it.

During the Algerian war Jacques Berque, the French sociologist and student of Muslim countries, gave us something to think about when he said: 'Perhaps it is just this that makes the struggle between France and Algeria so terribly bitter today. By their close contact with French civilization the Algerians have lost their own identity. They are almost French but yet not quite. They are waging a sort of war against themselves and with themselves, with that part of their self which today they want to suppress; it is this that makes the war so bloody, so tragic and so hopeless.'

Nevertheless one of the best political commentators in Beirut remarks that 'French training has brought it about that the young Tunisian and Moroccan politicians have a sense of realities which their emotional colleagues in the East lack. We in the Near East should learn from them.'

Of all the Arab countries it is the Lebanon that has had the longest and most intensive contacts with the West. The reason for this is that Lebanon comprises a large Christian community. The Maronite sect entered North Lebanon from the valley of the Orontes in North Syria in the seventh century. They found there another Christian sect, the Mardites, with whom they intermingled and on whom they imposed their special views on religion. During the Crusades the Maronites of North Lebanon made common cause with the Crusaders and at that time they came into contact with the Roman Church and entered into communion with it. After the Crusades the connection between Rome and the Maronite Church was for long broken but restored in the sixteenth century. The Maronite College was founded in Rome in 1584 and for centuries Lebanese priests and scholars have been trained and educated there. Branch schools in many of the Christian villages of Lebanon were set up.

Early on, because of the warlike energy the Maronite population showed, the Muslim rulers of the land began to settle the southern part of the mountain with tribes loyal to them. Arabs, Kurds, Turcomans and Persians emigrated into the country. After the first Crusades the Atabeqs of Damascus allocated areas of the southern part to Arab tribes. Many of these remained Sunnis, others adopted the Druse religion of their peasants and retainers. Still others remained Shi'ites while the Shi'ite sects, the Nusairis and the Ismailis came in from Syria.

During the Middle Ages the Druses knew how to organize themselves politically and submit to one leader. The Maronites of the north were con-tinuously quarrelling among each other and it was only in moments of extreme danger that they could unite for common action. This is the reason why Lebanon saw a whole series of Druse principalities from the thirteenth to the seventeenth century. The most renowned Druse Emir was Fakhreddin (1585–1635) who made an alliance with the Maronites of the North. He was a friend of the Medici and spent almost five years in exile at their court.

Later power in the land went to the Sunni Shihab house. The Druses split up and one of their tribes was forced to leave Lebanon and seek new places to stay in the Jebel Hauran, the 'Mountain of the Druses', in Syria. As the power of the Druses decreased the Shihabs came closer to the Christians and one branch of their family finally became Maronite. The famous Emir of Lebanon, Bashir II (1788–1840), belonged to this branch. He supported Muhammad Ali in his policies against the Porte and joined his son, Ibrahim, when he occupied Syria. The European Powers forced Ibrahim to evacuate Syria in 1840. This meant the fall of Bashir who died in exile.

At about the same time social revolutions began to take place in Christian Lebanon. The Maronites rose against their feudal lords, drove them out of their ancestral seats and took possession of their fields. We know very little about these events although there is much material about this period available which has only begun to be sifted in recent years as a first measure by a few young historians.

Since 1839 there have been regular steamship connections with Beirut and it is at this time that the emigration of Christians to the New World began. It is still going on today. The emigrants often return to their native villages as well-to-do men. Their children are educated in convent schools and the members of their families are supported by them. For all these reasons the emigration movement is a link with the European, non-Muslim world. At the present time there are about 1½ million Lebanese in Lebanon and almost a million abroad as emigrants.

When Syria was conquered by Ibrahim and the Emir of Lebanon made a compact with him the country was drawn into the whirlpool of the politics of the World Powers and the local communities began to establish 'alliances' with the great powers. France clung to the Maronites and Britain, in order to have a counter-weight, began to protect the Druses, while Russia tried to appear as protector of the Orthodox Christians. The Porte came to see the aspirations of the Christians who had made common cause with the Egyptian attackers as a threat to the Empire.

In 1860 a series of troubles and massacres ended in a frightful catastrophe. The Druses attacked the Christians perhaps in a last effort to recover the leadership they had lost. The Turkish garrisons assisted the Druses by first disarming the Christians and then handing them over to the Druses. A Protestant minister in Beirut, W. Krämer, described these events as follows:

The events which led to the outbreak of hostilities are still veiled in obscurity. On the 28th of May, the second day of the Whitsuntide holiday, the Pasha proceeded to the Mountains with two battalions in order to be nearer to the scene of unrest. Twenty-one cannon-shots announced his departure and when the last shot had died away we could see Beit-Mery (4½ hours away from Beirut) in flames as Christians and Druses fought fiercely. The fighting spread with terrible rapidity. For five days we saw the villages being burnt down, more than 100 of them being laid in ashes, while the refugees came down to the coast in unbroken streams. Very soon the Christians were seized with panic and they fell almost unresisting under the knives of their enemies.

On the 1st of June the Druses approached the town of Sidon (9 hours' journey south of Beirut). This town of 1200 inhabitants was five-sixths Mohammedan and had for long been a centre of fanaticism. The fleeing Christians had not been allowed to enter the town so that a large number of them was collected in front of the gates. They were all massacred by the Druses and the Mohammedans of Sidon, 800 on the first day, and the same number in the gardens on the following days. The next day Dair al-Mukhallis (San Salvador) monastery, which held enormous treasures, was stormed and all the priests and monks literally slaughtered.

So, unnoticed, the fighting between the two peoples had taken on a religious character and this became more pronounced when a Jihad (holy war against the unbelievers) was preached among the Druses of the Jebel Hauran. These, under Isma'il Al-Atrash, and in alliance with the Matawilah of the Bekaa and the Beduins of the desert, joined the Druses in Lebanon and war was waged on a large scale.

On the western slope of Mount Hermon are the two towns of Hasbaya and Rashaya, inhabited by Greeks (Orthodox) who had taken no part in the fighting between the Druses and the Maronites. Moreover, in both places there were garrisons of regular Turkish troops (Nizam). After burning down the villages in the vicinity the Druses reached the outskirts of Hasbaya on the 3rd of June. The Christians drove back the first attacks but Osman Bey, the Turkish commander, made his protection conditional on the surrender of their arms. The Christians obeyed and withdrew into the citadel where they remained confined for eight days. On the 11th the gates burst open and the Druses thronged in, massacring all the Christians before the eyes of the Turkish troops. With their hands still red with the blood of these un-fortunate people the Druses proceeded to Rashaya where the defenceless Christians were surrendered to the swords of their enemies by the very same treachery. . . .

The Druses advanced upon Zahleh, a bulwark of the Christians in all former wars, which is on the eastern slope of Mount Lebanon, half-way between Beirut and Damascus. Here the fighting was exceedingly violent but it was decided in the favour of the Druses by the grape shot fire of the Turkish troops. Still fighting, the Christians withdrew to Kesrawan and Zahleh was plundered and burnt down. From here the whole Druse force advanced on Deir al-Qamar which had in the meantime been closely surrounded by Turkish troops. Here, too, the Turkish officers committed the same treachery, disarming the Christians with solemn promises to protect them, locking them up in the castle and then themselves opening the gates to the Druses. In two days 2000 men, old men and children were mercilessly massacred.

The agitation which the report of all these massacres caused in Beirut was indescribable. While the Mohammedans rejoiced aloud at this brilliant victory of their brothers in faith, panic robbed the Christians of all presence of mind and composure. All the shops were shut and large bands of Druses and Muslims went in noisy processions through the streets of the city, mocking and maltreating every Christian. Even Europeans were not safe from such maltreatment. In spite of the presence of several warships the attitude of the Consular Corps did not inspire the Turkish authorities with any fear; the representatives of the various powers could not agree on any one course of action and every energetic step was nipped in the bud.

A short pause interrupted the series of bloody scenes, which had taken place before our eyes with great rapidity, but we had not yet reached the end of the terror. The blood bath began in Damascus on the 9th of July and lasted for four days. It deprived 7000 Christians of their lives, and the survivors of all their property, and the whole Christian quarter was given over to the flames.

But here (in Beirut) a limit had been set to the fighting by the presence of a French occupying force and the Turkish Government had, however un-willingly, to take steps against the attackers, at least in appearance. Some of those who were most seriously compromised were punished and Ahmed Pasha was shot in Damascus as was Osman Bey in Hasbaya; the others were brought to trial. But only then could one see the whole extent of the misfortune. From Beirut to Damascus, from Baalbek to the Jordan Valley, in an area of 70 square miles, not one town and not one village was left standing. Everything was devastated and burnt down; of the numerous and prosperous population about 20,000 had been slaughtered and between 70,000 and 80,000 had become destitute and homeless. Most of the refugees were crowded together in the cities on the coast, without clothing, without food, without everything. (From *Geschichte der evangelischen Gemeinde zu Beirut* by G. A. Kriener.)

Apropos of the massacres in Damascus Abd al-Qadir comes again to mind. Jurji Zeidan relates:

When the rising against the Christians broke out in Damascus in 1860 the Emir Abd al-Qadir was one of the first of the learned men who tried to put a stop to it after his many attempts to prevent it breaking out had failed. He did everything in his power to protect the Christians from harm. No sooner did he hear of the outbreak of the rebellion on the 9th of July than he assembled all the North Africans living in Damascus and sent them to the various quarters of the city to save whatever Christians they could. He had them brought to his house to be under his protection. When his house was full of refugees he had the neighbouring houses evacuated to provide quarters for all those who required help, especially the consuls of the foreign countries. He generously provided for all their needs and in this he was assisted by the Ashraf of the city, especially the two renowned scholars Mahmud Hamza and his brother As'ad who helped the Emir and his men in their efforts to ward off the attack the Kurds made on the third day of the confusion in order to seize these fugitives.

The Wali (Governor) of Damascus had announced that he would protect all Christians who sought refuge in the citadel of Damascus. About five thousand took refuge there. No sooner had they been quartered than the Emir learned that a crowd of Druses were on their way to the citadel to slaughter these Christians. He hurried to liberate them and he was able to force the band, who had come to kill them, to go back by threatening to fire on them.

During all the seven days of the troubles the Emir was ready to protect the Christians and to keep their enemies away from them. He spent nearly every night awake with his gun in his hand to defend those to whom he had extended his protection. On the 15th day of July of that year a new Wali arrived in Damascus, the old one was deposed and the situation quietened down. At that time there were about 7000 refugees in the citadel and about 4000 in the Emir's palace.

These massacres led to the intervention of the European Powers which resulted in the 'Règlement Organique' that conferred upon Britain and France certain rights to intervene in the administration of Lebanon. The French consul became the protector of the Christians in the Levant and the Porte undertook to appoint a Christian as Governor in the newly created Mutasarriflik of Lebanon. The mountain territories got a certain autonomy. An elected council sat with the Governor and the gendarmerie had to consist of Lebanese. The fifty-four years this 'Règlement Organique' was to last were perhaps the happiest, certainly the most peaceful, the country has so far seen in its history.

That was the time the missionaries came to Lebanon. They opened schools in greater number and of a higher standard than those existing in any other Arab country. It was also at this time that the large mountain villages of Lebanon developed into the unique phenomena they are today in the Near East; living village communities, comfortable and well-to-do mountain villages whose inhabitants are able and willing to carry on the business of their community themselves and in their own interest. It is in these villages that is rooted the strength which has permitted Lebanon to survive today as one of the last democracies among the Arab states.

The memory of the massacres is still alive in the Lebanese mountains and in the rebuilt Christian quarters of Damascus. It even plays a decisive political role, for the Christians of Lebanon do not wish at any price to put themselves under the rule of a Muslim majority. To be sure, economic and social considerations have something to do with this, nevertheless a strong mistrust, a naked fear, can be recognized deep in the attitude of the Christians; it is deeper than all practical reasons in support of independence for Lebanon. In times of confusion it becomes apparent. During the troubles of 1958 suddenly all the old atrocity stories were alive again. People recounted the horrible deeds of the Druses as if they had happened yesterday; indeed, some alleged, they had happened yesterday and they were talked about so much that new atrocities began to be committed—by both sides—through hatred and fear. . . .

But, at the same time, during the troubles of 1958 every politician, soldier or group leader had the year 1860 as a warning signal before him. Every attempt was made to avoid a new 'war of religion' between the Christians and the Muslims. Everyone knew that if it *did* break out there would be no place for reason and there would be no going back. They actually succeeded in preventing the parties to the quarrel from fighting each other as religious groups. Their quarrel was mainly about politics, not about religion and for this reason it could eventually be composed.

6

The Humanists of Beirut

THE TWO AREAS OF THE NEAR EAST, the beginnings of whose separate political development we have described, were also the centres which gave birth to intellectual innovations. Beirut became a centre for scholars who devoted themselves to the study of the Arabic language and the history of the Arabs. Old texts were rediscovered and published anew, dictionaries to help people to understand them, and encyclopaedias which were to give modern Arabic a more comprehensive and precise vocabulary, were compiled. These scholars were at the same time writers, many of them even poets, and the love of their lives was the Arabic language.

As opposed to them there developed in Cairo the first impulse towards religious reform, for Cairo is, contrary to Beirut, an Islamic city. In both countries politics played an important part in developments right from the beginning. This could not possibly be otherwise in any Islamic development, for Islam comprises both the political *and* (as we call it) the religious. In the field of Arabic studies one can understand the political undertone when one remembers that Beirut was the capital of a Turkish province. He who cultivated Arabic and spoke glorifying the Arabs thereby represented the local Arab world as against the controlling power of the Turkish Empire. Nevertheless, it must not be forgotten that most of the humanists and Arabists of Beirut were Christians. The study of their Arabic mother-tongue and the discovery of the great patrimony in the Arabic language gave them something like a province of their own, a cultural homeland, which belonged to them alone and with which they were more familiar than the Muslims who had followed the banners of the Turkish Ottomans. The Lebanese scholars sought a reason for, and a justification of, their autonomy and particularity as 'Arab' Christians, as opposed to the 'Ottoman Muslims', in 'their' Arabic language and 'their' Arab history. This was no doubt what engendered that burning zeal with which more and more Christian Lebanese have devoted themselves to the study of Arabic, Arabic literature and Arabic civilization and history ever since Faris Shidyaq's time. Men like the elder Yaziji and Butros al-Bustani remind us in many respects of the humanists of the Renaissance.

Nasif al-Yaziji (1800–71) was court poet and secretary of Emir Bashir II, but after his master's downfall he settled in Beirut and led the life of writer, literary historian, editor of ancient texts, school books and school anthologies, grammarian and poet. Today the works by which he is best known, along with his comprehensive anthologies of poetry, are his Maqamas, a classical 'genre' of Arabic literature consisting of short stories in rhymed prose. In his collection of Maqamas (Majma'al-Bahrain—'The Confluence of the two seas') Nasif al-Yaziji used a very great number of rare words which make it difficult to read these stories. Editions of this work consist of a few lines of text and innumerable notes and glosses. The whole is a piece of unsurpassed bravura. To appreciate its literary value one has really to exert oneself but, in return, one gets an idea of what it is to be a complete master of the Arabic language even in its more unusual fields.

Like their colleagues of the Renaissance in Florence the Beirut humanists were possessed by the joy of discovering a whole hidden world. Like them they did not only work with their attention on the past as 'scholars' but always at the same time with their eyes on the present with a view to turning the treasure they had dug up immediately into coin which would make their people's life easier at that time and in the future. Their achievement was enormous.

In order to get an idea of this one has only to look at the great Arabic dictionary ('The Ocean of the Oceans') which was compiled unaided by *Butros al-Bustani* (1819–83); it consists of two huge volumes and was not his only achievement. He was a teacher, first in the school of the Maronite Patriarch, then in the American missionary school in Beirut and finally in the 'national' school he himself founded and which was one of the most renowned teaching establishments in Syria. In addition he acted as translator for the British when they intervened in the country's destinies, as reviser for the Americans when they printed their great Arabic translation of the Bible and as interpreter for the American Consulate in Beirut. He had a thorough knowledge of Syriac, Latin, Italian, English, Greek and Hebrew as well as being a master of his own language, Arabic. He edited three newspapers and wrote a large part of these himself. In addition to his great dictionary he compiled an encyclopaedia in Arabic. He died having completed seven volumes of this and the last five were gradually issued during the subsequent twenty years (Da'irat al-Ma'arif). It is impossible to enumerate all his translations, technical books for teachers, sermons and literary writings. It was he, too, who drew up the School Law which was promulgated by Daud Pasha, the first Christian Mutasarrif of Lebanon, after the 'Réglement Organique'.

One must be careful not to brush aside these Beirut humanists as mere 'philologists'. To be sure, the Arabic language was the central field of their studies and writings but they cultivated more than 'philology' by their linguistic studies. They were conscious of the link existing between a nation and its language. They said: 'If the nation is to become conscious of itself again it has to be retaught its own language. Intellectual decay, which is mirrored in the formalism and barrenness of the Arabic of the later Middle Ages, can be halted and transformed into intellectual growth only when we put new life into our language.' *Ibrahim al-Yaziji* (1847–1906), the son of the afore-mentioned Nasif, describes the situation of Arabic as follows:

There is probably not one among the intellectuals of our nation working for the renaissance who does not feel how little the language of our times serves the needs of the people. Dictionaries do not comprise enough expressions fulfilling the requirements of writers and translators; writing has become in many ways a difficult task and a gate which it is not easy to pass through.

This is the language which every one who has described it says is the richest of all in ability to express ideas, which can assimilate the most abstruse concepts and which is the most pliable in depicting meanings. But today it proves itself incapable when a writer wants to use it to describe his bedroom; he has difficulty in finding words for his simple, daily food, let alone words he would need to describe the palaces of great kings or the mansions of great and rich men, or the streets of a well-to-do city and all the vessels, furniture, materials, and all kinds of tools, instruments and aids of civilization to be found there. He will find no words for all these in this language. For, if a Beduin had to describe all this he would stand there speechless and at a loss for words. The words that slip from his tongue must make sense in his heart and so it is not easy for him to express such things in language and he finds no way of putting them into words. He stands there like a dumb man who can see and distinguish things but who cannot speak about them except in sign language.

But what would one of us do if it occurred to him to visit a natural science or industrial museum and saw there how many names and designations there are for parts and for the whole of all sorts of animals, plants, and minerals? When he learns how many instruments, tools and other products of industry there are, how many individual parts and pieces they contain and how they are distinguished by different forms and different uses, how can he express anything of all that in Arabic?

Moreover, what shall he do when he wants to talk about the ordinary topics of everyday conversation, such as new scientific or industrial inventions? One cannot talk about all these things, neither in general nor in detail, without having the necessary technical terms.

Even in the dictionary he will find no words which he can use to speak about them. He will not be helped by the 80 different words he will find for 'honey', the 200 for 'wine', the 500 for 'lion', the 1000 for 'sword', the other 1000 for 'camel' or even the 4000 for 'misfortune'.

The reason for this is that language is the mirror of a nation, the image of its civilization, the expression of its society, the picture of its character and peculiarities and the register of all the knowledge, technique, and arts it possesses. It fixes everything that can be expressed in language, everything that can be conceived in the mind or all those ideas which touch upon their sensual life. Now, it is well known that the Arabs who first spoke this language were a people of the desert. Their houses were made of hair and leather, their materials consisted of matting and carpeting, their clothing of shirts and cloaks, their furniture of a hand-mill and a cooking-pot. . . .

When the campaigns and the conquests were at an end there awoke in the nation an interest in science and it desired to enjoy the arts of sedentary life. It gave up its tough, Beduin way of life and progressed as far along the path of civilization as was possible at that time. In doing so the Arabs took over practically no foreign words and they also were not forced to invent new words, but rather their language served them with the same words the Beduins had already used. They derived from it words for those things with which they had previously no contact, just by changing the meaning and applying it to things of which the Arabs had never spoken before. They surrounded themselves with the works of art of the Persians and with the sciences of the Greeks and adopted many technical processes of both Eastern and Western nations which they required; to all this they added what they themselves produced. Their language served them well in all these borrowings and its springs never dried up. Nor do we know that anyone ever complained that the language was too old or imperfect. This went on until the Arabs reached that change in their fortunes that was to lead to their downfall. The nation was destroyed, the curse (of God) and ruination followed one after the other and the sciences were blown away by the wind. At this point the language stopped developing and what is left of it today is no longer sufficient to be a worthy expression of the condition of a civilized nation.

From all this it can be deduced that, wherever there are signs of infirmity, the fault lies with the nation, not with the language, for the decay and impotence from which it is suffering are not because it is unfit and sterile but because of the weakness of those who speak it in the nation and their backward condition and lack of education. Had those who speak it remained at the level of their ancestors and continued to progress along the path of civilization the language would have served them well and expressed everything new they encountered; it would have carried them forwards right up to the latest currents of modern times.

Instead centuries passed without a single word being added to the language, indeed hardly anything was preserved in it which went beyond the needs of the home and the market-place. Moreover, these practical needs became narrower and smaller from day to day because those who spoke the language were exposed to the pressure of poverty and thus became a prey to the rule of ignorance, the decay of culture and the collapse of civilization, to such an extent that many of the town dwellers felt no more needs than did Beduins and peasants. (Selections from an essay in the newspaper *Al-Bayan*, Cairo, 1897, reproduced in *Manahil al-Adab al-'Arabi*, vol. 12, Beirut n.d., pp. 7–14.)

When one reads such treatises one may well ask oneself: Were the Beirut humanists not tying the horse up by his tail? If they were so anxious to 'give new life' to their 'nation' should they not have, in the first place, been out teaching rather than carrying on philological studies? Should they not have been trans-mitting to the youth of their country those modern sciences and techniques which would have enabled them to build a prosperous, able nation? Did they have, instead, to cram the heads of the young generations with all this historical stuff, the Beduin poets with their quaint language, the Umayyads with their drinking songs, with the subtle theology of the Abbasids and with Avicenna's old-fashioned philosophy?

The answer is that the Beirut humanists were anxious to achieve the rebirth of a 'nation', not the education of individuals. What did, or could in the future, hold this 'nation' together could hardly be anything other than its language. To be sure, the individual would have got off the mark quicker if he had forgotten his origin, if he had become europeanized and had learned a modern profession in a European school with the help of a European language and if, at the same time, he had been given a character training fitting him to become a useful and co-operative member in a society of men like him. But, in the course of this, what would have happened to the nation? Even if it had been possible to 'europeanize' every single member of it (for which there were, of course, no material foundations) would that not simply have meant self-surrender and the 'nation's' passing sentence of death on itself?

The Beirut humanists who stood at the rebirth of the Arab nation recognized one thing. If the nation did not wish to become lost it had to know its past, not only know it but go deeper and deeper into it with constant circumspection and ever new understanding. The gate and key to all this was the Arabic language. It was absolutely essential for these men to open up this gate and free it of the rubble of centuries, a task which they performed with enormous industry and great care, intelligence and skill; and yet it could still not be guaranteed that the existence of the nation was assured. The road has no doubt been opened up and the language now exists as a shining instrument which can express modern concepts; but it depends on the nation whether and what use will be made of it. Humanists can do nothing more than pave the way, spur on, give advice and seek to show where they think treasures lie—but it is the 'nation' itself that must follow the way they have newly prepared. It must be able to see itself in the mirror the humanist holds up to it, it must take pleasure and gain strength from recognizing itself. If the 'nation' is too lazy or too occupied with other matters and with 'more urgent' problems the sagacious humanist can be of no use to it.

Even if it honours him and sets up statues to him, as long as it cannot listen to him it runs the danger of losing not only him but itself.

When one reviews the generations of Beirut humanists one cannot escape the suspicion that these men became less and less able to win and hold the attention of the 'nation'. In the nineteenth century their influence was enormous. They not only dominated in the schoolroom as compilers of dictionaries and treatises on grammar, they also published newspapers, weekly magazines, translations from European languages, stories, novels and poems. All educated men in Arab countries read their works and even the foreign missionaries, American Protestants and French Jesuits alike, sat before them in class to perfect their Arabic.

But towards the end of the century this type of scholar and versatile man of letters disappeared from Arab literature and civilization. In their place came, on the one hand, the poets, story-tellers and novel writers of modern times and, on the other the journalists, publicists and propagandists. The scholar withdrew to the universities and even there he seems to have become a rare phenomenon. Where the standard of the teacher is still at the old high level he does not have the public; he is felt to be old-fashioned, pedantic and over-learned. All one wants to hear from him is that the Arabs produced a 'great civilization', greater than that of contemporary Europe; one does not want to be burdened with too many facts; there is hardly any time left for that. A hot wind of politics, sometimes tempered by religious undertones of polemic speeches, of accusations which sound like defences and of prophetic utterances, blows through the country.

7

Pan-Islam

THE FIRE, by which the more passionate aspects of Arab nationalism were to be fanned, had its origin in distant Afghanistan. *Jamal ad-Din al-Afghani*, who was born in Persia, close to the Afghan border, in 1839, belonged to a highly respected family of Sayyids or descendants of the Prophet. While still young he distinguished himself by his great talents and studied all the branches of learning which were available to him. After having spent over a year in India he went at the age of seventeen on the pilgrimage to Mecca. He then entered the service of the Emir of Afghanistan, the great Dost Muhammad Khan, and on the latter's death he lived through the confusion and struggle for the succession as first Wazir of one of the pretenders, Muhammad A'zam, who established himself for a time in Kabul. In the end Jamal ad-Din was driven into exile. Leaving Kabul in 1867 at the age of twenty-eight he had already gone through the whole political career of an Oriental wazir from the highest office of honour to the complete loss of every shred of power.

The British government of India received him with all honours but took good care to see that he left India again within one month.

On his way to Istanbul via Mecca Jamal ad-Din passed through Cairo for the first time but on this occasion (1868) he stopped for only a short while. He was well received in Istanbul, his talents were recognized and the Sultan appointed him member of the Council for Education. However, his modern ideas exposed him to the intrigues of the conservative divines and this ended in his being banished from the country. As a result he turned up in Egypt for the second time in 1871.

The Khedive's Government provided this famous man, whose brilliance and learning received general recognition, a small monthly stipend. He lived in constant intercourse with Azhar University circles and began to give lectures in his own home to students of the Azhar who came to him. It is difficult to comprehend today what an impact this outsider made on a whole generation of Azhar students with his private lectures. His most famous pupil, Muhammad Abduh, whom we shall deal with later, gave one of his own pupils the following description of one such lecture:

> The Sheikh (Muhammad Abduh) related to me: 'The first one who told me of the presence of Sayyid Jamal ad-Din was a foreign student from the

Syrian *riwaq* (hostel). He said: "A famous Afghan scholar has arrived in Cairo and is living in the Khan al-Khalili." I was pleased to hear this and went to Sheikh Hasan and requested him to visit Jamal ad-Din with me. We found him at table; he invited us to eat with him but we excused ourselves. He then questioned us about various verses of the Koran and what the interpreters of the Koran and the mystics had to say about them. He then explained these verses to us himself and filled my heart with amaze-ment and love for him for mysticism and interpretation of the Koran were my favourite subjects and the key to my happiness. . . .'

Later the Sayyid encouraged him, and also his other pupils, to publish and write treatises on literature, social questions or politics. He trained them in the art of public speaking and Abduh distinguished himself so much that he became even more eloquent than his teacher, for the Sayyid's style was, in spite of its strength and power of convincing, not quite free from touches of Persian and did not flow so correctly as the style of an Arab such as Abduh. (Tarikh al-Ustadh al-Imam.)

This same Muhammad Abduh, whom we have just heard telling of his personal acquaintance with Jamal al-Din, wrote a work on social conditions in Egypt during Ismail's reign and described in it, more from the point of view of the whole community, the influence the appearance of Al-Afghani had on the awakening Egyptian 'intellectuals' of the period:

(At that time) the Egyptians used to leave all their general and, indeed, their personal affairs to the will of the ruler and obey the orders of him who was delegated to supervise these particular affairs. In these matters this person acted according to his own lights and people were of the opinion that their welfare or misfortune depended on his uprightness and justice or on his deceit and tyranny. Not one of them thought he had a right to do something independent for the well-being of the nation. They had not the slightest idea how other states lived, neither Muslim ones nor the European ones.

Although very many of them had gone to Europe to study from the time of Muhammad Ali the Great up to the time of which we are speaking and although a large number of them had gone to the neighbouring Arab countries under Muhammad Ali and Ibrahim, still the people at home got nothing of the fruits of these travels and the advantage of the knowledge that had resulted from them. Although Ismail set up a Consultative Assembly in 1866 whose task it was supposed to be to convince the people that they had a voice in the affairs of their country, nevertheless no one, not even the members of the Consultative Assembly itself, believed that they really possessed those rights. . . . They felt that it was still the absolute will of the ruler (the Khedive) which governed their opinions. Was it possible for anyone to do or even think of the opposite of what he was ordered to do?

If he was firmly convinced that there was a better way of doing things than the Government's, was it possible for him to express his thoughts? Certainly not! On the contrary, he avoided any word that might have entailed for him banishment from his country, sentence of death or loss of his property.

While the people were in this condition with no writer to cheer them up and no orator to speak to them, there came to our country in 1871 a remark-able man, with deep insight into religious things, wise in the political affairs of states, full of information and knowledge and with an over-flowing heart; this was Sayyid Jamal ad-Din al-Afghani. When he took up residence in Cairo there gathered around him at first a number of students, then he was visited regularly by many officials and Ashraf, then all sorts of opinions of him began to spread. Thereby his fame increased so that everyone desired to meet him. Thereupon he occupied himself with teaching certain logical sciences and many students came to his lectures while he continued to be visited regularly by scholars and others. Whenever he met someone he spoke untiringly of things which fire the mind, purify belief, exalt the natural impulses to higher spheres, or turn people's thoughts towards the affairs of the community and to ways of achieving the well-being of the country and its inhabitants.

The students wrote down what they had learned from him and reported it in their own countries when they returned home for the holidays. Similarly visitors reported in their own quarters of the city what they had heard from him. Thus everywhere feelings were aroused, minds stirred and the veil of indifference became thinner in all parts of the country but especially in Cairo. All this was going on while the great Monarch was sitting on his high throne, too high for such radiations to weaken his position. This radiation did not cease but rather spread farther and farther until the war between Russia and the Ottoman Empire broke out in 1293 (1876).

At that time the people became more and more anxious to know who their sovereign was and how things stood with the Ottoman Empire and with the Russians and so they sought information about the war from whomsoever could give it to them. The great number of foreigners living in our country used to receive European newspapers regularly and the fact that they lived together with all classes of Egyptians made it easy for people to learn what the newspapers were saying. This also led some Arabic news-papers, which were at that time still on a very modest scale, to seek more exact information about what was going on and to publish it. These newspapers showed a clear tendency to underline and praise everything concerning the Russian troops and to disparage the Ottomans; some members of the public objected to this attitude and combated it. So there arose among the public a new and hitherto unknown type of discussion. New newspapers appeared and took up the cudgels with the old ones and more and more people wanted to subscribe to them so that it was no longer possible to restrain them.

What the newspapers published was not confined to the events of the war; many of them began to write about other countires, their political situation and their economy. They also contained reports of the bad state of Egyptian government finances which was beginning to be noticed. People talked more and more as the newspapers increased in number and Sheikh Jamal ad-Din began to encourage his visitors and students to publish literary and scientific articles about every topic under the sun which, however, did not go beyond intellectual matters and social criticism. In all this the writers competed with each other in the use of their pens until free expression became so apparent in the newspapers that one would almost have thought to be in a world of the spirit and not this corrupt world.

When the revolution or reform prepared by Jamal ad-Din broke out in 1878 as the Urabi revolt, the Sayyid was no longer in Egypt, for he had been turned out of the country the year before at the instigation of the British Consul and had returned to India.

Al-Afghani wrote while he was in India his only work of any size, the 'Reply to the Materialists'. In this work Al-Afghani sees the whole history of humanity as a struggle between 'religion' and 'materialism'. He gives an historical sketch. All great civilized peoples believed in their religions at the time of their greatness. They would never have become great but for their religions. Every time a civilization decays it happens because the 'materialists' have penetrated it and spread their ideas according to which there is no God nor any absolute laws nor any real difference between good and evil. By such teachings men become corrupt:

> Every one of them can say he believes in the Day of Judgement and re-peat to himself that his belief is just like that of his father but they act as if they no longer believed in a life in the Hereafter. The views of the materialists have entered into their hearts and they no longer have a care for their souls. Then, too, their egoism triumphs and they put their own personal well-being before that of the community, and they sell their families and their nation cheaply. Their desire for the good things of this world makes them fearful and their cowardice can go to such limits that they can fall into the abyss of the deepest self-degradation.

From the historic point of view the 'naturalists' (Al-Afghani uses this English word in Persian transcription) have appeared at different times under different names and guises. As 'Epicureans' and 'Stoics' they corrupted Greek and Roman civilizations and materialists in the guise of 'Mazdaists' destroyed Ancient Persia. Arabic-Islamic civilization was attacked and corrupted by naturalists calling themselves 'Batiniya'. Royalist France fell when rationalists like 'Voltaire' achieved prominence there and a short time before the Ottoman

Empire had suffered a severe defeat at the hands of Russia because the officers in the Ottoman army were infected with 'naturalism'. In modern times naturalists call themselves 'Socialists, Nihilists or Communists'. They busy themselves with opening and directing schools:

> They could find no surer means of corrupting souls than to found schools or to enter the schools of others as teachers with the pretext of spreading knowledge, but, in reality, to plant their principles in the brains of children while they are still innocent and while their minds are being formed.

This way of arguing may seem naïve to us and, above all, its historic basis is very weak. But in spite of the objections based on our more exact knowledge of history we should not ignore the fact that we have here in Al-Afghani's method of presentation something completely new in the Islamic world. A historical-empiric method is being used to prove the correctness of a religious thesis. Is that not 'materialism' also? At any rate Al-Afghani's method of arguing is based more on the European way of arguing scientifically from experience than on the theological argumentation of the East.

Its horizon is also absolutely new. 'History' had at bottom never meant anything for the scholars of Islam but the history of the Islamic religion and the Islamic peoples. Everything that happened before Islam or outside the Islamic lands meant for them little more than a senseless groping about in the dark. It was not worth while dealing with it seriously. And now we have Al-Afghani all of a sudden proving the superiority of 'religion' to 'materialism' from the history of the pagan Romans! 'Religion' is no longer exclusively Islam; other religions are shown in the same context. 'Civilization' is no longer only the Islamic way of life but there are other 'civilizations' which can also be considered of value and from whose experiences even a Muslim can learn a lesson.

This is one of the causes of the enormous impact Al-Afghani's appearance made on the Islamic World. He has certain intellectual weapons he has taken from the camp of the 'enemies' of Islam, the 'greedy Europeans', stolen by him, as Prometheus stole fire, and carried into the beleaguered fortress of Islam. By the light of his torch the young intelligentsia reared in the spirit of Islam began to take stock of their fortress, which had formerly been the only 'world' they had known. The forces which had assailed them from outside had been simply 'evil', 'incomprehensible' or 'not worth comprehending'. Al-Afghani was the first man to try to explain these forces to them. He dissected these forces showing their structure, origin and causes and so also it became clear that the people in the Islamic fortress had to conjure up counter-forces if they were to withstand the assault in the long run. All at once they realize that they can and must awaken similar forces, corresponding Islamic counter-forces, in their own nation. 'Renaissance', 'rebirth' (in Arabic 'Nahda') becomes vitally necessary. One observes how the European states achieved their 'rebirth'. Similar causes must have similar effects and the causes must be discovered.

Sayyid Jamal al-Din evolved a theory of how a people's 'rebirth' is brought about:

There were people in those times who thought that the ills of nations could be cured by the publication of newspapers, for newspapers awake thought and act as an incentive to improving manners. Is this correct? Even if we admit that the editors of newspapers aim at nothing but the well-being of their nation, yet there are only a few who will read them when care drives people to negligence and terror dominates the minds so that writers have no readers or, if they have, seldom one who can understand the sense of what he is reading. In this way the reader may perhaps be led to understand what he reads in a sense different from the one intended because his power of imagination is too limited or his mind is not independent enough; from this there can come nothing but harm. . . .

Others believed that a nation could be cured of its deadly evils by opening schools for all simultaneously in all regions and parts of the nation, that these schools would have to be set up according to the modern European fashion so that knowledge could be transmitted to all people within a short time. Once education was general, manners would improve, people would understand one another and would become strong through unity. But they are mistaken for such a great task must of necessity be undertaken by a government which is powerful enough and in a position to force the nation to learn for a time, when it has no desire to do so, until it understands the pleasure of it. . . . A great deal of money is required for this . . . but we are talking here of a weak state with no means.

If they say: 'One can progress step by step, but with perseverance and constancy,' this may be possible, but these methods take effect too slowly.

Moreover, even if a nation could take its time until knowledge had been absorbed by a few people and then gradually spread, it could still not be sure that this gradual increase would really benefit it. Can one assume that the knowledge which has been acquired by a minority can be transmitted in a way capable of raising the rest of the nation? It would be strange if this were so when the nation still has no knowledge of these foreign sciences. How is it to sow its seeds, plant them, water them and fertilize them so that they sprout and bear fruit? The nation does not know whence it received these sciences and if it has learned something of that, then only by hearsay.

The scholars who are to bring this foreign knowledge have (if they belong to a nation in such a parlous situation) preconceptions opposed to the preconceptions of their own nation. Esteem for the nation from which they have acquired their knowledge makes them foreign to their own people, and they can do nothing but corrupt the nature of their nation. These teachers who propagate the new learning are men who have not found their knowledge in their hearts. Even if they desired honestly to serve their country they could only give what they themselves possess. They teach what they have learned just as they heard it without regard for the needs of their nation, its situation, nature and ancient traditions. For this reason they also think that everything they have learned is perfect and suited to all minds.

The reason for all this is that the 'intelligentsia' are not the masters of their sciences but only their transmitters and middlemen. If God with his supernatural power does not come to their help, they are like a loving mother who likes a certain kind of food and immediately gives it to her child to eat, even if he is a baby in arms who cannot enjoy what she enjoys and is still so small that he has to have milk and nothing but milk suits him. So the child soon falls ill and dies.

The Ottomans and Egyptians opened a number of schools of the modern type and, moreover, sent whole groups of students to western countries to bring home all the arts, sciences, information and technical processes they needed, in short, everything one calls 'civilization'. And it is indeed a real civilization for those countries which have produced it naturally from their own society and human resources. But how much did the Egyptians or Ottomans get of what they brought home? Quite a long time has passed since then. Are they better off now than before, when they caught hold of this new lifeline? Have they saved themselves from the clutches of poverty and misery? Have they escaped from the abyss in which foreigners cast them by their tyrannical measures? Have they discovered among themselves hearts open to the spirit of patriotism? This is an attitude of mind which considers the well-being of the mother-country more important than everything else. It is for this that the patriot strives even if he has to lay down his life for it. and if he dies for its sake another succeeds him as has been the case in many nations.

So what should one do now? What way out can one find? Newspapers are of little use and have not much influence even when they are well-intentioned. As for the modern sciences we have seen to what bad use they are put. In addition there is not much time and the need is pressing. What raising of voices will suffice to awaken those sleeping in the corners of heedlessness? What storm can awaken their numbed bodies and set their rusty brains in motion? What breath can put life into them and rally them around the banner of their own salvation?

I will show you the cause which includes all causes and the means that comprises all means. Imagine a state, humbled after having been glorious, weak after having been powerful, plundered after having ruled and oppressed after having once been flourishing. Then try to discern the causes of its first rise to power, imagine the blows which led to its disintegration and the seeds of its sickness. Is it not religion that caused that state's most important principles to flourish, that united its individual members, that raised its head high above other nations and led it by well-chosen laws? Is it not religion, with strong principles and fixed rules of conduct, comprising all types of government and calling aloud for unity in friendship and love, keeping hearts pure from sensual things, lighting up the mind with the rays of truth from the origin of all things and supplying stones enough to build the edifice of human society! Men need such a religion, it preserves this society and at the same time it preaches faith in all types of civilization.

Al-Afghani religion is the origin of all civilization and of all forms of political community. It has to be kindled and stirred into life if the 'renaissance' of the nation is to be brought about. In his book against materialists he expresses the same idea in other words:

There can be no real unity without, to a certain extent, restraining the impulses of egoism. There are four different ways of disciplining these impulses; force, ambition which seeks for power, ambition which seeks glory, and religion. The first three means of keeping egoism in check have in the long run a destructive effect. Therefore only religion can provide a permanent foundation for a state.

The way in which Al-Afghani describes how things develop along wrong lines when one tries to transfer the achievements of European civilization to the Muslim countries of the Near East is most remarkable. In seeing this experiment from a critical point of view he is far ahead not only of his compatriots in the Near East but also of all his European contemporaries. It is only the ethnologists and sociologists of our generation who have arrived at opinions such as Al-Afghani held and tried to express.

Modern cultural sociologists have developed a special technical vocabulary for the whole circle of problems connected with the transference of a culture. Today they say: Every 'civilization' is a living unity in itself. Relatively small and unimportant fragments can be taken over from another civilization and incorporated in the receiving one, but it is only rarely that more complex transfers of larger fragments of a foreign civilization are successful. They entail a fundamental change of direction of the receiving civilization and often lead to its collapse because it is no longer contained by its vital circle. The adoption of essential parts of the virulent, so-called 'western' civilization has so far led to the collapse of nearly every 'non-western' cultural circle that has attempted it.

The sagacious Afghan was able to express all this with the aid of an Arab friend in Paris without all the modern technical terminology and that in a language which for centuries had been used more for rhetoric than for analysis, at a time when Europe believed that its specific culture was the only civilization and the only way of progress.

The long quotation on 'adoption and revivification of culture' has been taken from the periodical *Al-Urwa al-Wuthga* which marked the next step in Al-Afghani's life. During the Urabi rebellion he had been detained in

Calcutta by the British, but when their difficulties in Egypt were over Al-
Afghani was set free and allowed to go wherever he wanted. He went first to
London and then a short time later settled in Paris, where his friend and pupil
Muhammad Abduh joined him. Abduh had remained in Egypt during the
revolt and had been imprisoned for a short time after its failure. Paris was chosen
as the place in which to publish the new periodical because the best prospects
for the liberty of the press existed there. The enterprise was financed from India
and the language of publication was Arabic so that it might be available to all
Muslims. Muhammad Abduh, the Arab, was responsible for the language
but the contents and thoughts were no doubt mainly Al-Afghani's. A third
collaborator, who knew English and French, looked through the European
press and wrote up all the news that dealt with the Islamic countries. The
periodical appeared for only eight months and copies of it had to be smuggled
into most Islamic countries even during this short period. It ceased publication
when the British Government protested to the French Government.

This periodical was later published as a book but is read far too little in
Europe and has never been translated, not even partially. The reason for this
may be its extraordinarily difficult and prolix language. It contains very sharply
formulated political articles which are directed mainly against the British.
Britain was for Al-Afghani the main opponent whom he had to encounter
again and again, from Afghanistan and India via Persia and Istanbul to Egypt
and Paris. The powers which are now accused in the Near East as 'colonialists'
are generally dismissed in Al-Afghani's paper as 'the greedy ones'. Again and
again Al-Afghani exposes the 'greed' of the European states as the main motif
of the Western 'colonial expansion' which was then in full swing. If one
takes the trouble to pass an objective judgement one cannot say that the Afghan
was completely wrong.

Side by side with the purely political articles there are considerations of a
more general, cultural and cultural-political kind. These articles centre around
religion and the state. Some people have sought to sum up their contents under
the slogan 'Pan-Islam'. They all deal with the fact that 'Islamic civilization' in
its weak and barren state would succumb to the assault of the covetous European state if it were not able to turn with renewed enthusiasm to the religion on
which it was based. With the 'religious' renaissance there also had to be a
'political' one, for the two are always inseparable in the Islamic world. The
strengthening of 'religion' automatically led to a revival of the Islamic state.
Al-Afghani was described as a revolutionary, a conspirator and an agitator in
Europe but, in my opinion, this view is over-simplified. He was striving to give
new life to Islam and 'Islam' is always a state or an empire. As an Islamic
reformer he *had* also to be a politician.

However, it is clear that Al-Afghani was anxious to apply the lever of his
action predominantly to political matters. He did not fight with sermons and

discussions nor did he seek to stir up religious fervour as a dervish but rather worked as a politician, in co-operation with governments when this was possible or as a political controversialist and agitator against those governments which opposed his aims. It is clear from his writings that he was always conscious of the fact that pan-Islam had to be realized on two fronts: one internal, that of the 'revival' of religion and the whole spiritual world of Islam, in which it was essential to build a bridge to modern life, the science and 'progress' of the nineteenth century—and another external, political front on which the struggle was waged against the covetous oppressors from Europe and along which all the Islamic states were to be linked up.

When his periodical was banned Al-Afghani's political career by no means came to an end. But what was to follow had less influence on the Arab countries than his stay in Egypt and his paper in Paris. He went to Persia where a series of ups and downs at the court of Tehran, then in Russia and again in Persia, ended with a 'bast' or retreat in a mosque in the neighbourhood of the Persian capital. Finally the Sheikh was escorted in chains over the Persian frontier by a detachment of cavalry. In Persia, too, a revolution followed shortly after his stay there. The events in Persia have been described in great detail by the British orientalist E. G. Browne in a book (*The Persian Revolution*) which also contains the best appraisal of the great Afghan by any European writer. Jamal ad-Din spent the last years of his life at the court of Abdul Hamid in Istanbul.

The principal result of the appearance of the Afghan firebrand in the Arab countries was that problems and questions were shown in a clear light, problems the existence of which had previously only been dimly felt. Europe and the superiority of the European nations as far as the technique of war, technical processes, organization, commerce and education were concerned had already been 'disturbingly' noticeable in the Arab Muslim world before Al-Afghani, but it was he who first formulated the Europe-Islam relationship as a competitive struggle, indeed as a struggle for the very existence of Islam. It was Al-Afghani, too, who first showed the Arab Muslims that they would be weaker than the Europeans in this struggle unless they revived their own religious, social and national life. Under Al-Afghani's influence evolution and revolution were recognized for the first time by the Arabs as a vital necessity for their states, nations and communities.

Throughout his life Al-Afghani worked for evolution and revolution (by means of religion). Twice he unleashed revolutions but the execution of these revolutions, the attempt to contribute to a real development and to the 'progress' of the Arab nation, was to be left to others.

8

Reform of Islam

AL-AFGHANI'S GREAT PUPIL, Muhammad Abduh (1849–1905), was one of the most important personalities whom the whole world produced in the latter part of the nineteenth century. He was the son of a peasant from the Nile Delta and was sent by his father to the provincial town Tanta for religious studies. Early on he conflicted with the traditional method of teaching there:

I spent a year and a half there (in Tanta) without understanding anything at all because the teaching methods were so bad. Then I became a prey to despair and I thought I should never be successful. I ran away from school and hid myself for three months with my uncle's family. Then my brother found me and brought me back to the Ahmad Mosque and wanted to force me to study. However, I refused and said to him: 'I am sure I shall never apply myself to study successfully. There is nothing for me but to return to my village and till the fields as so many of my kinsfolk do.' This discussion ended in me getting the better of my brother so I picked up my clothing and baggage and returned to our village Mahallat al-Nasr with the intention of never going back to my studies and so got married in 1865.

This was the first time the methods of instruction in Tanta affected me. They are exactly the same methods as those of the Azhar (in Cairo) and 95 per cent of all the students are exposed to this influence, that is to say all those who are not fortunate enough to have comrades who are following another method of instruction. Moreover, most students who understand nothing at all deceive themselves into imagining that they have grasped something. So they continue to learn until they have reached man's estate continuing all the while to live in boyhood dreams. Then the public is afflicted by them, the community suffers from them and great damage is caused by them because all they do is heap one foolishness upon another. They lead astray those who call out for good guidance and by their boasting harm even those who have a certain amount of learning and prevent them from gaining any benefit from it.

The young Abduh was later forced by his father to go back to Tanta again but once more he ran away from the useless teaching in the Mosque, this time to a village where he came into contact with a mystic, Sheikh Darwish. Darwish had been in Libya where he had accepted the doctrines of the

Shadhiliya Order, returning later to his village in Egypt. Abduh relates how this first master of his affected him:

I felt my ego flying into another world, a world quite different from the one I had believed in. What had been narrow for me now became wide and everything in the world I had previously imagined great now became small. Everything that troubled my soul left me all but two single cares: that I might become perfect in mystic knowledge and complete master of my soul.

Mysticism helped the young man to make sense out of his other religious studies but it remained his real field of interest up to the time when he was to meet Al-Afghani at the Azhar. We have already dealt with the work they did in collaboration with each other. When their periodical had to cease publication Abduh turned more and more to the life of a scholar and theologian, leaving politics to others. He taught at the Azhar, worked as editor and contributor to newspapers and in 1899 was appointed Mufti of Egypt. The mufti of a country is the highest authority in matters concerning Islamic Law and the government asks for his opinion (fatwa) when it has to take decisions in questions connected in some way or other with religion.

Muhammad Abduh's life-work was that of a thinker. In *Islam and Modernism in Egypt* (London, 1933), C. C. Adams has tried to present a picture of the mental world in which he lived and to point out the influences he has had on the 'modernist' movements of present-day Islam. One of the Imam's writings, *The Message of the Unity of God*, has been translated into French but, in spite of this aid, it is not easy for a westerner to see in what Abduh's special greatness lies.

Perhaps one can get an inkling of it when one turns to his main work, an enormous commentary on the Koran. This commentary, while following the tradition of Islamic philosophy and theology, contains the deepest thoughts of this 'modernizer' of Islam. We choose an extract, almost at random, from Abduh's *magnum opus*, which he did not live to complete:

Explanation of the verse of the Fatiha:

'Lead us . . . on the path of those who have found favour in Thy Sight, not of those on whom wrath is brought down nor of those who have gone astray.'

Some scholars have explained that 'those who have found favour in Thy Sight' are the Muslims, while 'those on whom wrath is brought down' are the Jews and 'those who have gone astray' are the Christians. But we say that the Fatiha is the first Sura which was revealed. This was the opinion of Imam Ali (may God be pleased with him) and he should know this better than anyone else for he was brought up in the lap of the Prophet (may God bless and give him peace) and he was the first man to believe in him. Even if the Fatiha was not the very first sura which was revealed it is certain that it must have been one of the first.

When the first revelations came down the Muslims had nothing to cling to for their guidance and had no other guidance but the Revelation. They are commanded to beg God to lead them on this path, the path of those 'who have found favour in God's Sight'. The others are on other paths. Clearly what is meant is His word (Exalted is He): 'Those are they whom God guides, so follow their guidance!' (Koran, Surat al-An'am (VI), v. 90, a reference to the patriarchs of the Old Testament).

So those who have found favour in God's Sight are the prophets and friends of God and the martyrs and pious men of former nations. This is indicated by the whole context of the Koran and the rest of the Koran proves it. Are not almost three quarters of the Koran stories about this and directions to learn from the experiences of nations in their disbelief and belief, their misfortune and fortune. Men have no better guidance than examples and facts proved by experience. If we listen to this command and obey it we shall look around us at what has happened to past nations, at the causes of their knowledge or ignorance, their strength or their weakness, their power or their impotence, and at everything that happens to peoples. If we do this these considerations will have an influence on our souls and lead them to seek the best means and the good in the nation which is the basic cause of its happiness and permanence. We shall try to avoid every-thing which is a cause of misfortune, corruption and destruction.

He who has some intelligence can see and understand from this how important the science of history is, and what benefits and fruits it contains. He will be seized with stupefaction and confusion when he learns that many scholars of religion in the Community of this Book (the Koran) are opposed to history in the name of religion. They have an aversion to it and say that history is unnecessary and profitless. How can one not be horrified and stirred up, knowing that the Koran announces that a knowledge of the circumstances of divers nations is one of the most important things demanded by our religion? 'And they bid thee hasten on the evil rather than the good, when exemplary punishments have indeed been meted out before them.' (Koran, Surat al-Ra'd (XIII), v. 6.)

Here we have another problem: How is it that God (Exalted is He) commands us to follow the path of those who have preceded us, whereas we have ordinances and directions previously possessed by no one before us, so that our Law is more perfect and more suitable for our times and for all later times? The Koran gives us an answer to this: it makes it clear that there is only one Religion of God among all nations. The only difference is in the prescriptions according to the various branches of religion which differ from each other as times change. But they do not contradict each other in their basic essentials. He, Who is High, has said: 'Say to the people of the Book: Come to a word which is the same for us and for you.'

He, Who is High, has also said: 'We have sent to you what We previously sent to Noah and the other prophets.'

They all have in common a belief in God and prophethood and that one should desist from evil and do what is good and that one should adopt good customs.

But God has commanded us to take heed how the situation (of earlier peoples) was and to learn from this how they fared. From this we can proceed to build on good foundations. It is a command which contains a hint that salvation and happiness lie in this (history and what is to be learned from it), the method of the Koran being to link those who are led with him who leads them, cause with effect and foundation with what is founded. The details, however, of what is thus generally prescribed are known to us from our Law and from our Prophet (on him be Peace and Blessings). . . .

Every European has long been familiar with the fundamental ideas on which these statements are based. They may be called 'Liberal Theology' and one can easily imagine the smile of disdain which plays around the lips of many a modern theologian when he hears this word. For they know by experience that one cannot 'liberalize' religion without finding oneself on a slippery slope down which man slips and in the long run finds himself without any 'positive' religion. Perhaps they are right. Abduh, however, approaches the question of liberalizing religion from the opposite direction. For him it is necessary to bring his religion into harmony with the facts of a life which already exists.

The modern life of the West has burst into Egypt and it is there with over-whelming force. For long the men of religion turned their backs on it but it is now clear that the 'modern' way of life will prevail and is winning over the best forces in the country whether the scholars like it or not. If religion is to remain alive it must somehow or other adapt itself, collaborate and become up-to-date.

But is Religion not an absolute value? Can one still be a believer when one presumes to 'adapt' God's Eternal Revelation, His Word, as the Koran says, even if this is done to maintain the vitality and actuality of God's Word? Does this not mean that one has already lost all real belief in that Word?

An escape from this dilemma is to be found in 'interpretation'. Every age has a duty, one can say, to come to a new understanding of God's Eternal Word according to the spirit of that age. This is why Abduh's commentary on the Koran is his real life-work.

But it is not so easy to get over the difficulties. What is the 'spirit of an age'? 'Nothing', a theologian of old Muslim school would reply, 'but corruption caused by the long lapse of time since the Prophet and his first followers and by the weakness of man's character. One must strive to reintroduce the conditions of that first period. The age must be adapted to religion'. Abduh forsook this point of view which he saw as hopelessly barren, and discovered his own way by reading the Holy Book. This he sees as a summons to approach the world as it is, to argue with it, penetrate it and learn from it. There can be no contradiction between the commands and views to be derived from the Koran and the knowledge one acquires when one explores the outside world.

What part does the interpreter's desire play here not to see such contradictions and to read 'modernity' into the Koran? There are some quite ludicrous and untenable interpretations in modern apologetic literature and some scholars have done their utmost to prove that inventions like the railway and the telegraph are already to be found *in nuce* in the Koran. Democracy is also said to be a Koranic invention because in a well-known sura we read: 'Take your decisions by consultation one with another.' Such interpreters are not lacking in good intentions; they would like so much to be both 'modern' and 'Koranic' that they become sophistic. It was Abduh's greatness that he did not succumb to this temptation. His arguments are not only logical but also reasonable and bear all the marks of arguments not invented towards an end but produced by a mind for which it is important to understand and to concentrate objectively on 'God's Word'.

At the same time one must not underestimate the pressure to which a 'modern' Muslim is subjected. The onrush of what is new, strange and power-ful is enormous and is too much for many people; these are sorely tempted to go over to 'modernity' by intellectual acrobatics and to persuade themselves that they have always been 'modern'. But only very rarely do they succeed in really persuading themselves and, moreover, no attempt is made to make a deep study of all 'modern' phenomena.

Abduh was able to resist this temptation. His attitude was never 'I already know' but always 'I want to understand'. Faced with the innumerable diffi-culties a mediaeval theologian faces when suddenly confronted with the modern world, he never attempted to argue away contradictions but always made an effort to get far enough beneath the surface of things to that point where con-tradictions disappear.

In our small extract from his great commentary we have followed only one minute argument, but what seems to me important in it is its solidity. To be sure, from the view point of a modernizer of Islam it is *desirable* to emphasize that 'those who have found favour in God's Sight' does not mean only the Muslims and 'those on whom wrath is brought down' not only the Jews, for after all people are being forced more than ever to live together in this 'modern world'. But who dares to assert that Abduh's arguments against these doctrinal views stemmed from the necessity of protesting against 'old-fashioned' doctrinal views. Abduh's arguments are independent, to the point and strong.

Nor did the Imam permit himself to overlook the new difficulty which arises when one accepts his interpretation: 'How can Islam be the "more perfect" religion when it is enjoined on the Muslims to live according to the teachings of prophets of former religions?' The solution of this difficulty again leads him into a 'modern', 'liberal', indeed, 'philosophic' train of thought, by force of circumstance and by consideration of the facts, without the decisive factor being the desire to be modern at any price.

Abduh's great commentary is a strong bridge, built up stone by stone surely and reliably so that the mind of a Muslim reader can pass honourably from a 'mediaeval', absolutist-exclusive religious frame of mind to a conception of religions which includes the modern world. It was his greatness that he succeeded, in a spirit of surpassing objectivity, in uniting 'mediaeval' faith and a 'modern' inquisitive mind without artificial feats of logic or seductive rhetoric.

*   *   *

One other question is how profound an influence Abduh's life-work exerted on the Arabs' intellectual life. Abduh became the precursor of a movement which has been called 'modernism'. One of his pupils, the Syrian *Rashid Rida* (1865–1935), was editor of the periodical *Al-Manar*, which in its time exercised great influence throughout the Muslim world. Throughout his life Rida had the greatest respect for Imam Abduh and to him we owe a very detailed work of reference in three volumes on the life and work of the great Egyptian reformer. He also edited and completed his master's commentary on the Koran. Nevertheless one has to consider Rida's *Manar-modernism* rather as the product of his own spirit; Abduh was only the god-father. It seems to us characteristic of Manar-modernism that as the years passed it confined itself more and more to doing honour to the Prophet's companions and to the Prophet himself as the great examples, and to reject all later 'accretions' to Islam, especially mysticism and its 'excrescences' as manifestations of degeneration. A puritanical movement of 'return to the origins' arose which rejected all kinds of spiritual life that could not be attributed to the Prophet and his companions as impious. Manar-modernism locked itself up in a restrictive religious life whereas Abduh had demanded an open attitude of mind, not 'defence' of religion by 'returning to the origins' but a 'revival' of religion by opening up new spiritual worlds and the 'modern times' the West had just introduced and permeating these with religion.

So Manar-modernism is no longer a living spiritual force of any importance today. Because of its defensive attitude it sank to the level of those classes of the Arab peoples who still lead a traditional Islamic life or who did so until yesterday, the lower middle classes, workers and peasants. These lived until recently in a spiritual world which still seemed intact enough to be worth defending. But the Arab *élite*, those who lead the 'modern' life of the West, from the students to the merchants, from the politicians to the officers and from the civil servants to the technicians and engineers, all of these can do very little in 'defence' of their traditions and their traditional Islamic spiritual world for they already live to a great extent outside these traditions, in the 'modern' world. What they require is not protective walls but bridges by which they can pass over organically from the traditional world from which consciously or uncon-sciously they *derive* to the 'modern' world in which they *live*.

Abduh's life-work was dedicated to constructing such a bridge; but what is strange, indeed tragic, is that few any longer appear to use it. Here we come to a point on which Islamic scholars and observers of political and social conditions in the Arab countries do not quite agree. 'A religion', says the experts on Islam, 'that is capable of producing masterpieces of the calibre of Abduh's works, cannot have said its last word. Just think how often and with what brilliance Islam was able to deal with new circumstances and spiritual con-ditions!' 'We are glad to hear this,' reply the political observers, 'but as far as we can see, religion is becoming more and more of secondary importance. In many nerve centres of the Arab countries where Islam was, just one generation ago, the decisive power which gave pattern to life, such as Cairo or Baghdad, it seems to have become merely incidental. No doubt there are still a few pious men but it seems that Islam as a social force is allowing itself to be pushed aside more and more. It seems to be retreating under attack from nationalism and communism. It is only in the typical areas of retreat that it has any importance as a living social force; in Jordan, on the edge of the desert, in the countryside among the "uneducated" so long as these do not obtain a town education, among the elder ladies in the harems of the middle classes and among the private and retired gentlemen of the old generation. It seems that Islam is often called in by the governments merely as their submissive tool to play a purely propa-gandist role only to be pushed aside when it has done its work, to lead a forgotten life on the edge of the nation's consciousness.' 'You are too impatient,' retort the Islamists. 'A great religion with a tradition and history of centuries behind it follows its own laws. Perhaps a new revival will come. The present atmosphere of political unrest naturally does not make it easy for the masses to come to a new realization of religion but the political storm could one day die down and Islam might survive it.' The politicians will not fail to point out that the political eddies will not necessarily pass away and could very easily end up in a Soviet-materialist channel. Many Islamists concede this, 'but', they say, '*sub specie aeternitatis* the struggle for survival with communism under the pressure of a materialist régime could force Islam to adapt itself really to the "modern" world. Perhaps, during the next two or three hundred years, there will be a most interesting and fruitful struggle between communism and Islam.'

To most political observers such views hundreds of years ahead seem a little too abstract and general. For someone who is endeavouring to get a view of the present-day situation the political observer's point of view is of prime importance; namely that Islam is in retreat before the storming forces of 'modern' life. Communism, materialism, liberalism, nationalism, socialism and laicization, in all possible connections and obscure combinations, determine the intellectual horizon of the leading classes much more than do the traditions and principles of Islam.

This is not altered by the fact that most educated Arabs say that they are Muslims, for in many instances such declarations appear to have little value in practice. One does not get the impression that those who make them think very much about their religion. I have rarely met a student or professor at one of the 'modern' universities who said his prayers. Many of them are more or less consciously ashamed of their religion. They let slip no opportunity of declaring that 'real' Islam has nothing to do with the 'superstition' of the uneducated classes. But, apart from this, they seem to think very little about the positive value of Islam. In general the picture such an educated 'Muslim' draws of his religion is so superficial and incidental that it horrifies even Westerners who themselves are as a rule not exactly distinguished by their highly developed religious culture.

When one sees this state of affairs in Islam's modern life one cannot avoid coming to the conclusion that Abduh's work of uniting modern life and traditional religion has, from the sociological point of view, so far been fruitless. His works are little read and less acted on, at least insufficiently to be an influential force in the life of the Arabs. This appears all the more tragic since Abduh himself was no bookworm. He had a better eye for sociological contexts and for the importance and development of the human milieu than most of his contemporaries; even those who, during his lifetime, were groping to found the 'science' of sociology in Europe.

Abduh himself was aware that he had lost a decisive battle, perhaps the decisive battle, if not as an intellectual forerunner at least as a practical reformer. He did not succeed in revitalizing the Azhar although he exerted himself to do so for years. He had the vision that the Islamic University of the Azhar should be expanded until it comprised all branches of learning in the modern world. He himself showed in his work how the bridge between theology as taught there and the modern sciences was to be built. But Abduh's reform was to be broken even in its initial phases by the resistance of the conservative sheikhs in the Mosque University. The sheikhs never rested until they had finally excluded Abduh from Azhar matters by their intrigues. For them he was an 'unbelieving' sheikh, for he copied foreign customs, asserted that, without a mastery of at least one European language, no one could claim to be educated (the Azhar sheikhs knew no French and read no European books), and was intent on destroying the traditional methods and doctrines. They could not see, what Abduh had understood, that 'modernization' was inevitable and that there could only be one choice: modernization with or modernization without Islam.

The University of Cairo was later to become the symbol of modernization without Islam. It has grown into a gigantic institution with thousands of students and with no connection whatsoever with the Azhar, as a parallel, indeed, a rival enterprise, an import from Europe with no roots in the land in which it stands.

The University of Cairo and similar institutions in Egypt and in Damascus, Beirut and Baghdad are today more important than the Azhar. They turn out the technicians and scientists the state requires so urgently. Their professors enjoy enormous prestige, especially if they are native-born. The Azhar and other less well-known religious institutes vegetate side by side with them. In wide circles they are felt to be anachronisms, unmodern and unhygienic; their students come from the country districts and live the life of despised Kasbah dwellers. They wear the traditional dress of the country folk and of the 'dirty' old quarters of the town, whereas the students of the 'modern' universities set great store by immaculate European dress, for it is this that bestows prestige. One learns nothing 'useful' in the religious institutes; one 'only' becomes a sheikh when one leaves them after years of exacting memory work. To be sure, the sheikhs are still respected and admired by the peasants but they earn very little money and the 'educated' classes tend to laugh or sneer at them.

Several attempts were made to modernize the Azhar after Abduh's death but any renovation could, and even today can, hardly produce anything more than a change in the curricula, reorganization of courses and the introduction of a few lectures on general education into the purely theological curriculum. The 'lay' universities live and flourish—at least in the material-quantitative sense. A fusion of the Azhar and the 'modern' institutions, as Abduh envisaged it, would on the other hand, have pulled theology out into the whirlpool of 'modern' science and would have made it play its part in the problems of modern times.

The separation of the two institutions has driven the Azhar more than ever into a stagnant backwater and even if it is reformed on more rational and modern lines this will never restore it as the centre of Egyptian intellectual life, such as it had been for centuries.

People may here object: 'But do the lay universities not represent an advance on purely theological universities? Is it not desirable and right that they should today be at the centre of Arab intellectual life?' It is not for us to discuss here the value or otherwise of European or American lay teaching establishments, but it is important to point out that the word 'lay' means something a little different in the Arab world from what it means in a Western or European context.

'Laicization' was imported into the Arab countries from the West but has no real roots in the civilization of the lands into which it has been introduced. The same can be said of many related concepts such as 'liberalism', 'objectivity', 'enlightenment', etc. (Apologists for the Arabs and Arab civilization may at this point object that the beginnings of such an attitude of mind became apparent in the nineteenth century but their argument does not affect the context we are dealing with at present: The Azhar of the eighteenth and nine-teenth centuries was so opposed to objective, liberal knowledge that nothing was left but to transplant alien 'modern' institutions *en masse* to Cairo with European teachers and according to a European pattern.) In Egypt or any other Arab country 'laicization' does not have the same cultural tradition as it has in Europe. It does not have the values which it acquired in France, for example, in the course of its development: values such as a puritanical concentration on the object, criticism and self-criticism on the basis of what can be comprehended by logic or established by experiment, a limitation of one's interest in meta-physical matters, which is not the same as disinterestedness in the metaphysical, and humanism in the form of sympathy with one's fellow-men and recognition of their rights, etc.

Only a very little of all that has been transplanted to Egypt by western laicization. That word, as it was understood in Europe, contained undertones which were not necessarily preserved when once it was transported overseas. In Cairo 'laicization' meant indifference towards 'religion and superstition', nothing more. Thereby it denotes a void, something that does not exist. The finer nuances, which have given the word its positive content in European intellectual history, have been lost or are as good as lost on Afro-Arab soil.

This void is also the main feature of a 'modern' Arab university. Not in the sense that there is nothing to learn—there is indeed so much that ought to be learned—but in the sense that students confine themselves strictly to what seems of interest for financial reasons or for reasons of individual or national prestige. What has been called the 'urge to discover' can be found only in a very few exceptional personalities.

The traditional paths of discovery are perishing in poverty and contempt but the 'modern' paths of discovery are followed almost exclusively by those individuals who succeed in isolating themselves from their traditional back-ground and native environment and emigrate to the West spiritually and, if possible, physically too.

Where no discovery and no search for discovery fill the mental vacuum created by a hollow laicization, other forces creep in, doctrines instead of religions, self-confident pseudo-knowledge instead of the search for knowledge. These are the forces that are rampant in the institutes of higher learning in the Arab World, as in few other places. It is at these institutes that the two political doctrines now current in these countries, nationalism and communism, are hatched. Every year they produce thousands of half-educated graduates, many of them imagining themselves better than their 'uneducated' compatriots, because they have acquired some technical knowledge or other, men who are less principled than the 'people' they despise, foreigners in their own country, undisciplined and arrogant 'colonialists' who arrogate to themselves the right to live better than their compatriots, to order them about and 'lead' them, to determine the politics of their country, to take its 'development' in hand and to blame Europe and the West for their failures. . . .

The bonds of knowledge, character, education, a sense of responsibility and self-criticism which make up that whole we call an educated man may, in many cases, have become remarkably loose in Europe, but in the Arab countries they very frequently do not exist at all.

Abduh pointed out and embarked on a tack which would have allowed the 'whole man' in the Near East to 'modernize' himself without becoming a split personality. But up to now Abduh has found no one who really followed him. Spiritually a reform of Islam was achieved by him, but so far it has failed sociologically.

9

Conservative Reformers

IN CONSIDERING THE LAY UNIVERSITIES in the Arab countries we have run ahead of Muhammad Abduh's times. The tone of his period, that before the First World War, is essentially different from the mood of the modern intellectuals and semiintellectuals. The intellectuals of his period were by temperament and descent aristocrats. At the same time they were reformers for, owing to their privileged position as educated men, men who travelled and came into contact with European diplomats, administrators, businessmen and government experts, they realized the necessity of 'modernizing' their country. But many of them were also so deeply rooted in their own civilization and sufficiently aristocratic and experienced men of the world to somehow or other regret that these 'renovations' were necessary. More or less consciously they felt that much of positive value, indeed the very character of their countries, was being jeopardized by these reforms.

In their view it was absolutely necessary that the traditional way of life of the East, and especially of the Arab countries, be reformed politically, culturally and scientifically, but they also sensed the danger that lay in a sterile imitation of European examples, which they knew were not always worthy of being imitated. This fact led them to formulae like: 'One should take what is good from Europe but not allow what is bad to come in.' However childish such statements may sound—they surely forget that civilizations are very complicated and intricate entities which cannot be so easily dissected for such purposes—it is not profitless to read the writings of these men of enlightenment and cultural critics who lived before the First World War. These writings contain something more and deeper than one might expect from their simplifying recipe for adopting a foreign civilization. The best of them are full of honest apprehension; they observe their own country and its manners as well as their western partners and opponents with the same eye for detail. They try to describe, to understand, to find out motives and causes so that their division into good and bad may be well founded.

Muhammad alMuwailihi was the perfect example of such a conservative man of enlightenment or careful reformer. He was descended from an important family of Turkish officers who had been close to the Khedive of Egypt for several generations and had played a decisive part in state affairs. His father had accompanied the Khedive Ismail to Italy after his abdication and the young Muhammad grew up in the ex-Khedive's palace in Naples. He travelled all over Europe on the business of the former Khedive and for his own edification. At the same time he contributed to all the important Egyptian newspapers. His pen described the Paris World Exhibition of 1900 and also produced one of the most detailed descriptions of Mecca, to which he had been invited to be present at the ceremonial opening of the Hijaz Railway which the Germans and the Turks had built.

Muhammad al-Muwailihi has left us a book which can very well be compared to the great works on social criticism of classical Spanish literature, like Quevedo's 'Dreams' perhaps. A 'Pasha' of Muhammad Ali and Ibrahim's time rises from the grave and is taken around Cairo by a modern Egyptian 'Isa ibn Hisham'. In doing so the two have all sorts of adventures and the 'Pasha' continuously asks questions about what all these innovations mean. In this the opportunity is seized to evaluate each single institution. Many judgements are more negative than positive. Muwailihi is at pains not to depart very often from reality. The two-volume work is full of description in rhymed prose and one milieu after the other passes before the observers' eyes. The evaluations are contained mainly in the descriptions of facts and customs, theoretical discussions are sparingly used and it is only towards the end of the book that a general analysis of the causes of social conditions in Cairo and the whole 'East' is attempted.

Isa ibn Hisham related: We had scarcely arrived home (after an evening at the theatre which had deeply shocked the Pasha) when the Pasha went to his bedroom seeking to drive away his grief and care by sleep. I left him in his room as I, too, desired sleep. While I was deep in sleep and swimming in a sea of dreams I suddenly heard the Pasha call to me several times. I got up and went to him and said: 'Here I am!' He told me that he had been thinking so long that sleep had been driven from his eyes, and now he could not sleep. He asked me to spend the night in conversation with him and to help him to kill it by keeping awake. We sat down together and talked about all sorts of things from old and modern times until the night had reached the last stages of her youth and until she made light her veils and cloaks: grey hair appeared at her temples and traces of the dawn were to be seen on her body; she began to despise her necklaces and earrings, her pearls and jewels and removed from her breast every piece of jewellery, the pearly planets and the jewels of the stars. She tore the two Pole Stars from her ears and removed the signet ring of the Pleiads from her finger. Then she tore her wide upper garment and rent her veil, appearing before our eyes like a grey old woman, leaning trembling on the staff of Gemini and trying to draw out the last moments of her existence. Then the twilight wrapped her in its bluish mantle, the morning swathed her in a white sheet of linen and buried her in the belly of nothing. The pigeons rose up above her like mourning maidens; they sighed for her with their cooing and chanting. Then suddenly the funeral gathering became a triumphant wedding, the mourning became song because the day had arisen in the East and because the queen of the full and crescent moons had departed. . . .

The next thing we knew was that our 'Friend' had come to us with the Sun as we had arranged the day before. He asked us how we had spent the night, whether we had slept and rested well. I told him what had happened, how we had remained awake until morning and I told him what we had conversed about and what our minds were constantly preoccupied with. To sum up: The Pasha was still filled with amazement at what he had seen on his journey, things of which there had been no trace when he was alive. He had asked me how things had changed so rapidly and what were the causes and reasons for the spread of so much corruption and disorder. I told him what I knew about it but you, O friend, are in a position to reveal to us the true state of affairs. Tell us what you know of the real causes!

The Friend: The true cause is that western civilization has suddenly burst into the lands of the East and the orientals are blindly imitating the Westerns in all particulars of their life, not submitting to the light of examination, not following any rule or measure and not looking around with clear eyes nor heeding the differences between natures, tastes, countries and customs. They have not separated what is sound from what is false, the good from the bad but have taken it all together and believe they have found their happiness and well-being in it. They imagine that thereby they will have strength and supremacy and have therefore given up all the sound principles, good habits and clean manners they had. They have rejected the Truth their forefathers followed. The foundations are ruined, the pillars are weak and the edifice has collapsed. They no longer have anything to hold on to and are wandering blindly in error, toying with worthless things. They are satisfied with the impermanent whitewash of Western civilization, submitting to the rule of foreigners which they think is the fate decreed for them by God. We have destroyed our houses with our own hands and have become in the East as if we belonged to the West, although their way of life and ours are as far apart as the East is from the West.

The Pasha: That may be so but I do not know why the orientals have taken what is worthless in Western civilization and donned its garments, never thinking of returning to their former sound civilization and culture which are really theirs. . . .

The Friend: I know no other cause than the indifference and remissness, which has followed upon former greatness, and the weakness and decay they have engendered. They did not think about their past and forgot their present state and cared not about their future. They were too unambitious to take upon themselves those hard tasks which their forefathers bore to the last degree, and were proud to undertake. They were quite happy to take over this whitewash of Western civilization, without giving themselves any trouble, without effort and without work. They paid great respect to the people of the West and imagined them to be a class higher than them, so they humbled and abased themselves while the Westerners became mighty and all-powerful.

The conversation goes on. The Pasha expresses the desire to see Western civilization. The three travel to the World Exhibition in Paris, and its wonders fill them with amazement although they also discover its weak points.

In the extract quoted above we have translated the detailed description of the passing-away of night and the daybreak—as well as possible without reproducing the rhymed prose of the original. This description follows the traditional laws of near-eastern poetry. Night is represented as a woman, its ending is described as ageing and new and surprising parallels between a woman, her life and character and night and its ending are discovered. There is an abundance of brilliant ideas and daring pictures and concepts.

Psychologically speaking there is at the root of such poetry—along with a centuries-old tradition of poetry and artistic expression—a feeling that man and nature belong together, held within one frame-work. This makes it possible to move backwards and forwards from a woman to night, from a woman's necklace to the stars in the southern firmament and from the morning twilight to a shroud. We have already spoken, while dealing with classic Muslim civilization, of a basic sense of harmony which this civilization seemed to bear and be characterized by. Muwailihi appears to have retained something of that. No doubt he borrowed the concepts woman=night and stars=necklace from classical literature; nevertheless we feel that his is not a spiritless imitation but that he feels it and so doing is able to invent new variations.

At the same time he asks the most unoriental question about the *cause* of Muslim decadence and answers it in phrases a modern sociologist might well employ. If anyone thinks Muwailihi's analysis does not go far enough or deep enough let him remember that even present-day sociologists with all their learning can in the long run find no other explanation for the phenomena of decadence than 'a certain enervation' or 'a certain weakening of the powers of mental concentration' (that is, unless they belong to the school of materialism).

What is characteristic of a man like Muwailihi seems to us to be that he has both traditions at his command. He still knows something of the old culture of his country and he proves this by writing rhymed prose, and very good rhymed prose at that, and by succeeding in drawing here and there a picture based on 'harmony with the cosmos' which has a living and true effect. At the same time he is a complete realist in the European sense and he is in a position to print an analytical picture, to observe objectively and to present sceptically.

The two types of presentation are opposed to each other. Muwailihi's traditional description unites what is incongruous and unidentifiable in the 'everyday world of realists'. He uncovers the hidden relationship between night and a woman and this is made possible by his knowledge that there is a cosmic harmony between the two. The realistic descriptions of Cairo or Paris his book contains ultimately rest on the fact that the author isolates himself from his 'object'; he stands back from it in order to give a critical appraisal and invents for himself a series of different characters, the Pasha, the Friend, etc., who see and express the same facts sometimes for a second or third time, in order to reach a 'more objective' presentation. The separation of object from subject, the concealment of the observer behind what is observed and the attempt to exclude one's own person are all methods of the West. Al-Muwailihi's book is a work of art because he has succeeded in reaching a balance between the two methods he mastered so thoroughly: the oriental one in which the poet takes part and moves with and mixes up the categories (rhymed prose which advances like waves plays a part in this) and the European one in which he excludes his own person and concentrates on the object while keeping the categories and differences strictly separate (and in this the form of the dialogue makes its own contribution).

But only rarely have the two intellectual types worked together fruitfully in one individual. For this one has to be an aristocrat for whom it was possible to be educated in both worlds and at the same time one has to be extraordinarily gifted and skilful in order to unite the two contradictory views into a whole. The vast majority, even of those for whom this was physically possible, arrived at no synthesis. Rather, they became the first orientals 'with split personalities' in whose minds two worlds struggle with each other—a painful process which occasionally led to a representative of the upper classes abstaining, as far as possible, from every sort of intellectual activity. . . .

The Hour of the Minorities

AFTER HAVING SEEN how an aristocratic Muslim attributed the decay of his country to the fact that the inhabitants of Egypt were trying to take over the 'whitewash of western civilization' without themselves taking any trouble or making any effort, and remembering that Muwailihi's book was primarily about Muslims, we now have to ask: What were the *Christians* of the Levant doing, when even the Muslims seemed inclined to throw over their traditions?

The Christian communities in the Ottoman Empire had been accustomed for centuries to look to the European states to protect and preserve their interests with the Porte. France played the main role as protector of the Near Eastern Christians. France was also the state which exercised this function in the most selfless manner, perhaps even more in the interest of those requiring protection than in the interest of the protecting power (at least up to the moment, immediately after the First World War, when she acquired direct territorial interests in the Levant). Besides France Russia was the great power protecting the Orthodox Christians and knew how to harness these for her plans for expansion. In the half-century of wars with the Ottoman Empire which were temporarily halted by the Crimean War of 1853, the Russian relations to the Ottoman Christians, especially the Orthodox 'nation' among these, helped to a great extent to pave the way to the Ottomans' many and painful defeats. For this reason Russian peace treaties, dictated to the Porte after each new Russian victory, always contained a clause which expressly aimed at strengthening the influence of the Tsarist Empire on the Christian subjects of the Porte.

Britain had early on taken a part in the 'protection' game because she felt she had to stand up to French and Russian competition at the Porte. Association with the minorities in the Turkish Empire provided one of the most important levers by which the 'Eastern question' was kept delicately balanced by the Great Powers of Europe. When the Great Powers were associated with these minorities 'humanitarian' motives were so closely interwoven with 'political' and 'religious' ones that they were almost inseparable. At that time America had no interest in the political struggle of the 'Eastern question' and it is still enjoying in the Near East that capital of goodwill which her missionaries and school teachers were able to accumulate as men with 'no political axe to grind', a capital, which is, however, being rapidly expended.

The great majority of Levantine Christians were drawn into the vortex of the 'Eastern question'. They were influenced by the constantly rising prestige of the Western Powers, especially of that power whose protection their own community enjoyed, for it was, after all, their 'brothers in faith' who had acquired so much power, respect and influence. The anglicized Arab, Edward Atiyah, gives a very vivid picture of the feelings of such a community in a book which traces his own development from a Levantine Christian to an Arab nationalist, then to a British administrator and to an author writing in English:

When the Turko-Italian War broke out in 1911, my mother and I were again living with my grandfather in Beyrouth. The sympathies of the Christian Syrians were entirely on the Italian side. I was then just old enough to take notice of such an event, and from what I heard came to take a keen interest in it. Our detested sovereign Turkey was at war with a Christian power, and naturally I wanted the Christian power to win. I would sit and listen to the war news being discussed in privacy (for no one dared discuss it in public) by my grandfather and his friends, and exalt over the defeat of the Turks. And then occurred the most exciting event in my young life—an event which at once appealed to my sense of adventure, and filled me with the utmost thrills of triumphant joy.

An Italian naval squadron came to Beyrouth in the course of the war, and after a short bombardment sank two Turkish destroyers at anchor in Beyrouth harbour. It was a day in early February. The Italian cruisers were sighted on the horizon at dawn, and the news rapidly spread over the city. I happened to go out of the house after breakfast, on an errand to the grocer's, and soon gathered that there was something unusual in the air. There was a stir and a hum in the street. People who should have been at their work in the town were coming back, walking hurriedly, as if trying to reach their houses before something happened. Some of these stopped for a second here and there to impart hurried information to a friend or acquaintance whom they chanced to meet proceeding on his normal way. Shopkeepers were standing outside their shops, communing quietly with one another, stopping new arrivals from the town to ask questions in an undertone. Some of them who had just opened their shops were closing them again, turning customers away. On everybody's face there was an expression of suppressed excitement, of fearful anticipation. At the grocer's shop I heard one or two words from which I began to understand what was happening, or about to happen. I hurried back home and at the gate met my grandfather, who had been out too and brought with him definite news. An Italian fleet was coming to bombard the Turkish boats in the harbour. It was not likely that the town would be molested, unless the land batteries were to fire at the Italians. In any case the safest thing for us to do was to go to the British School, where we should be under the protection of the Union

Jack. My grandfather had seen the Headmistress, and she had told him that she had received instructions from the British Consul to hoist the flag over the school, in case the Italians were to bombard the town.

A few minutes later my mother and aunts had shut up the house, and we were all hurrying to the British Mission Girls' School, say rather to England's protective bosom for sanctuary, and as we approached it, this school, which I had hitherto looked upon as a school and nothing more, appeared to me as an inviolable fortress, defended by the great might of England, more inviolable than any sacred place of the Middle Ages, defended by the Holy Ghost, could have seemed to those who sought refuge within its walls. I could not have felt safer if I had seen the British Fleet at anchor around its walls. I imagined the Italian admiral spotting the Union Jack as he scanned the horizon with his telescope, and shouting out to his men not to fire in that direction on pain of their lives.

And were we not privileged creatures, I and my mother and my grand/father and aunts, to be admitted into that sanctuary, when so many other people were left defenceless in their homes or were fleeing from the town altogether, seeking refuge inland? Those were the Moslems, whose fear was quite different from ours on that day. We were only afraid of being molested accidentally, by a stray shell that should be unable to distinguish between Moslems and Christians. But we did not fear any intentional injury from the Italians, for they were our friends, since they were Turkey's enemies, and were coming to humble her under our very eyes.

But the Moslems felt differently about it. The Italians were their enemies, the enemies of Islam, since they were waging war on the Caliph. Moreover, it was in consonance with the mentality of those days to imagine that the Italians would raze the town to the ground, or land a force and put the inhabitants to the sword. Hence the Moslems were in a state of panic. Large numbers of them took to cabs and carts, and fled towards the interior. We could see them scuttling away—cartloads of children and women all in black, and men, fleeing from the wrath of the Christian Power. One spectacle impressed me particularly. On our way to the school we met our milkman, a Moslem called Yusef. He was hurrying past, a milk/pail in his hand. He did not take any notice of us. He had a look of panic in his eyes, and was murmuring audibly: 'El Yom Yomak Ya Rasul Allah'—Today is your day O Prophet of God.

Safely installed within walls protected by the Union Jack, within hearing of the Italian guns doing their glorious work, I exulted over the defeat and terror of the Moslems. It was our turn at last to feel exultant; theirs to tremble and flee. The Christian God had after long ages heard His people's prayers.

The bombardment was over by noon. In the evening we went back home and began to hear the details of the action—how the Turkish destroyers were hit, how they sank, how their men perished, details over which I gloated with a sense of triumph unsoftened by any feelings of pity for the slain and wounded, or for their people. And yet I am sure that had I heard of a dog killed in the street outside our house, and his end had been described to me with half that wealth of detail, I should have cried. (Edward S. Atiyah, *An Arab Tells His Story*, *A study in loyalties*, London, J. Murray, 1946; a most instructive and entertaining book.)

Such was the condition of the minorities in the Ottoman Empire, not only of the Christians but also of the other minorities, Shi'ites of all schools, Sabaeans, Yezidis, Druses and Jews who lived within the frontiers of the Empire. Each of these made up a closely knit 'nation' (Millet) with its own spiritual and temporal 'government', its traditions and law. When the Turkish sovereigns began to rely more and more on the Turkish element in the state, when, indeed, they began to transform the state from a feudal structure personally subordinated to the Caliph into a Turkish national state, the religious 'nations' felt that the bonds were broken which had held the old structure together. Their inclusion in the Ottoman Empire was felt to be a merely arbitrary act and they no longer felt any loyalty to the Porte but rather felt free to associate with their brothers in faith outside the Empire. The Porte, for its part, saw its authority over the minorities disappearing and had recourse to violent measures, indeed to massacres, in order to retain a shadow of its authority. Massacres such as those perpetrated against the Armenians in 1893 or the Assyrians, only led to the minorities waiting for the hour of 'freedom' from the 'Turkish yoke' to strike.

At about the same time as the idea of a national state, engendered in the Balkans, began to spread in Istanbul and before it became a reality as a result of the revolution of the Young Turks, we find it appearing in the Arab countries. It was an Arab Christian, *Nejib Azuri*, a former civil servant of the Porte in Jerusalem, who wrote the first important work advocating an Arab national state. His book, published in 1905, has the very formal but nevertheless precise title: *Le Réveil de la Nation Arabe dans l'Asie Turque, en présence des intérêts et des rivalités des Puissances étrangères, de la Curie romaine et du Patriareat oecuménique.*

In those days it was easier for an Arab Christian than it was for an Arab Muslim to anticipate the birth of an Arab national state. The Christian felt no ties of religion to the Porte and to the (Turkish) Caliph. When a congress of Arab nationalists was held eight years later in Paris, we again find it was attended by many Christians. The manifesto issued after the congress contains not a word about religion, neither Islam nor Christianity; it states:

We Arabs in Paris . . . shall show to the nations of Europe that the Arab nation is a living social unity. It is indivisible and has a special place among nations. It occupies a political position of supreme importance and is a power that will have to be reckoned with.

In this, no religious decision was demanded of a Christian but for a Muslim the proclamation of an Arab nation demanded a religious decision, the decision to separate from the (Turkish) Caliph and the Muslim state he ruled. But in both communities, Christian as well as Muslim, it was the europeanized intellectuals who first seized upon the idea of a national state. In the years just before the First World War the great masses of both communities still kept to two separate camps. The Christian villages of Lebanon dreamed of union with France while the Muslims in the hinterland discussed whether the future Arab nation should be joined by federal ties to the Turkish nation, whether one should agree to recognize the Caliph in Istanbul or whether the close collabora- tion of the Young Turk Government with the German unbelievers justified a final break with the Ottoman Empire. The answers to all these questions were not at all unanimous. Even the representatives of the Arab nation at the Paris congress were not all of one mind. They wanted to get rid of the Turks, all were agreed on that; but should not certain regions have a special position even within the Arab nation, like, perhaps, Christian Mount Lebanon which already had a separate administration and had, thanks to its autonomy, developed successfully? Should the Christians demand that their rights be guaranteed?

In a few pages of his book *The Seven Pillars of Wisdom* (Chs. 58 and 59; London, 1935), T. E. Lawrence presents a brilliant survey of the variety of different religious communities and towns in the Levant, which gives some idea of what was peculiar to each one of these immediately before the outbreak of the war.

II

THE ARABS IN THE MODERN WORLD

I

The Founding of the Arab States

WITH THE OUTBREAK OF THE FIRST WORLD WAR the development of the Arab Near East entered an acute political phase. If one had the impression from the period preceding the political Arab Renaissance that the Arab peoples had experienced a new and energetic intellectual development under the Turkish 'yoke' or under the Khedive which had also stimulated certain political developments, the World War brought about a different state of affairs. From then on politics were to dominate the Arabs' thinking and feeling to such an extent that they seem to have determined the course of intellectual development too.

This preponderance of politics over all other fields of human activity made itself felt just when the Arabs won *a part* of their liberty and their right of self determination. The fact that it was only a part makes the lack of the other, certainly more important, half all the more painfully felt. Complete independence which they had not achieved became an obsession and the idea became widespread everywhere that, if only liberty were achieved, all other problems and unsatisfactory situations could be easily solved.

As the Arabs say, the battle for independence now entered an acute phase. Not only what they themselves did, but also what happened elsewhere in the world, was significant to them mostly in so far as it affected their struggle for independence.

The history of how the Arabs achieved semi-independence during the First World War is too well-known to need telling in detail here. *Husain*, the Sharif of Mecca, who was a descendant of the Prophet, an Arab prince and high dignitary of the Ottoman Empire, rebelled against his sovereign in far-off Istanbul. From the beginning of the war he had been in contact with Britain which held Egypt and the Suez Canal against a first Turkish offensive. Supplied with British money and arms the Sharif's revolt broke out in 1916. Among the handful of British specialists, acting as advisers, there was one extraordinary man, T. E. Lawrence, an archaeologist Arabist and romantic genius with self-destructive tendencies, but wonderfully gifted in dealing with the Arabs. He acquired decisive influence over the military leader of the revolt, the Sharif's son, Faisal. The *Revolt in the Desert* became, in Lawrence's own eyes and to a great extent also in those of later Europeans, Lawrence's Revolt.

It succeeded beyond anything that could have been expected. While Allenby's army advanced along the coast through Palestine to Beirut, the revolt of the Arabs mopped up the Arab hinterland from Medina to Aqaba, from Aqaba to Der'a and from there to Damascus (1918).

The Turks remained in occupation of the largest part of the Arab countries for the first three years of the World War, only Egypt being outside their control. Parts of the desert were controlled during the last years of the war by the Beduin armies of the Revolt. Between 1914 and 1917 the British advanced in Meso-potamia with fluctuating fortunes from Basra to Baghdad. It was during the war years that the Turks appeared for the first time indisputably as an occupying power in the Arab countries. In 1908, shortly before the war, the Young Turks had come to power in the Ottoman Empire and had tried to abolish the old Turkish policy of diverse 'religious states', or 'millets', which had previously lived together, each with its own leader and internal administration, and to replace it by a new, 'Ottoman' policy. Each subject of the Porte was declared an 'Ottoman' citizen for which 'honour' he had now first and foremost to perform military service. This had earlier been a privilege of the Muslims. The 'religious states' opposed this abolition of their privileges and not only these, but also the ethnic groups living in the Empire, the Kurds, the Arabs and the Armenians, stirred and began to appear to the ruling Turks as unreliable 'Ottoman citizens'.

Moreover, the Young Turks thought in racial concepts. European 'national' concepts had reached the Balkans and it is significant that the Young Turk movement began in Salonica. They must also have been influenced in this direction by their co-operation with the most national of all European national states, the German Empire. The fact that the Turkish element began to appear more and more as the most reliable element among all the 'Ottoman citizens' had its effect on the racial policy of the nationalists. In practice it amounted to the first-class 'Ottoman citizens', the Turks, being differentiated from the second-class 'Ottoman citizens', the religious and ethnic minorities. The minorities, the largest and most important of which were the Arabs, reacted to this with the increasingly audible desire to separate from this Empire, in which they could be nothing but second-class citizens, and to set up their own states.

The Arabs of today are inclined to make the conditions, which became especially noticeable in the Ottoman Empire after 1900, applicable to earlier centuries too. Most of them still believe that they were subordinated on the grounds of race and nationality during the 'four centuries of Turkish rule'. But the historical facts indicate rather that any real nationalist discrimination only began later and, as far as can be observed, under the influence of European ideas.

Professor Z. N. Zeine of Beirut describes in his clear-sighted book, *Arab-Turkish Relations and the Emergence of Arab Nationalism* (Beirut, 1958), the relations the Turks had with the Arabs towards the end of the nineteenth century and in the Young Turk period. He comes to the conclusion that a sense of Arab nationhood and Arab nationalism only developed later. A first, preparatory period of this development began with the Young Turk Revolution and as a reaction to their nationalism. Arab nationalism only became effective in breadth during the World War, under the pressure of the Turkish occupation and the methods used by the Turkish generals against the (Arab) civilian population. It then grew under the pressure of the European mandates, which were established after the war, into a general movement for emancipation.

What happened in the Arab countries 'occupied' by the Turks during the First World War cannot be imagined in sufficiently horrible terms. If one wishes to be just one should add that conditions in the Turkish territories were not much better and perhaps towards the end of and after the war became even more dreadful as a result of allied and Greek action. Lebanon was no doubt the Arab country that suffered most, famine being widespread in the mountains and terror in the cities. Arab patriots and liberals were executed and the mountains given over to anarchy. It has been estimated that about one third of the mountain population died of hunger in the last two years of the war. The old peasants of Lebanon still speak of those terrible days. 'If smoke were seen rising from someone's chimney,' they say, 'that man could be sure that starving neighbours would break into his house and steal everything eatable they could find. He could consider himself lucky if he himself were not murdered while this was going on.'

Into all the Arab countries there poured a stream of Armenian refugees, 'deported' by the Turks to the 'under-developed' Arab provinces. Only the toughest of these reached Baghdad, Damascus, Beirut and Jerusalem, driven along by Turkish soldiery. Those who died, were shot or beaten to death or ill-treated on the way became drastic examples of what minorities which rebelled unsuccessfully had to expect.

All this makes it understandable why Arab officers of the Turkish Army went over to the enemy, wherever they had the opportunity to do so, and put themselves at the disposal of the 'Arab Revolution'. They even began to organize a regular Arab army. One of the most gifted of those Turkish officers of Arab descent, who risked their lives for the 'Arab Revolution', was *Nuri al-Sa'id* who later became the 'strong man' of Iraq and, after forty years of political ferment, the victim the enraged masses of Baghdad dragged by a rope through the streets. . . .

While the Arab Revolution was taking place in the Arab countries in Asia there was quiet in Egypt. Cairo was a British strong-point and headquarters of operations in the Near East and the Egyptian politicians had to wait until the 'state of emergency' was over in order to raise their demands. It was for this reason that their voices could be heard all the more clearly in 1919.

We, in the West, are accustomed to see what happened then through the eyes of western witnesses. For this reason it is good to give here a description by an Arab; to be sure, it is not less biased than the western description but it shows us a side we generally hear nothing about. Descriptions of this type are also the source from which the young Arabs of today derive their view of history.

In 1882 the English, with the help of Egyptian traitors, condemned us to death, politically. We remained dead until 1919. Then we arose and began to find our way back into history. We made our return to it by means of a revolution with bloodshed and destruction.

All the classes of the nation were in revolt. The peasants, who for four years had been robbed of their crops and many of whom had been deported, hated the English. The middle class, especially the officials, hated them, too, for having deprived them of all functions in political leadership, just as had been the case in the days of Tawfiq, when all leadership belonged to the foreign Turks and Circassians to the exclusion of the native Egyptians.

So the poor classes of the nation and the middle class were all in a state of turmoil, and when the latter assumed the leadership of the revolution the peasants and the workers were ready to follow their lead. After all, patriotic consciousness had never been quite dead since 1882; it had only been asleep. Mustafa Kamil had stimulated it to new life, but his effort was premature, and he was still young when he died, in 1907. After that, there had been a pause, a period of intellectual confusion due to historical reasons, when to many minds it had not been clear whether Egypt was to remain part of the Ottoman Empire or adhere to a league of Islamic nations.

This confusion of thought greatly weakened our patriotism. Therefore it was easy for the English, when the First Great War broke out, to dispose of our state with a simple gesture as if they were gods high up in the clouds, and to proclaim the 'protectorate' of Egypt. Next, they deposed the Khedive, and intended to raise on the throne of Egypt the Sultan Husain in his place. They restrained our freedom of association and writing and they censored our newspapers so that not a word could be printed without their permission.

The majority of the nation was of the opinion that the year 1919 was going to be a decisive one in our history. So thought all those who had lived through and taken part in the 'Urabi Revolt. Sa'ad Zaghlul was the leader of all these. . . .

Sa'ad began to call for a new policy in the country, one of the basic conditions of which would be independence. A wave of rage against the English spread over the land. In March 1919 they arrested Sa'ad and his companions and banished them to Malta. Thereupon the people's anger increased and strikes of students and officials spread. The railways went on strike and telephone and telegraph wires were cut. Then the English permitted the Wafd, that is, Sa'ad and his companions, to go to Paris but at the same time they sent a commission to Egypt under the chairmanship of the hated imperialist Milner. This was to destroy the national movement by bringing pressure to bear on its principal representatives, apart from those who had gone to Paris, until they accepted English rule. The nation was to be scourged with fire and sword so that it should accept English Imperialism and humble itself before it.

The Milner Commission managed to persuade Adli Pasha to begin negotiations with the English, Sa'ad and the Wafd having previously demanded independence for Egypt as part of the general peace negotiations in 1919. Adli Pasha then joined Sa'ad and convinced him that it was necessary to go to London. This happened in May 1920 and changed our position. Sa'ad thought that the other states should have something to say in the question of our independence but Adli Pasha's point of view was narrower: that there should be negotiations with the English only.

Sa'ad and the Wafd then returned to Egypt and he began to stir up the spirit of the people with his speeches and publications. In the meantime Adli Pasha had failed in his negotiations with the English and Sa'ad said of these negotiations that they had been a case of George V negotiating with George V. The strikes spread and the English had recourse to violence. They arrested Sa'ad and his companions and banished them to the Sey-chelles Islands and proclaimed the 'independence' of Egypt on 18th February 1922, stipulating four conditions according to which the English reserved the right to:

Protect the Imperial communications in Egypt,
Defend Egypt against foreign aggression,
Protect aliens and minorities,
Keep the status quo in the Sudan. . . .

In 1923 the Government appointed thirty prominent men who drew up the Egyptian Constitution. Sa'ad and his companions had returned from exile and in 1924 he formed Egypt's first constitutional government.

In the years of the revolution, while Sa'ad and his companions were active, the people were as if intoxicated and a new spirit arose. It was then that the foundations were laid. Students, officials and merchants vied with each other to instil spirit into the populace to stand up to the English and win independence. At that time there were demonstrations by school children and women and even the peasants sabotaged the railways and telegraph lines. All this, however many victims it demanded, helped to awaken and instil new life into the nation. (Salama Musa, Salama Musa's Education, Cairo, 1958.)

The Peace Conference was to give rise to severe disappointments and unrest in the Arab part of Asia, too. The history of the double promises made to the

Arabs who took part in the revolt has been dealt with too often for it to occupy us for long here. The famous Sykes-Picot Agreement which had already been concluded in 1916 provided for the division into two spheres of influence, one French, the other British, of those Arab territories which were to be detached from Turkey. What was to be understood by a sphere of influence was never laid down. The Sharif of Mecca received promises from Cairo that he could keep those Arab territories which fell to him during the revolt, along with an obscure formula according to which the rights of France in the Levant, the rights of Britain in Palestine and also the right of the Jews to a 'national home' in Palestine were to be preserved. The Jewish claim to a 'national home' was based on the likewise much discussed 'Balfour declaration', a promise given in 1917 by the British Foreign Secretary, Balfour, to Lord Rothschild, the president of the Federation of British Zionists.

Faisal, Sharif Husain's son, was present at the Peace Conference at Versailles as an 'observer', but his visit was kept so well under control that he went on a trip to the battlefields in the Ardennes on the very day on which the Peace Conference discussed the Arab questions! Lawrence felt himself betrayed by the diplomats as he had given the Arabs his personal word that they would receive 'their' Arab kingdom. He resigned from the army as a protest. It was in Versailles that the idea of 'mandates' was born and the Allies proceeded to translate the spheres of influence promised to France and Britain into mandates. Palestine and Iraq became British mandates and Lebanon and Syria French ones. All that was left to the Arabs was the Arabian Peninsula, and this in its turn was divided up among several tribal chiefs who had to reach some sort of understanding with the British who were dominant in the whole area.

The future of the former Turkish Liwa of Mosul, the northern province of present-day Iraq, was especially uncertain. Was it to be conceded to Syria, to Turkey or to Iraq? Or should it form a separate state? Although an investigating commission, the Crane Commission, came to the conclusion that the majority of the population of that province, Kurds in the mountains and Arabs, Assyrian Christians and Yezidis in the plain, demanded their independence, the Liwa was in the end given to Iraq (and thereby to Britain). This decision was the first step in a bloody tragedy which has not yet come to an end.

The Arabs consider this division of their lands among the victors of the First World War a betrayal. They insist that an Arab kingdom was promised to them, that they liberated themselves, to some extent by their own efforts, from their Turkish overlords and that they remained loyal to the allies in the World War, only to be made 'subjects' of the victors when the war was over.

The Western Allies can quote all sorts of separate points in their defence. One is that they honestly believed that the Arabs were not in a position to rule themselves. This could be true in so far as a series of revolutions, revolts, and even massacres would probably have broken out in the Arab countries, had the allied occupation troops not been there to see that 'peace and quiet' were maintained. However, one has to admit that even this state of 'peace and quiet' was not maintained without massacres. And today, now that we can look back on developments up to and beyond the Second World War, we know that those revolts and troubles, which were at that time suppressed, were bound to explode a generation later under much higher pressure and in circumstances much more dangerous for international peace. They are still doing so.

In addition the West refers to the 'benefits' which have been conferred on the Arab countries under its administration. What is meant thereby is that a more or less civil administration was set up in these countries, roads built and hospitals opened, that economic development was to some extent cared for (up to a limit where the interests of the 'motherland' remained of first importance), and that schools and universities were opened. This has all to be taken *cum grano salis*. It is also good for the Europeans to be reminded that the 'mandated territories' *paid* for all these benefits which were financed from local taxation. The Arabs believe that they paid very dearly for them and that the same amount of money would have produced much more, had they not been compelled to accept those services and goods which the mandatory power forced upon them. . . . From this point the argument becomes unreal and all sorts of hypotheses are made. The West might answer: 'If the Arabs had had a free hand to spend their own money this would have resulted in nothing but an enormous mass of corruption.' To which the Arabs retort: 'The corruption which existed was brought about by the mandatory powers which were compelled, in order to carry out their "exploitation", to collaborate with the most corrupt and character-less elements in the country and to set them up as puppet governments' . . . and so on. There is no end to such discussions. If one tries to stick to facts one must admit that the Arabs exaggerate enormously the misuses of the mandatory authorities, that they see bad and treacherous intentions everywhere, whereas it was often just a question of incompetence, and that they are inclined to ignore those colonial officials who really devoted the best of their knowledge and conscience to their tasks—however limited such knowledge and conscience may have been in many cases. The Arabs are inclined to belittle the initiative, intelligence and enterprise of individual Europeans in the mandated territories. To be sure these brought the Europeans wealth and well-being but they also provided the Arabs with certain new enterprises and institutions. On the other hand it is clear that no mandatory administration *per definitionem* could care so well for the welfare of a mandated territory as a *good* national administration could have done.

In practice a mandatory administration was provided by the 'motherland' and could not avoid putting the interests of its own country before those of the mandated territory whenever the two came into conflict. The 'best' mandatory officials in the eyes of the 'motherland' were no doubt those who were incapable of recognizing that the interests of the mandated territory and the mandatory power really conflicted or those who were always able to suppress any doubts that might arise in their minds.

In all this the Arabs have the benefit of the doubt. One can argue that they themselves would not have been in a position to set up a 'better' administration than the one imposed on them by the mandate system. But one must admit that they were never given the opportunity to try to do so. On the other hand the abuses of the mandatory administration (whether these be 'important' or 'unimportant') are not just hypotheses, but facts.

Then there is the more philosophical argument: What is a good administration? Perhaps, after all, it is the one those who are administered themselves desire, even if an administration according to foreign standards might work 'better'.

Another line of defence in the West is the question: 'What were the *real* wishes of the *people*?' Here, too, we have many 'honest' and upright colonial officials and experts who have been able to persuade themselves and others that 'in reality' the 'people' and the 'great majority' *wanted* to be administered and guided by them. However, the facts speak for themselves; no mandatory power ever dared to carry out a clear plebiscite either for or against the mandate principle.

*   *   *

Let us turn away from speculations and return to the history of the mandates, against which the Arabs were opposed from the very beginning. Palestine and Lebanon found it easiest to submit to the inevitable. In Lebanon this was partly due to the feelings of anxiety of the religious minorities (Christian churches, Druses and Shi'ites), an anxiety they had received from their forefathers and which was not altogether unfounded. Likewise there was the old tradition according to which France was the special protecting power of the Christian minorities. Palestine, too, was a country with strong Christian minorities and with long established connections with Europe. In this context one should remember that Lebanon and Palestine, owing to their old connections with Europe, were by far the most educated of the Arab states.

Egypt possessed the two largest and most highly 'westernized' Arab cities, Alexandria and Cairo. But Egypt was, and still is, outside its two centres of culture and commerce, a huge 'agricultural slum'. Palestine and Lebanon were the only two Arab countries which had produced an educated middle class of professional men and intellectuals spread over the greater part of the country and in both of these the percentage of illiterates was much less than in the other Arab countries. Only in Palestine and Lebanon did there exist something like living and active village communities, led by citizens who were proud of their village or little provincial town and were attempting to develop it.

These two coastal countries were 'educated' enough to accommodate themselves to the superior power of the mandatories. Their leading men knew enough about the true ratio of power to recognize that not much could be achieved through armed revolts. Many of these people perhaps had enough trust in the mandatory powers, to whom after all they owed much of their education and general outlook on life, to hope that they would in time prove to be open to reasoned argument (a trust which was to be justified by later history to an astonishingly small degree). In the case of Lebanon there was really a relatively peaceful development, broken by only occasional uprisings and demonstrations, but just in so far as these were necessary to remind the mandatory power from time to time that no one was thinking of putting up with it 'indefinitely'.

In Palestine peaceful evolution was seriously disturbed in the latter years of the mandate by the question of a 'national home for the Zionists' and had finally to be completely interrupted and abandoned.

Things were much more turbulent in Syria and Iraq. The British had persuaded the French in Versailles to install Faisal, the commander-in-chief of the revolt and son of the Sharif of Mecca, as 'king of Syria' in Damascus. However, Faisal proved to be a king little to the French liking, for he wished to rule. A few months after his installation he was driven out of Damascus by French troops (25 July 1920).

Bitter fighting took place between the French troops and Syrian insurgents and the Druses of the Jebel Druse. Finally, after a war lasting for two years, 1925-7, and involving the whole of Syria and after massacres in the Damascus oasis and in the Jebel Druse, the French were able to impose their authority. A part of the Druse fighting men under the Emir Al-Atrash took to the desert and sought refuge in the neighbouring districts of Transjordan and Arabia until the French should leave Syria. After Faisal's eviction the real power in the country was the French High Commissioner in Beirut. It was he who controlled the operations of the French troops and of the so-called 'troupes spéciales' which was a professional unit of Beduins under French officers. These troops were the last argument in all 'political' discussions. There were many crises and once, in 1936, a 'state treaty', such as the British employed, was almost concluded between the mandatory power and the people who had been put under her protection. This, however, came to nothing at the last moment because the authorities in Paris regretted the concessions they had made, whereas the Syrians themselves could only be persuaded by all sorts of manipulations to accept the treaty as a temporary measure which still did not seem to grant them sufficient liberty. 'Parliaments' were elected and 'governments' appointed although everyone knew that the real power of decision lay with the military and the High Commissioner. It was only after the Second World War and under British threats to fire on them that the French could finally be persuaded to hand over the 'troupes spéciales' and thereby the real power of government to the Lebanese and Syrian governments.

In Iraq there took place much earlier, in 1920, a rebellion against the British government which spread over the whole country. The British fell into line; they gave up the idea of a colonial administration and connection with India and showed that they were prepared to conclude a state treaty with Iraq, that is, to recognize her independence, at least in theory, and to give her a government which would be assisted by British 'advisers' and experts and the presence of British troops.

The then Colonial Secretary, Winston Churchill, decided that Faisal should be installed as king for, after all, much was owed to him and great promises had been made to his house. A 'plebiscite' was held but first, so that this plebiscite should run according to plan, the Iraqi candidate, Saiyid Talib, had to be removed for he had the greatest following in the country. So he, who was at that time Minister of the Interior, was banished to Ceylon. One British official in Iraq who saw the Faisal operation at close quarters, found it so unethical that he tendered his resignation. This was H. St John Philby who later became the friend and consultant of King Ibn Saud.

One cannot avoid the suspicion that the British had a further reason to prefer Faisal, who was foreign to the country and to whom they owed a debt of gratitude, to a native candidate for the throne: it was clearly easier for them to support Faisal than to hold a strong, Iraqi king in check.

The Arab state of Jordan owes its existence almost to chance: in 1921 Sharif Husain's youngest son, the Emir Abdullah, marched against Syria to avenge the insult the French had offered his brother Faisal and, probably, just to try his luck. The British managed to halt him at the present-day Syrian frontier with promises to give him his own emirate in the region on the east bank of the Jordan, which was already occupied by his forces, namely Trans-jordan.

The Emir received sovereignty over this desert territory and concluded a treaty with Britain, undertaking to accept British protection in foreign affairs and to keep order in his territory so that Palestine should no longer have to suffer from marauding Beduins. The capital of Transjordan was at that time a village inhabited by Cherkesses and Emir Abdullah held court in his black Beduin tents in the hills above. In 1946 Transjordan became a kingdom and in the Palestinian war Abdullah fell heir to those parts of Palestine which the Israeli armies were not able to occupy, the pockets of Hebron and Nablus along with the old city of Jerusalem. Thus Transjordan became Jordan.

The only Arab state of modern times, which developed outside the formative 'influence' of the victors in the First World War, was Saudi Arabia. In British eyes the Arabian Peninsula had fallen to Husain, the Sharif of Mecca and they would have liked to see him extend a sort of hegemony over the Beduin chiefs of the whole peninsula, but fate was to decree otherwise. Ibn Saud, the unknown son of a petty prince of Najd (the eastern part of the peninsula), who had been driven out of his domains by a rival and was living as a refugee in Kuwait, won back his ancestral capital, Riyad, in a surprise attack in 1902. He was able to remain neutral during the World War but on good terms with the British and in the years after the war he built up again the old Wahhabi empire of his forefathers not only by conquest but also by a purposeful policy based on the Wahhabi religious brotherhoods, settlement plans, battle formations and propaganda.

The old Wahhabi Empire had been gradually built up by an ancestor of Ibn Saud's in collaboration with the religious reformer, Muhammad ibn 'Adb al-Wahhab (1703–91). This reformer had been driven out of his own land because he had preached a purified form of Islam in which only God was worthy of veneration. He had sought to abolish the cult of saints, Sufi practices and the decoration of mosques as being contrary to the Spirit of Islam. His followers, the Wahhabis, were to return to the pure basic principles of Islam and live strictly by these. Attendance at public prayers in the mosques was made obligatory and smoking condemned as a sort of mild intoxication. By 1806 the Wahhabis had conquered almost all the towns in Arabia but Muhammad Ali's troops wrested their empire from them and destroyed their capital after long and bloody fighting.

In the early 'twenties Ibn Saud came into conflict with the Sharif of Mecca who, as Prince of Mecca and descendant of the Prophet, even laid claim for a time to the Caliphate and was not at all disposed to leave the eastern part of Arabia to a 'heretic'. There were two short wars, in 1919 and in 1924, which ended in the Sharif's complete defeat. Mecca and Medina were occupied by Ibn Saud's troops and so present-day Saudi Arabia was born.

2

International Policy in the Years
between the Wars

AFTER THE ARAB STATES had been formed and the troubles of the early years
had died down, each country gradually began to build up its own internal
political structure. The administration was set up according to a French or
British pattern and, indeed, was to a certain extent successful as a simple copy
of a European example. However, this order which was introduced by foreign
advisers does not tell us much about the political development of the Arabs
themselves in their new states.

It was different with the *parties* which the Arabs began to form. These were
their own creations and were often founded in a spirit of opposition to the
mandatory authorities or to the dominant 'mother power', with the expressed
aim of mobilizing the Arab forces against the foreigners.

Roughly three 'generations' of Arab parties can be recognized. Two of these,
the generation of 'machine or business parties' and that of 'authoritarian parties',
were founded in the years between the two wars. The third generation, that of
the 'propaganda parties', is a creation of the period after the war and will be
dealt with later. We call them 'generations' because each of these three categories was born within a fixed period of time, although their life-span has
been very different according to the various countries and according to their
social conditions.

The 'machine or business parties' of the first generation are overgrown bodies
in which the old feudal world combines with the 'modern' world of finance.
They are formed around a local 'boss', a great landowner, the richest and most
energetic man in a certain district, who often bears a small 'title of nobility':
Pasha, Emir, Sheikh (in Lebanon), etc. Their 'members' are on the whole
simply the influential man's peasants. They vote for him in political elections
and expect him to treat them well, to help them to get certain advantages or
simply to let them till 'his' soil, if he is successful in the elections. In particularist
lands like Lebanon, Syria and pre-revolutionary Iraq each 'boss' fights his own
battle. He has himself elected to parliament by using his 'clients' as voters. Only
occasionally do several 'bosses' unite to form a section of the parliament which
they then call a 'party'. In this case what arises is a loose structure in which

several local bosses wish to pursue a common aim, to work against a common enemy or to assist a common friend to come to power.

In a centralized country like Egypt the individual 'bosses', who were practically all landowners, tended to come together into rather large and stable organizations. They gathered into large groups under a patriotic slogan, originally no doubt through perfectly honest if somewhat superficial and idealistic enthusiasm. One 'boss' is made the leader of the 'bosses', a party fund is opened and a party organization developed. The aim of such a consolidated party is to get the reins of government, at first in the hope of being able to realize its ideals: the evacuation of the British, union with the Sudan, etc. As the years passed and it became clear that these aims could not be realized in the face of Britain's superior power, the groups contented themselves more and more with exploiting the financial possibilities offered them by their participation in the government. So the party gradually developed into an instrument of political poker. Money was spent on propaganda, bribery, the purchase of votes, news-papers and the subvention of clients and party hangers-on, in the hope that such monies spent would be recovered (of course, with the highest possible margin of profit) when governmental power had been acquired.

The game soon became so difficult to understand that it could only be played by full-time experts, the 'politicians', and in a short time stakes became so high that the 'parties' which put up and shared in these stakes grew into huge structures covering the whole Valley of the Nile. The largest of these Egyptian 'machine parties' was the *Wafd* which had been created by Sa'ad Zaghlul during the Revolution after the First World War. It soon became a 'business party', always in an idealistic guise, and remained one of the main powers in Egyptian political life until 1952 when Nasser's revolutionary junta suppressed it along with all the other parties. Other parties vied with it for the golden apple of governmental power: the Destur, the People's Party, the Sa'adists and so on.

In those Arab countries which were not centralized the stakes were not so high and for this reason the 'parties', that is, the individual 'bosses', each one of whom aimed at finding a place for himself and his men in the government and administration, were all the more numerous. Here, too, money played an important part. Votes had to be paid for and clients satisfied. This money could then be recouped in the government or in executive or political jobs. Family politics played a direct part in this system. A man's most reliable 'clients' and 'protégés' are always the members of his family and whenever a man as head of the government or as a minister could not himself recover his outlay he saw to it that the profits went to a cousin or son-in-law.

In these districts, too, 'politician' soon became a profession and, indeed, often developed into an hereditary family prerogative. One was initiated into the mysteries of 'politics' while still a child, one learned how to deal with one's 'clients' with the right admixture of tact and strictness, one learned how to weigh correctly one's 'business friends', how to put the right amount of pressure on them or entice them with the right rewards and one learned how to cultivate one's friends inside the government and to 'support' them (for government salaries are so small that one would starve, if one had to depend on that alone). At the same time one perhaps studied law or managed a part of the family estate, one perhaps travelled to Paris or London and waited for the stars to enter the constellation under which one could become member of parliament for 'one's' village, chair-man of an important parliamentary commission, minister or Prime Minister.

In Lebanon, which contains nothing but minorities, this system achieved its fullest blossoming and was supported by an economy which was developing upwards owing to the industry and intelligence of the country's inhabitants. Lebanon avoided all too violent tensions and never came under the complete dictatorship of any one group of interests. In these circumstances the advantages of the system were able to prove themselves: periodical elections distributed huge sums of money among the masses of the electors and the state was a sort of 'leasehold estate' occupied in turn by the various leading families of the feudal, ethnic and religious groups. The 'leaseholders', as a professional group, showed enough realism not to reduce the state to unproductivity, but rather saw to it that a certain measure of productivity and soundness was maintained. If anyone did not respect the rules of the game he would be pushed aside by an *ad hoc* coalition of his rivals after having held the 'lease' for a certain length of time.

The disadvantages of the system also became clear. These seem to us to be more of a spiritual than of an economic or political sort. In such a system money is the goal of all ambitions and the standard by which all success is measured and beside which even the satisfaction of the urge to power takes second place. Spiritual aims, ideals and emotions run the danger of being smothered by the introduction of this tendency to measure everything in money.

This system of 'business politics' was broken into by the emotionalism of the 'authoritarian parties', the second generation of Arab parties which began to appear in the late 'twenties although the period when they really flourished was the 'thirties up to the Second World War. That they were modelled on European Fascism is clear from their ideology and their organization but one should be careful not to brush these parties aside as 'Fascist', for even in Europe we have had German National Socialism, Italian Fascism, the Spanish Falange, etc., which should all be kept separate. The parties of this second generation can only be understood if each one of them is considered as a special phenomenon, each in the social and political context of its country.

The Arab forms of Fascism frequently grew out of youth movements and many of them always retained something of the 'Scout Movement' about them. The enthusiasm of youth for patriotic nationalism, semi-military, uniformed and centrally directed movements has to be understood against the background of the 'business and machine parties' of the first generation. It was partly a reaction against the cynicism, egoism and businessman's mentality of the professional 'politicians'. The leaders of the new movements were not 'politicians' like these but generally men of the middle class, from the youth organizers of 'clubs' and 'unions'. The growth of such a patriotic union into a 'movement' made them, overnight and almost against their will, political 'bosses' of a new type.

The members of their movements were primarily schoolboys, students, young men of the lower middle classes, apprentices, young employees and minor officials. The new parties recruited their members predominantly from the new middle schools which were increasing greatly in number just at that time.

These 'movements' participated in the general agitation against the mandatory powers. They provided 'strikes', as held in the East, with pickets and agitators. After every such 'strike' and during every crisis and period of unrest the 'movements' gained new members and new esteem. These frequent 'strikes' were by no means social and economic struggles; they had a political character and were demonstrations against the occupying power or against the European powers in general. By persuasion and threats the 'nationalists' forced as many shops as possible in an Arab capital to close and large sectors of the local industry to be brought to a stand-still. Processions of demonstrators went through the streets and shops which remained open were in danger of being stoned. The favourite targets of such demonstrations were the European embassies, especially the British and French ones, which were also stoned whenever possible. A large part of the population approved of these 'demonstra-tions', especially if they did not last too long and did not cause any serious set-back to trade in the bazaars and economic life.

It was the new 'movements' which provided the activists who took part in the demonstrations, forced the bazaars to close and, where necessary, fought it out with the police. Their intellectuals were the orators who moved the masses. They had their own newspapers which they brought out in an amateur-like fashion. They were the aggressive element in the nationalist press and the less material interests they had behind them the more violent was their language. On the other hand the great newspapers of the East which were well-established institutions could not afford to annoy the governments or the mandatory powers to the point where they might be confiscated or suppressed.

These 'movements' arose and died out in the various Arab countries under the most diverse names. There were the 'Green Shirts' in Egypt, the 'Young Men' (Futuwwa) in Baghdad and Mosul, the 'White Shirts' and the 'Steel Shirts' in Damascus and Aleppo, the 'Phalanges' in Lebanon, militant 'socialist' groups in Syria, the 'PPS' (Parti Populaire Syrien) in Syria, Jordan, Lebanon and Iraq, the 'Najjade' in Lebanon and, more important than all the others, the 'Muslim Brothers'.

The more important of these movements which managed to continue to exist after the Second World War not only preached an indefinite, if enthusiastic 'nationalism', but also developed a definite ideology with concrete political aims.

The Lebanese *Phalange* was founded in 1936 and is led by Pierre Gemayel, a pharmacist of Christian Lebanese origin, who is at present Lebanese Minister for Public Works and Social Affairs. The 'Phalanges' are a nationalist Lebanese party which advocates the establishment of a modern, socialist inclined democracy on the Western pattern in Lebanon. It stresses Lebanon's links with the West and is ready to co-operate with the 'other Arab countries' but only if it is a question of co-operation between equals and on an independent basis. The Phalanges are prepared to meet with arms any attempt to transform this co-operation into any sort of Islamic predominance. In theory the movement is open to nationally minded Muslims but in practice its members are almost exclusively Christians. Towards the end of the mandate the Phalange fought street battles with the 'gendarmes' and was a factor in gaining independence for Lebanon. During the civil war of 1958 the Phalange supported the constitutional and pro-western President Chamoun and when, after American troops had landed and his period of office had come to an end and the pro-Arab forces in the country seemed to be winning the day, it started a counter-revolt which in the end led to the establishment of a new balance between pro-Arab and pro-Western (roughly, Muslim and Christian) forces in the country.

The Phalange's party centre in Beirut reminds us in many respects of the boy scout clubs of our youth; in it earnest political and economic experts, who are thoroughly versed in Lebanese conditions, hold their meetings and discussions connected with the party programme. In a new reception room, the only one in the centre, Minister Gemayel receives the country's industrialists and dignitaries. Parades, assemblies of the youth organization and ceremonies of all sorts are held in the courtyard; by torchlight oaths are taken by the flag, women's groups meet and delegations from the mountain villages are received.

The PPS (Parti Populaire Syrien), today officially renamed the PSP (Parti Social Populaire) is a party of a most headstrong kind. It was founded in 1932 by Antoine Sa'ade, a Syrian Christian, who was Professor of German at the American University in Beirut. Its aim is to unite 'Greater Syria' into a modern, lay and nationalist state. 'Greater Syria' comprises all those lands which were once ruled by the Assyrians; Lebanon, Syria, Jordan, Palestine, Iraq and even Cyprus. The PPS believes that these countries form one ethnic unity to which Egypt, as a part of Africa, does not belong.

For them the cult of a greater Syrian motherland has a mystic, religious character although they themselves insist on the rationalism and 'scientific nature' of their national and political theories. Blood and fighting are an important element in this mystique. Every member of the party must be ready to be called up sooner or later for 'action', that means for the defence by arms of his political ideals. They have special training centres where the use of hand grenades, machine pistols, rifles and explosives is taught. In PPS circles it is

believed that a Greater Syrian motherland can only be achieved after Syrian soil
has been soaked with the blood of its sons. The party is proud of having both
Muslims and Christians in its ranks, the only political party in the Near East, so
they say, which has.

As was to be expected, the history of the PPS is a bloody one.

From 1932 to 1935 the party was a secret society and when, after 1935, it took
the stage openly its founder was regularly thrown into gaol by the mandatory
authorities whenever trouble broke out in Beirut or Damascus. Sa'ade left the
country in 1938 and did not return to Beirut until after the war. However,
the party continued to grow during his absence, recruiting its members from the
students, pupils of the middle schools, young artisans and business people.

In 1947 Sa'ade returned to Syria and began again to agitate and build up
cells. In 1949 he tried to get control of the Lebanese government by a *coup d'état*.
The putsch failed and Sa'ade fled to Syria but was, contrary to the usual
practice in the Near East, handed over to the Lebanese by the Syrian Government. He was shot under martial law.

The party rose again and was accused of a series of political attentats in
Damascus. It suffered and is still suffering severe persecution in Syria. In
Lebanon, however, the PPS achieved something like the favour of the Government by helping Chamoun's new government to bring about the fall of the
previous government of Bishara al-Khuri which had had Sa'ade shot. It was not
officially recognized as a party but had one member in the Parliament and was
in a position to keep its training camps and to carry out its armed exercises more
or less openly in the mountains.

The PPS played a decisive part in the Lebanese crisis of 1958 shortly before
the American landings for it was its 'volunteers' who stopped the Druse march
on Beirut while the army observed the fighting from a distance.

The PPS is opposed to Arab unity under Nasser's auspices for it is of the
opinion that the Egyptians are not 'Syrians' and have no business in a 'Greater
Syria'. Their supporters, who are violently anti-communist, also reproach
Nasser with having opened up the way for the communists to the Near East.

Encouraged by the detachment of Syria from Nasser's United Arab Republic
in September 1961 the PPS attempted a further *coup d'état* in Lebanon on
New Year's Eve 1961. It attempted with the aid of two army captains and their
men to occupy the War Ministry in Beirut, to arrest President Shihab, to intern
the leaders of the forces and in this way seize power. In this the party had
completely misread the general political situation in the country. Their attempt
failed, the soldiers who took part in the attempted putsch and the whole cadre
of the party were arrested and brought to trial in the summer of 1962. Whether
the PPS will be able to survive this setback only the future can show.

The most interesting of all the parties of the second generation is without
question the *Society of Muslim Brothers*. In its case there was no imitation of

foreign, mainly European Fascist organizations but rather something that grew directly from the Muslim soil of Egypt. The 'Brothers' were founded in 1928 by an Egyptian teacher Hasan al-Banna.

There is no doubt that Hasan al-Banna was an exceptional man. Since his youth he had devoted himself to setting up and leading 'clubs' and 'societies', and had come into contact early on with the popular mystics of the traditional religious life in town and countryside and also with the fundamentalist reformers or advocates of 'original Islam' and a return to the early 'pure' decades of their religion, a movement which has often been given the comprehensive name of the 'Salafiya' (=followers of the early, 'orthodox' Caliphs). Hasan al-Banna possessed in a high degree the gift of inspiring and leading his fellow men by his oratory. He was extraordinarily well-read in Koranic and religious literature and knew how to bring out his gift of oratory in his own writings.

He founded the first society of Muslim Brothers in Ismailiya where he was then living and the movement was from its inception more than political but at the same time not unpolitical. In this it followed the traditional Muslim articles of belief according to which politics and religion cannot be separated. The 'Brothers' met together to maintain the Islamic values and precepts of the Koran. The mosque of their village or quarter was their place of assembly and the members of the brotherhoods were generally simple people, workers, dwellers in the Souks, peasants, small shopkeepers, minor officials, simple people to whom the Islamic religion was near and dear, presenting no problem. It was this very inability to see any problem that was in time to prove one of the greatest weaknesses of the movement. It was enough to live an Islamic life and promote Islam, but no one asked himself, which Islam? It seemed to be laid down in the Koran, in the life of the Prophet, in the Sacred Traditions and the traditional laws. These theological data had simply to be accepted in their 'purity' and fought for determinedly, thought the Brothers, and one could not go astray, for one was surely doing God's Will.

Thus they contradicted such prominent Muslim intellectuals as Muhammad Abduh who quoted passages of the Koran in support of his opinion that: 'One of the most important tasks a Muslim is faced with is to concern himself, to ponder, investigate and strive (*Jihad*=striving is a keyword) to grasp the meaning of Islam.' On the other hand the brothers stressed that they did not want to be 'philosophers'. For them 'Islam' was a fact that had simply to be 'accepted'. To ask questions about its deeper meaning, to try to 'understand', appeared to them not only unnecessary but even dangerous. In this way one could lose one's faith.

So the Brothers turned away from the spiritual and intellectual part of their religion and at the same time too from the intellectuals of their country. Their movement was destined to remain a movement of the common people and it was on this rock that it was to break in the end.

This deficiency was not to be so apparent in the beginning as in later years.

The Brothers concentrated on practical works, on prayer and Koran reading. They believed they could, indeed must, spare themselves intellectual effort but in the practical field they were remarkably successful. Their societies spread quickly over the whole country. They opened schools, soon possessed wide business interests and published their own newspapers. Around 1946 the number of members in the Valley of the Nile was estimated at two millions and each member was in contact with many sympathizers so that they can really be estimated at between six and eight millions. In the whole of Egypt only the Wafd could count upon an equal number of supporters.

For a long time the brotherhoods played no direct part in politics, but confined themselves to issuing instructions to their members. In their relations towards the unbelievers, their power, their unislamic methods of government and economics and their social and political ideals, the brothers were advised to adopt an attitude in conformity with the religious precepts of the Koran and the Tradition —as the Brothers understood these. A prayer, composed by Al-Banna for use by the Brothers, runs as follows:

> O God, Master of the worlds, security of the fearful, Humbler of the proud, Subduer of the tyrants, accept our prayer, answer our plea, grant us our rights, and restore to us our freedom and independence. O God, these British usurpers have occupied our lands, denied us our rights, tyrannized our country, and increased the corruption therein. Therefore, O God, drive from us their tyranny, confound them, disperse and punish them along with those who aid them, help them and temporize with them; punish and afflict them by Thy might and power. O God, turn against them, visit them with injury, humiliate their state, and drive their authority from Thy lands; let them have no means against any of the believers. (*The Moslem Brethren* by Ishak Musa Husaini, Arabic ed. Beirut, 1955; English transl. Beirut, 1956: a richly documented and scientifically objective book.)

After the Second World War the will of the Egyptians to rid themselves of 'foreign' rule became more and more evident but the King and the Government seemed to take little or no account of this will, using the presence of foreign armies and foreign political representatives as an instrument to support and consolidate their own privileged position. In these circumstances the Brothers decided to intervene actively in the political struggles of the times. The first result of this was that their popularity increased enormously, and when, in 1951, the students elected their University representatives (a good measure of the popularity of a party among the 'intellectuals') the Brothers received about 80 per cent of all votes.

In view of the events which were to take place in the following year we can today give a different interpretation of such an electoral success from that which the Brothers gave in 1951. The votes of the students were not for an 'Islamic state' but, without the electors being necessarily aware of it, for the Brothers' uncompromisingly anti-foreign 'political' programme, for in that year they were on the extreme wing of all 'anti-colonialist' parties. Moreover, they appeared to the students who cast their votes as the only group which was really anti-colonialist. The Brothers had fought in Palestine against the Zionists, and in Egypt had been the heart and soul of those forces which began to oppose the King when the scandal became common talk in Cairo of how the armaments of the Egyptian troops had proved defective in the Palestine campaign and of how the King and his friends had thereby pocketed enormous sums. They seemed to be the only group one could trust to transform their words into deeds if they came to power. It was for this reason that the students elected Brothers to represent them, while taking into account their religious tendencies, in many cases with a shrug of the shoulders.

The Brothers made it easy for many of their own members to put the 'political' side of their programme before the 'religious' one, for did this not consist merely in keeping to certain outward forms. Indeed, it seemed enough to follow the Koranic precepts 'in public'. Remnants of outward conformism, a certain hypocrisy, which had existed in many petit-bourgeois Islamic circles, received a new lease of life.

This is the deeper reason why the Brothers' political success lasted just as long as it had no competitor who could be trusted to have the same honest anti-colonial attitude, that is, until 1952 when Nasser and his officers' junta came to power. The 'intellectuals', the students and the modernists were to forsake the Brothers at the moment when it was possible for them to support a radical, 'anti-colonialist' programme with no religious undertones.

There are other reasons for the swift collapse of the Brotherhood and for the astonishingly final defeat Nasser was able to inflict on it. The Brotherhood had entertained too close relations with terrorism and the Egyptian bourgeoisie had no sympathy with terrorists. It possessed a 'secret organ', a special group of selected members who were sworn to obey their superiors without question, the oath being taken at their initiation on a copy of the Koran and a revolver in a dark room in the presence of the group leader. There is no doubt that members of this secret organ were used in assassinations and several prime ministers were murdered, not to speak of less important politicians and non-political men.

To be sure, the Brothers were not the only group who used the weapon of assassination and it appears very probable that, apart from groups with criminal business interests such as opium and hashish smugglers, arms traffickers, white slavers, etc., even persons in high places occasionally employed hired assassins. Since it was known that the Brothers had a secret organization, practically every political or semi-political murder which was not cleared up was liable to be attributed to them.

Of the series of assassinations the following, especially, were to prove fatal to the Brotherhood. On 8 December 1948, a military decree banned the

Brotherhood for the first time and on the 28th of the same month the Prime Minister Nokrashi Pasha, who was responsible for the ban, was murdered. On 16 February 1949 Hasan al-Banna, the founder and leader of the movement, was shot dead in his car in the centre of Cairo. (The Brothers accused King Faruk of having instigated his murder.)

Al-Banna's murder was a decisive factor in the collapse of the Brotherhood. His successor was officially Al-Hudaibi, a judge of the Cairo High Court. He had good relations with leading politicians, with many of whom he had family ties, and, apart from this, was in good odour at Court. His appointment as Supreme Leader of the Brothers was no doubt intended to help in healing the break between the Government and the Brotherhood. Al-Hudaibi then made contact with Faruk and it seemed for a short while as if the King were trying to use the Brothers as a support in his struggle with the ambitious group of 'young officers' which was later to become known as the Nasser group. But in reality the Brotherhood was never completely behind its new 'leader', for from the beginning certain groups had doubts about the 'politician', Al-Hudaibi. They did not wish to see the Brotherhood reduced to the level of an Egyptian 'political party'. There were dissatisfied elements which sought contact with the opposition of the Left and the various communist splinter groups, at that time operating in Egypt, were only too happy to conclude an unholy alliance with the Brothers. This gave them an opportunity to restore their own popularity because their anaemic Marxist theories meant very little to the Egyptian 'proletariat'.

The cells of the 'secret organ' found it very easy to avoid being controlled by the Supreme Leader of the Society and inside this 'secret organ' several leaders fought for power so that the cells became nests of intrigue. Contact was made, not only with the Communists and 'Nazi' elements but also with every imaginable group of armed ruffians of the Cairo underworld. Now the Brothers were paying for having no real spiritual leadership.

Their end came suddenly. In the struggle for power between General Naguib and Colonel Nasser the Brothers sided with Naguib, presumably in the expectation that he would give them the liberty to agitate they needed in order to eventually come to power, and realizing correctly that Nasser was of a mind to rule himself. After a critical period of manoeuvres, demonstrations and counter-demonstrations and Naguib's resignation and reinstallation (February 1954), Nasser organized the 'Liberation Cohorts' who demonstrated as a counter-weight to the Brothers. Nasser won the day and, after an unsuccessful attempt on his life on 26 October 1954, the members of the 'secret organ' were arrested wherever they could be seized. The Brotherhood was tried before a Military Court and a number of Brothers 'confessed'. Six Brothers were hanged, and several thousands were thrown into prison or concentration camps.

In this way the power of the Brotherhood was broken in Egypt and all circles which had any sort of ties with them are under close observation. For years it will be dangerous even to mention their name in Cairo and any reorganization of the Brotherhood can easily be nipped in the bud by Nasser's capable police.

In the other Arab countries where the Brothers set up branches, there exist residual societies and in the Jordanian troubles of 1955–1957 they took part in the game of high politics as forces inimical to Nasser. They have come to the fore again in Syria, after the break with the United Arab Republic, and their leader, Isam al-Attar, is at present one of those politicians who are working most energetically for the reintroduction of a parliamentary system.

Looking back on the history of the movement one can say that the Brothers broke on one of the basic spiritual difficulties of the present-day Islamic world. They were unable to really bridge the gulf between what is 'modern' and what is 'Islamic'. Their society did not take what is 'modern' as its starting-point like the other parties and it is this that makes their experiment especially interesting. They tried to build up their organization from Islamic tradition and on the masses who lived by that tradition and for this reason were and have remained the only Muslim party which has true roots in the people. It is this that gave them their success: the remarkable speed with which the organization grew, the popularity it enjoyed both in the countryside and in the 'Arab' quarters of the cities, the loyalty of large sections of the people to their ideals and the enthusiastic work done by a large number of activists and propagandists such as no other Near-Eastern party has known, the enthusiasm for work of *idealists*. The remarkable economic success of the Brothers in all their undertakings, newspapers, schools and their own factories and business houses, is also to be attributed to the real popularity of the society and its principles.

But the Brotherhood was unable to win over the intellectual *élite* of Egypt, for their interpretation of Faith was too narrow to appeal to 'modern' men. The fanatical 'modernists' deserted it when a lay movement with its anti-colonialism proved successful. The real intellectuals, whose educational make-up contained and—let us hope—still contains a goodly dose of European Liberalism, could never agree with the 'fanatical', 'reactionary' Brothers and were not prepared to accept their religion like pure 'fundamentalists' as literally absolute. Many of them—and today there must be even more—were no longer able to work up much enthusiasm for religion.

In the long run, however, the Brothers were not able to do without the fertilizing spirit of the 'intellectuals'. After the death of their founder, who was without question a great intellectual personality, they very quickly sank into the tragic swamp of 'empiricism'. Not only did they act according to the principle 'the end justifies the means', but they very quickly forgot which was 'end' and which 'means'. It became more and more difficult to distinguish between Brothers and 'politicians' (in the worst sense of the word), and between Brothers and terrorists or organized criminal gangs. It was these shady zones which finally led the whole society to its destruction.

3

Mandate Mentality

TODAY, NOW THAT THE COLONIAL PERIOD can be considered ended, it is especially interesting to call to mind the spirit in which the Arab countries were ruled at the time of the mandates. Around the time when the authoritarian parties were being formed in Syria and Egypt a ruling group of French and British officers were busy playing their own game in the mandated territories. In his novel *La Châtelaine du Liban*, Pierre Benoit gives a detailed description of the officer society under the Syrian mandate. Whoever reads it today and knows present-day Lebanon, discovers a world of travesties and distortions, an unreal, almost surrealist Lebanon that fills him with amazement. Benoit's novel is the story of an officer in the French intelligence service who falls in love with an 'Asiatic' *femme fatale*, a half-Russian countess, who charms him so much that he is about to sell military secrets to the British. However, he is saved from the disgrace of treason by an attack of fever and later returns to his unit in the Syrian Desert. In his story, told in the first person, this officer draws for us his romantic picture of Lebanon, a 'mysterious, Asiatic mountain land,' whereas the modern traveller finds it rather a typically Mediterranean mountain country, not unlike the French Côte d'Azur. He spends his leisure hours in Beirut on the 'Corniche' which is still called the 'Avenue des Français'. Today, however, the 'cafés chantants' are 'night clubs'. For the hero the real Lebanese are as good as non-existent. Only the 'Syrian women' in the cafés are worth noticing for their 'mollesse'. Among the men only a 'Syrian chauffeur' plays a subordinate part: he is afraid to drive into the dangerous mountains but the officer addresses him with 'tu' and gives him such sharp orders that he overcomes his fear of the savage Druses. In addition to him there is the businessman who is intent on becoming a contractor to the French Army and to whom the officer turns, first to find a profitable investment for his private income and later for a loan—for the *femme fatale*. Then there is a Jew whose business is smuggling gold. The Beduins, too, figure in the novel because of the attacks they occasionally make on the French troops. In one instance there is a dark hint of the methods used against them. It seems important as an indication of what was to happen later in Algeria:

'Have you caught Colonel Lacaze's murderers?'

'Yes, I caught them!'

'How was that?'

He laughed aloud: 'You still find the time to worry about such unimportant things?'

'How did you catch them?'

'Oh, quite simple. We had a Beduin guide of the tribe Tai between Tell Kankab and Hassatche. One evening around the camp fire our Beduin was careless and dropped his knife. It was Colonel Lacaze's knife.'

'What then?'

'I gave orders for him to be left alone with me and two men of the Camel Corps, two strong young fellows, friends of Lacaze. You understand?'

'I understand. He talked.'

'He talked. The murderers were Tai Beduins from a tribe which was in camp just near by. I myself did what was necessary along with ten men and Ferrières, who will have to be trained. You can imagine the scene. The false dawn, quite a small tribe, hardly twenty tents, the dogs giving the alarm, the women fleeing on all sides, the men tripping over their tent ropes. It barely lasted five minutes. There were four murderers.'

'Did you take them alive?'

'Yes. And I learned that the devils didn't bat an eyelid before the firing squad in Aleppo.'

As he spoke he didn't miss the smallest part of the effect his short report had on me. His eyes were shining.

The narrator of this feat is the 'real' hero of Benoit's novel, 'Captain Walter', who in the end saves the intelligence officer and restores him to the 'pure' life of the desert. Of course, torture has been used in all wars and perhaps more in the Beduins' campaigns which are more like raids. Writers like Benoit made literature out of it. But that was in 1924 and after the theme had become an accepted topic of literature other French officers, like Massu, were able to indulge in carefully thought out struggles with their consciences: 'Should one torture and thus save the lives of comrades in peril or should one not torture? What a terrible dilemma!'

But in the eyes of the officer telling the story the real enemy is not the Beduins or the Arabs in general. These people have no political will, let alone any political rights. The real enemy is the British. Our narrator's antagonist is the British intelligence officer Hobson, a cold, rude cynic and tippler whose bloody intrigues lead the noble French soldiers to their deaths in the Syrian Desert. He is successful because he has unlimited money at his disposal. Gold seems to flow of its own accord into the hands of the British antagonist:

Two or three offices of this type had been betrayed to us in all the larger towns in Syria: Damascus, Aleppo, Tripoli, Beirut and Lattakiye. Gold flowed drop by drop into these secret reservoirs, where it heaped up and lay in deep layers. Millions of pieces stamped with every imaginable effigy slept in these new bays of Vigo. Then, one day, at the right moment, when a rift in the net of surveillance had been reported, they disappeared like a flash. Mysterious motor-cars, phantom sloops, placid camels transported them to foreign safes in Egypt and Palestine where they were used to strengthen all the formidable financial artillery trained on the French credit. It was one of the most harmful if not the most odious aspects of the gigantic intrigue which was being spun around us.

The 'gigantic intrigue' was the net of agents and trouble-makers which the French officers believed was being organized and fed by Britain. It was to blame for all the troubles in the Syrian mandated territory. It was created to 'drive the French out of *their* mandated territory'.

'Thank you,' says his congenial superior to the intelligence officer, 'your information is most important. Ha! They are doing everything they can to make things impossible for us in this wonderful country. But we'll oppose them tooth and nail. By God, we'll not make way for others here!'

The 'others' are not the Arabs but the British. The Arabs are simply a bunch of poor devils to be ordered around at will; they would know how to deal with them if only there were no British trouble-makers.

Here, in my small office in the Grand Serail, much more than when I was in pursuit of a Beduin raiding party with my Camel Corps, I took pride in the great task I had to do. In these hundreds of files, notes and many coloured slips which I was constantly rearranging and reclassifying with meticulous care lay the whole epic of France in Syria, a constant target for the monstrous intrigues of our enemies, our allies. Every one of these documents spoke of blood, gold, treason or loyalty and by them I knew that such and such a high placed person to whom I had to bow, for a little while longer, was a traitor, a swine; that such and such a sailor on Ruad Island or such and such an unknown peasant in the Beka'a was nothing less than a hero. . . . With an emotion made up partly of horror and partly of pride, something like what one feels when one weighs a bomb in one's hand, I manipulated the tragic slips, blue, red, green and white: the machinations of the Sharifs, the British, the Americans. . . . Oh, what a world of concealed enemies I have to protect you from, my beloved country!

It is easy to see nowadays how completely false was the idea these officers and colonial administrators had of the East. There is no doubt that everything that they saw and which Benoit tries to describe, existed. But colonial society was so engrossed in itself and 'those like it' that it lost sight of the real East, the East which consisted of Arabs whose aim was to create themselves the civil, independent and comfortable existence they had learned to value in Paris and London and other Arabs who in their multitudes silently and attentively watched the new developments and wanted nothing else but to eat . . . and eat their fill.

With true insight Benoit describes how the officers arrived at their false picture of the Orient when he makes the hero of his novel say:

> All my past rose up before me, my childhood as we went from one garri- son to another; relationships which were no sooner tied than they were untied; new towns where we arrived one rainy night; Abbeville or Castres as was decided by some petty official in an office in the Rue Saint-Domi- nique; the haphazard schooling I had, and the prize-givings in which I never had anything but an honourable mention because I had always arrived too late after the work of the first term had already been done; the Baccalauréat which I just managed to pass, then Saint Cyr; the war which put me, while still almost a child and terrified of responsibility, in charge of sixty men. . . . What a paradoxical fate! When did I ever have the time or the opportunity to learn the terrible secrets of life? What an excuse for nerves which have suffered such chaotic shocks from early youth! . . . And sud- denly, after a nightmare lasting four years, the East, pale and rose-coloured, the respect enjoyed by the victors, the perfumes, the women and the flowers on the shore of a resonant sea, the apparently high pay, a mirage which deceived better and stronger men than me. . . .

It was, indeed, a mirage and a most dangerous one at that. It was especially the 'little man' in the 'colonies' who seemed most incapable of seeing political facts in their true light. Paris generally judged matters better, Paris of the intellectuals at least; but the Parisian intelligentsia was unable to put its ideas across to the Government in sufficient measure and to the bourgeois in the provinces and colonies not at all. It was this, in short, that brought about France's ruin. In the case of the Arabs the result is that the Syrians hate the French in spite of everything that individual Frenchmen have done for that country, perhaps, indeed, because of that.

4

Palestine

THE STRUGGLE OF THE ARABS in Palestine is directly connected with the growth of the authoritarian parties of the second generation. For the Arabs the Palestine question goes back to the Balfour declaration, an assurance given in 1917 by the then Colonial Secretary in a letter to Lord Rothschild. Even before the Balfour declaration there had been Zionist immigration into Palestine, to a large extent fostered by philanthropists, and about 80,000 Jews were already in the country in 1914. In the Balfour declaration Great Britain pledged herself to give official support to a Jewish 'national home' in Palestine. The official interest taken in the Jewish national home in London also served to support Britain's claim to the mandate for Palestine which was put before the 'Supreme Allied Council' (at least the Arabs are convinced of this and the argument has, indeed, often been used).

The persecution of the Jews under Hitler made the Jewish National Home of much greater topical importance than the early Zionist movement which had been before that time relatively small, unpolitical and idealistic. Jewish emigration to Palestine grew beyond all proportions and large sums were collected by Jews throughout the world to build up the National Home. Zionist circles in Palestine began systematically to acquire land from Arab landowners with the clear aim of carving out a consolidated, 'Jewish' area in the country. As the Zionist interests operated as unified, centrally directed financial blocks, while the Arab landowners faced these interests at first in complete disarray, later with an improvised and financially weak Arab land bank at their backs, it can be easily understood why the Zionists were successful in their purchases of land.

Zionist methods of cultivation were as superior to the Arab methods as, in general, western technical skills were to the ancient Arab traditions. Since the Arabs were afraid of being reduced to a minority in their own country their reaction to the spread of Zionism was exceedingly bitter. As in the struggle with the mandatory powers it was the educated and half-educated middle classes who were in the forefront of the opposition to the Zionist movement. 'Strikes' began to be proclaimed as a protest against the growth of Zionist power (1936).

It was only a step from 'strikes' to open battles between Zionists and Arabs and the British troops intervened in an attempt to put an end to acts of violence.

The result is that the Arabs are still convinced that the British purposely helped the Zionists to win in Palestine, whereas the Israelis boast of having wrested their country from the British troops 'who were always on the side of the Arabs'. What actually happened is that the fighting and troubles had, already before the Second World War, transformed the country into a police state of a most unpleasant sort, in which the police themselves were only superficially masters of the situation.

The British changed their Palestine policy just before the war. From 1939 Zionist immigration was to be limited and the purchase of land was forbidden. This was done in an attempt to safeguard the rights of the weaker party, namely the Arabs but Britain's attempt to stabilize the situation by an artificial preserva/ tion of the status quo came too late.

The status quo was just as unsatisfactory from the Zionist point of view as it was from the Arabs'; they had invested too much money and energy and made too many sacrifices to be satisfied for all time with a 'national home' under British or Arab supervision. The dreadful conditions of the German, and after the outbreak of the war also of the East European Jews made it morally impossible for them to agree to a limitation of immigration. They saw therein a threat to their whole idea at a moment when the Jews were exposed to the greatest persecution of their history. But for many Arabs, too, the mere limitation of Jewish immigration was no longer enough. These foreigners had acquired important key positions in their country. They were living there, distinct from the real inhabitants and at a higher economic level thanks to foreign capital, foreign know/how and foreign technical skills. They seemed to be determined to use their superiority to 'exploit' the Arab majority. In the eyes of the Arabs the Arab labour force seemed destined to become in time labourers on the Zionist farms and a market for the products of Zionist factories. The simple Arab labourer may have seen nothing bad in that but the leading Arab intellectuals, made wiser by their experiences under the mandate, feared a new colonial rule in which the colonial upper class would this time consist of people of a foreign faith both indigenous to the country and continuously increasing in numbers by immigration from abroad.

The war brought a sort of armistice between the two sides but in the years after the war there were new outbreaks, more violent and more ugly than ever. Both sides trained battle and terrorist groups. There were bombing incidents, attacks and reprisals from one 'sovereign' territory to the other. Wherever the British authorities applied a curfew more or less normal life went on during the day, occasionally interrupted by bomb explosions, while by night the irregular troops of both sides carried out their campaigns and attacks.

Since Britain tried to block the import of arms, smugglers and black marketeers did brisk business; and since the Zionist immigration was, according to the new rules laid down by the British authorities, to be drastically reduced great numbers of Jewish refugees from Central Europe tried to get to Palestine in ships chartered in Marseilles or in Italy. When the British authorities stopped these illegal immigrant ships their passengers were interned in special camps in Cyprus. Because of the absurdity of this situation and the sufferings of the Jewish refugees who had just been freed from camps and hiding-places in Central Europe, the whole Western world brought strong pressure to bear on the British authorities to abolish the quota system or at least to raise the quotas. In all this the Zionist point of view had much more effective representatives in the West than had the Arab point of view, for Zionism had at its disposal a great many talented men and first-rate links with the press. But, above all, it was in those very years that the full measure of the sufferings of the Central European Jews became known and awakened the conscience of Europe. However, the European states and the United States of America refused to accept more than a small number of Jewish or other refugees, insisting that the British should let more Zionist immigrants into Palestine than had been laid down in 1939 and thus disregard the interests of the Arabs who had been put under their protection. President Truman strove more than anyone else in this direction and, again and again, his personal intervention caused the British temporarily to relax the restrictions on immigration.

The Arab point of view was less spectacular than the Jewish one for the Arabs had suffered less than the Jews had under Hitler and his accomplices. To be sure, no right thinking person can accept the fact that the Palestinian Arabs suffered less than the Jews did under Hitler as an excuse for committing an injustice against the Arabs. Moreover, Western Europeans have no personal experience of the complex of 'colonialism'. On the contrary, they, as inventors and profiteers from this system are accustomed to stress the so-called benefits of colonialization. For this very reason the Arabs' complaints would have fallen on deaf ears even if they had had better advocates of their cause.

However that may be, the British Government decided, under the pressure of pro-Zionist European and American public opinion, to return their mandate as quickly as possible to the United Nations as the successor to the League of Nations. The British found themselves caught up in an increasing conflict between the Arabs, whose goodwill they believed they needed to assure Commonwealth communications, and the Jews who had fought on Britain's side against Hitler. Moreover, American interest in the Palestine question deprived the mandatory power of some of her liberty of action. Truman's part in all this derived to some extent from electoral considerations, for the so-called 'Jewish vote' was a Democratic vote. Thus one can understand why the British were not willing to use their own troops, their financial resources and political prestige in vain attempts to prevent a civil war, while Western public opinion was almost without exception on one side.

By giving up their mandate in the critical years after the war the British took the first step in their disengagement from the Near East; this was to lead to further steps which brought about the liquidation of the British political position in almost the whole area. Britain undertook under the mandate to further the maintenance of law and order and free political development in Palestine. In 1918 she was not asked to play this part, but her statesmen used all the means of pressure at their disposal in order to obtain the mandate in spite of Arab opposition. For twenty-six years Palestine was occupied by her armies and administered by her officials and they are directly responsible for the development of Palestine in a direction other than that of peace and liberty. To be sure, Britain could hand back her mandate to the United Nations and thus formally salve her conscience, but in reality the surrender of the mandate was not only a confession of political failure but was also equivalent to a veiled invitation to civil war, for it was clear that the United Nations was much less in a position to force obedience to its decisions than the Great Power Britain which already had her troops on the spot.

On the other hand the Israelis are convinced that it was the British intention to surrender them to the Arabs, whereas the Arabs believe that it was just a treacherous manoeuvre to hand Palestine over to the Zionists. Indeed, the Arabs are convinced that behind this manoeuvre lay the further intention of the 'colonial powers' to turn Israel into a 'western bridgehead' on Arab soil.

When the war broke out the Arabs—or at least the majority of their propagandists and politicians—were convinced that they could beat the Zionists militarily. The disappointment when this did not happen and the resulting bitterness against all those powers and forces which are held responsible are still decisive factors in Arab political life.

Explanations of the failure of the Arab armies in the Palestine War in the post-war years produced an enormous pile of literature, none of it very profound. Certain, rather superficial, errors have been discussed and written about, among them faulty arms, and insufficient supplies and financial reserves. Political causes have been discovered: not only did the armies of the five Arab countries, which took part in the war, have no apparatus at all to co-ordinate their efforts but the politicians of the Arab countries were at cross purposes with each other in their attempts to claim those areas of Palestine they were going to conquer. An inter-Arab cold war was fought at the same time as the Israeli-Arab hot war.

The least publicity has been given to the purely military errors of the Arab armies and their leaders. The reason for this is no doubt that the army took over power either openly or behind the scenes practically everywhere in the Arab world and was not willing to take upon itself the odium of defeat. But there is no doubt that serious military errors were also committed.

The Arab critics of the Palestine War practically ignore the achievements of the young Israeli state and its army. Even today Arab propagandists and ideologists cannot admit that the hated Jews have made or ever can make any positive achievement and Arabic writings on Palestine always have an almost completely apologetic character. Similarly the individual Arab in all Arab countries will always try to explain away the success of the Zionists by the Western 'betrayal' of the Arabs and 'unconditional support' of Israel.

Very few Europeans who do not have personal experience of these countries realize what the loss of Palestine meant and still means to the Arabs. First of all there are those who have lost their homes, their jobs, their lands and family possessions. Many of these belong to what was once a relatively large class of educated and professional men and most of these have since managed to find new jobs in the other Arab countries or abroad. Since the time when they emigrated or were driven out coincided with a period of expansion in most Arab countries and there was everywhere a dearth of educated and enterprising men, they have generally been able to build a satisfactory new life after some years of deprivation. Some of them have become royal advisers in Saudi Arabia and others have risen to diplomatic posts of great importance and to positions of decisive influence in education and in the new industries.

However, all this does not mean that they have forgotten their old homeland. On the contrary, it is the educated and relatively well-off Palestinians who feel themselves as guardians of the 'Palestinian idea'. They see to it that it is never forgotten in any Arab country that 'Palestine belongs to the Arabs and must be won back by them.' They control a part of the Arabic press and it is easy for them to influence other newspapers. The rest of the press would never dare to show the slightest softening in its attitude to the Palestine problem and even governments have to bow before this influence.

This upper class of Palestinians forms a sort of brotherhood of the like-minded spread over all the Arab countries. The majority are supporters of Nasser since they see in him the most effective opponent of 'western colonialism' and believe that he can bring about the union of all Arabs and in the end launch a successful campaign against Israel.

The best measure of the irreconcilable hatred these circles have for Israel is their treatment of their own compatriots, the Palestinian lower classes. These form the great bulk of the Palestinian refugees who now with their descendants are said to number more than a million and live in camps or improvised huts, and some too in the houses of relatives, in Jordan, the Gaza Strip, Syria and Lebanon. Most of them receive rations, primitive shelter and education from UNRWA. It is their own compatriots, the well-to-do Palestinians, who are loudest in their demands that they must continue to live under these conditions until they are able to return to Palestine.

All the plans which aim at permitting the refugees in the camps to be incorporated to a certain extent economically in the organisms of the states harbouring them—whether great comprehensive projects like the Hammarskjöld plan of 1959 or minor advances in individual countries and for certain categories of refugees such as UNRWA sometimes undertakes—are systematically thwarted by the Arabs. Typical of this state of affairs is the fact that it was leading Palestinians who held a pre-conference on the Hammarskjöld plan in Lebanon in July 1959 as 'experts on Palestine questions' and decided that the plan could not be put into effect since the economic incorporation of the refugees was practically tantamount to their becoming ordinary citizens of the countries in which they were living. This could not be tolerated since the refugees, the most effective symbol of the wrong done to Palestine, had to be left in their misery until they once again found themselves able to return to their homeland. At the time of the conference there were some signs that the Arab governments, or at least some of them like those of Amman and Cairo, would not have been displeased to see the Hammarskjöld plan accepted and would have been glad to seize the opportunity to welcome large sums for development into their needy countries. It is clear, however, that they had to agree with the 'Palestine experts' for all Palestinian questions are of such great propaganda value and importance that even 'strong men' like Nasser and King Husain have to be very careful how they deal with them.

Since it is not possible in practice to set a term for the return of the million Arab refugees to Israel, those who control Arab public opinion on Israeli questions are simply condemning the refugees to remain propagating themselves in the mud of their camps for an unforeseeable time.

If any fault lies with the Arabs in the Palestine question it is in this. It is the fault of the intellectuals who are not willing to recognize the fact that Israel exists and who have, for the past ten years, been keeping their unlettered brothers artificially in a situation which makes it impossible for them to adapt themselves to the facts and to develop their own creative work. Whenever foreign relief organizations, whether sponsored by private bodies or by UNRWA, attempt to do something to overcome this situation they are blocked at the instigation of the Palestinian bourgeoisie, whose consistent strategy it is to keep alive the Arabs' hatred for Israel and to prevent at all costs any sort of accommodation with her.

Many leading Israeli intellectuals express the opinion that Israel cannot tie herself to any policy which excludes the possibility of an understanding with the Arabs. They point out that Israel is at pains to remain neutral in the East-West struggle so as to be in harmony with her Asiatic hinterland. But whatever the views of Israeli moderates, the Arabs are firmly convinced that Israel is making common cause with the West against them. They see in Israel a colonial power whose urge for expansion they fear and such views are pumped into the Arab public day by day. It seems most improbable that, after ten years of constant indoctrination, there is the slightest possibility of a different picture of Israel appearing in any Arab country.

One may ask what the seemingly inexhaustible sources of hatred are with which the Palestinian Arab intellectuals conduct their propaganda campaign. Material and political losses seem to play a smaller part than psychological factors, for the upper class Palestinians have acquired comparatively good positions in the other Arab countries.

At the time when Zionism appeared the educated Palestinians were in the process of becoming 'westernized' and had every reason to be satisfied with their progress for Palestine was, along with Lebanon, in many respects the most advanced Arab country. Then the Zionists came to their country and proved themselves more able to use western, modern methods than the Arabs. To be sure, the Palestinians try to argue away this fact by pointing to the financial preponderance of the Zionists and 'international Jewry's control of the European press' but in their heart of hearts they know that they were beaten by the Zionists in the field of 'modern life', a field they were anxious to master and which they believed they had already mastered.

The leading Palestinians refuse to admit their defeat, considering it merely a reverse, but they are also not sure of themselves and of their power over their own people. Today they feel that they are still inferior and want to gain time, for tomorrow, so they hope, they will perhaps be equal. Until that day there is only one thing for them to do: to engage in no contest, but rather to isolate and cut themselves off. This their hatred helps them to do.

Behind this barrier of hatred to which the welfare of the great majority of the refugees is being sacrificed, they hope that in the long run they will have advanced so far with their own development that they will be able at last to resume the struggle with their dangerous opponent and bring it to a successful conclusion.

5

The Second World War
and the Post-War Years

UNLIKE THE FIRST WORLD WAR the Second World War was a relatively peaceful time for the Arabs. In the occupied countries behind the front, Egypt, Syria, Lebanon and Palestine, the war economy led to a strong development of local industry and to a rising standard of living, especially in the towns, which was only partially offset by inflation. Destructive military operations occurred only in North Africa. In Syria and Lebanon there was the bitter, but short, struggle when a Gaullist administration took over from the Vichy authorities. In Iraq a military revolt led by Rashid Ali al-Gilani, who was for neutralism in favour of the Axis powers, was quickly crushed, after two months, in April 1941 when British troops from Palestine and the Arab Legion from Transjordan marched in.

On the other hand the years after the war brought far-reaching changes. Syria and Lebanon very soon freed themselves from French tutelage and the way in which this came about explains to a great extent the hatred still felt for the French, especially in Syria. The commander of the Free French, General Catroux, proclaimed the end of the mandate immediately after his victory over the Vichy French in 1941, but for two years he saw to it that Syria and Lebanon were ruled by pro-French governments which in the last analysis were dependent on the French troops in the country to keep their own people in check.

After El-Alamein in October 1942, the British began to support the right of the Syrians and the Lebanese to really free elections and in 1943 the 'nationalists' came to power in both countries. These were led in Damascus by Shukri al-Quwatli and his colleagues and in Lebanon by the 'constitutional block' under Bishara al-Khuri and Riyad al-Sulh. Both governments really tried to exercise their sovereignty. In November 1943 the French decided to depose them by force of arms but were prevented from doing so by the intervention of Britain and the United States. In the subsequent years the 'nationalists' forced the French administration step by step to surrender its privileges to the local governments.

But the French refused to surrender their most important privilege, namely the command of the 'Gendarmerie' and the 'troupes spéciales', except in exchange for a state treaty, like those between Britain and Iraq in 1931 and Britain and Egypt in 1936, giving them special strategic and political rights.

When the 'nationalist' governments of both countries refused to enter into negotiations for a state treaty before the troops had been handed over to them, the French once more attempted to resort to force. Damascus was bombarded in 1945 and Senegalese troops landed in Lebanon and in 1946 the French High Commissioner had the Lebanese government locked up. An order of the British Government to the G.O.C. Middle East to intervene, if necessary with force, strengthened the opposition of the Syrians and Lebanese to such an extent that they were finally able to achieve the evacuation of their countries. By April 1946 all French troops had left Syria and towards the end of the same year Lebanon, too, was evacuated.

The French may defend their policy of that period by pointing out that Britain, too, had refused to withdraw her troops before the 'state treaty' was agreed on, but what may have been considered a 'progressive' policy in the 'thirties could no longer be forced upon the Arabs after the Second World War.

The British, too, were soon to be faced with demands for the revision of the treaties with Egypt and Iraq. The Egyptian situation was complicated by the double problem of the presence of British troops and the Sudanese question. During the war, in February 1943, the British had used their troops to encircle King Faruk's palace with tanks and compel the installation of a pro-allied government. In this way the Wafd had come to power and bravely supported the allies during the most critical years of the war.

But after the war the Egyptian nationalists, that is, every party which had a mind to appeal to the nation, demanded the evacuation of Egypt and the union of Egypt and the Sudan. Negotiations between the then Prime Minister Sidqi Pasha and the British Foreign Secretary Ernest Bevin would probably have been successful had not the Sudanese question prevented their agreement at the last moment.

The *Sudan* had been conquered for Egypt by Muhammad Ali in 1820 but the Egypto-Turkish administration, whose main aim was exploitation and the taking of slaves, led in 1881 to the rebellion of a religious sect, the Mahdists, who conquered Khartum in 1885. As is well known, the British General Gordon was thereupon sent to Khartum where he lost his life.

In 1898 Lord Kitchener reconquered the Sudan with British and Egyptian troops and Egyptian money, France having also attempted in the years just before to gain a footing in the Sudan. The Sudan was declared an Anglo-Egyptian Condominium, according to Cromer 'a hybrid form of government so far unknown in International Law.' This condominium lasted *de facto* until 1924. The higher officials were British and the great majority of the District officers (Ma'murs) were Egyptian officers who had been seconded to the civil administration. In 1924 Sir Lee Stack, Governor-General of the Sudan and G.O.C. the Egyptian Army was murdered in Cairo and at the same time mutinies broke out in the Egyptian garrisons in the Sudan. Thereupon the British gave the Egyptians an ultimatum to withdraw all their troops and officials from the Sudan and from then on the country came under solely British administration, while remaining a condominium *de jure*.

The Egyptians never gave up their claim to the Sudan which was from then on, along with the problem of the British military occupation 'to safeguard the Suez Canal', the main obstacle to every agreement with Britain. The policy of the Wafd, according to which the two problems could only be discussed together with Britain, was only ended in 1952 by General Naguib.

After the Bevin-Sidqi negotiations had come to nothing the British with-drew their troops from the Egyptian cities to the Canal Zone in 1947 which they had already undertaken to do under the Anglo-Egyptian Treaty of 1936(!). One reason for the British troops remaining so long in Cairo was the Italian conquest of Ethiopia and another was the imminent threat of a general war. When this at last did break out Egypt became a base for the campaigns in North Africa. The Egyptian Government accused Britain before the Security Council of the United Nations and demanded the evacuation of Egypt and the Sudan; the Council adjourned the case until it was overtaken by events.

In the following year came the Palestine War and the resultant confusion and shame of defeat. This crisis had perhaps a greater effect in Egypt than in all the lesser Arab countries because Cairo had claimed to be the leader of the Arabs and because the population of Egypt was forty times greater than that of Israel. The Palestine situation along with the uncertainty of the legal position *vis-à-vis* Britain led to a period of constantly increasing political confusion.

In internal politics the Palace was opposed to the parties, especially the Wafd and the Muslim Brothers, the King relying on lesser parties like the Sa'adists, a break-away group of the Wafd, and on 'independent' politicians. His con-siderable constitutional prerogatives allowed him to appoint ministers and dis-solve parliaments, he was Commander-in-Chief of the Army and received financial and political support from all sides, for a time even from the British and also from his actual opponents, the Wafdists. The Wafd was forced to appear as anti-British as possible so as not to lose its popularity with the masses and to counter the increasing complaints of corruption by posing as patriots. No Egyptian government could afford to be anything but anti-British although there was no earthly possibility of using force successfully against Britain.

After a period of fruitless political and diplomatic manoeuvring by both British and Egyptians a Wafdist government unilaterally abrogated the Anglo-Egyptian agreement of 1936 in October 1951. A 'Middle East Defence Plan' and Britain's undertaking to evacuate the Suez Canal Zone in the event of Egypt's agreeing to join this planned Four-Power Defence organization came too late. King Faruk was proclaimed King of the Sudan and the Egyptian Government gave their blessing to all sorts of extremist groups which set about 'liberating' the Canal Zone from the British troops.

The Egyptian Army took no part in the actions against the Canal Zone, the main weight of the fighting falling on units of the so-called 'auxiliary police'. A sort of state of siege began in the Canal Zone in October 1951 and the isolated British troops undertook reprisal measures against various Egyptian villages which had caused them trouble. On 25 January 1952 they surrounded the headquarters of the 'auxiliary police' in Ismailiya with tanks and armoured cars and called upon the policemen to give themselves up. The Wafdist Minister of the Interior, Serag ed-Din, gave his men orders by telephone to resist and in the fighting which developed forty-five auxiliary policemen were killed.

The next day is still known in Egypt as 'Black Saturday'. It began with a mutiny of auxiliary policemen in Cairo and the disappearance of policemen and soldiers from the streets. Later there appeared separate groups of terrorists and fire-raisers which began systematically to set fire to certain buildings in the city. Their targets were British clubs, Shepheards Hotel and a number of foreign businesses, bars, cinemas and other hotels. More and more people rushed to take part in the plundering.

It is evident that 'Black Saturday' was organized, for it is said that the fire-raisers even carried with them lists of targets to be attacked and consulted each other in the streets. But it has never been established who was behind it all. Several interests coincided on that day at a moment of extreme political excite-ment: those of the King, who profited by 'Black Saturday' in so far as the Wafd government was forced to resign after it, those of certain extremists among the Muslim Brothers and also those of individual protection and smuggling gangs of the Cairo underworld. Added to this the police, made bitter by the useless loss of forty-five of their comrades in Ismailiya, refused to do their duty. The fact that the army did not intervene throughout the day seems to be directly attributable to the King's attitude.

As a result of 'Black Saturday' the Egyptian economy, which was very much under the influence of foreigners of all nations, practically collapsed. Even before the troubles Egypt's economic situation had suffered very badly from the Wafd government's prices policy on the Alexandria cotton market. Attempts to boost the prices artificially had led to the whole 1951-52 cotton harvest remaining unsold. This economic and external trade crisis helped to bring about a certain lull in the anti-British agitation.

After the British had withdrawn from the Egyptian cities and the Wafd had been discredited, King Faruk was the most important political power in the country. He appointed and dismissed government after government but even his position had become weaker in the years following the Palestine War. On 23 July 1952 a group of officers led by Colonel Gamal Abd an-Nasir with

General Muhammad Naguib as their ostensible leader, seized power in a bloodless *coup d'état*.

As in Egypt, there developed in Iraq after the war, strong pressure against the 1931 treaty with Britain. Here, too, there was no revision because a new draft treaty which was drawn up was all too violently rejected by the people. Troubles in Baghdad in the early summer of 1948 forced the Regent Abdul-Ilah to reject the draft of a revised treaty which his Prime Minister had already signed. According to the provisions of this new treaty, Britain had undertaken to evacuate Iraqi military airfields after the conclusion of the peace treaties with the former Axis powers, Iraq was to grant British aircraft transit rights and an 'Anglo-Iraqi Joint Defence Board' was to be set up to co-ordinate the defence of Iraq. As there was no final agreement the old treaty of 1931 remained in force until it was abrogated after the revolution of 1958.

After the war political parties were allowed in Iraq for a short time and socialist inclined left groups were formed in the cities. Their leaders, who had 'nationalist and socialist' leanings, were generally lawyers who had studied abroad. On special occasions these groups in conjunction with the nationalists were able to call the Baghdad masses 'into the street', but once trouble had broken out it was difficult for them to direct the 'movement'. These parties were of no account in the countryside where the great majority of Iraqis live as peasants. In the countryside the laws of Iraqi feudalism still held good, laws according to which the landowner ordered 'his' peasants how they should vote and in most cases had himself elected as their member of parliament.

Two politicians of the old school, Nuri al-Sa'id and Salih Jabr, but primarily Nuri, were the real power in the country, and the parliaments which consisted of landowners laid down only one condition for supporting them, namely that the government should not touch their feudal privileges. Iraqi ministries and military dictatorships in which Nuri had no part followed an uneasy course of political excitement, intrigues and struggles until Nuri (and the elements supporting him) thought fit to reassert their authority again. In such moments the left-inclined, small 'nationalist', that is, anti-British, parties in the towns were banned or had their liberty of movement severely restricted. Their newspapers were censored, banned or taken over by a group which was friendly towards the government. The parties avenged themselves by casting a double accusation at Nuri and his friends, of being feudalists and of collaborating with the British. The accusation of feudalism was no doubt justified in so far as the great landowners and sheikhs from the country districts saw to it in the parliament that the state acted first and foremost in their own interest. But feudalism stirred the people to anger much less than did the accusation of collaboration with the British 'colonialists', although this second accusation was much less justified than was the first. To be sure, Nuri preferred to get his foreign specialists from Britain and the Iraqi Petroleum Co. was a company in which most of the shares were held by Britons, primarily the British government. But the country needed foreign technicians, industrialists and foreign capital. The assertion that foreigners derived disproportionately high profits from their enterprises in Iraq has never really been proved. It may be that certain 'services' were dearly paid for, yet one cannot escape the impression that, on the whole, Iraqi state business, especially that of the powerful Development Board, progressed in the main on a commercial basis and that bribery and 'colonialist pressure' played a far smaller part than they did in most other Arab countries. The revolutionary régime in present-day Iraq, which has terminated most of the old agreements as being 'too expensive', has so far been able to produce little but economic chaos in spite of substantial Russian aid.

Although the accusation of collaboration with the colonialists could only in part be justified, it was all the more effective politically and could serve at any time to provoke a riot in the streets of Baghdad. In the cities, it was very easy for foreigners to arouse envy by their ostentatious and, to the Iraqis, most luxurious way of living.

The leaders of the nationalist troubles, especially the secondary schoolboys and students, were generally the sons, cousins and nephews of the great landowners and politicians of the old school and, since the feeling of Arab solidarity in effect favoured the feudal classes, their activity could more easily be turned against foreigners. In this way foreigners and 'colonialists' acted as a sort of windscreen for the great landowners. Even the communists could only develop their activities on a wide front when their agitation was directed less against the 'feudalistic exploiting classes' than against 'colonialism'.

The political champions of Arab unity were to be found long before Nasser among the leading Iraqi politicians for, besides the interest of the privileged classes in pan-Arab agitation as a diversion from social questions, there was no doubt also a sincere pan-Arab idealism. Had not Nuri himself been in his time one of those Turkish officers who rebelled against the Porte?

After the war Britain decided that a certain measure of Arab unity could well be considered compatible with British interests in the Near East. It was expected that this would create greater stability in the whole area and it was more important to have a friendly and prosperous Arab Near East on the side of the West, than to exploit it economically for a limited period of time with the risk that the whole region might finally go communist. Arab unity within reasonable limits seemed to be a practical condition for a policy of prosperity and stability. Anthony Eden, who had once studied oriental languages, was the champion of this new British policy towards the Arabs but perhaps London underestimated the intensity of mistrust and hatred which Britain's former policy had evoked among the Arab masses. However, in the years just after the war this hatred was not so apparent for up to then no one had appeared who knew how to revive it and use it for his political aims.

After several projects for uniting all or some of the Arab states had come to nothing the Arab League was founded in Cairo in 1945. Its greatest weakness was, and still is, that it had no executive power whatsoever. The political or economic committees of the League or the extraordinary meetings of Foreign Ministers or even Heads of State take 'decisions' which for the individual member states have only the value of recommendations. Even when decisions are unanimous, which is not very often, that does not mean that they will be ratified and carried out in each country. They are often subsequently opposed in parliament, or governments keep postponing their ratification, or the execution of a decision which has already been ratified is postponed until the neighbouring state has ratified it. In this way the League's more radical decisions, taken unanimously in a moment of enthusiasm in Casablanca, Beirut or Cairo, have remained partly or wholly on paper.

Soon after its foundation the League became a sort of propaganda forum in which the two largest countries, Egypt and Iraq, competed and strove for hegemony over the other Arab states. As long as Egypt was under the monarchy, whose more or less corrupt methods kept the other Arabs somewhat unsympathetic to the Land of the Pharaohs, the balance was more in favour of Iraq, although some caution was shown towards Iraq, too. Hashimites, descendants of the Sharifs of Mecca, ruled in Iraq and Jordan and this was enough to fill the Saudis, the old enemies of the Hashimites, with misgivings. For this reason Saudi Arabia tended to support Egypt as soon as the possibility arose of Syria being drawn into a Hashimite state, for the policy of King Abdullah of Jordan was officially one of a 'Greater Syria'.

The Syrians themselves kept their distance from Iraq, because they were afraid of British influence in Iraq and Jordan and despised the Iraqis for tolerating it. Many of their politicians had become sympathetic towards republican ideals in French schools and mistrusted the British inspired monarchical system.

The balance of the League changed against Iraq when the Egyptian monarchy fell before an officers' conspiracy, for these officers could then outdo their Iraqi rivals in 'anti-colonialism'. Supported by the middle and lower classes of their country they felt that they need no longer follow a policy of caution and collaboration with the Western powers. Nasser no longer needed to protect the privileges of a special class, the great landowners, against the demands of the middle classes and the peasants. This made it possible for him to stand up much more firmly to these powers than was possible for the Hashimites.

This attitude won for Egypt the admiration of all the Arabs. The Iraqi (and later the Jordanian) government stood angrily aside while Nasser transformed the League into a propaganda forum of Egyptian 'anti-colonialism'. The Baghdad Pact was the main target of attack, the nationalists in the League seeing in it a proof that Iraq was controlled by the imperialist west and so a traitor to the cause of the Arabs. In view of this policy of the League which was directed by Cairo, Iraq, in the few years before the revolution of 1958, did not even pay its contributions to this League which her statesmen had decisively helped to found.

*   *   *

The years after the war were a period of unrest for *Syria*. Disappointment because of the defeat in Palestine awakened in the army the urge to interfere more than before in politics and *coups d'état* against the republic were carried out several times by officers. As a rule it was easier for the officers to seize power than to keep power and remain alive subsequently. It is no easy task to rule a turbulent country like Syria. The more energetic and far-seeing of the military dictators, Husni Za'im and Shishakli, tried to introduce a certain measure of social reform in the hope that the country's development would be more regular and intensive. But social reforms in Syria have so far mostly miscarried because of the fact that the state and its administrators are much less in a position to develop the country or to provide work for the Syrian day-labourers than the powerful and rich, but at the same time active and capable, big landowners, merchants and industrialists of Damascus, Homs, Hama and Aleppo. While the state had neither capable planners nor sufficiently trained and energetic executives at its disposal and the authorities possessed neither the means nor the initiative, the private economy of Aleppo developed on its own initiative the extensive desert areas of the Jazira (between the upper Euphrates and the Tigris) and thereby increased the country's cultivated area by a full third in the ten years after the war.

These same ten years were spent by the politicians and the military in intriguing against each other, in carrying out or uncovering *coups*, in throwing each other into gaol or—if only very occasionally—in shooting each other down. Husni Za'im and Shishakli created for themselves political organs in the form of state parties. Husni Za'im, the first of the military dictators (1947) fell in 1949 to a rival, Colonel Hinnawi, who in his turn was removed after six months by Lieut.-Colonel Shishakli. Shishakli ruled for four years as dictator and the 'strong man' behind various governments but in 1954 had finally to give way to a *coup d'état* whose instigators once more proclaimed the republic and reinstalled the first Syrian President, Shukri al-Quwwatli. The republic became more and more dominated by the complicated intrigues of a minority party, the leftish, pan-Arab Baath Party which until 1958 was in collaboration with the communists. The principal military associate of the Baath Party in its game with the parliament was Abdul Hamid Serraj, chief of military intelligence. When the communists tried to gain the upper hand with the aid of a new associate, the politician Khalid al-Azm, the Baathists brought about the union with Nasser's Egypt in 1958 as a sort of rescue manoeuvre.

If the Palestinian defeat had a decisive influence on the politics of all the Arab states, it completely changed the aspect of one of these, for as a result of the Palestinian War Transjordan became *Jordan* by annexing those areas of Palestine which at the end of the war were occupied by the Arab Legion: the old city of Jerusalem and the 'pockets' of Hebron to the south and Nablus to the north of the holy city. The acquisition of these new territories brought about a sharp rise in the population of the Kingdom. Instead of ruling over half a million Beduins, King Abdullah now found himself with a million and a half subjects of whom a third were peasants and another third refugees from 'occupied Palestine' as Israel is officially called in Jordan.

The Palestinian war and the subsequent blockade destroyed Jordan's modest economy. Her natural port had been Haifa and now a long detour had to be made by way of Beirut. This long route was too expensive for certain heavy transports, like alfa-grass, one of the principal export products, to continue to be exported. The refugees—a third of all the inhabitants of Jordan—were kept and are still being kept just alive by UNRWA, an international aid organization which was created for them. Nevertheless, they have no work and for Jordan they are more a burden than an advantage.

The former Palestinians living on the right bank of the Jordan had little sympathy with the Beduins and their ruler Abdullah. Moreover, many of them held him responsible for the defeat of the Arabs in Palestine and accused him of 'treason' for having concluded a separate peace with Israel permitting him to keep the territories his Arab Legion had conquered. Practically all of them hated the fact that Abdullah relied on British technicians, advisers, training officers and subventions.

Abdullah was assassinated in the Mosque of Jerusalem in July 1951 and it appears that his murderers were in touch with the family of the 'Mufti of Jerusalem', Hajj Amin al-Husaini, friend of the Nazis, leader of the Palestinians against the Zionists and political intriguer in Cairo, Damascus, Baghdad, and Berlin. The Arab Legion was able to keep order in the country and Abdullah's son, Talal, accepted a revised constitution according to which the government is responsible not, as before, to the King but to parliament. Nevertheless, the King reserved for himself the office of commander-in-chief of the Army and the right to appoint ministers and, in certain circumstances, to dissolve parliament. After only six months Talal had to give up his powers as his mental health was not up to exercising royal power. He was succeeded by his son, Husain, who was then sixteen years old and for whom a council of regency ruled until May 1953.

In that period the Jordanians suffered many headaches because of their 'long frontier' with Israel. Refugees showed a tendency to return secretly across the border to Israel in order to live on their former fields or simply in order to harvest part of their produce and smuggle it across the border. This resulted in fighting between such 'infiltrators' and the Israeli citizens or frontier guards. The Jordanian Government say that they not only advised the refugees not to infiltrate but that they even had the frontier patrolled by Jordanian soldiers and that severe sentences of imprisonment were meted out to infiltrators who were caught. The Israeli Army made reprisal attacks on Jordanian frontier villages, the most brutal of which was against the village of Qibya in 1953 in which the Israelis massacred sixty-six persons, mostly old men, women and children, by blowing up their houses (cf. Glubb, *A Soldier with the Arabs*).

With the rise of Nasser's 'Pan-Arabism' a new development took place in Jordan. The view spread among the 'Palestinians' and also a fair section of the 'Jordanians' that it was Britain that was preventing Jordan from forging closer links with the 'other' Arabs—in this case the Syrians and the Egyptians. This pan-Arab influence was inspired mainly by Syria and the King himself came under it. A young colonel, Ali Abu Nawwar, had been removed from the Legion for nationalist machinations and had been sent off to Paris as military attaché. There he was able to influence the young heir to the throne when he spent his holidays in the French capital. Shortly after his accession Husain summoned the colonel to Amman as his personal adjutant and with his arrival there began within the Legion serious wire-pulling between officers of the 'old guard' with British sympathies and the 'young officers' with nationalist pan-Arab ideas. It seems, to judge from his *mémoires*, that the commander of the Legion, Sir John Glubb, had less talent for politics and intrigues than his Arab subordinates. He gives the impression of being a 'soldier of the old school' who believes in God and his King in the conviction that he must do his duty as a soldier and an officer, while gladly leaving politics to the 'politicians'.

Towards the end of 1955 trouble broke out in Amman, beginning as a demonstration organized by the nationalists against the Baghdad Pact. The British General Templer had visited Amman in order to persuade the Jordanian government to join the pact. The court and the government were intimidated by the demonstrations. The Legion received orders not to intervene and the government announced that Jordan would not join the Baghdad Pact.

Encouraged by this success the nationalists in Amman organized further demonstrations and 'strikes' but this time the Arab Legion took energetic counter-measures since the court began to fear that the 'demonstrators' might become dangerous. It appears that this first successful intervention of the Arab Legion convinced the nationalists that their immediate task would have to be to get control of the Legion itself. They were successful in getting King Husain to dismiss Glubb in March 1956 and in his place Ali Abu Nawwar became the Legion's commander-in-chief. New elections were held throughout the country and a parliament was elected with a 'nationalist' majority (the Baath and socialist, nationalist, pan-Arab parties of a like mind). A government consisting of Palestinians was appointed, which came to an understanding with Syria, and Nasser and Husain were photographed together as 'two friends'. Egypt, Saudi Arabia and Syria undertook to provide together the financial aid essential for Jordan's continued existence as a state, aid which had up to then been granted by Great Britain, and the Jordanian government actually terminated the treaty of subvention with the British.

Of all the Arab countries of the Near East, *Lebanon* suffered least of all from troubles which can be considered a direct result of the defeat in Palestine. The balance between the various large and small religious communities gives Lebanon its particular character and stability. In Lebanon politics are first and foremost internal politics and foreign politics or 'Arab politics' do not excite all Lebanese so directly as, for example, their Syrian neighbours. Thus the first generation of politicians after independence was relieved of office in Lebanon more from internal political than from 'pan-Arab' motives: President Bishara al-Khuri was accused of nepotism and corruption. When, in 1952, he sought to have an alteration of the Constitution adopted by the parliament which he dominated, allowing him to stay in office for a further three years, armed opposition broke out.

The commander-in-chief of the Army, General Fuad Shihab, refused to order the army to fire on the rebels. Thereupon Bishara al-Khuri resigned and General Shihab became 'non-political' interim President. One of the rebels, Camille Chamoun, became the new president as a result of the elections and his period lasted in Lebanon until 1958 when he came into conflict with the rising high tide of Nasser's pan-Arabism.

6

The Egyptian Revolution

AMONG THE MANY BOOKS on Nasser and his movement a French work, *L'Egypte en mouvement* by Simone and Jean Lacouture, is the best that we have seen. It is a report by well-informed eye-witnesses of the Egyptian revolution. It is critical but not, like so many writings of European observers, hypercritical or accusatory. In our treatment of this theme we have little to add to the material they have collected in their book and whoever wishes to make a deeper study of Nasser and his movement should turn to the Lacoutures' book.

The man the European press calls Nasser is called in reality Gamal Abdu-n-Nasir. Names beginning with Abdu are very common in all Arab countries. 'Abd' means 'servant' or 'slave' and names containing this word always refer to God. 'Abdu-n-Nasir' is the 'Servant of Him who gives victory' i.e. God. Similarly 'Abdu-l-Wahid' is the 'Servant of the One (God)', 'Abdul Hamid' the 'Servant of the Praised One' and 'Abduh' 'His Servant'.

The Egyptians are naturally pleased when European papers call Abdu-n-Nasir simply 'Nasir' or (in the French-influenced Egyptian transliteration of Arabic) Nasser 'the giver of Victory', especially when the papers in question are unsympathetic to the head of the Egyptian state. It then becomes a sort of tribute through ignorance.

'Nasser' belongs to a lower middle-class family. His father seems to have been a postal official who came to Cairo in this capacity from the country. The assertion one hears so often in Egypt that Nasser is the 'son of a peasant' is correct only to the extent that his origins are in fact peasant ones.

Like many children of minor Egyptian officials young Gamal went to a military academy and in this way was educated by the state to be an officer. That so many of Egypt's best specialists, administrators and senior officials are products of the state academies for police or army officers cannot simply be explained by the fact that it is the 'officer class' that is in power today. One should not lose sight of the fact that, during the years and decades of unrest which Egypt suffered, the students in the military and police academies were almost the only ones who really learned something. In the military academies the students were soldiers whose orders were to go to school and study, not like the pupils of all other secondary schools and students at the university who were almost daily 'on strike' or 'demonstrating'. Student officers were compelled by military discipline to treat their instructors, even if these were foreigners, with respect and to try to learn something from them. (Foreigners who have taught in Cairo University assure me that this was not the case there in the years before the revolution and even today such discipline is still insufficiently observed.)

In his often quoted little book 'The Philosophy of the Revolution' Nasser describes among other things his own inner development. He gives us to understand that, as a young lad, he was sympathetic towards the ideas of the Muslim Brothers, which was only natural in a young man of his class:

> I thought of attempts on the life of the King and on the lives of those of his advisers who were tampering with our sacred traditions. In this I was not alone. When I met others our thoughts crystallized into definite plans. In those days I drew up many projects and spent many a sleepless night in devising methods for so long awaited positive action.

Nasser then goes on to describe one such attempted assassination in which he took part and then tells how he was assailed with doubts after having escaped from the scene of the shooting: 'I lay on my bed in the dark and lit one cigarette after the other. Had I done right?' He comes to realize that the 'glory of a nation' cannot be achieved 'by the disappearance of one who should disappear' but by preparing the way for one who must come.

> Glory is something that has to be built up. We must change our methods. What we have done is not the positive action which we feel is our duty. The problem has deeper roots and is much too significant to be tackled in this negative way.

> Suddenly I called out: 'I hope he will not die!' It is strange that the dawn found in me the desire that a man might live whose death I had wished for the evening before!

> I anxiously waited for the morning papers. I was relieved: the victim of our planned assassination was out of danger.

> But that was not the basic problem. The main problem remained, namely to discover what positive action was now required of us.

> From this time on our thoughts were concentrated on doing something more radical, more serious, more effective. At that time we began to sketch the outlines of the picture which then took shape on the night of the 23rd of July: the outlines of a revolution which was to spring from the heart of the people, expressing its longings and leading it forward on the same path along which it had already taken its first steps towards freedom. (From *Die Arabische Revolution, Nasser über seine Politik*, edited by F. R. Allemann.)

Nasser considers these first steps to have been the 'revolution' of Saiyid Makram by which Muhammad Ali came to power, the 'Urabi Revolt (cf. p. 167) and the Revolution of 1919 (see p. 218). None of these achieved their aims; it was only his revolution, that of the 23rd of July, which was destined to do so.

Now, what really happened on the 23rd of July?

A group of young officers, calling themselves the 'Free Officers', rebelled against the King, the Palace circles, the commander-in-chief, whom the King had shortly before forced upon the Army, and against a recently installed government on which the King exercised considerable influence. The *coup d'état* was well organized and carried out without bloodshed. On the morning of the 23rd the whole of Egypt was in the power of the 'Free Officers'.

It appears that the group of Free Officers came together as a result of the Palestine crisis. According to Nasser, their first plans were hatched in support of the Arab cause in Palestine. Nasser describes in detail how the realization dawned upon him in the beleaguered fortress of Falluja that the Egyptian Army's real battle front was not in the field against Israel, but first and foremost in Egypt. The officers of the Egyptian Army in Palestine felt that they had been left in the lurch by Cairo; not only this, but business had been made out of supplying them with faulty or insufficient arms and ammunition or even with no arms and ammunition at all. On their return to Egypt Nasser and his associates became every day more convinced that the existing régime had to be removed by force and the whole system with its ruling classes done away with. They believed, perhaps naïvely, that, when the 'corrupt' elements were removed, the pure and selfless would come forward and help in administering and developing the country.

In reality the Free Officers' 'positive action' only began after their *coup de main* had succeeded. Nasser himself describes in his little book how, contrary to what he expected, the 'good and pure' elements did not automatically come forward as soon as the 'corrupt' ones had been got rid of. However, for the details, for the various phases of the development and for the many intrigues leading up to them the enquirer should not consult the 'Philosophy of the Revolution' but observers like the Lacoutures.

In an early phase the Free Officers seem to have been willing to remain in the background. Forced to some extent by the special circumstances of the intrigues within the Army, they sought out a nominal chief, General Naguib. When King Faruk learned shortly after the end of the Palestinian War that an opposition group had been formed in the Army he decided, quite typically, to create a counter-group of officers loyal to him and of court favourites. General Naguib came into conflict with the officers of the 'court group' although he had only loose ties with the group of Free Officers. The direct cause of the Free Officers' rebellion was elections in the Officers' Club in Cairo. The King had dismissed the club committee elected by the 'Young Officers', including the President General Naguib, and had installed his own candidates in their stead. When the 'putsch' took place the Free Officers, who were completely unknown young men, needed a figure to lead them who was politically experienced and in a position to negotiate with the professional politicians. Their choice naturally fell on General Naguib since it was obvious that the General was on bad terms with the court, himself required support and would thus be ready to collaborate with them.

In this first phase the Free Officers went even farther in preserving their 'anonymity'. They tried to find politicians to lead the country along the lines they deemed right but this experiment was soon to fail. Politicians of the old school, like Ali Mahir, the first Prime Minister of the Revolution, resigned as soon as it became clear to them that the Free Officers were determined to keep power in the stricter sense in their own hands in order to enforce their own ideas. Slowly but surely the Free Officers were made to realize that, if they were to determine the policy of the new Egypt, they would also have to take upon themselves the responsibility for that policy.

They then tried to persuade the political parties to 'cleanse' themselves. The Wafd gave the impression of complying but in the end stood out against the land reform project launched by the officers. Land reform was contrary to the principal interests of the great landowners whose party the Wafd had become. Finally all political parties were dissolved. The Muslim Brothers, who had supported the revolution from the beginning, were allowed to function for a time as a 'religious organization'. The king was sent into exile, a council of regency was formed and later re-formed and in the end the monarchy was declared abolished. The revolution was marked in its first year by the fact that it gradually spread, as it seemed, almost reluctantly. The Free Officers found themselves faced again and again with situations in which they had to choose between surrendering power or enforcing their own ideas. Everything indicates that many of their conceptions only crystallized fully in such moments of crisis. They emerged and were formulated more or less clearly because they were required if the 'revolution' was to continue. At the same time it is clear that during this process the more active of the Free Officers, especially Nasser, by then already the recognized leader of the group, acquired a taste for power.

Nasser was then—and certainly still is—honestly convinced that 'his' revolution has fulfilled the desires and dreams of the Egyptian people, even if the Egyptian people has from time to time to be forced or persuaded by propaganda for its own good. But it seems clear to an unprejudiced observer that power for its own sake, the possibility of commanding and enforcing his commands, has become more and more one of the driving motives of Nasser's actions, perhaps unconsciously or only half consciously.

It was the battle for power which finally brought about the rift between the organizer of the revolution, Nasser, and the head of state installed by the revolution, Naguib. Naguib demanded a policy of returning quickly to a democratic system while Nasser tended more and more towards a policy of social, economic and psychological reforms. For him a 'return to democracy' could only be considered after carrying out radical changes in the social body of Egypt. Presumably it was not these theoretical attitudes of the two leaders of the revolution which were important but rather the fact that Naguib did not wish to take orders from Nasser, having gradually become convinced of his own popularity throughout the country. He found himself winning support in increasing measure from the most varied political elements, ranging from remnants of the Wafd and parliament to the Muslim Brothers, and was ready to do battle with the Free Officers.

As for Nasser, he was not popular at that time. He was not a great orator and he seems to have developed his nowadays famous charm only later. On the other hand the outcome of his struggle with Naguib showed that the latter much under-estimated support for Nasser in the Army and his talent for organization. On 25th February 1954 Naguib tendered his resignation and Nasser became Prime Minister. After huge demonstrations in Cairo Naguib became President again on the 27th. On 9th March Nasser tendered his resignation as Prime Minister. At Naguib's instigation the edict banning political parties was rescinded on 25th March, but on the 29th the revolutionary council under Nasser's chairmanship decided to postpone execution of this decree. Then began the long negotiations with Britain over the Canal Zone which will be dealt with presently. These led to the conclusion of a treaty on 19th October. On 26th October certain elements among the Muslim Brothers tried to shoot Nasser. But by then he had found sufficient support to checkmate Naguib. On 14th November the General retired for the second and last time from the Egyptian political scene. Since then he has been living under guard in a villa in the vicinity of Cairo.

Egypt's official propagandists and historians still do not like to talk about that year of struggle between Nasser and Naguib. The reason for their silence can easily be guessed: it is clear from the reports of contemporary observers that Naguib was by far the more popular. He enjoyed the support both of the 'politicians' and of the masses. His smile and his friendly personality dominated the political scene. Nasser stood in the wings, little known and little liked, shy of the people. However, he knew how to keep his influence over the Army and after his initial failures made it his aim to organize 'popularity', too, for himself whereas Naguib seemingly relied too much on his being a man of the people and neglected to assure for himself a reliable following.

The Nasser-Naguib struggle is a good example of a political situation in which an 'immature' people has, in Nasser's opinion, to be *forced* to choose what is good and right for the country. At the same time Nasserist theoreticians maintain that he is not a dictator and so do not like to talk about those happenings. Since Naguib's fall the 'compulsion' which weighs on Egypt has been exercised, well hidden under the velvet glove of a skilled propaganda organization with practically a monopoly of all channels of information. It was only in the critical year 1954, in which Nasser had to get rid of his rival for power, that it appeared undisguised.

7

Nasser and the British

WHILE IN THE FIELD of internal politics the struggles for power and manoeuvres between Nasser, Naguib and the old parties, principally the Wafd, were running their course, the Egyptian state was carrying on tough negotiations with the British, aimed at nothing less than the abolition of the colonial heritage. For decades the main obstacle to the conclusion of a new treaty had been the Egyptians' insistence on discussing simultaneously the two main prob-lems, the Sudan question and the problem of the Canal. When the revolution came to power Egypt's international reputation was very low; international trade relations were still suffering from the effects of 'Black Saturday' when Cairo was set on fire, and trade itself had suffered badly from the speculation of Wafdist circles with cotton prices.

In this situation General Naguib seems to have seized the initiative to negotiate with Britain first over the Sudan question and later over the Canal Zone. Naguib was the son of a Sudanese mother and had himself seen long service in the Sudan. He showed more understanding of the Sudanese than the average Egyptian. Most Egyptians, even the educated, cannot quite rid them-selves of the centuries-old prejudice of seeing the Sudanese as ''Abid', the dialect word for 'blacks' and for 'slaves', and of believing that they must necessarily rejoice over everything coming from Cairo, the great Arab capital.

Naguib had enough understanding for the Sudanese to know that conditions in the Sudan had changed radically since Muhammad Ali's times. In Khar-toum there had grown up a generation of capable young civil servants, repre-sentatives of the liberal professions, technicians, officers and administrators who for their part demanded their freedom from both the British and the Egyptians.

In addition there was in the field of traditional politics coloured by religion the powerful sect of followers of the Mahdi, called the *Ansar* or Helpers of the Prophet and led by a grandson of the Mahdi, Saiyid Abdur-Rahman al-Mahdi, which since the time of the Mahdist revolt had been anti-Egyptian. The rivals of the Mahdists, the *Khatmiya*, had as their spiritual leader the head of a Sunni mystic order and as their political leaders pro-Egyptian politicians like Isma'il al-Azhari. They were for collaboration, even union with Egypt.

Naguib, who was on friendly terms with the leading personalities and fully conversant with the politics of the Sudan, seems to have taken it upon himself to concede to the British in principle that Egypt was willing to recognize the Sudanese right to self-determination. On this basis it was possible to open negotiations. The practical details of how power was to be transferred from a British to a Sudanese administration were laid down after lengthy discussions and in this way the Sudan achieved her independence sooner than she could have done through direct negotiations with Britain. A three-years' transition period was agreed upon after which all British officials were to leave the Sudan and the Sudanese to elect their own government. This government would then take a decision on the question of 'union' with Egypt or independence.

After the Sudan question had been settled negotiations were begun on the Canal Zone which at that time was still occupied by British troops. The British declared themselves ready to evacuate the zone provided they received guarantees for the security of the canal, for the maintenance of the military installations in the zone and for a possible return to the fortified zone in the event of war.

The negotiations which were conducted by Nasser were to prove exceedingly long drawn out and difficult and were broken off and resumed several times. Britain's attempts to win Egypt over for the anti-communist defence pact which the West desired came to nothing and in the end Nasser succeeded in having his point of view accepted: British troops would evacuate the Canal Zone, civilian technicians would look after the military installations, Egypt guaranteed Britain entry into the zone in the event of an attack 'from outside the Middle East' and Egypt undertook expressly to make no changes in the existing Canal treaties and even envisaged the extension of the Canal Company's concession after its expiry in 1969.

When the Suez agreement, which was very favourable to Nasser, was finally concluded in October 1954 it was opposed by the extremist 'nationalists' who demanded that Britain evacuate Egypt unconditionally. They felt that the more conciliatory, but also more realistic attitude of Nasser and the revolutionary government was a 'betrayal' of the old traditions of the nationalist party. This phenomenon is characteristic of the Near East: popularity is won by drawing up a grandiose programme and putting forward enormous demands and the masses do not worry very much whether those demands can be achieved or that programme carried out or not. Nasser himself was soon to become a past master in the technique of gaining and using this type of popularity. But in the case of the Suez negotiations he proved himself an 'unpopular' realist and a practical man.

8

Internal Politics and Economy

AFTER NASSER had got rid of the two main obstacles which had stood in his way, the presence of the British and the claim to leadership of the 'nominal' head of state, Naguib, he again found himself faced with the old question which had troubled him *post factum* as a young terrorist—'to find out what positive action now demanded of us'.

At first it seemed that internal politics more than anything else could give the answer. Egypt was poor; her national income per head and per year is reckoned to be between 120 and 140 dollars and in the Near East the national income of 'oil-rich' Saudi Arabia is the only one which falls below it. The country was over-populated and births were greatly in excess of deaths partly owing to the rising standards of hygiene. So the revolutionary régime decided that the 'revolution' had to be first and foremost a social revolution.

But it was a social revolution ordered 'from above' and such directed 'revolutions' are not easily brought about. The régime's greatest success in this field has been in land reform. A law was brought in according to which a landowner together with his sons could hold no more than 300 feddans (300 acres approx.), which was still quite a considerable amount. Land in excess of this had to be either sold, surrendered to relations or put at the state's disposal in return for government bonds. The great land holdings of court officials and the royal family were taken over without compensation. The state then proceeded to 'distribute' the landed property so acquired, in theory as small holdings of under 5 feddans to individual peasants. In practice, however, owing to the highly specialized and industrialized nature of Egyptian agriculture, this meant that a government official took over the functions of the former estate adminis-trator. He provides the peasants with the seeds for their cotton plantations, determines how much cotton each one must grow and buys up the cotton when it is picked at a price fixed by the government, which also controls the export and sale of cotton. The sums the peasant earns with his cotton seem on the whole to cover his tax debts to the state and the payment for 'his' land, irrigation, union services, etc. The products he grows in addition to cotton cover his own consumer requirements or, to a lesser extent, are sold in the markets.

In earlier times it was normal for the lease holder to surrender all of his cotton and about half of all other produce to his landlord and so a state-regimented 'landowner' of today is considerably better off than a former lease holder, even though he does not have full responsibility for his land and its management, and thus freedom in the European sense.

The lands which were distributed in this way came to about 10 per cent of all land cultivated in Egypt, the great majority of peasants continuing to live on as tenants. Three hundred feddans are still quite enough for a 'middle-class' Egyptian or village sheikh to let and live comfortably on their oncome, for in Egypt 300 feddans bring in a yearly income of between £4,000 and £5,000.

In practice the land was distributed among its former lease holders but these reforms did very little to reduce the number of unemployed or under-employed which is estimated at about 5 millions in a population of 26 millions.

The greatest gain—from the sociological point of view—achieved by the reform is that farm rents fell throughout the country. Maximum rents had already been fixed by the state but had not been adhered to any more than minimum wages. The pressure of those in need of work and of land was too great and everyone knew how to get around the regulations: nominal rents plus additional sums which were not mentioned or nominal wages minus the same. But when the land reform brought about the fall of land prices and at the same time of farm rents it could be foreseen that a new rise in prices could only be avoided if the state were able to find ways and means to reduce the pressure of the population on the land. Doreen Warriner (from whose two brilliant treatises on agriculture in the Near East we have taken our information: 1 *Land and Poverty in the Middle East*; 2 *Land Reform and Development in the Middle East*, London, 1948 and 1957) cites a further fact which is worth noting from the point of view of economics: According to the theories of modern economists the improved situation of the Egyptian peasants should have led to an increased consumption of consumer goods of all kinds and so to a general cranking-up of the Egyptian economy. This, however, does not seem to have been the case. Doreen Warriner gives an explanation of this which in itself is enough to throw light on the situation of the Egyptian peasantry. She believes that when the peasants' economic situation improved they simply ate their fill. After they had satisfied their hunger a little better than before the surplus of profit taken from the 'rich classes' was all eaten up and there was hardly any money left over for an increased consumption of consumer goods.

The other projects which the revolutionary government had undertaken have been even less successful than the land reform.

Liberation Province is one very costly undertaking to obtain new land from the desert. So far about one twentieth of the area envisaged has been brought under the plough—which is not to say that it is already productive—and the cultivation of this twentieth has cost many times the sums estimated. Today Cairo maintains a discreet silence about this project—the first director, an officer of the Revolutionary Council, has been dismissed and it is emphasized that the plans can only be proceeded with after the Aswan High Dam has been constructed.

The *High Dam* is a major project which has lacked money right from the start. The first plan was drawn up early in the nineteenth century. It was envisaged that Britain and America would provide part of the requisite financial aid and it was the withdrawal of their offer which conjured up the Suez crisis. Thereupon the Russians undertook to finance the first two stages of the construction but from the purely economic point of view it remains to be seen whether the Egyptians will succeed not only in damming up the waters of the Nile but also in putting them to good use for the cultivation of the desert. The experiences of Liberation Province are not a good augury of this.

In addition there is the problem of dividing between the Sudan and Egypt the water 'which will be preserved for irrigation by the High Dam'. This question was finally decided in the winter of 1959 after long intrigues and arguments by an agreement which does not seem to be in Egypt's favour. The Sudanese military régime, which came to power to some extent as a reaction against Egyptian intrigues, used its position of strength to obtain two thirds of the water 'which will be preserved for irrigation' by the High Dam to be built by Egypt.

The Egyptian Revolution turned its attention only gradually to *industrialization projects*, perhaps under the influence of the friendship with Tito and Soviet Russia which will be dealt with later. Today, as projects, they constitute an essential of Cairo's policy. They are considered, perhaps rightly, the only means of mastering the increase of population and the chronic under-employment in Egypt. But so far little of real importance has been achieved.

The basic danger, which always threatens when a state tries to carry out at one and the same time an expansive and a 'social' economic policy, is especially apparent in Egypt: new industries are planned and set up which only pay for themselves when the state provides markets for them at home by means of customs barriers or simply when the state owns and manages them and ensures for them a monopoly. The prices of these 'artificial' industries are then higher than those on the world markets. Now, since Egypt is in many respects dependent on world markets Egyptians must pay excessive prices for certain products which the state produces, whereas the best prices they can hope to get for their own products are those current on the world markets.

9

Pan-Arabism

ALTHOUGH THE EGYPTIAN revolutionary government was unable to achieve direct successes in the fields of internal politics and economics, one branch of their policy was to prove so successful that it grew within a few years into a mighty tree. Nasser's approach to pan-Arabism was, as in the other aspects of his policy, not that of a doctrinarian but that of an empiricist. The strategic experiences of centuries had taught him that Egypt is dependent for her military defence on the collaboration of her (Arab) neighbours. In a frequently quoted passage of his 'Philosophy of the Revolution' he himself describes how military considerations had led him to the conviction that it was essential for all Arabs to make a common defence against 'colonialism' and all other possible enemies.

At the same time Nasser mentions two other circles in which, in his opinion, Egyptian policy has an important part to play: the African 'circle', because Egypt is geographically part of Africa, and the pan-Isamic circle, because Egypt is an Islamic country and one of the most important Islamic universities is situated in Cairo. However, experience has shown that not much can be achieved politically with the African and pan-Islamic 'circles'. Propaganda platforms for both of these have been set up in Cairo. African 'freedom' congresses of all sorts are held there and anti-colonialist negro politicians are readily given asylum and often financial support as well. Cairo Radio broadcasts in many African languages and an African review is published in Arabic and in English. As experience has shown, the young African states willingly accept Egypt's financial and diplomatic support but as they progress along the road to independence they make it quite clear that they intend to manage their own affairs and refuse to allow Cairo to influence their policies.

The Egyptians have not been more successful in the pan-Islamic 'circle'. The Egyptian ulema of the Azhar are usually at the Government's disposal when it wishes to make a demonstration on the pan-Islamic platform but, in spite of the great prestige enjoyed by the Azhar throughout the Islamic world, their solemn declarations seem to make little impact outside Egypt. Most Muslims see the difference between 'political' and 'religious' manifestoes and, for example, are fully aware that the ulema of Cairo only declare 'Holy War' against communism when that is the line taken by the Egyptian Government. It has not been forgotten that these same dignitaries visited Moscow not long before and praised in their writings and speeches the lot of the Muslims living in the Soviet Union. In Pakistan and Afghanistan, for example, Nasser's political stock is high with the secularized educated and half-educated classes because they admire his adroitness in manoeuvring between East and West, but at the same time Egypt does not enjoy a high religious reputation with the common people or with those intellectuals who are interested in religious matters. It is felt instinctively that Egyptian Islam is in the service of Cairo's policy.

The extension of Cairo's influence upon the Arab sister states is another story. In these Nasser's reputation increased enormously and the point of view put out by his propaganda machine became a power which no politician could afford to ignore.

As late as 1958 pan-Arabism emanating from Cairo seemed about to sweep away all other political tendencies in the Arab countries but since the rise of Qasim and his followers it has found a counter-balance in Baghdad. No one can say as yet whether this dam will be swept away sooner or later by the high tide of Egyptian pan-Arabism or whether Qasim's resistance to Nasser, which has hardened since the spring of 1959, means a final halting of pan-Arabism as preached by Cairo.

How can we explain the success of Nasser's pan-Arabism with the 'other' Arabs in the years following its proclamation? It can be assumed that it satisfied the deep need of most Arabs for a new political line of thought. After the defeat in Palestine they saw themselves faced with bankruptcy of two kinds. It seemed clear that the politicians of the old school had failed and they were blamed for the defeat and, out of hand, for all social, economic, military and political grievances in the Arab world. It was they who had *ruled* and now others had the right to try their hand.

It was not so clear that the proto-fascist 'authoritarian' parties of the second generation had failed. These parties had never come to power and had never had the opportunity to disappoint the people. However, they suffered from the eclipse of international Fascism after the Second World War and were reduced to playing the part of merely secondary movements.

Pan-Arabism had, of course, existed long before Nasser but what transformed it from a rather sluggish ideal into a political power was the fact that Nasser began to couple 'his' pan-Arabism with 'neutralism'. This had been in the beginning an almost chance result of political circumstances and, especially, of the tactless insistence of the West that the Arabs should join a defence alliance directed against the Soviet Union. In addition the rivalry between Nuri's Iraq and Nasser's Egypt was a contributory factor.

In the beginning the young dictator, Nasser, would not have been averse to a defence alliance with the West but soon the suspicion arose that this would force Egypt to accept the 'tutelage' of the 'colonialists'. Moreover, Nuri showed himself as the champion of an alliance with the West and the lack of tact of Western negotiators and diplomats and Western collaboration with Israel did all that was required to make the Egyptian head of state, if not averse, at least more and more sceptical towards Western proposals for an alliance. Then, in a second phase, it seems to have dawned on him what an enormous propagandist potential there was to be gained from an Arab 'neutralist' attitude.

His 'neutralism', which was put forward at first tentatively and in obscure terms, proved unexpectedly popular right from the start. This was clear at the time of the unrest in Amman when not only the 'street' demonstrated against joining the Baghdad Pact but even young King Husain was influenced by the 'nationalists' and decided to break with Britain and the British commander of his 'Beduin army'. King Husain was to be the first 'neutralist' to be forced a little later by the instinct for self-preservation to draw closer to the 'West'. In the last few years the dangers of their course have become obvious even to the two 'great' neutralists, Nehru and Nasser. This was done for Nasser by Iraq and for Nehru by Tibet and Red China. Even though they have not, for the time being, given up their neutralist line both of them have, in fact, been forced to modify it.

There was no trace of all this in 1955 when 'neutralism' was officially baptized in Bandung. At that time neutralism filled a deep want felt by the 'under-developed' countries. The more limited the individual's political horizon was the more imperative did it seem to him not to get drawn into the conflict between the 'West' and the 'Soviet Union'. He was faced with quite different tasks and might indeed, in the long run, act as intermediary between the two camps. Why, he asked, should he spend money for armaments, when he needed it so badly for development? Why should he join the Western armed camp whose great powers were still for him a symbol of oppression, whose politicians and nations he mistrusted and whose economy sought to 'exploit' him?

The man in the street *could* not, and the politicians *did not want* to know that the opposite camp concealed quite other dangers and temptations for they had not yet had actual experience of its onrush. They comforted themselves with the fact that the two great opponents seemed to be evenly matched.

The combination of Afro-Asian 'neutralism' and nationalist pan-Arabism was to become Nasser's special line. It was perhaps Israel which led Nasser to this for massive retaliatory attacks by Israel on the Gaza Zone in February and October 1955 most probably faced Nasser with the necessity of acquiring arms at all costs if he was not to be faced with a revolt by his own officers. After fruitless negotiations with the United States he got these arms from Czecho-slovakia and, as was later openly admitted, from Russia.

The so-called 'arms deal' immediately received loud acclaim from the great majority of the Arabs. 'If the West refuses to sell us arms we can get them from the Russians!' was the general cry of joy. The Levantine business acumen was stimulated and there was opened up a possibility to exercise a new sort of pressure on the 'colonialist' West. It flattered the Arabs to be able at last to show the Western powers that they had caused themselves most harm by supporting Israel. 'Now they will see to what their actions have led. In future Russia will espouse the Arab cause.'

10

The Suez Crisis

THE SUEZ CRISIS is indirectly connected with the 'arms deal'. The purchase of
Russian arms along with a series of manipulations of the Egyptian state
finances which Washington considered highly unorthodox led to the Secretary
of State Dulles's brusque withdrawal of the offer to provide a loan to finance
the High Dam. Nasser's answer to this American step was to nationalize the
Suez Canal and after a period of international conferences, manoeuvres,
accusations and counter-charges lasting from 26 July until 29 October 1956
Britain and France decided to resort to the use of arms.

At the same time Israel attacked in the Sinai Peninsula. It is still officially
maintained that there was no, or little, collusion between Israel and the two old
colonial powers just as it is still not clear how far and at what level American
statesmen were informed of the Israeli-French-British plans.

In a well-conducted, three-day long campaign the Israeli Army succeeded in
occupying the whole of Sinai and in destroying the Egyptian bases and
capturing the arms dumps there but the French and British military machine
proved less effective and much too slow and clumsy. It took longer to organize
the attack on the Canal in 1956 than it had taken Nelson 150 years earlier to
plan the Battle of Abukir and destroy Napoleon's fleet. This gave the Egyptians
the opportunity to gain time and to appeal to the Russians and the whole world
for help. Whereas the Israelis were able to achieve their strategic aims in the
Canal Zone within three days with their 'unorthodox' army, the British and the
French were unable to occupy the Canal before the politicians of the United
Nations, Moscow and Washington began to protest and intervene in unison.

However, it is doubtful whether the total occupation of the Canal would have
caused the action to succeed. Too little consideration had been given in
government circles in the two western countries involved as to what was to be
done once the Canal was occupied. They no doubt thought that its occupation
would be a fatal blow to Nasser's prestige and that he would be forced to
resign. But in this they were greatly deceived for, on the contrary, Nasser was
able to turn his military defeat into a propaganda victory, and that within a very
short time. Nasser himself wrote an article in the leading Egyptian illustrated
weekly describing how the main bulk of the Egyptian Army had been saved by
the successful strategic withdrawal in Sinai and the Egyptian propaganda

machine inflated the 'resistance' of the 'martyred city' Port Said into a great popular national epic. Both versions that of the strategic retreat and that of the 'martyred city', are still believed word for word in Egypt. Official publicists have repeated these two themes in innumerable versions, in public speeches, 'eye-witness' accounts and film versions of the events for so long that even the most sceptical have become convinced that at least a part of all these stories must be true.

But, if one refrains from speculating as to what might have happened if the Western military men had acted more resolutely and more quickly, one thing is nevertheless quite clear: Nasser's fame became immeasurably great in Egypt and—still more—among the Arabs outside Egypt after the Suez adventure. In the eyes of all Arabs he was the one man who had succeeded in challenging the Western powers which had for so long lorded it over the Near East and in standing up to them in spite of their use of force. No Arab since Saladin had been able to do that. Very few Arabs know that Saladin was by race a Kurd!

The High Tide of Nationalism

i JORDAN

THE FIRST ARAB COUNTRY in which Nasser's increased prestige seemed to bear fruit was Jordan and in February 1957 the union between Jordan and a pro-Nasser Syria appeared about to take place. Elections in the previous October had brought pro-Egyptian and anti-British elements to power and the army was controlled by the 'nationalist' Abu Nawar. Young King Husain seemed faced with the choice of either abdicating or of playing the part of a 'nationalist' and surrendering much of his independence.

But instead of the expected union with Syria or Egypt it was the king who struck a counter-blow. A rift appeared between him and his pro-Nasser government on the question of diplomatic relations with the Soviet Union. After dramatic events in the army camp of Zarqa Husain was able to reassert his personal influence with the Beduins of the Arab Legion, to brand the pro-Nasser elements as 'traitors' and banish them from the country. Parliament was dissolved and a government of East Jordanians loyal to the King was set up.

The Egyptians were inclined, perhaps not quite without cause, to see the hand of America in this *coup* against the nationalist forces. The United States had succeeded Britain as the power affording Jordan protection and financial support and King Husain could at least count on America backing him up. But Cairo went even further. Violent attacks were made on the American 'imperialists' for having planned the *coup* of the Jordanian 'reactionaries' against the 'nationalists'.

Although the United States had been instrumental in saving Nasser and his régime during the Suez crisis, they now became the main target of Egyptian propaganda attacks. That may not say much for the gratitude of the Egyptians but it was an almost inevitable result of the new division of political forces.

After the failure of the Suez action, Britain and France ceased to be decisive factors in middle-eastern politics and the United States was the only major power left which could counter the increasing Russian influence in the Near East. In doing so America had to take over a large part of the political heritage of the former colonial powers. Egypt, as champion of anti-colonialism, could by no means accept the western theory of a 'power vacuum' in the Middle East for she maintained that Nasser's Arab nationalism had already filled this vacuum.

ii PRESSURE ON SYRIA AND UNION WITH EGYPT

Within a year Egypt was called to fill the power vacuum where it threatened to be most dangerous. Increasing Russian influence in the Near East threw the always unstable political situation in Syria off balance. Looking back we can sketch as follows the political forces which were active behind a thick veil of propaganda in Damascus during the winter 1957–58. Since the end of Shishakli's dictatorship Syria had been ruled by a weak combination of politicians and officers with political ambitions. In addition to old style 'freedom fighters', like President Quwwatli, who were mostly patriarchal anti-colonialists and nationalists of property, two modern parties became increasingly influential owing to the modern methods they employed. These were the *Baathists* and the Communists. Both knew how to stir up the masses for their purposes and make political capital which bore no relationship to the actual strength of their parties.

In the main their technique was to outbid all their rivals for power in radical, nationalistic and pan-Arab declamations. Until their failure in Jordan Communism and the Baath were in alliance but during the summer of 1957 they parted company. It appears that the Baath renounced the Communists in order to pursue its pan-Arab aims whereas the Communists hoped to come to power quickly with the help of a feudal politician of the old school. It is difficult to decide which of the two, the Baath or the Communist Party, was the first to break off collaboration, but what is clear is that these former partners have been deadly enemies ever since and pretend that they never had anything to do with each other.

Thus there were formed two camps, on the one side the Baathists with old-style 'nationalists' under Quwwatli as their more or less willing allies and with the head of the Syrian Secret Service, Sarraj, as 'their man' in the army, and on the other side the Communists and the 'old style' politician *Khalid al-Azm* played into each other's hands, having their link, too, with the army in *Afif al-Bizri*.

Khalid al-Azm is one of the richest landowners in Damascus, scion of the Turkish family from which the Ottoman governors of the city were once chosen. He is an ambitious politician and an old rival of Quwwatli's for the presidency. He appears to have determined to come to power on the wave of Russian favour. As the outcome of a quarrel with King Saud in the summer of 1957 he had been forced to leave Damascus but, nevertheless, without losing his job as Foreign Minister. He went on convalescent leave to Europe and, apparently to the surprise of some members of the government to which he belonged, paid a more or less official visit to Moscow. On his return a change took place in the attitude of the army: an 'American conspiracy' was uncovered, a number of politicians were thrown into gaol and the fellow-travelling Afif al-Bizri became

Chief of the General Staff. Khalid al-Azm's party seemed to be in the ascendant and in the autumn and winter of 1957 managed to improve its position by putting out warnings, supported by Soviet propaganda, of an imminent Turkish attack. It systematically worked up the hysteria of the masses in Damascus so that trenches were dug and a people's militia organized.

The Baath-Quwwatli party saw itself challenged with its own weapons. Whichever side was able to stir up the passions of the Syrians most successfully could count on exercising decisive pressure on the government by mobilizing the masses. Faced with the imminent success of the Khalid al-Azm-Communist combination the Baathists and the politicians around Quwwatli made a desperate counter-move: in order to snatch their prey from their opponents at the very last moment they surrendered Syria's independence and offered Nasser the union of Syria with Egypt. This union was enormously popular for it seemed to bring the realization of the dream of Arab unity at last within the foreseeable future. Nasser was the symbol of the success of nationalism and the Syrians saw him, as many still do, not as an Egyptian but as an Arab. Union with other Arab countries seemed to have become possible and the Damascenes in their enthusiasm already saw 'Arab Unity' as an accomplished fact.

Nevertheless, the Yemen was the only country to establish loose ties with the newly formed United Arab Republic. For the moment the communist danger was exorcized in Syria and Khalid al-Azm was forced to leave Damascus. All parties, including the Communist Party, were banned. Ex-president Quwwatli was designated First Citizen of the UAR. The Baath, although officially dissolved, was given the most important ministerial posts in the new provincial government in Damascus and was intent on gaining influence in the Central Government in Cairo, too.

As a reaction to the foundation of the UAR Jordan drew closer to Iraq and the two Hashimite kingdoms came together in a short-lived 'Arab Federation' whose purpose was to ensure the continued existence of little Jordan between the two 'regions' of the UAR, Syria and Egypt.

iii LEBANON

The pressure of pan-Arab propaganda was now transferred to Lebanon. The peculiar composition of that country, consisting half of Christians of various churches and confessions and half of Muslims of various sects and communities made it especially sensitive to internal divisions. President *Chamoun* (Sham'un) had adopted a decidedly pro-Western attitude and Lebanon was the only country which had declared itself in agreement with the Eisenhower Doctrine. During the Suez crisis Chamoun had refused to follow Syria's example and break off diplomatic relations with Britain and France.

At that time a series of explosions in British and French business houses in the Lebanese capital demonstrated the sympathy of the 'people' with Egypt's sufferings. Raw materials for bombs were discovered in the Egyptian military attaché's car and incidents like this naturally did not help to improve relations between Lebanon and the UAR.

In Lebanon, too, there was an opposition consisting of politicians for whom Chamoun's last electoral victory had been all too radical. First among the President's personal enemies was the Maronite Patriarch Méouchi, a cousin of the previous President, Bishara al-Khuri, whom Chamoun had been instru-mental in deposing. Chamoun's opponents naturally comprised the minority of young enthusiasts and Muslim 'nationalists' who were working for Lebanon to unite with Egypt as Syria had done. Large quantities of arms were smuggled over the frontier with Syria which for a long time had been practically un-controlled. The Druse community, especially, the larger part of whom live in Syria, had never taken the frontier seriously.

When Chamoun had his supporters spread the report that he intended to stand for election for a further term of six years as President by altering the constitution to this effect with the help of his parliamentary majority, demonstra-tions and strikes took place in the Muslim towns, Sur (Tyre) and Saida (Sidon) and in the Druse areas. After a journalist opposed to the President had been murdered a general strike was proclaimed on 9th May and large Muslim areas of the country came out in open revolt.

The army confined itself to preventing, as far as possible, looting and similar acts but the commander-in-chief, General Chéhab (Shihab), refused to use force in the interest or on behalf of one part of the country against the other. He had adopted a similar attitude six years earlier on the occasion of the uprising against President Bishara al-Khuri. On the latter occasion Chéhab's inactivity had been in Chamoun's interest but this time it was against it.

For some months the country was in a state almost amounting to civil war, the opposed areas corresponding in the main to the Muslim or Christian areas of the country or quarters of the cities. The army and the police strove to confine and encircle the rebellious areas but not to pacify them. The areas bordering on Syria were practically governed from Damascus through the local tribal chiefs and poli-ticians. In vain the Lebanese Government complained to the United Nations of 'massive infiltration' from Syria. UNO sent observers who patrolled certain rebellious areas in white jeeps by day and saw nothing of this infiltration!

Only when revolution broke out in Iraq on 14th July 1958, thus creating a new situation in the whole Near East, did the Americans answer the appeal of Chamoun's government and disembark troops in Beirut, while King Husain called for the support of British troops which were flown in.

iv REVOLUTION IN IRAQ

The bloody revolution in Iraq came very suddenly. Most observers had for long known that many of the middle and lower middle classes were dissatisfied with the state of affairs in Iraq and it was also clear that their dissatisfaction was exploited and stirred up by radio propaganda from Cairo. This dissatisfaction of the growing middle and lower classes in the towns had two main causes: they complained that the wealth from oil merely went into the pockets of the ruling upper class and the government's policy, compared with that of the government in Cairo, seemed subservient to foreigners and too little Arab and national. Britain was still considered the power 'colonizing' and 'exploiting' Iraq, even if this was being done in a subtle manner.

Nevertheless, the revolution came as a surprise to most observers. It was prepared, launched and carried out by an army officer whom Nuri al-Sa'id's government had considered completely reliable and non-political, Brigadier *Abdul Karim Qasim*. The revolution in Baghdad was to prove a spark which caused those basic destructive forces, from time immemorial especially strong in Mesopotamia, to explode and commit acts of violence.

The effect of the revolution in Baghdad was not less violent outside Iraq. For a moment it seemed that Arab nationalism was about to win the last battle. The union of Iraq with the United Arab Republic was thought very probable and the nationalists believed they would gain the oil-fields of Kuwait in the Persian Gulf at the same time. The balance of power between Iraq and Egypt which had existed since the end of the First World War threatened to collapse all of a sudden and it seemed that all the governments in the Near East must soon collapse or change their policies in favour of Cairo and even of Moscow.

But the American landings with heavy war material, a hundred times more than the local situation required, brought some stability into the fluid political situa-tion and when the American troops left Beirut three months later without having fired a shot a solution of the Lebanese conflict was in sight: the arbitrator of the situation, General Chéhab, had been elected president. At the same time Western diplomats in Baghdad had become convinced that Qasim was not at all anxious to unite his country with Egypt and Syria and subordinate himself to Nasser.

Indeed Qasim and Nasser have since become completely estranged. In addition to the Iraqi military dictator's desire to rule his country in his own way the tactlessness of the pro-Nasser party in Baghdad and the attitude of the Egyptian politicians and press have both contributed to the estrangement of these two Arab rulers.

Colonel 'Arif, who represented the pro-Nasser school in the revolutionary government in Baghdad, was dismissed and the 'nationalist' politicians who were well disposed towards 'Arif were checkmated by Qasim. Thereupon pro-Egyptian elements attempted to launch a revolution in Mosul in February 1959, but this was suppressed with great cruelty by the army, the people's militia and pro-Qasim left-wing and Kurdish elements. The Baghdad government accused Cairo of having stirred up this revolt and in any case the Egyptian papers showed clearly enough at the time of the revolt that their sympathies lay with the insurgents. In September 1959 an attempt was made on Qasim's life, again probably by pro-Nasser elements, from which Qasim was lucky to escape with only a wounded arm. Naturally such happenings only served to increase Qasim's mistrust of Egypt and the pan-Arab party in Iraq.

The Communists knew how to profit by this state of affairs, placing themselves at the government's disposal as a counter-weight to the 'nationalists'. For his part, Qasim made, indeed had to make, use of the Communists and their ability to mobilize the 'rabble' for him since after the July revolution there were only two forces left in Baghdad able to influence the masses: (Nasserist) pan-Arabism and Iraqi Communism disguised as nationalism.

The Communists managed to get a considerable number of their supporters into strategic jobs in the government and in Qasim's immediate entourage. They got almost complete control of the Ministries of Information and Education and also acquired great influence in the trade unions and peasant unions which latter they created. Their deceptive humanitarian organizations with international ties like the 'League for Women's Rights', the 'Society of Democratic Youth' and the 'Union of Peace Partisans' were tolerated, indeed supported by the state and became very popular with the people of Baghdad.

Nevertheless, like the pro-Nasser nationalists, but in a less drastic manner, the Communists also turned upon Qasim in the first year of the revolutionary régime. This was shown most clearly in the Kirkuk troubles from 15th to 18th July 1959. The diverse ethnic groups, Turcomans, Kurds and Arabs, living in that provincial town came to blows and the Communists in alliance with the Kurdish troops stationed in Kirkuk seized the city. They proceeded to massacre the Turcomans who were celebrating the first anniversary of the Revolution under the banner of Qasim and Iraqi nationalism. For three days the red flag of Communism flew above Kirkuk which was governed by an executive committee of the Communist-led 'National Front' until the Iraqi Army forced its way in with tanks and took control of the situation.

In the following weeks it was dangerous to mention the Communists in Qasim's presence but the Communists, more skilful in such matters than the pan-Arab nationalists, submitted themselves to self-criticism in public. They proclaimed aloud that they were ready to follow Qasim and that they had had nothing to do with the monstrous crimes committed in Kirkuk. Since then they have known how to keep to their own hunting-grounds, the information services, the schools and University and the trade unions, without coming into direct conflict with the government. But the Communists faced a further difficulty in that their party split into two groups, one minority group apparently more national and Iraqi under Sayigh and a second group which follows the Moscow line. It is typical of Qasim's methods that he has recognized only the weaker 'Iraqi' group officially as a party. He clearly would not be sorry to see it win ground in Iraq at the expense of the more dangerous orthodox Communists.

12

The Ebb of Nasserism

IT WAS NOT ONLY IN IRAQ that Nasser's pan-Arabism suffered setbacks, a certain weakening of Egyptian influence has been noticeable throughout the Near East since the summer of 1959, and especially in *Syria*. There was no end to the dissatisfaction and unrest in the 'Syrian Region' of the United Arab Republic. At first the attacks of the dissatisfied were directed at the Baath Party which had concluded the union and which was held responsible for the failure of the land reform in Syria. There was no end to the complaints against the Baathists in Cairo and it seems that even Nasser's Plenipotentiary for Syria, Marshal Abdul Hakim 'Amir, harped on against them until Nasser finally decided to get rid of the Baath. In the winter of 1959–60 all the prominent Baathists were relieved of their ministerial posts in the Central Government in Cairo and in the government of the Syrian Region. From then Syria was in the main ruled by the Egyptian Marshal and the former associate of the Baath, Sarraj, who became Minister of the Interior, Chief of Police and the man at the controls of a brutal machinery of oppression.

A quarrel, not the first, between 'Amir and Sarraj was the prelude to Nasser's loss of his 'northern Region'. In August 1961 the government of the Syrian Region was abolished and all governmental power was concentrated in Cairo. The Minister of the Interior, Sarraj, was to leave Damascus and take over a ministerial post in Cairo. 'Amir arrived in Damascus to take control of the 'Region' as Nasser's plenipotentiary. But Sarraj, unwilling to give up his post at the centre of the web of the Syrian Secret Services without a fight, returned for a short time in September to Damascus and tried to induce his Syrian subordinates to take orders from himself, not from 'Amir. The attempt failed, Nasser summoned the two quarrelling officers to Cairo, confirmed 'Amir in his post and, after a quarrel, accepted Sarraj's resignation. No sooner had Sarraj resigned than he flew back to Damascus.

While this was going on and while the Syrian information services and nets of secret agents were paralysed by the struggle for power, Colonel Nahlawi proceeded to carry out his military rebellion. Colonel Nahlawi had been 'Amir's personal adjutant ('Amir, in addition to being Nasser's representative in Syria, was commander-in-chief of both armies of the UAR), and had used his position to plan the conspiracy against Egypt along with his colleagues in the First Army which consisted of Syrian troops. It is probable that many of the Syrian conspirators did not envisage a separation of Syria from Egypt but only a partial autonomy for the Syrian Region and, especially, fixed rules safe-guarding the interests of the Syrian officers as against their Egyptian colleagues. It was Nasser himself who provoked the separation of Syria from Egypt after the rebellion had broken out by his sharply negative attitude when in the first days of the revolution the Nahlawi officers offered to keep Syria subordinated to him, under certain conditions.

But after the separation had become inevitable men decidedly opposed to Nasser took over the government in Damascus. Dr Ma'mun al-Kuzbari, a lawyer, politician and member of one of the leading business families in Damascus, became Prime Minister and proceeded with calmness and assurance to plan the reintroduction of a constitutional régime with elections two months after the revolution and the re-establishment of the democratic régime of pre-Nasser times. The Parliament, elected honestly and freely (to be sure no candidate was allowed to present himself under a party label, but only in his own name), looked very like the one which had existed before Nasser and was even farther to the right than its predecessor. The Communists were not represented in it since the leader of the Syrian Communists, Bakdash, had been forbidden to return to Damascus and none of his party comrades were influential enough to be elected as private individuals. Such personal influence was possessed by the landowners and professional politicians of the old school and these came to dominate the new parliament.

On 28 March 1962 it was shown that the officers around Nahlawi were not willing to tolerate such an old-fashioned parliament; its policies and its liberal and conservative draft laws did not please them at all. So Nahlawi and his friends carried out another putsch, parliament was dissolved, many politicians were imprisoned, the government was dismissed and the President was interned.

But then the officers ran up against a sort of boycott by the politicians, all the politicians, even the most 'progressive' among them, the Baath group under Akram Haurani's leadership. The Baath seemed to have learned that authori-tarian methods are more dangerous for their country than democratically elected governments which young men believing in progress might consider too 'reactionary'. The politicians refused to form a new government for Nahlawi and his colleagues. This led to unrest, to dissension within the Army, to a two-day-long counter-revolt of dismissed officers in Aleppo who declared themselves for Nasser, to an accommodation within the Army (the Congress of Homs) after which the Nahlawi group were exiled and finally to the semi-re-establish-ment of legality. The President, Dr Nazim al-Qudsi, was reinstalled and he appointed a government consisting of politicians who were considered 'progres-sive' and who mainly followed the Baath line. This government was to pave the way for a transition to a democratic régime. A promised plebiscite on the question of reunification with Egypt proved to be a somewhat theoretical measure for Nasser had no intention of having anything to do with a Syria not completely submissive to himself. Instead, he embarked on attempts to stir up trouble in Syria by violent propaganda and bomb-throwing. The attempts—mostly organized by Sarraj who had fled to Egypt—did not succeed, but only led to a reaction in Syria. The Damascus government complained to the Arab League about Egyptian subversion and this resulted in a quarrel of such violence that it nearly caused the League to founder. Egypt walked out of the last remaining pan-Arab association and has not since participated in its activities. In Syria a new government took over; the old politician Khaled al-Azm, now far from any communist alliances, managed to convince parliament—dissolved previously by the officers of the Nahlawi group—to reconvene and to grant him exceptional powers for one year in order to lead the shaken country towards social evolution and a liberal parliamentary régime.

Nasser reacted to Syria's defection by taking flight to the left. A 'self-criticism', published shortly after the revolution, said that the Egyptian Government had not given sufficient consideration to 'the danger of internal reaction'. Nasser also hinted that his régime had up to then not known how to let the 'Egyptian people' participate in the country's politics. Both 'errors' were now to be corrected: all land holdings above 100 feddans were distributed, large fortunes confiscated, industries nationalized, certain 'capitalists' were thrown into gaol and others lost their civil rights.

In order to mobilize the 'people' politically a new unity party was created which sent an enormous 'National Congress' to Cairo to 'discuss' and approve a 'National Charter' drawn up by Nasser. This charter is Nasser's most important political programme since his 'Philosophy of the Revolution' and has been made compulsory reading in all secondary schools and universities. It contains promises of a social and political Utopia which is depicted as if the Egyptian authorities considered it already almost achieved. Analysis of this voluminous document reveals that it contains two contradictory principles of government: on the one hand Nasser insists that the elected popular councils must take precedence over the executive organs of the state and on the other he talks of a 'real leadership' (of a collective type) which 'senses and expresses the aspirations of the people', no longer mentioning control by elected organs of the people. When he talks of this 'real leadership' Nasser naïvely equates himself and his régime with the 'people' and also asserts that this monolithic people possesses only *one* political will, that of the 'Revolution'.

The concrete constitutional rules, according to which the new 'popular régime' in Egypt will work, are at this moment being worked out by Nasser. If experience does not prove false they will be formulated so that the real power will be concentrated in the hands of the 'leadership' and the most the 'people' will get will be nominal control of the state's power apparatus.

Hand in hand with the new internal political tendency—towards the left—there went a new Arab policy. The head of the UAR decided to emphasize his new inclination to the left by violent attacks on those Arab Kingdoms he considered reactionary. This led first of all to a rift between Egypt and the Yemen and then to violent polemics with King Saud which have gone to the extent of Cairo Radio's openly urging the people of Saudi Arabia to rebel against the King.

Throughout the Arab world Cairo, having once been the mouthpiece of Arabism, has now become that of Arab Socialism. It is by no means clear just what this socialism will consist of and how far it will differ from Tito's socialism or that of the Soviet Union. Even the 'National Charter' gives only quite indefinite and somewhat contradictory information about it. Only the future can show what attraction it will have for Arabs outside Egypt. This will be put to the test by the attitude of Syria whose politicians immediately recognized the doubtful nature of Nasserist Socialism without democratic liberties, without freedom of the press, parties and the trade unions. The Syrian officers for a time seemed to be much more receptive to the rhetoric of this new Arab Socialism. A lively debate is going on in the Baath Party on the tactics to be used in the face of Nasser and his socialism. One wing of the Baath, under Michel 'Aflaq and Salah al-Bitar, is for negotiating with Nasser on the possibility of an Arab federation. The other, under Akram Haurani, declares Nasser a dictator and aims at realizing Arab socialism without him and according to democratic principles.

13

The Yemen

IN SEPTEMBER 1962 a military revolt broke out in the Yemen. The revolutionaries had since 1948 made periodic attempts to gain control and had been energetically suppressed by Imam Ahmed, who seems to have outwitted them regularly. Imam Ahmed's son, Imam Mohammed al-Badr, had been in the saddle less than a week when he was overthrown by his Army Commander, Colonel as-Sallal.

As a prince, al-Badr had shown reformist leanings; he had associated with Yemenis of modern outlook, tried to introduce welfare schemes in his country and been largely responsible for the Yemen's temporary association with Nasser's state. Now he was overthrown by the very elements he had favoured and brought to power. They attempted to murder him but they failed. Very quickly the country turned into an arena for the competing Arab régimes. As-Sallal proclaimed a republic and called Nasser to help him. The Imam and his uncle al-Hasan took to the mountains and received tribal support inside Yemen and some moral encouragement, financial help and military advice from the two Arab kings most endangered by the pressure of Nasserism: King Saud and King Husain.

Cairo could not resist a new pan-Arab venture; solidarity with the Yemen Republic was proclaimed and Egyptian troops poured into the country. The stakes on both sides were high; if Nasser dominated the Yemen and as-Sallal's Republic, he might achieve an overthrow of the monarchy in Saudi Arabia and finally put his hands on the petroleum regions of the Arab world. If the Imam could manage to reimpose his sovereignty, not only the kings of Arabia and Jordan were safe but the Egyptians would face a military and political defeat possibly severe enough to have serious repercussions at home.

However, after two months of intermittent military and propagandistic struggles a kind of stalemate in the Yemen seemed to be reached. The revolutionaries and their Egyptian allies appeared to be unable to capture the Imam and to pacify the mountainous parts of the country; while, for their part, the tribal forces of the Imam proved unable for the time being to occupy the cities defended by Egyptian tanks, planes and artillery. Nasser, under severe economic stress since Egypt's weak economy seemed unable to bear much longer the cost of

285

his military expedition, showed himself ready to accept an American plan calling for the retreat of the Egyptian forces from the Yemen and the cutting-off of the support which the kingdoms had been affording the Imam. But, at the time of writing, neither the kings nor the Imam have agreed to the American project; judging that time is on their side they have preferred to go on with the struggle.

14

The Kurdish Question

THE PROBLEM OF THE KURDISH MINORITY in Iraq—and to a lesser extent in Syria—has come to the fore as one of the major problems which the Arab states will have to cope with in coming years. In its modern form the Kurdish question is largely of General Qasim's own making. The Iraqi régime encouraged the autonomist aspirations of the Kurdish minority in the northern mountains during the years of its struggle with Nasserite Arab nationalism. General Qasim had permitted Mustafa al-Barzani, the old Kurdish warrior and national leader, to return to Baghdad from the Soviet Union where he had taken refuge after the troubles following the Second World War. At one time Barzani, although an Iraqui Kurd, had been commander of the army of the short-lived Kurdish Republic of Mahabad which had been conquered by the Persian Army (together with the bigger Republic of Azdharbaijan) after the withdrawal of the Russian army from northern Persia in 1946. After his return to Baghdad Barzani proved himself to be rather sceptical of communism, principally by excluding the Communist wing from his 'Kurdish Democratic Party' in line with Qasim's own curbing of Communist influences in Iraq during 1959. But in 1961 an open conflict broke out between the Kurds and the Iraqi régime. The Kurds under Barzani insisted on the fulfilment of the promises made to them. They particularly demanded linguistic, cultural and a limited administra-tive autonomy and development aid for their parts of the country. Their insistence provoked the government into using bombs, and soon a state of insurrection ensued. The government tried using anti-Barzani Kurdish leaders to combat Barzani's followers, but they were beaten and dispersed several times. At the same time, the brutal bombing of Kurdish villages by the Iraqi air force helped to create a spirit of national resistance and to unite all Kurds under the leadership of Barzani and the Democratic Kurdish Party, designated by the Kurds with the French word 'Parti'.

By the summer of 1962 all anti-Barzani Kurds had been defeated and the warriors of the insurrection held a considerable part of the mountain regions in the face of the regular Iraqi army, small units of which were regularly surrounded and destroyed by Kurdish partisan forces.

The Kurdish insurrections became not only a military problem for the Iraqi army but also the major political question for the whole of Iraq. It was to be expected that the army would, as the result of ignominious defeat by the Kurds, become discontented and might eventually turn against the régime itself—a régime that had come to rely almost exclusively on this very army for support.

From claiming partial autonomy the Kurds have gone on to call for the downfall of Qasim and for complete autonomy 'in the framework of the Iraqi Republic'. Their independence movement affects not only Iraq but also Turkey and Iran, which have large Kurdish minorities. Iraqi air raids across the Turkish frontier have brought friction between Baghdad and Ankara, and this same problem has made its appearance in Syria. The government in Damascus has felt impelled to take severe measures against alleged Kurdish infiltration into Syria, while the Syrian Kurds, living mostly close to the northern and north-eastern frontier of the country, maintain that they have 'always' lived in Northern Syria, and that the government wishes to break up their settlements in order to create local Arab majorities in traditionally Kurdish regions. Notwithstanding their own fervent nationalism, none of the Arab governments seems to have grasped the nature of the Kurdish nationalism which has clearly begun to make its appearance in opposition to their own. Instead of coming to terms with it in the cultural, linguistic and administrative fields they attempt to suppress it, thereby only increasing its bitterness and combativity.

15

A Second Pan-Arabic Upsurge

IN FEBRUARY 1963 the long expected revolt against Qasim broke and succeeded. The *coup* was directed by the Baath Party with the help of army officers and 'nationalist' allies. The militia of the Baath played a considerable role in it. The nuclei of this private army must have been formed in the long years of underground struggle and internecine war between Iraqi Communists and Baathists. Qasim was bombed by the Air Force in his Ministry of Defence after the Baathists had killed the general in command of the Air Force, Awqati, a pro-Communist. Eventually Kassem had to surrender and was executed by the officers of the Baath.

The Baath Party took over the country; it had managed to develop during its years of underground existence a closely knit party structure extending well into the army. A revolutionary council was formed which assumed the highest power in the country including the installation and dismissal of governments. In the government officers and party members dominated; the membership of the revolutionary council was kept secret. The new powers persecuted the Communists and blamed Qasim as a tyrant who had caused the Iraki revolution of 1958 to deviate from its true aims. These aims, they said, were to be 'socialism' and Arab unity in close collaboration with Egypt and the other 'liberated Arab states'. This term was applied to Egypt, the revolutionary Yemen, Algeria, and Iraq itself.

One month later a *coup* in Syria inspired by the same Baath party ended the democratic and liberal experiment in government that had lasted a year and a half in Damascus. There too the Baath took power but found itself much weaker than in Iraq. It seemed to lack wide popular support and managed to stay in power because of its close links with some of the army officers who had risen to prominence through the *coup*. The simple people preferred to follow the 'Nasserite' slogans of some politicians who called for the immediate return of Syria to her old union with Egypt and for handing over all power to Nasser. The liberal and bourgeois politicians of the previous régime suffered 'civic isolation', the loss of their civil rights.

The Baath party called for Arab unity; but it reasoned that unity under the existing circumstances ought to be threefold, consisting of a federation of the three countries, Iraq, Syria and Egypt with a possibility for Algeria and the republican Yemen to join later. The Baath spoke of 'mistakes' that had occurred during the first experiment in unity. According to their doctrine these mistakes had afforded the 'separatists and reactionaries with their backer, colonialism' an opportunity to destroy the union. The principal mistake, according to the Baath party, had been the lack of 'popular organizations'. Such organizations, had they existed, or had Nasser permitted the Baath to found and animate them, would have given the people of Syria sufficient strength to resist the 'criminal attempts of the reactionaries' to separate Syria from Egypt.

The Baath intended to keep this time some degree of power in the two countries which it had come to dominate. It desired the collaboration of Nasser in a large Arab federation; it did not want him to dominate unconditionally. After some projects of loose collaboration originating in Baghdad had been repelled by Nasser the Baath proposed a federation of the three countries and Cairo declared itself ready to treat about it. But at the same time Nasser, his agents and his propagandists in Syria made a great effort to overthrow the Baathist government of Damascus and to replace it by forces entirely submissive to the Egyptian 'raïs': the Syrian 'Nasserites'. Damascus was soon the scene of noisy demonstrations for 'Nasser' and 'immediate unity'. All kinds of pressures were brought to bear on the Baathist majority of the Syrian government. But the Baath party avoided counter-charges and loud polemics. Michel 'Aflak, the party's chief ideologist and general secretary, explained this attitude saying that Arab unity was well worth controlling one's nerves. In an atmosphere of great tension and insecurity in Syria talks about federation went on. The main difficulty seemed to be that Nasser intended to dominate the planned federation in one form or another, claiming that this was 'the will of the people'. The Baath appeared decided not to permit such domination and equally decided to include Egypt in the proposed federation.

During the eighteen months of separation from Egypt it had come to be axiomatic with 'Aflak and his Baathist followers that it must be possible to bring Nasser to collaborate as an equal with the Baath. 'He must have learned something from his experience with the previous "union"', they reasoned. They staked their policy on this assumption promising their nations and army officers that they would achieve 'unity'. They intended to defend their own position in Iraq and Syria against Nasserite bids for power by means of the separate entities granted to each member state under the proposed federation agreements. But clearly the envisaged federation could only work if Nasser could be convinced to collaborate sincerely and disinterestedly with the leader-ship of the other two states. Would he be willing and able to do this? Only the future can show; but if past experience is any guide the prospects are not very encouraging.

III

ANALYSIS OF THE PRESENT

I

The Parties of the 'Third Generation' and the Reaction to them

IT CANNOT YET BE PREDICTED how the struggle between Nasser's pan-Arab nationalism, Arab nationalism of the Iraqi type, and nationalism of the democratic variety as attemped in Syria will end. For the moment it seems that those Arab countries which have not yet achieved stability are more inclined towards Nasser than towards Qasim or towards a Syrian-style régime. But on the other hand, provided he can stay in power and bring some sort of calm to Iraq, Qasim has in the long run better prospects of developing his country economically than has Nasser in the over-populated valley of the Nile.

Although the struggle for power has not yet been decided one can see a fundamental structural change in Arab political life: it is the 'parties of the third generation' which dominate large parts of the Arab world today.

Political life on the level of the 'third generation' was first organized by Nasser in Egypt and it was already well established there while the neighbouring Arab states were still governed by the 'first' and the 'second generations'. This gave Nasser and his political methods the advantage they enjoyed in the Arab world until 1958, the year in which Iraq underwent revolution and thus passed over to the third political level.

The methods of the 'third generation' consist in making full use of modern means of influencing the masses, for the first time in the history of the Arabs. These means are at the disposal of the state alone both in Egypt and in Iraq and are used by it as one of the most important instruments of governing. The 'parties of the third generation' tend toward one-party systems but for psychological reasons they permit a certain amount of diversity of tendencies. For example there is a 'left' wing and a 'right' wing, both speaking for the Government but whoever wishes to speak *against* the government finds that he is not permitted to use the public means of communication.

The Suez crisis showed drastically what feats of 'reinterpretation of the truth' and 'shading of the facts' the Arab propagandists are capable of and the amazing effect their interpretation is able to have on the public. As far as the Arabs were concerned, defeats became victories, victories which have become 'realities' even for those Arabs who are able to get their information from other than Egyptian sources.

State propaganda has proved equally effective on the internal political fronts. It has been shown that it is not difficult to 'reinterpret' the past through propaganda and to transform the new opinions and evaluations into 'truths'. The Muslim Brothers, who were once looked up to far and wide as champions of the Islamic and national idea, became 'reactionaries' and 'fanatics'. The revolt in Kirkuk in 1959 was the work of Communists but when the opponents of the Communists, the nationalists, fired on Qasim two months later they were pronounced guilty of the outrages in Kirkuk, too.

It has even been demonstrated that the opinion of the masses as to the conditions in which they actually live can be influenced to such an extent that they see 'improvements' where an outsider can see that conditions have only remained as before or have even deteriorated slightly. This magic trick is performed by presenting 'plans' or 'projects' as already carried out or at least by presenting their realization as already assured before they have been embarked upon. So one reads: 'The Aswan Dam will make it possible to cultivate two million feddans,' not: 'Provided the necessary means can be found and the plans carried out there is a possibility, after fifteen years of hard work, of increasing Egypt's agricultural land by, at the most, two million feddans.' Every day the Egyptian papers are full of such promises: 'The national income to be doubled in the next ten years,' 'Industrialization of the country.' The Baghdad papers use the same technique: 'Millions of new houses for the poor,' 'Planned industrialization of the country,' etc.

A rosy view of the near future, which 'has just begun', or which 'will be realized almost immediately' or which has already 'been scientifically planned', is given not only in the sphere of economics but also in all fields of political and social life. Scapegoats can always be found for failures, the most important of these being the colonialists and the Zionists. These can even be held responsible for existing evils and any unsatisfactory state of affairs by proclaiming that it was they who conditioned the mentality of the 'backward classes' of the Arabs by their former oppression.

Propaganda must always 'express the wishes of the people'; if it goes too much against controllable realities or against the aspirations of the lower middle class, who set the tone in the main cities, it has to be adapted. When such adaptations are made it is most important that there should be one theme in which one can be sure of the whole-hearted enthusiasm of the Arab lower middle classes. This theme is anti-colonialist, anti-Zionist, anti-feudalist and anti-regionalist, that is to say pan-Arab, agitation. One can be certain of achieving an effect on this sounding board which will, no doubt, continue to be used until the masses become interested in other, less negative propaganda themes, too.

There are many examples of this type of propaganda which is designed to let off steam, the best known being the Suez *coup* by which Nasser reacted to the loss of prestige inflicted on him by Dulles. The nationalization of the Suez Canal also shows that such recourse to demagogism is not necessarily the result of cold consideration. It is perhaps most successful and is acclaimed most loudly when it is the leaders' spontaneous reaction, which awakens a similar spontaneous reaction in the masses they lead.

Qasim has used more considered demagogic tactics in a different way, such as proposals for a 'Palestinian Government', arms to assist the Algerians, propaganda attacks on Persia over the Shatt al-Arab, anti-French agitation and so on, but such tactics could always be seen as diversionary moves.

The dangers of this kind of demagogism are well known: successes are anticipated and promised when, in reality, even greater efforts are necessary in order to achieve these successes.

In defence of the politicians of the 'third generation' it can be said that, if there are no real successes, at least apparent successes are necessary to stoke up the lethargic Arab masses, inspire them with hope and direct them along the road of real successes. In the long run it is a question of how far this can be safely done and it is clear that the correct mixture of 'hope' and 'self-knowledge' is different for each nation and its state of development.

Observers still hold very diverse opinions of the success or failure of those Arab governments depending on appeals to the people and state propaganda. Although it cannot be denied that Nasser and Qasim (and Bourghiba, too) are enormously 'popular' with their peoples there are very diverse estimates of their objective achievements and their chances of achieving in the near future the goals they have set for their peoples.

An independent observer might also ask whether 'success', even should it materialize, is worth the means employed to achieve it. In other words, does a possible economic, political and military advance justify the systematic depreciation of 'truth' and 'objective facts' under state guidance of opinion?

The Arabs are not much interested in such theoretical considerations. For them 'development' comes first and foremost. Many consider their goal to be one large, unified, Arab state, others confine themselves to seeking power and wealth for their own country. Still others, the most 'modern' of all, have learnt to talk of 'classes' and seek power (and wealth) for themselves as representatives of a 'working class' which has still to be built up. Even those who are tolerably comfortable are filled with deep dissatisfaction with the existing state of affairs and the best of the nationalists have a somewhat biased, but nevertheless honest, concern for the fate of the nation. The great peasant masses, which still have no way of making their voices heard, are dissatisfied too, and all this makes 'development' and 'emancipation' the watchwords of the times. 'Truth, which serves to retard this development, is clearly not truth for us,' so reason the Arabs of today.

Foreign observers have often been tempted to trace the political institutions of Nasser's state back to foreign prototypes. For far too long the thought and utterances of western statesmen (including Anthony Eden) were influenced by the idea that Nasser was another Hitler and this idea led the West to make many mistakes. Nowadays one feels tempted to see in Nasser's and Qasim's methods Russian influences at work. To be sure, one cannot close one's eyes to the fact that the Egyptian state propagandists, like all state propagandists, have adopted a policy of distortion of the truth for propaganda purposes, a process which Hitler developed into an instrument of government, and in this they have proved apt pupils of Goebbels. There is also no doubt that Communism has reached new and confusing heights of distortion of the truth by setting itself up as the only valid standard for 'objective truth' and describing and analysing the world consistently from this perspective.

It is clear that Nasser's state gradually changed from being an 'old-fashioned' Fascist one into one much more towards the left, whereas Qasim's revolution was from the very beginning under the Red Star of Russian and Chinese methods. At the same time it is well to recognize that Arab state propaganda has its own particular pitch which is modulated to the special psychological condition of the people towards which it is directed.

This pitch varies from one Arab country to another. In Egypt it is best characterized by the clever satirical political periodical *Rose el-Youssef*. Iraq expressed itself much less articulately in *Mehdawi's People's Court*. In Tunisia propaganda follows rational and dialectical lines which betray the nearness of France; this propaganda is nearer to reality than that of the two countries in the East. Of course the nearer state doctrine and propaganda are to reality, the more possible it is for them to influence reality.

*   *   *

Political forces developed in the Arab countries after their foundation in a manner different from that expected and hoped for by the liberally minded West of the League of Nations era. In general power went from client groups under their leaders to agitation parties with extremist programmes and then to state parties with a monopoly of means of propaganda and supported by the army. Democratic institutions, which were a foreign body in the Arab countries, have, for the time being, proved scarcely viable. Only in Lebanon has a sort of precarious democracy balanced between two equally strong power groups been preserved.

Since the political liberties of the populace have never been anything but a façade, few tears are shed for democracy when a totalitarian Arab state abolishes it. One simply declares that the Arabs are not yet ripe for democracy or even that a special kind of 'Arab democracy' must first be developed. For the present it is better in the interest of the Arab national struggle to avoid parties and political divisions. In contrast to these arguments of Nasserist nationalists, Qasim has announced, following the Communist technique, that 'true demo-cracy' now prevails in Iraq. In February 1960 the pretence of Iraqi 'democracy' was strengthened by the licensing of several parties, all of them pro-Qasim. But all of them disappeared again in the following years.

Nasserist political ideologists declare that there can be no liberty before all Arabs have been liberated which in the past meant above all the evacuation of Arab countries by foreign troops. Since this has been achieved and still no real liberty has been gained they are coming more and more to the belief that economic liberation must also be achieved as a prerequisite of liberty. By economic liberation they mean above all sufficient work for everyone and an assured income for the whole people, indeed, a welfare state on the European socialist pattern. At the moment we can see how the two competing Arab propaganda states are striving to divert the eyes of their citizens from purely political matters to this economic 'liberation'.

In Cairo, as in Baghdad, it is taken for granted that it is the state's duty to direct, even carry out the necessary economic liberation. 'Who else has the means to do so?' is the naïve question. 'Only the state can see to it that within a short period every Arab will have enough to eat and be sure of a job!' In this they ignore or refuse to recognize that the desired economic emancipation by the state will result not in the liberation of the individual but, rather, in the still more absolute subordination to the power apparatus of the state.

A symbol of what is being worked for is the collective farms of the Egyptian 'Liberation Province', a self-administered state enterprise where selected peasant families lead a life regimented from early morning gymnastic exercises to the wearing of uniforms and the institution of children's crèches. The only pleasing fact is that the strictness of the regimentation is gradually being loosened owing to the humane laxness of the Egyptian officials while the whole enterprise is allowed to be forgotten, because it cost the state far too much. However, industrial or agricultural enterprises under the management of officials did not come to an end with 'Liberation Province'. The agricultural and commercial 'co-operatives', which are always sure of official backing, are not very different. As for the Egyptian state factories, these are controlled by expertly managed state or semi-state banks and holding companies.

Such organs of state management, nevertheless, make it possible for the Egyptian lower middle class to become emancipated. Members of this class can become civil servants in the economic sector and so 'managers' of the whole economy. The civil servant replaces the former landowner and since he belongs to a class which formerly had practically no power this means an advance for him. This class of semi-educated 'literates' is at the same time the sounding board for state propaganda; on the other hand the supervised peasants and the workers employed by government officials are of no political account, for they have, as yet, no opinions of their own.

The machinery of state control of the economy is not so well developed in Iraq as in Egypt but promises to become all the more dominant in the future. Here, too, the managerial class is recruited entirely from the lower middle class in spite of all their Communist or semi-communist terminology. It is they who are taking steps to achieve their economic liberation under the aegis of the propaganda state. In most cases these officials and agitators are fully convinced that the 'uneducated' peasants and workers entrusted to their direction are infinitely better off than under the former 'colonialist feudalist' ruling class. Throughout history most ruling classes have held the same opinion of themselves.

In Syria in the wake of the military *coup* of Colonel Nahlawi a return to democratic forms of government and liberal ways of economic development has been attempted. Time will tell whether this spells a return to an old-style liberal régime, such as existed before Nasser's and the Nationalists' peak period, or whether the Syrians will prove capable of evolving a modern style of economy and government comparable to European models. Many tergiversations during the first year of the new Arabic Syrian Republic have shown that it will be by no means easy to reconcile the liberal, socialist, nationalist and pan-Arab aspirations that co-exist in the country. Even so, Syria represents a major hope for an Arab breakthrough to a more responsible and more contemporary kind of politics. The aims are to develop the country which has great potential resources, to return to a multi-party system and a parliamentary form of government. Some of the over-excitability of bygone times has abated; at least some of the leading statesmen appear capable of differentiating between propaganda-mirages and real possibilities. The Syria of today has perhaps the period of the 'parties of the third generation' behind her. If in the coming years she can evolve freely and constructively she will be a model of immense significance for the other Arab countries.

2

The Danger of Communism

A DESCRIPTION OF THE ATMOSPHERE in which the leading forces and tendencies develop in one of the absolutist Arab states is in itself sufficient to show how closely related such a state system is to communism in its tendencies and political practice. The official goal of development is in the one case the 'dictatorship of the proletariat' and in the other the 'creation of a socialist, co-operative, Arab society'. But if one considers the practical means by which these aims are pursued one finds that they are startlingly similar.

In both societies it is considered the role of the state to direct the development of the community and in both it is considered harmful if individuals or groups try to discuss non-conformist ideas. The only 'right' path is the one laid down by the ruling power.

In practice the ruling power is able to alter radically the direction of develop-ment as long as it keeps to its theoretical goal and manages its propaganda machine with sufficient skill. Thus the goal often appears to an outsider as a mere pretext behind which in reality power groups and power-hungry in-dividuals chase after their own dreams. But seen from the inside, Khrushchev in all probability considers himself just as much the embodiment of the 'working class' as Nasser considers himself and his régime the symbol of the Arab nation.

Both societies create classes of officials in whose interest it is that they control the life of the nation ideologically, organizationally and technically. In both, in addition to the totalitarian character of the government, the slogan 'progressive' plays a decisive part.

Of course, there are also differences: First of all both Nasser's United Arab Republic and Qasim's 'Eternal Iraqi Republic' are not only infinitely weaker in comparison to the Soviet Union but are also much less stable bodies. They have not had so long as the Soviet Union to establish the 'system'.

The individual in Egypt can still save himself from the 'system' if he wishes to do so. Some private economy still exists in which one can find an escape, foreign newspapers can still be read and the private citizen can still withdraw into his house where he can receive his friends and discuss any topic with them. There are still foreign firms and economic interests in the Arab countries which are indispensable to these countries. The most striking example being the IPC (Iraq Petroleum Company) in Iraq. There are still whole groups of minorities which crowd around such islands, trying to share in their European or western, liberal way of life.

But more important than all this is that there is still a powerful group of liberally minded Arabs, generally independent professional men, whose services are indispensable to the government. They may understand and sympathize with the state and the Arab aspirations it represents but they refuse to accept the state propaganda blindly as the 'truth'. However, this class of educated men have no political power left, indeed no means of expressing their opinions on political issues in Egypt or Iraq, unless they themselves become whole-hearted champions of the state by accepting government employment. If one belongs to a more or less secret opposition group one has to go underground and use the means of conspirators. Of course, the most effective, the boldest, best organized and best led 'conspiratorial group' is the Communist Party. This holds both for Iraq where it is at present collaborating with Qasim's régime and for Egypt where it is subjected to severe persecution.

The great majority of educated men feel that they neither belong heart and soul to the state nor to the opposition. They are content to live for their own work and hope that the government will one day introduce the 'democratic institutions' which it every now and then promises. It is enough not to have one's personal liberties further restricted and in return the 'state' is not criticized too loudly. It is also honestly believed that—on the whole—the Arabs are 'progressing' and wide circles are pleased by the apparent rise of Arab prestige in the world.

However, one's judgement should not be swayed too much by the amenities of a middle-class, liberal way of life which is still possible in the totalitarian Arab states. These liberal men of education may still be in many cases indispensable to the state as individuals but they no longer have any political power or means of influencing government policies.

The development which the state is furthering is proceeding without the collaboration of the liberally minded educated *élite*. This development is advancing very fast and one cannot see it leading to anything but a closely knit, authoritarian, bureaucratic, state. There may still be many difficulties of organization along this path but there is no trace of any counter forces willing and able to lead development along other paths. The irony of the situation is that even the opposition, in so far as it can be seriously considered a power, which is in practice only the Communist opposition, would be forced to follow the present line of political development if it came to power. All it would endeavour to do would be to canalize and speed up the movement and make it more consistent, brutal and practical.

Western newspapers and political books have discussed at length Soviet penetration in Egypt, Syria and Iraq, quoting arms deliveries, trade pacts, Russian diplomatic influence and support, the presence of Soviet experts and officers, cultural agreements, state visits and Soviet gifts and loans. In all this they see a sort of net in which the cunning Russians are gradually entangling the naïve or too self-confident Near-Eastern demagogues.

However, it would be far too simple to try to measure the chances of com-munism in the Near East by these outward signs of Soviet influence for trade relations, loans and even arms deliveries will by no means necessarily lead to a complete take-over by the Soviet Union. When, a hundred years ago, the West started its colonial conquests, in Egypt, for example, by economic manoeuvring its economic organizations were backed up in all colonial territories by infinitely superior military power which it threatened to set in motion immediately should the 'debtor' in China, Africa or the Near East prove insolvent. The Soviet Union cannot indulge in such manoeuvres today for direct military pressure, for example on Egypt, should she become insolvent, would bring about counter-pressure by the West and at the same time the prestige acquired by 'unselfish gifts' would be thrown away.

The real danger threatening a modern Arab state in its relations with the Soviet Union is a moral one. It is that the aims and methods of the 'Arab' social, political and economic way of life will become so like those of the Soviet countries that in the end an 'Anschluss' will take place more or less auto-matically.

No one can yet foresee how such a union might come about in practice but several possibilities can be seen. For example, if the Arab state were not in a position to keep up, even approximately, with the promises of its propaganda, the contrast between the reality and the promises could be so strong as to unloose a revolt. Such a revolt would most probably lead to a move to the left, for the Communist Party is the only one which has been able to keep sufficiently alive, illegally or semi-legally, to take control of the revolt at the given moment. The Arabs' political thinking has for so long been directed towards material development, 'progress', state industrialization and state welfare that any revolt might easily lead to this path being followed even more consistently, perhaps under direct Russian or Chinese orders.

But one can also imagine the development running its course without any revolt. In order to keep its promises to a certain extent the propaganda state must have recourse to an ever more absolute penetration, to more and more severe measures of compulsion and to the liquidation of even the last traces of intellectual independence. Externally with their 'economic aid' and internally with the help of their cells and their experience in leadership the Communists are prepared to collaborate in this development until their organizations become indispensable to the state. They would then be in a position to take over power practically from the inside. At one time Qasim's Iraq came close to this danger.

What keeps the present-day propaganda states, Egypt and Iraq, from joining the Communist block seems to be above all the desire of their ruling personalities and their followers to wield power themselves and not to deliver themselves over to Moscow. In this the army plays an important part both in Egypt and in Iraq and in both states the means of influencing the masses are directed first and foremost towards maintaining the popularity of the head of state.

But the point is that when one head of state tries to outbid the other the most effective way of doing so seems to be to 'move to the left'. To begin with Qasim was only able to stand out against Nasser by relying on the Communist Party, its slogans and its jargon and letting the pro-Nasser nationalists clash with it. Then Nasser moved to the left when he found himself in difficulties owing to the collapse of the UAR. The reason for this continuous shifting towards the left is that a real liberalization of the authoritarian propaganda states would be considered by the very victims of their propaganda, above all the younger generation who have heard nothing else all their lives, as a retrograde step to the 'old-fashioned', reactionary bourgeois 'capitalist' system which for years has been pilloried as the tool of western 'imperialism' and colonialism.

Their own propaganda prevents such totalitarian régimes from progressing towards western-type, liberal institutions. If they run up against economic or political obstacles they are forced to go 'left' around them. So, even with the best will in the world, it is difficult for them to avoid the clutches of Communism. For the present they differ from the satellite governments in that they govern themselves and so are able to consider their own interests. The crux is that those Arabs, who are victims of state propaganda, hardly ever see these interests to be other than what Moscow would like them to be. Moreover, whenever they encounter difficulties they are forced by the inner logic of their own development to take one step closer to the communist system of government.

3

The Nationalists Faced with the
Danger of Communism

IN RECENT YEARS it has become clear to the intellectuals, especially in the UAR, that they must justify their political positions intellectually. This can be seen from the many writings which appear almost daily and which discuss on the one hand Arab nationalism and on the other Communism. Communism is rejected, generally with very limited arguments, the most important of which is the argument that Communism is opposed to religion. The citizens of the UAR also received detailed photographic reports with Arabic text of the suppression of the Hungarians three years after these events took place. But the propagandists find it difficult to deal thoroughly with the evils prevalent in the Soviet Union without drawing attention to the lack of liberty in their own country.

The nationalists of the UAR have developed a special doctrine on liberty according to which the experiences of pre-revolutionary Egypt showed that, the country being where it is socially and educationally, there could be liberty only for the few rich and educated persons whereas the majority of the people would be so poor and restricted under a European-type liberal régime that the words liberty or slavery would mean nothing to them. For us, they say, as for the other under-developed nations, there can be no liberty, but only 'liberation' (emancipation and development). In order to become generally effective this 'liberation' has to be centrally planned and organized. This task can only be done by a state which does not tolerate any opposition because the low standard of the country could easily lead to the uneducated and the poor being diverted from their real task of 'development'. In practice any sort of opposition is always obstruction and moreover, the nationalists assert, Arab liberal government always showed that the opposition was prepared to collaborate with foreign countries and with 'colonialism'. Members of the opposition are potential traitors and saboteurs and so, in the interests of 'liberation', there can be, at least for the moment, no freedom of criticism.

In view of such a doctrine one cannot reproach the Communists if they, too —and much more consistently and effectively—suppress the political liberties of their subjects for the sake of 'development' towards true Communism. For this reason what is said against the Communists is always remarkably general and indefinite:

Let no one imagine from what we have said about our failings and the successes of the Communists that we think that it is the inescapable fate of all mankind for these failings and these successes in spite of their importance are transitory. Communism is in fact completely ideological, materialist and social but in spite of its universality and blatant social levelling it is totally erroneous.

Communism seeks to uproot man from the seeds of divinity which are the deepest, most noble and most permanent thing in him. It seeks to explain history in terms of class war, reducing it to simple terms although history is wider and more comprehensive than mere class wars. It explains the composition of society and the moral structure of this composition by the type of means of production prevalent, ignoring all the psychological and social factors which affect this composition. It depicts man as a prisoner of his material needs and strips him of all the spiritual, mental and psycho-logical needs of his senses. While promising to free man from being a mere cog in the wheels of the economic system it turns him into a soulless, materialist, ideological instrument. For this reason, although it appears in the immediate short run to be a liberator, it is in the long run an enslaver and man will pass over it sooner or later even in its original homelands.

There lies in man, whoever he may be and no matter what passing enslavement he has to submit to, an eternal spark of revolt for liberty and emancipation, a spark which fires all, Arab or German, African or European, black or white or yellow alike. We have living examples of that in the African and Asian nations closest to us, in the van of which are Indonesia, India and Japan. All of these suffered greatly from western colonialism and are faced with the conflicting aspects of their social and economic situations but are, nevertheless, determined to go their own way, not that of Communism, towards progress and complete emancipation.

The mistake of the Communists, in which they vie with western colonialists, is that they are unable to conceive of any way of emancipation other than their way. Moreover, they are incapable of understanding the primary human facts that awakened man finds his happiness in choosing his own way towards complete emancipation no matter what obstacles he may encounter and rejects completely the path which is imposed upon him by others no matter what enticements it may offer. This lack of imagination and this psychological error may cause the Communists to lose all the friendship they have so far won among the Asian and African peoples which are beginning to wake up. (Dr Hasan Sa'b, a young, European educated political scientist and spokesman of 'moderate' nationalism, in *Al-Ādab*, Beirut, June 1959.)

It will be seen from the passage quoted above that the author and those who think like him are quite prepared to stand up to Communism. In doing so they use certain arguments they have learned in Western schools, that the Communists neglect the 'spiritual' aspects of human life in favour of the purely 'material' ones, etc. At the same time Dr Hasan Sa'b admits, at least implicitly, that even Communism is a 'road to emancipation'. He seems to believe that the Communists will sooner or later 'automatically' detach themselves from their restrictive ideology, a hope which is shared in many Western quarters, too.

On the positive side Dr Sa'b confines himself to noting that the Arabs must follow their own path of development. How this path of development should be is discussed in the whole essay only in the most general terms, e.g. 'the liberation of all Arabs and all men and peoples', 'social development', 'progress', etc. If forced to answer, Dr Sa'b would no doubt say that the Arabs must first reconnoitre their path empirically and then gradually find it.

'Empiricism' in pan-Arab politics is a contribution of Nasser's. His revolution developed empirically right from the beginning; it had no programme and asked itself, as soon as one 'goal' was achieved: 'What next?' When it seemed that pan-Arabism was triumphing the programme of the Baath party overshadowed the lack of programme of the Cairo government but with the failure of the Baathists and the postponement of their hopes for 'unity' to an uncertain future Nasser's empiricism has turned towards its own brand of 'Arab Socialism'.

If one asks what are the principles guiding this empiricism the nationalists usually answer that it is the history of the Arabs which in the long run determines the direction of pan-Arab policy. But the picture many nationalists have of their own past and which they conjure up on this occasion has remarkably little in common with objective historiography and is rather an essay in political self-justification, indeed, in self-glorification.

In the rich and brilliant history of the Arabs (or, to be more exact, of the mediaeval Muslim Near East) it is not difficult to find single events or whole epochs which justify the Arabs' pride in their own past. But when the nationalists take the stage as historians they generally do not take the matter seriously enough. Whenever they find something in their Arab past derived from the standards of nineteenth-century Europe which suits their personal taste, they take these details out of their historical and sociological context and put them forward as a proof of Arab greatness and, if possible, of Arab superiority over the West 'which at that time was still sunk in barbarism'.

To quote just a few of the most common clichés: The so-called religious *tolerance* of the Muslims of the Middle Ages is heavily underlined but in reality it was a relatively tolerant religious legal system which was in spirit quite different from our modern 'tolerance' founded on humanism and which was also applied very differently in different epochs. They explain how Christians and Jews lived among the Muslims in perfect freedom in the Islamic Middle Ages whereas, as they seldom forget to emphasize, 'Jews and Muslims and even heterodox Christians were subjected to constant persecution in Christian Europe'. Such generalizations are far too rough in view of the diverse nature of historical episodes and manifestations both in the East and in the West. But the Muslim's 'tolerance' serves as a proof of the superiority of the 'Arabic' or Islamic spirit over the Western one and at the same time is considered a guarantee that in the pan-Arab Empire to come the rights of religious, even ethnic minorities, will be scrupulously protected. And if minorities view with anxiety and doubts the planned pan-Arab Empire, as they frequently do, this is taken as a proof of their backwardness and of their lack of understanding of history. The nationalists go so far as to make statements like the following: 'If the Copts today complain of being given a secondary place in the Egyptian state (as they do occasionally and not always without cause) they must be mistaken for we Arabs are known for our tolerance. This is proved by our history.'

The part played by the 'Greek sciences' in the Arab Middle Ages is greatly magnified. One can read generalizations such as: 'The Arabs took over Greek culture "almost completely", developed it and transmitted it to the West which was completely ignorant of it in the early Middle Ages!' In reality the struggle of the Greek spirit with the Spirit of Islam was a most intricate one which lasted for two or three centuries and finally ended with Greek methods of reasoning being in many cases banished from official Islam. They do not say in which cases Greek ideas and methods found acceptance and do not ask what sort of Greek thought was adopted nor how it was transformed in the process. All that is said is that 'Greek culture' was adopted and developed 'by the Arabs'. They like to convince themselves of great Arab achievements and to remind the 'West' how much it owes to them. Indeed, they assume that the West has reached its stage of development and dominant position in the world on the whole only because of the Arabs.

Self-encouragement is no doubt a necessity for a people which is preparing to take its own fate in its hands and to solve its own difficult problems and, after the experience of 'colonialism' the need for self-glorification is quite understandable. For the colonial powers created a reaction by their constant use of their double standard for 'Europeans' and for 'natives' in conjunction with their superior power and technical methods. In view of the 'colonialists'' conceitedness the desire of the Arabs to preserve their individuality compelled them to repeat to themselves that their nation, too, had been capable of considerable achievements.

However, the generalizations they indulge in are so grotesque and clumsy that they make the historical facts almost unrecognizable.

The desire of nationalist historians to justify and glorify their nation prevents them from studying and recounting their history for its own sake. The foreign model, which was formerly imposed on them by force and which they imitate today half-consciously, weighs heavily upon them and so again and again their attention is diverted from their own past to the history of the West and to the search for arguments against the 'colonialists'.

The standards applied to their own history are those by which they imagine their 'rival' measures his achievements, and they try to prove themselves at least equal to this opponent. In their heart of hearts they are so convinced of the superiority of their opponent and his methods that they avoid standing up to him as another people which follows its own laws. They try to justify themselves by asserting that they themselves helped in days gone by to create their opponent's achievements.

Thereby they undermine their own nationalism for, when all is said and done, the only purpose of nationalism is to convince people that they follow their own laws of life as a 'nation', as a sort of individual among the other nations. But the Arab nationalists confine themselves to considering the history of human civilization purely quantitatively without paying attention to differences in character: 'We were civilized *before* you were. You owe your civilization to us. We shall again be civilized because we were once civilized', and so on.

From all this it can be seen that 'history', as the majority of Arab nationalists understand it, cannot be a pointer towards a sound Arab policy. What really determines their desires and aims?

The most important factor seems to be the Arabs' wounded pride. They desire Karama (honour) above everything else. Collectively and as a nation they seek to escape from the disdain they suffered from so terribly in colonial times and which they believe the 'colonialists' still have for them. But the means by which they hope to recover their honour have been borrowed from the West. Above all they run the danger of forgetting completely who and how they really were as 'Arabs'.

We see the question of the immediate future of the Arab countries as at bottom a spiritual problem. We think that the decision between nationalism and communism in the long run depends on whether Arab nationalism can develop sufficient spiritual strength to become a real counter-weight to communism and the vortex of the Communist power *bloc*. If the Arab nationalists discover new ways of their own on which their historical heritage and the human peculiarities of their nation can be reconciled with the aspirations of a modern state or if they decide to profit boldly by the experiences of the West as the Turks have done under Atatürk's leadership, there might develop for them, too, a spiritual climate in which they could live and work fruitfully. For the present only one thing can be said with some certainty: this spiritual climate does not (yet) exist. One thing more: the Arabs themselves must achieve this. No one can do it for them.

At the moment all that exists is fragments of a way of life stretching into the present from times gone by. This is the great tradition of Islam as it is preserved in the habits of the lower classes. Everything else is overshadowed by the façade of Arab nationalism which serves above all the need for self-glorification and self-justification. Side by side with this goes the western liberal current of a western educated *élite* which practically always thinks and writes in a western language, not in Arabic. Finally, still thinly spread, there are the young communists or fellow-travellers who already have a decisive influence on the formation of public opinion in Iraq and dominate a fertile sector of literature in Egypt, young intellectuals who have turned their backs on the West and its civilization, its policies and its concepts of liberty and human rights, who do not wish to be reminded of Islam and envisage an eastern model for the construction of a new Arab society.

The zones of transition between these various typical currents are extensive and many Arabs shift easily from one zone to another or live somewhere between two zones. At present the liberal-western type has only very limited possibilities of expressing its opinions. In Egypt 'Arab Socialists' who follow Nasser receive the total patronage of the state. In Iraq, now that the pro-communist wave has receded, pure opportunists, who know how to flatter Qasim, dominate the press, the schools and the universities almost completely, so that there prevails in intellectual life a monotony which it is difficult to imagine more sterile. Practically everywhere the 'people' continue to live at an impoverished and proletarianized level with no leaders of their own—the traditional Islamic life which only remains alive because of its roots among the people.

4

The Problem of 'Humanism'

IT IS POSSIBLE TO SURVEY the present complex situation of the Arabs by picturing to oneself the role of 'humanism'. An important ingredient of western life is the belief in man and his inviolable rights, in his uniqueness and his link with the divine.

Of course, the idea of a divine inspiration in man is not foreign to Islam and mediaeval Islamic tradition developed its own type of humanism. But the two types of humanism tend in basically different directions: one might describe Islamic humanism as theocentric and the western one, especially since the Renaissance, as anthropocentric. The special nature of both attitudes may perhaps best be illustrated by reference, on the one hand, to the myth of Prometheus who stole fire from the gods and was punished for his action and, on the other hand, to the attitude of a Muslim Sufi whose earnest desire it is to be lost in God, or to a work of Islamic art in which both harmony and secret correspondences are expressed.

But now, under the influence of the West and western civilization the Islamic world, especially the Turkish and Arab nations, has begun to lay aside its own type of humanism which was valid for it until the later Middle Ages and which was directed towards God or the divine cosmos. It seemed after all not to be worth the political and social sacrifices made for its sake. Its symbol, the wandering mystic, suddenly seemed 'primitive' and 'ignorant'. A whole social order which sought to realize the divine commands on Earth had to collapse when a few leading individuals and later all 'educated' men took it into their heads that there were more important things in the life of man than the search for submission to God's Laws.

However, the Muslims themselves hardly noticed this change in their attitude. Just as a traveller may change direction completely in a tunnel without realizing it except when he follows the movement of the train with a compass, so did the Muslims remain unaware of their change of direction for it was a gradual process both in time and in its social implications. But the change is apparent if one compares the present-day attitude to religious, political and social questions with the earlier one. The Arab Muslims are now 'discovering' in the Koran all sorts of prescriptions for an active Islam dealing with one's intercourse with fellow men, indeed, the basis of a socialism founded on religion, of democracy and of a scientific attitude of mind, all commandments of which they were previously either completely unconscious or only insufficiently aware. Coming out from the tunnel in which their change of direction took place they look around in the spiritual landscape surrounding them and discover that their history and the Koran itself 'really' held a quite different message from what they had previously believed.

The change of direction was not so much consciously initiated by the Arabs (the Wahhabis are an important exception) as forced upon them. This was done internally by 'tyrants' like Muhammad Ali and from outside by the 'colonialists'. The change began on the material surface of Arab Muslim civilization and only gradually did the radical 'revolutions' in daily life bring about a new attitude of mind.

One knows first and foremost what one does *not* want. The Arabs no longer wish to live as they formerly did. Nor do they wish to live as a cultural, let alone a political, appendage of the West. So the long dead epoch of the Caliphs is idealized in the spirit of 'modern' ideals.

They set their sights very high materially, demanding a high standard of living for the whole people such as the West possesses and Russia claims to possess and they wish to be honoured and respected as a nation. They regard these as basic demands in the light of ideas which became popular in Europe in the nineteenth century. But they are little aware that such achievements were realized even in the 'rich' West only by fulfilling certain spiritual preconditions and have to be constantly earned anew if the whole edifice is not to be undermined.

One of the spiritual forces which hold the Western social structure together can be described in the widest sense as humanism. It is a complex moral and spiritual structure rooted partly in Christianity and partly in classic tradition. It influences the behaviour of 'modern, civilized' man, his attitude to weaker persons and those dependent on him, his relations to the sciences, the arts and the state and his intellectual and many of his economic pursuits.

The tradition of theocentric humanism has been interrupted in the Arab countries and in its stead certain *élite* groups have turned to western anthropocentric humanism. But the Arabs themselves often admit that they do not understand traditions like the practical civic spirit of the Anglo-Americans. For this very reason, they often add, the state must take upon itself the task of development which private individuals have performed and still do perform in the West. There is no tradition of Prometheus-like, scientific asceticism, no art directed towards man and his dramatic potential, no tradition of civic spirit to create a community.

'Abduh tried to include 'humanistic' values in his reformed Islam but these reforms have (so far) not struck deep roots among the Arabs. All politicians and ideologists are obsessed by the problem of how to 'create' a better community life and a climate of objective scientific mentality. The Arabs know, too, that the spirit of practical altruism in the West, as far as it exists, was the result of a long and variegated historical development, not the product of a propaganda campaign or a single politico-cultural movement. This is one reason why communism and its methods are attractive to them.

It appears to the Arabs that communism in Russia and especially in China has succeeded in creating by state intervention a citizen with a new mentality. It seems that a spiritual change of mind took place after the revolution, especially in China, a turning-away from 'oriental' empiricism to a 'modern', 'scientific', anthropocentric life directed towards the welfare of the community. It is not for us to discuss here whether this is a mirage of propaganda or an actual attitude of mind in these two communist societies. However, it is a fact that many Arabs, especially the youths, believe it. It is just the young, active and intelligent persons, ready to grant that the West is striving for objectivity, method and social justice, who doubt in their heart of hearts whether the Arab peoples can arrive at these virtues by the same road as the West.

The development of the European community spirit followed a centuries-long, winding path full of snares, dangers and false trails. The Communists laud their path as a 'short cut'. 'Have they not progressed', the Arabs ask, 'in less than fifty years from being a half-enslaved agrarian society to creating a modern state which is so all-powerful that it can make better lunar rockets than the Americans?'

Many go even farther and ask: 'Was it not after all the chaotic Western concept of "liberty" and the rights of the (moneyed) individual that prevented the Europeans from developing more quickly?'—'Do they perhaps want us to put on the straightjacket of human rights because they fear we might otherwise develop too fast or because they wish to continue to exploit us?'

Such arguments against the West and for the 'methods' of communism are completely reconcilable with a belief in 'Arab nationalism'. 'Of course, we are nationalists', say the leftish intellectuals of Cairo whenever the state allows them to express themselves. 'We believe we are better nationalists than those who would introduce uncongenial and hypocritical Western methods into Arab nationalism. All that we suggest is that they consider the other side, too, communism, and adopt from its system whatever suits us Arabs. In any case, we are fully convinced that Chinese and Russian methods are more suited to us than Western ones.'

Arab nationalism has nothing with which to counter such statements, unless it be ideas borrowed from the West. It is even possible for the communists to pose as patriots whose only desire it is to purify Arab nationalism of 'colonialist, capitalist' concepts. They do not need to extol 'Eastern socialist' ideas over much for these will 'automatically' enter the vacuum of Arab nationalism as soon as 'Western' ideas are driven out.

The Eisenhower Doctrine annoyed the Arabs when it was proclaimed because it spoke of a power vacuum after the supposed exclusion of Britain from Near-Eastern politics after the Suez crisis, a vacuum which the United States had to fill. The Arabs felt that they themselves had sufficient military power to fill this vacuum but today it seems that it is not so much a question of a power vacuum in the Arab World as of a vacuum of *ideas*. For the Arab nationalists are still searching feverishly for an 'ideology' to make the slogan 'Arab nationalism' mean something and fill the vacuum caused by the collapse of the old Islamic world of ideas.

For the present the slogan 'Arab nationalism' seems to the outsider to be mainly an expression of negative tendencies; they do *not* want to belong to the West (nor to the East either), but what they themselves as 'Arabs' really want is still obscure. The nationalists say that experience will provide them with concrete aims. But one cannot live without ideas: every step one takes is directed, if not by a conscious, at least by an unconscious or subconscious idea.

At the beginning of Nasser's revolution the junta still thought like the slightly socialist, liberal-nationalist West but even under the name of Arab nationalism these transplanted ideas met with resistance. The idea of liberty which had spread among the *élite* of the Near East towards the end of the Ottoman Empire is now considered discredited and un-Arab. Only a few Arabs, even among their leading men, are aware that 'Arab nationalism' is no substitute for it and, since new intellectual guiding lines are needed at least in order to envisage a future, the ideas of the East are ready at hand. . . .

5

Documents illustrative of
Present-day State of Mind

IN THE FOLLOWING PARAGRAPHS we shall try to quote a series of documents which may serve to illustrate the situation we have described. Every newspaper printed in the Near East is full of such material. While trying to indicate the various layers of modern Arab 'ideology', from more popular to academic and critical essays, we keep to the higher level. What the press shouts 'on the street' from day to day is much more primitive and one-sided than most of the writings we quote here.

i GREAT EXPECTATIONS: 'THE ARAB WORLD IN THE YEAR 2000'

The two-generations-old periodical *Al-Hilal* (The Crescent Moon) is published in Cairo and reminds us both in its format and content of the *Reader's Digest*. The first number of the year 1950 gave a preview of the future in which an attempt was made to depict conditions in Egypt and throughout the world fifty years later. On 1 January 1959, nine years later, *Al-Hilal* published a second preview of the year 2000, since, as the editor remarked in his foreword, one result of the Revolution of 1952 was that the preview of 1950 had to be revised in favour of even bolder dreams.

> Not three years passed before a new renaissance began and a rapid process of development saw its beginning throughout the Arab World. We witnessed a stirring leap forwards which led to a change in political, social and economic conditions. Important events occurred which the politicians and observers of the fates of nations had not foreseen. It was not long before we brought about revolutions against corrupt régimes in several parts of the Arab World, north, south, east and west. These revolutions brought about great changes: a new will showed itself to destroy the corruption which was the cause of decadence and servitude, to build a new life and work for a better future.

The 1950 number was prefaced by the Minister of Education as follows:

> We must undertake a great task which is nothing less than a total cultural revolution. We have to find the money, earmark taxes and contract loans for this purpose. We must recruit all the intellectuals for this and declare

unremitting war on ignorance. We shall not stop at combating illiteracy but shall strive to raise the culture of the people to a level which befits it so as to create an enlightened people conscious of its duties and of its rights. . . .

If we can realize this hope we shall have taken such a step forward in our history that no later generation can destroy what previous generations have built up. If no obstacles are placed in the path of the caravan and no false moves divert it from the right path we shall be able—and I am known for my pessimism—to bury our last illiterate in the year 2000. In every village in the country we shall have a school producing good citizens with a good education, well trained for agriculture or a handicraft or with a solid scientific foundation. These schools shall provide a spiritual, moral and scientific education, spreading brightness in the villages and turning their deep shadows into broad daylight. . . .

The preface to the 1959 number is by Nasser himself and the UAR Minister of Education Kamal al-Din Husain (one of the officers of the original junta) contributes the first article. There is no longer talk of the Egyptian village but of the 'Arab Nation'. It begins:

Today the greatness and brilliance of our Arab culture can be seen far and wide. No one any longer has the right to ask what it is and what its special characteristics are. It is somewhat different from what we used to call the 'science of the Arabs' when all the Arabs knew was what was for-bidden and permitted (by God) along with a little literature, philology and history. . . .

But at one time the Arabs had stood on the summit, their science had been *the* science and their culture *the* culture. They were masters of the science of what God has forbidden and permitted and the arts of language, literature and history and were the first to distinguish themselves in many sciences. They specialized in these and were either their founders or made such important new contributions to them that they are still a reminder of them and are ascribed to them in the great centres of science in the East and in the West. . . . Some of them made innovations in mathematics, engineer-ing, medicine and pharmaceutics. In chemistry and physics they opened doors which had been closed and even attempted to split the atom.

In the institutes of Cordova, Cairo and Baghdad those European scholars were trained who were later to become the founders of the European Renaissance. . . . If Arab culture had continued to develop it would have reached a degree of advancement with which the present-day culture of Europe and America could not be compared. But when the Arabs had reached that height of progress, time stood still for them for long. . . . But present-day Arab culture must reunite what was torn asunder by that historical development. It must advance and must not flag until it has caught up with and surpassed the culture which overtook it. It must catch up with it and surpass it. . . .

We have already determined the road to this goal. We have drawn up a plan and provided the means. We already have an Arab civilization whose brilliance and greatness can be seen far and wide. It is not the 'Arab science', which was formerly studied nor is it wholly European civilization. It is something different from both of these when one considers each of these separately but which, looked at as a whole, comprises both of them.

It is an extension of the past as it would have advanced had it followed its own course in those by-gone times and not met with obstacles.

Arab civilization is a pure inheritance from our ancestors along with the light which emanated from that heritage, which illuminated the European mind and helped it to build up its civilization. There is a place in it for the science of what God has allowed and forbidden for it is a part of our life, of our being and the basis of our society and belongs to humanity in whom we believe and for whom we pray to God. Our civilization also comprises our language, literature and history for these are a possession of our people, images of its perception, relics of our past and light illuminating our future. Arab civilization will compromise new branches of science which we shall discover just as our ancestors discovered sciences. We shall take what we need from the Western sciences and develop and expand them so that we may preserve our individuality. Thus we shall use to our own advantage the progress of science which was formerly made in Europe and so we shall overtake Europe and not limp after it as was formerly the case.

Our past and our present, the hopes we have for the future, the examples we have before us, our merits and our understanding of the cause of those things which worked against us and let others overtake us, all these are elements which we shall use to build our new Arab civilization.

In 2000 the definition of Arab civilization will not be very different from what it is now. . . . But it is possible that the characteristics of that civilization will be more clearly visible and more clearly and precisely definable. A further difference will be that that civilization will have a stronger influence on the Arab nation. . . .

New Arab civilization has already begun to create a new history for our Arab nation. Electric turbines in Aswan, iron and steel works in Helwan, the atomic pile in Inshas and the new oil pipeline along the Canal, the flourishing gardens of Liberation Province in the Western Desert and hundreds of factories, observatories and scientific institutes with their various tasks—all reflect the image of the new Arab civilization.

Our great homeland (i.e. all Arab countries) has in its soil and in its air, in its oceans, deserts and mountains riches such as can be boasted by no other land. It possesses unused natural resources which have not yet been discovered. Nothing is easier than to exploit these riches and possibilities in order to create wealth, power and a high living standard. Thus we shall be able to live a good life and help those friendly nations around us, achieving peace and wealth for ourselves and for our neighbours.

The scientific level of the Arab nation will be raised. . . .

When an Arab author in Baghdad writes a book and a reader in Fez, Cairo, Damascus or the Hadramaut reads it, it will be like a reflection of what is in his own heart. The view of the one will hardly differ at all from that of the other except in so far as the views of two comrades differ when they look at something from the same point of view. The frontiers and barriers between minds will disappear as the frontiers and barriers between all Arab countries will have disappeared. . . .

There will be public libraries in every quarter. . . .

There will be specialist societies for each art and for each science. . . . Our language will grow, expand and become stronger. It will be an international language for the sciences and the arts. It will be able to express any idea and describe anything and will resound in every international gathering. Translations will be made from and into Arabic, lectures will be given in Arabic in all universities, in every land inhabited by man. . . .

Thus the Arabs prepare for the second time to take a mighty step towards the development of human civilization and the ordering of relations between men.

We are living in a time of unity. Unity is the road to progress and its first cause is the unity of thought and the unity of civilization. It is the road to unity of sympathies, hopes and feelings, to the unity of planning and of aims. We have taken the first step along this road and lo! we have arrived. . . .

This does not mean that we have to wait until the year 2000 in order to achieve all that we have described . . . the gospel of unity has already begun to spread; the moment in which all these hopes can be realized has come.

Certain motifs and ideas are expressed again and again in nationalist propaganda in constantly changing forms. 'Progress' is thought of as a continuous develop, ment. The Arabs had helped to advance it and had then become tired. The Europeans had succeeded them but now it is the Arabs' turn again. There is already a plan for the Arabs to take their turn and the author claims to know already how long this will take and in what conditions it will be fulfilled. The 'plan' plays an inordinate part in nationalist propaganda and in nationalist thinking. What is 'planned' is already as good as achieved.

The 1950 number of *Al-Hilal* on the future contains a little essay on the uncertainty of the future by Al-Maufaluti, the well-known traditional essayist:

The future is an uncertain phenomenon. You see it indistinct in the distance. Perhaps it is a merciful angel, perhaps, too, a stoned devil. It can happen that when a cold wind blows upon a black cloud its component parts dissolve and disappear. It is then no more, as if it had never existed.

Man has desecrated every corner of this world. He has dug holes into the ground and climbed on ladders to the heavens. He has joined East and West with apparatuses of iron and wires of copper. In his spirit he has ascended to the upper world and lives among the planets, studying scientifically the most distant stars. . . . With his intelligence he has penetrated every veil and opened every door. But before the door of the Future he came to grief and is helpless and defeated, not daring to open it, for that door belongs to God and God permits no man to acquire knowledge of what He keeps hidden.

This is an echo of the traditional Islamic world. The 1959 number contains nothing like it. Instead one can read a long essay on 'scientific planning' by Dr 'Abd al-Halim Muntasir, Dean of the Faculty of Science of 'Ain Shams:

The Renaissance (of the Arabs) must be surrounded by scientific planning, not for five or ten years, but for fifty, so that we may achieve what we need for these millions (of people): food and water, land to cultivate, towns and villages to live in, factories to work in, arms to be strong, power to drive the machines in the work-shops and factories, schools of different grades and universities to train specialists: farmers, engineers, pharmacists and doctors, researchers in chemistry and physics. . . .

The purpose of scientific planning is to provide the possibilities and forces and direct them towards the goals, needs and economic development of society. For such a plan to be drawn up it is of course necessary for all the fundamentals to be collected by the President's collaborators and it is inevitable that scientists and specialists should be called upon to draw up the plan.

Great emphasis is given to 'science' and 'specialization'. The lower middle classes and perhaps even the governments have no idea which of the 'scientific specialists' really has some ability and which is also willing to do the work. So long as 'world famous specialists' are engaged on a plan or undertaking it cannot go wrong. Often orders, the result of military thinking, take the place of methodical and objective instructions: 'A new civilization *must* be created', says the Minister of Education, 'indeed, it already exists!'

The 1959 issue also contains a purely materialist theory of literature formulated by the well-known writer 'Abbas Mahmud al-'Aqqad. Al-'Aqqad's numerous writings deal mainly with the traditional Islamic past. Many of these are accounts of historical events or biographies of great Muslims. When the Congress of Arab Writers was held in Cairo in 1958 Al-'Aqqad opposed the attempt to include some leftish, socialist minded young writers in the official Egyptian delegation but did not himself take part in the congress although his wish was deferred to. His book *Neither Communism nor Colonialism* is 'nationalist' and anti-communist. His main ideas on the future of Arabic literature are as follows:

In 2000 Arabic literature will be a world literature for the following reasons: When a literature serves only a small number of readers it is difficult to include it among the literatures of world-wide importance. Its writers are not able to 'specialize' enough and the volume of literature they produce is too small. In the future the Arabs will form a state of 100 million souls and so their literature will flourish like that of America or Russia.

Seventy years ago the Russians had no literature of higher standing than the Arabs have today. Yet they raised their population to 70 millions or more, all held together by one language and not divided by geographical or political barriers. Thus the population of that remote land became large enough to produce a world literature which specialized mainly in narrative. . . . The Arabs, too, concludes Al-'Aqqad, will develop a world literature once they have become a unity of 150 millions (as they will probably be in 2000).

Salvation is expected from unity and at the same time even the traditional Muslim and the conscious anti-socialist supports their hope of salvation by purely materialist theses. They want to be 'modern' and have 'learned' that nationalism should be kept free from religious considerations. (Whenever nationalism is combined with Islam the Arab Christians get up and protest violently.) And just because they are Muslims they do not like to seize upon theories or ideas of European origin such as, for example, a simplified form of Hegelian national idealism as liked by the Syrian nationalists. Only those who have had a French or an English education are familiar with such ideas and so 'plausible' materialist arguments are seized upon.

On a more popular level, but characteristic of the psychology of salvation produced by Arab propaganda, is the following piece from the 1959 number:

Recollections of a tourist visiting the Arab World in 2000 (by *Habib Gamati*)

We welcomed the New Year in in New York, then at about midday went on board an aircraft of Misr-Air, and dined in Cairo. Cairo, which was formerly the capital of Egypt, is now the capital of the United Arab States. We only spent an hour or two there and at 10 o'clock in the evening we and about twenty other passengers went on board that wonderful vehicle which an Egyptian invented in 1995 and which they call here the 'Sari'a' (the swift one). It can skim over the land and the surface of the water just as the passengers wish. After a journey of two days we arrived in Aswan, having passed by many towns which lie along the banks of the great River Nile.

That part of Egypt is called Upper Egypt. It has changed very much in the past forty years especially since scholars discovered there hundreds of ruined cities and treasures and historical monuments buried under the sand. Every town in Upper Egypt has a museum in which the monuments found in the neighbourhood are collected. . . .

But the wonder of wonders in Egypt are the dams, bridges and reservoirs which control the water of the Nile and put it to the service of this people.

It is they which cause their fields to flourish all around. The most important of these miracle constructions is the High Dam with the reservoir of Aswan and that of Jebel Awliya. It was only when I visited these wonders that I realized how backward we in America are. . . .

Cairo, 15 January 2000

What a wonderful city this is and how fitting is its name: Al-Qahira, the Conquering. Betsy said to me the very first night we spent in the Salam (Peace) Hotel at the top of Muqattam mountain: If only we could come back to this country every year to renew our pledge of love.

We determined to see everything a tourist should see in Cairo. We spent a whole week there but didn't manage to do everything we intended to do. We had to be satisfied with just a little and to imagine the rest. We visited one of the 20 universities, one of the 130 hospitals, one of the 90 theatres and five of the 500 factories which have shot up around Cairo. We drove twenty kilometres along the promenade which runs along both banks of the Nile. It is the longest promenade in the world beginning at the estuary of that wonderful river on the Mediterranean and following the course of the river right through the country as far as Shallal in Upper Egypt. Now that this gigantic promenade has been built the modern Egyptians are convinced that they, like the Ancient Egyptians, are the greatest builders in the world. The Sphinx, the Pyramids, the Temple of Luxor, the Tombs of the Pharaohs, the Suez Canal, the Aswan Dam and the Nile Promenade all testify to this. . . .

Jerusalem, 22 January 2000

We came here in a new kind of automobile we have bought. It can fly when you press a button and can be turned into a bedroom when required. It has an atomic motor instead of a petrol engine.

Jerusalem is dear to the hearts of all Arabs for it is a reminder of the birth of the great religions and also because the Jews had their own state there during a certain period of Arab history. They set it up, helped by the Western powers, in a part of Palestine they called 'Israel'. However, the Arabs were able to liquidate it less than twenty years after its foundation. Palestine became a unified Arab country again and is today part of the greater Arab unity.

Baghdad, 5 February 2000

In our last two weeks we made a tour by air of the Arabian Peninsula. We saw the miracles which have been achieved in Central Arabia. Where there was formerly nothing but sand today we see stretches of cultivation, towns, farms, fields, factories, asphalted roads, reclamation work which was begun some fifty years ago and which is still going on. All this is provided for by the revenues from oil which the Arabs are today exploiting for themselves in contrast to the state of affairs in the distant past. . . .

What a wonderful and delightful thing it is that the desert is being transformed into cultivated land, fields and gardens! It is one of the greatest miracles the Arabs have achieved with their own hands ever since their renaissance began and they liberated themselves from foreign domination. I often thought during our flight of the time when my country, America, and my wife's country, England, called that part of Arabia 'backward' and tried to take possession of it and enrich themselves with its treasures.

Iraq, which was for decades the throne of western colonialism in the Eastern Arab World and in Asia is today an outpost of Arab enlightenment directed towards the Asian continent. . . .

In the book (I intend to write) I shall explain how remarkably advanced the Arabs are today, whom we Americans and Europeans wanted to keep at the level of shepherds and peasants. In the past forty years they have made progress which we could never have expected and which would normally have required at least a hundred years.

ii REALITY

The following are extracts from the semiofficial Cairo newspaper *Al-Gumhuriya*, which were reproduced in the French quarterly *Orient* (No. 3, 1958). It was only owing to special circumstances that such realistic reports could appear in a Cairo paper. In July 1958 Nasser touched on the lot of the peasants in a long speech. 'We all know what living conditions are like in the country districts. . . . If we do not worry about these facts we shall be made, perhaps by force, to reconstruct our society.'

The following August *Al-Gumhuriya* published some articles on the life led by the peasants:

Four questions we would like answered:

Here are the questions we wish to put today so that they may be answered:

First question:

Have the peasants' living conditions really changed since the revolution of 23rd July? Was the revolution not made for the peasants? Is the attitude of mind prevailing in the countryside—which in the final analysis decides the lot of the peasants—the same as it used to be? Do the same despotism and tyranny still prevail, the same desire to keep the peasant in misery and the old resignation which finds its expression in the words: 'It is my fate!'?

Second question:

Are the plans of the revolution to improve the lot of the peasants complete and have they been carried out in its spirit? Have the sums which were earmarked for these plans and for the achievement of the aims the revolution set itself been spent? Have they not rather drifted away in all directions without benefiting in the least the peasants who toil and sweat for the whole country?

Third question:

Do the high officials in Cairo who have American cars and air-conditioned offices perform their duties in a manner justifying the high salaries they receive? Do they really control everything that is going on in the countryside? How many of them leave their offices in Cairo and go and live in the country to supervise and direct the carrying out of the great agricultural projects?

Fourth question:

If things have not changed at all in the country do the high officials who bear the responsibility know what the final outcome will be? Do they think the peasant still does not know what rights he has? Can he not follow how the world is developing on the modest radio he possesses? Do these gentlemen, who live so comfortably in their air-conditioned offices and travel about in government cars, think that the pleasant life they are leading will last much longer?

These four questions are not specifically answered in *Al-Gumhuriya* but those who know what life is like in the Egyptian country districts already know the answer. The descriptions, a few of which follow, are intended for those who do not know or do not want to know the answer, namely the majority of Egyptian town-dwellers:

The Land Rent Act:

At first I could hardly believe my ears when I was told that the law fixing land rentals at seven times the yearly land tax was not really operative.

I refused to believe it because this law which has been on the statute book since the beginning of the revolution is one of the most important items of legislation on land reform, the land reform which abolished feudalism and put an end to the exploitation of small landowners by big ones. . . . But in the end I had to believe it.

Intimidation:

I was told the following:

Seven times the land tax means £E26 per feddan. But can any peasant rent a feddan for such a fair and modest price? No one will let him land at that price! What do they do instead? The landowner gets the wretched peasant to sign a note for the legal sum but at the same time he has to sign a bond undertaking to pay the difference between the legal rental and the rental the landowner can extort from him. In this way the £E26 often rises to £E50.

I asked: 'Can you give me a name?'

The peasant's face clouded over with fear and he begged me not to write anything of what he had told me. . . .

'Are you afraid?'

'Of course. I could suffer a great calamity if it became known that I had given the secret away.'

How the peasant lives:

We visited Ma'sara village (in Daqahliya Province), a little place with 3000 inhabitants, 1750 of whom own little plots of land from a sixth of a feddan to five feddans. 1250 are really poor with no land, no aim in life, resigned and wretched. This village is typical of the unemployment in the country districts. There are 12 similar villages in the vicinity and together they have 50,000 unemployed.

The unemployed and semi-employed only find something to do when a disaster hits the village, for example, when the cotton weevil attacks the cotton crop. They then work for 7 piastres a day. They are also needed to clean out the canals but these tasks occupy them for only 60 days in the year. . . . Might I also mention that Ma'sara and the neighbouring villages have not benefited from the land reform because 80 per cent of the lands which formerly belonged to the feudal lords have been used up (by the state) in building roads and for other construction purposes. . . .

. . . We had to stoop down to enter his dwelling, which he shares with his mother, his wife, and three brothers, all living in one room where they sleep and eat. What do they eat?

Cheese and dry bread.

'Is this all you have to eat?' I asked.

'Yes, provided we can get even that,' answered the old woman.

A cage made of palm branches serves them as a cupboard in one corner. But what have they to keep in it? Clothes? All they have is the rags with which they cover their emaciated bodies. What else? A few empty tins, which they use as cups and tea-pot, and a cooking pot!

The young peasant and his brother are unemployed and can find nothing to do for there is no work anywhere. The oldest had been employed for some time by a contractor constructing one of the buildings for the (Helwan) steel works. But when the work was finished he was dismissed and he has been unemployed for a year. When he does find work it is for at the most 6 or 8 days in the month and so he earns from 70 to 80 piastres (14/– to 16/–) a month. So we could see just how serious the problem of unemployment is in the villages. It is a problem which does not seem to interest those responsible. . . .

Three persons I have met:

Zainab Mahmud Halawa, 65 years old, beggar, has not eaten meat for six years. . . .

Muhammad Musa, 63 years old, father of eight children, four of whom are dead; he is himself paralysed and so forced to beg. His daughter works carrying tiles and so earns two piastres (5d) a day.

Zainal Ali, 80 years old, beggar; has a son but he cannot support him because he has a wife and five children and only earns £E5 a month.

Villages are dying. Hordes of peasants are waiting to be liberated from unemployment so that they can fill their bellies and build a great nation.

iii THE INDUSTRIAL PARADISE

The following are extracts from a newspaper article published by Khalid Muhieddin, the then editor-in-chief of *Al-Masa* newspaper in November 1958 (French translation in *Orient* No. 8, 1958). Khalid Muhieddin was one of the officers of the original junta but had always been on its left wing. During Nasser's struggle with Naguib he supported the latter who was promising to reintroduce political parties. After Naguib's resignation he used the troops subordinated to him to force Nasser to reinstate him and when Nasser was finally victorious he had to leave Egypt. He was allowed to return in 1958 and Nasser made him editor of *Al-Masa*.

This paper, more popular than *Al-Ahram* which is read by the business world, has since become the mouthpiece of the left. Forced to work under a cloak of nationalism, it went just as far in friendship to communism and in propagating communist ideas as the government allowed. A few months after the publication of the above-mentioned articles Khalid Muhieddin fell victim to the anti-communist line of Egyptian internal politics occasioned by the quarrel with Baghdad and had to resign from the editorship of 'his' newspaper. Nothing has been heard of him since. Zakariya Muhieddin, Minister of the Interior of the UAR and Nasser's expert in police matters, is his cousin and protected him during all these storms.

We are not so much concerned to point out Khalid Muhieddin's (pro-) communist line as the sort of hopes engendered in the minds of the vast majority of Egyptians by the word 'industrialization'.

Kladno, centre of the steel industry (Czechoslovakian).

This city, which has distinguished itself in the heroic struggle with the forces of reaction, owes its fame and its prosperity to its workers. Many Czech poets have sung of its fame and self-sacrifice. The first strike against the social-democratic government took place here and the Czech Communist Party was born here.

Ten thousand workers work in the coal mines and 20,000 in the steelworks.

Their average wage is 1,800 crowns (£E90) a month but specialist workers and engineers can get as much as from 12,000 to 22,000 crowns, that is to say from £E600 to £E1,100, a month.

In addition to the wages there are family allowances.

There follow further enticing details: free education and free medical treatment, pensions up to 90 per cent of the wage at the age of fifty-five, paid holidays and trade union benefits.

Large buildings surrounded by gardens are put at the workers' disposal. A still childless newly married couple is given two luxurious furnished rooms (radio, television, central heating, bathroom). The furniture is simple but tasteful and there is always a well-filled bookcase (Balzac, Tolstoi, Gorki, Shakespeare). The rent for such an appartment is 160 crowns (£E8) which is not much when one considers that their combined income is 4,000 crowns (£E200). In addition to the rent they pay 70 crowns (£E3) a month for heating and lighting.

The young wife said to me:

'We have chicken and meat for lunch and dinner, with a drink, vegetables, cakes and fruit.'

'Once a week we go to the cinema and once a fortnight to the theatre. On Sunday we go to the country.'

'We dress well and I have a fur coat!'

Mr Franlick told us that 80 per cent of the workers in Kladno are party members. It was the party that was able to guarantee them this living standard which they had formerly never dared to dream of, not even in their times of greatest optimism.

iv A SHEIKH VISITS MOSCOW

An answer to the much discussed question as to whether Islam is a counter-force to Communism is given by the 'sermon' delivered in Damascus by Sheikh *'Abdur Raziq al-Homsi* and broadcast by Damascus Radio shortly after his return from a journey to Moscow in August 1958 (Extract in *Orient* No. 7, 1958).

Brothers!

We thought we would find in the territory of the Soviet Union naked, starving, ignorant peoples subjected to a reign of terror behind the notorious Iron Curtain as mean and dirty propaganda asserts for its own filthy and base purposes. Instead of the so-called Iron Curtain we found a curtain of air which we easily passed through, as our Mufti said in his speeches. We flew through this curtain of air to find on the other side civilized and cultured peoples living prosperously in perfect freedom. They lead a quiet, disciplined life, knowing no theft, murder or false oaths, loving peace above everything else and working to assure it.

The shops and stores are full of life, many welcoming every day more than 50,000 customers who, owing to the liberal wages they receive, buy there everything they require, what is necessary as well as what is superfluous. It is not true that there is, as has been said, no money in the Soviet Union and that nothing is bought and sold there.

We visited Moscow University, an enormous building of thirty-two storeys, and passed through its museums, libraries and lecture halls. In twelve seconds we went up to the twenty-second floor where 22,000 students live. We discovered that the University has 47,000 rooms and that a student wanting to spend a day in each one of them would need ten years to visit them all. . . .

V GOING ONE BETTER. A VOICE FROM IRAQ

The following newspaper article from which we give extracts, again from *Orient* (No. 9, 1959), was written by the Iraqi writer *Dhannoon Ayyub*. Ayyub, whose first name would read Dhu an-Nun in classical Arabic as it sometimes appears in Europe, is at present Director-General of the Propaganda Ministry ('Ministry of National Guidance') and director of Baghdad Radio. In Nuri Pasha's time he was one of those intellectuals of the left whom the government branded as Communists and persecuted. He spent the last few years before the revolution in Vienna and his short stories are well-known in all Arab countries.

Advice to 'Abd al-Nasser.

. . . Dear President, I do not think you are so naïve as to be unaware that your reputation does not stand very high here in Iraq. But should you not be clear about this I advise you to ask your agents and spies in Iraq for you have no doubt quite a lot of these.

You would perhaps like to believe that it is our government that is responsible for the collapse of your reputation in our country. But do you really think that there is any government on the face of the earth able to stir up in the hearts of the whole people disgust and resentment ending in deadly hatred? Nuri al-Sa'id, too, thought that the Iraqis' hatred of him was only a result of propaganda.

You wanted to spread your hegemony to our country for reasons known to everyone. Again and again you proclaimed that Arab unity demanded the submission of Iraq to your commands. But the Arabs, and especially the Iraqis, asked themselves: How is it that Mr President does not address his call for unity to the 'Anglo-Egyptian Sudan' which should have become simply the 'Egyptian Sudan' after getting its freedom? Why does the President not try to bring about the union of Libya with his country? And why does he not exercise his heroism by trying to liberate Algeria which is so near? No, the President has forgotten all his neighbours and turned his desires upon a country that is remote from his.

Only after the heroes of our revolution had driven the imperialists for ever from our country did President 'Abd al-Nasser get up and proclaim that he was the 'Liberator'. He reminds me of the dwarf in the fairy tale who, when the battle was over, drew his sword to cut the feet off the corpses. Someone asked him why he didn't cut their heads off and he replied: I didn't find a single head I could have cut off!

But that isn't all. There are reasons for the President's attitude. Having annexed Syria 'Abd al-Nasser found himself in a bad way. He had, by hook or by crook, to find money for his industrialization plans and markets for Egyptian capital goods. Instead of asking for Iraq's help in the name of Arab brotherhood, our hero simply decided to take possession of our country in the name of 'Arab unity', imagining that our country was led by naïve and ignorant men. Because he suffered from such hallucinations, the President made his intentions and secret plans known a little too early. And as a result he found suddenly all Iraq giving free reign to its hatred of him.

... When you took leave of Faruq you accompanied him to his yacht, your eyes full of tears. You fired the gunshots in his honour and then you called that 'revolution'! But then straight away you had to find another master. .... You offered yourself to the Americans and requested their aid, but they were deaf. So you tried to entice them by turning to their enemies (the Russians). Just as a woman who has been deserted tries to arouse her lover's jealousy by flirting with someone else. The leaders of the East to whom you turned were ready to help you, not for your sake but through pity for your people.

They decided to come to the help of your people, which is trying to recover its human dignity after centuries of slavery, and to protect it from those attacking it. But you quickly realized that the rulers of the East are not prepared to recognize one man as superior to another and so were not prepared to help you to extend your authority over others. You said to yourself: They are stupid and don't understand anything.

... But the great revolution broke out in Iraq and you recognized that this revolution was quite different from yours. It was free from intrigues and falsity. It was a power breaking out and shining like daylight. The imperialist world was terrified and America was stunned. She turned whining to you and implored you to forget the past. You puffed yourself up proudly and said to your master: These scoundrels ... I'll deal with them ... who are they to stand up to 'Abd al-Nasser? So you began to look for a henchman who could carry out your dark plans and you found him in 'Abd al-Salam 'Arif.

By acting like this you proved you knew nothing about Iraq and the Iraqi people. You were like your masters, the Americans, who write a book about a city they have driven through without even getting out of their car. The moment your pretensions became clear the people in their anger tore your agent to pieces. All those who wanted to belong to you or who bore your name were liquidated in a very short time because they were only a very small minority. .... (*Al-Zaman*, 23 March 1959).

Setting aside his manifold distortions of the truth the director of Iraqi propaganda nevertheless utters some fatal truths both for Nasser and for the anti-communist world.

'Nasser', says Ayyub, 'has proved that, in the middle of the twentieth century, he is dreaming dreams worthy of the Middle Ages. Not only by dreaming of an Empire but also by using political methods completely alien to our times.'

vi COMMUNIST TACTICS

Although propaganda attacks on Nasser, like those made by Ayyub, are meant for the general reader and the 'people' of, as the Communists say, 'elements belonging to no party', the Iraqi Communists also published documents for internal party use during the first year after the revolution. These are written in the communist 'scientific' jargon and sometimes make very unpleasant reading. But if one can read between the lines they are exceedingly indicative of the new tactics and aims of the Iraqi Communists. We give here some short extracts from a voluminous report of the Central Committee of the Iraqi Communist Party of July 1959. The entire document has been published in French in *Orient* (No. 11, 1959).

. . . Our party considers the events of 14th July (the Iraqi revolution) as a people's revolution, a revolution of all anti-imperialist and anti-feudal classes of the people, not as a *coup d'état* from above. Our party also considers that these events were only a continuation of the national revolutions and uprisings of our people in the last forty years. They were nothing other than the continuation of the long, hard struggles of the national forces.

With this assertion a distinction is drawn between the Iraqi revolution and Nasser's revolution. Occasionally the Iraqi Communists have defended the thesis that they were the 'decisive' force behind the revolution. Nevertheless, Qasim has taken sharp exception to such claims and has proclaimed on various occasions: '*I* am the revolution. *I* am the symbol and essence of the people.'

As a matter of fact there is no doubt that Qasim was the 'father and instigator' of the revolution. As far as we know it was he who planned it and carried it out whereas the 'people' would have been powerless without the intervention of the Army.

While considering what kind of revolution it was to be, our party worked out a definite political line for national co-operation. Our policy is based on the unity of all national, anti-imperialist, anti-feudal and anti-reactionary forces. This was expressed first and foremost by the masses and our party giving full support to the national government (Qasim). It was also expressed in new forms of collaboration with various patriotic and democratic organizations. Finally it is reflected by the political and economic slogans which our party has proclaimed.

The close solidarity which arose between the party and the leading men in power has contributed fundamentally to the preservation of the republic and the development of the benefits gained by the revolution, thus strengthening and consolidating the power of the nation. It was this solidarity which made it possible to mobilize the greatest masses and to achieve great victories one after the other.

In other words: It is mainly due to us, the Communists, that Qasim's régime has been able to survive certain crises like Shawwaf's revolt in Mosul and the alleged attempts at revolution of 'Arif and Gilani in Baghdad. But again it was actually the Army which played the really decisive role in all these. To be sure, once things had been decided, the Communists knew how to mobilize the 'street' for monster demonstrations in favour of Qasim and in this way gain credit for their party.

The Egyptian upper *bourgeoisie*, who have distorted the meaning of Arab nationalism, tried even in the first days of the revolution to extend their domination to Iraq, taking advantage of the fact that a large number of nationalists of the right were in the government and outside it. . . . The Baath Party and, to a lesser extent, the Istiqlal Party, took up a hostile attitude to the National Front. Once they were expelled from the National Unity Front we spared no efforts to collaborate with the National Democratic Party. But unfortunately during our promising negotiations we were surprised by the news that the National Democratic Party had suspended its political activities. Owing to the negative effect of this decision on the democratic development of our republic and on the unification of the national forces, we were forced to oppose their decision although we feel solidarity with the National Democratic Party and although we justify the position they adopted in the past.

This refers to the following events: After the pro-Nasser forces had been driven out of the government and also the National Front which had been formed in secret even before the revolution, the Communists desired to form a new 'National Front', comprising themselves, the so-called Kurdish Democratic Party and the National Democratic Party. Qasim's government consisted half of officers who are officially attached to no party and half members of the National Democratic Party. The purpose of the Front was obviously to surround and dominate the National Democrats (and so important ministries) by means of the Communists. Qasim saw through this manoeuvre and called upon all parties to suspend their political activities.

. . . The victories achieved by our revolution in spite of external and internal threats and the great activity we displayed in supporting the national government led our party to make mistakes and underrate the capabilities of the national government. We judged the national forces by their traditional political organizations which were in the main parties, but we neglected to analyse the role of the national government in detail although it had become practically the centre around which the national forces gathered.

This is 'self-criticism' but not a very honest one. What the Communist Party calls a sin of omission was in reality rather a miscalculation whereby they considered the government too weak to impose its will on the parties.

When news went around that a redistribution of the ministries was intended our party seized the initiative and circulated the slogan of participation in the government.

A plenary assembly of the central committee emphasized that participation of representatives of all classes of the nation in a coalition government was the form of government best suited to the (then) stage of the revolution. Political experience in many countries has also proved that coalition governments are suitable forms of government. . . .

So much for general principles. However, in practice our request (for participation in the government) came to nothing because it had not reckoned with concrete reality, the proportion of the (various) forces in the country and the development of the revolution *vis-à-vis* the Arab situation and the international situations of the moment.

The last sentence is particularly informative: The Iraqi Revolution had already gone too far '*vis-à-vis* the Arab situation'. If the Communists in Baghdad had seized power that would have done too much harm to the Communists in the rest of the Arab world. Moscow wanted a relaxation of tension and the Iraqi Party had to fall into line and bide its time.

After the revolution a revolutionary government was appointed which followed a policy of anti-feudalism and anti-imperialism. But this government, whose members were determined by the leader of the revolution, has up to now only a provisory character. In these circumstances the call for participation in the government, which the party made without the approval of its leaders, was an abortive and sectarian act. It reckoned neither with the concrete reality of the revolution nor with the proportion of forces in the country. As a result this action damaged the unity and solidarity of the national forces in their fight for the defence of the republic.

The massive propaganda made to express the desire (of the party) also heightened the negative results for the country. . . .

This situation was the result of a miscalculation by us, namely the overrating of our own strength and the underrating of the role of the Government and the other national forces in defending the republic. As a result of this miscalculation our party concentrated its efforts on mobilizing the masses with the intention of taking the defence of the Republic in hand and leading it on the path of democracy. This is in itself right and proper. But from time to time this was pursued too strictly and another problem which is just as fundamental was lost sight of, namely lasting solidarity with the government and with the other national forces. . . .

No Communist could say more clearly: We tried, alone and against the government, to take control of the country but we overrated our strength. Now we want to be readmitted to the protecting bosom of 'solidarity with the government and the other national forces'.

The event which led the Iraqi Communist Party to indulge in this self-criticism was the Kirkuk revolt of July 1959, an unquestionably Communist-inspired uprising accompanied by fighting between Kurds and Turcomans. For three days a committee of the 'National Front' ruled in Kirkuk and massacres were perpetrated before the Iraqi Army managed to occupy the city.

The Communist Party officially denies all responsibility for these events. Its report speaks of certain 'spontaneous features' which showed themselves 'among the people' but which could not be condoned. Lenin is quoted: 'Deviations to the left are an infantile sickness of revolutions' and a promise is given to preserve order better in the future. In reality Kirkuk was an attempt to seize power, probably not confined to that locality alone.

The Communists profited by their self-criticism. Qasim's government did not take strong measures against them. All it did was to condemn to death some of the 'anarchists' responsible for the Kirkuk massacres. When, in the following September, what were most probably 'nationalist' elements made an unsuccessful attempt on Qasim's life, the Communists were again in a position to mobilize 'the street' for Qasim, the 'Republic' and the 'Revolution'.

However, Qasim's government seems to be on its guard against the Communists. Their party continues to be illegal in theory although in practice it controls whole ministries.

What will happen if the 'other' national forces are not prepared to collaborate with them as they demand? The Arab communist parties must then reckon with more or less severe persecution, but this hardly reduces the general prospects of communism in the Arab Near East. So long as there are tensions and rivalries between individual states, the party will always succeed in flourishing in one country because it is being persecuted in another. But should the unification of the Arabs actually come about (a not very probable supposition at present), the Communists could in the long run profit even by such a development: namely in the event of the pan-Arab paradise, which is hoped for and confidently expected by the more primitive Arab nationalists, not materializing after the unification. . . .

6

Hope

IN MAY 1959, when the troubles in Lebanon had hardly subsided, a young Arab authoress, Leila Baalbaki, gave a public lecture in Beirut. Leila Baalbaki had suddenly become famous in the Arab world through her novel *Ana Ahya!* (I live!).[1] In diary form she describes the inner life of a young Muslim girl of good family. Her father and mother will not admit that their daughter has a right to her own personality and to lead her own life. The struggle is bitter, for the memorable conceptions of respect due to one's elders are still upheld in traditional Muslim families, at least to all outward appearances. Many of the younger generation submit to this but make light of deceiving their strict father and coaxing money out of their worried mother. 'When my father finally dies I shall go for a trip around the world' and the like can often be heard.

But the heroine of Leila's novel fights back. Leila Baalbaki herself tells how a mother in Syria wrote the following letter to her after she had read *Ana Ahya!*:

If only Lina Fayyad, the heroine of *Ana Ahya!* had shown a little decorum and education and a minimum of respect when speaking of her parents even if she had only done so in her heart. For example if she had said: 'I silenced my mother' and not 'I shut her up', or if she had said she could have torn her father to pieces with her fingernails and teeth or, for all I care, with a knife. Can she not spare us such words as 'I could have stamped on his face in my rage!' That is too much.

So the young novelist stood 'for the first time in my life', as she says, in front of a large audience in a country which had been shaken to its roots by a revolt a few months before. She was speaking in a course of lectures dealing with the problem of a future, better Lebanon, on the theme of Lebanese youth: 'We without masks'.

A fifty-year old acquaintance of mine said to me: 'The most remarkable aspect of this book (*Ana Ahya!*) is the victory it finally wins over the slack traditionalism which up till now has degraded our young people to servile subjects of their parents. I still cannot bear to have to bow before my old father and kiss his hand. I detest this comedy just as much as my father enjoys it, glorifies in it and persists in demanding it of me, considering it more important than eating and drinking. This comedy satisfies his lust for

[1] French translation by Michel Barbot, Aux Editions du Seuil, Paris, 1961.

329

power and his pleasure in autocracy. At the same time he humbled himself all his life before aggressors and tyrants, from the Ottomans to the period of the Mandate. . . .

We are not fans of the late James Dean, nor the followers of the marvellous Brigitte Bardot, nor the clique of the bobby-soxers' idol, Anthony Perkins. All of these are merely a superficial reflection of our sorry plight.

We are harder, more violent, more unhappy than young people in Europe or America for we are waging a merciless battle for liberty—for the individual, the state, and the nation—while they enjoy their liberty as easily as we drink a bottle of lemonade. . . .

They can protest against anything they do not like but our lips are sewn up tightly. The very thought of this infuriates us. . . .

For this reason the struggle we are waging within our narrow limits aims at loosening the grip which the fictions concerning our history, society and state have on people here.

One can see how the problem of emancipation from 'the older generation' spills over into the greater community, and one wonders: 'Will this young girl who fights so strongly against hypocrisy and restraint in her family be caught by the fictions of the state? Along with liberty, man and the service of man are first in her scale of values. Nothing is said about the Arabs and the Arab nation. The state has to serve man, not the other way round.

If the state is small it must fight to liberate itself from the yoke of colonialism, from the powers which oppress it and the servitudes it has too long suffered.

If the state is great it must avoid, in future, meddling in the affairs of others and it may no longer try to swallow up small countries.

The state, no matter what the régime, for all peoples and especially the youth of every people are working for the establishment of universal brotherhood, must extend the kingdom of peace and respect for human beings and human life all over the earth. . . .

Here, as in all other Arab countries, we are ready to collaborate with the state to achieve the sovereignty and well-being of the people but we consider that open discussion of the laws and decrees elaborated for us and for our future is absolutely essential. For the state, as we understand it, is nothing but the sea, a crust of bread, a bunch of flowers; I mean that it only becomes important when it serves human beings and human life. . . .

We ourselves can satisfy our need for political institutions, a need which stems from our most inner nature, within our own limits and from our liberty. Our inner nature is our heritage.

Many a one will be surprised that we young people recognize the past in this way. But heritage is something different from the past; it is the warmth-giving wall which protects us and is a vital necessity for us. The past is the colour of the wall which disgusts us and which we absolutely reject.

We believe firmly that the confusion between heritage and past has caused us great harm throughout history and that certain states have exploited this for centuries using it as a bogy-man to frighten us.

It seems inevitable that the problem of the past, of history, must crop up as soon as one begins talking about the state and its organization and our young novelist, too, cannot avoid it.

But she approaches the history of the Arabs as a free individual. She does not feel in duty bound to accept this past as a whole and to paint it in lovely colours as the doctrinaire nationalists do. She feels free to reject whatever 'disgusts' her.

She also has passages which show a certain hypersensitivity towards the West but she shows quite clearly that she is by no means of a mind to keep pondering the problem of this 'superiority' of the West for the rest of her life. She envisages something much greater and passionately demands liberty for herself and for her generation. But liberty to do what?

The only truth we are conscious of is that we shall never be in a position to achieve respect as members of the great human family unless we tear down the dark veils enshrouding our history and, having reached the last stone our ancestors added in times gone by to the general edifice of human society, help with our shoulders and our hands to establish the new state.

In view of such a testimony of undeniable individuality and unlimited thirst for freedom we must ask ourselves: Have we not misjudged the Arabs by analysing their present situation mainly at the popular level of newspapers and state propaganda? Should we not rather have tried to deal with the *élite*? And are not the achievements of real intellectuals a better yardstick by which to measure the 'Arabs'' intellectual situation than state propaganda?

Do such real intellectuals exist? To be sure, they crop up here and there but Paris is still the spiritual home of many of them, Paris or Cairo—or Moscow.

Many of them write in French, for example, the Lebanese Coptic philosopher René Habachi, the Algerians Bennabi and Bencheneb, the Algerian novelists Chraibi and Yacine and the Tunisian Jew Memmi. Something of the spirit of French 'existentialism' goes into their writings with the language. Their basic themes are the individual, his liberty and his free choice.

A second group of true intellectuals can be observed at work in Cairo. They draw their inspiration from the Egyptian villages and their doctrine is 'socialism'. They do not accept that the peasant's life should be as it is with all its terrible hopelessness. Their passionate interest in the concrete reality of Egyptian country life (perhaps also a silent criticism of the 'nationalist' government) expresses itself in their use of the colloquial language. Their stories and novels are full of colloquial expressions and they make their peasants speak more or less as they really do. They do not translate their speech into classical Arabic which was fixed by the religious scholars a thousand years ago, and which is still essentially the same.

THE ARAB EMPIRES

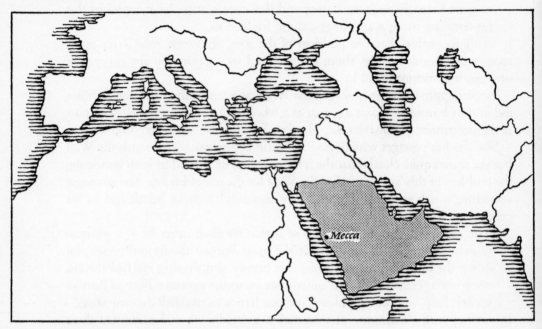

The Arab national state at the time of Muhammad's death in 632

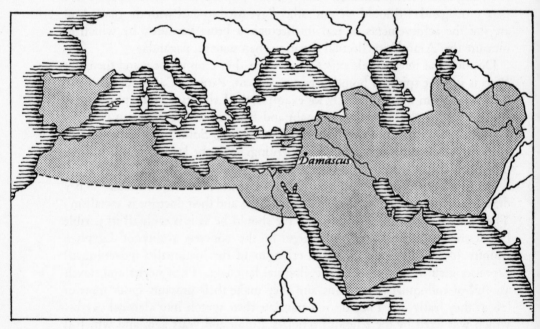

Extent of the Umayyad Empire in 750

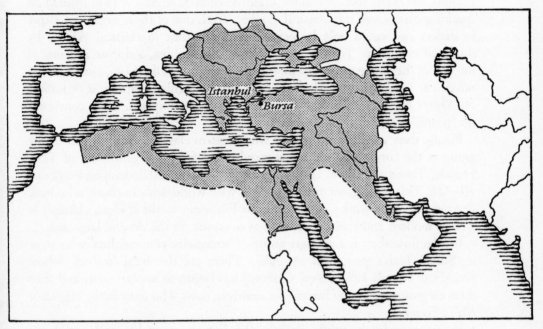

Extent of the Ottoman Empire at the end of the sixteenth century

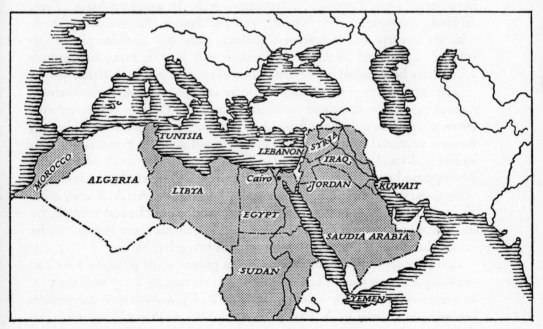

The member states of the Arab League

With that impressive consistency, so noticeable among the Oriental communists, the Arab 'socialists' at the Cairo Writers' Congress of 1958 insisted on
speaking dialect and not classical Arabic. Each one of them began his paper
in dialect and could only be persuaded to continue in classical Arabic by
threats of expulsion. To this group belong Yussef Idris, a doctor and one of
the best of the young Egyptian short story writers, Al-Sharqawi, author of the
novel *The Land*, and also Marduk, editor of the openly Communist periodical
Al-Sharq (The East) which is published with Soviet support. Their concern is
the 'people' and the life of the people.

Finally there are also intellectuals who write in classical Arabic. This is the
group of the famous but already somewhat old-fashioned generation of Taha
Husain, Tanfiq al-Hakim, and Albert Adib with his still flourishing magazine
Al-Adib. This is the generation of patriots with world-wide horizons who have
devoted their life's work to expressing the European world of ideas, classical as
well as modern and scientific as well as romantic, in the Arabic language.

Besides these there is a younger group of 'nationalist existentialists' who write
in Suhail Idris's periodical *Al-Adab*. There are the Iraqi 'realists' whose
periodical *Thaqafa Jadida* (New Culture) has begun to appear again and then
there are groups of 'young literati', for example, those who write in the magazine
Shi'r (Poetry).

In an exceedingly subtle analysis the French orientalist and sociologist
Jacques Berque has described all these Arab intellectuals as being under the
influence of 'Qalaq' (anxiety) ('L'inquiétude arabe des temps modernes', *Revue
des Etudes Islamiques*, 1958). 'Qalaq', explains Berque, has something to do
with the concept of incoherence—'quelque chose qui n'adhère plus à son
contour'. In the case of the modern intellectuals it is the unrest and anxiety
which have been caused by the destruction of the firm bonds of Islamic life.

'The men of letters, the *Udaba*, feel more subtly and express more actively
those things which drive and move the masses. For this reason they are even
better at explaining and testifying than our own intellectuals are. The very
moment a national demand achieves its end, new discussions begin, all the more
violent and cruel since, if I may say so, they are not the result of a natural
development but break out abruptly, with the force of a revelation; revelation
of the social struggle or economic necessities, for example. An Arab and, above
all, an intellectual, questions himself in his very being. His real strength, his
strength which belongs to the present day, lies in his inner tension, in his
values, the values of a sundered existence. His strength is his cry.'

Can some general direction be seen in this ground swell of 'unrest'? At least
one thing is already clear. The true intellectuals are moving away from the past.
In many instances this movement is being masked and overlaid by nationalism
but when one comes to the intellectual *élite* of the Arab world one finds that
their special kind of unrest is following the same lines as the unrest of the rest

of the world. To be sure, 'socialism' and 'existentialism' are both given a specific Arab accent according to the cultural climate of the country, but the basic themes occupying creative Arabs are nevertheless 'socialism' and 'existentialism', not 'Modern Islam' and 'Arabism'.

The two motifs which, according to Berque's analysis, characterize the present are humanism and history. *Man* appears as the goal and meaning of life. But what sort of man, the collective or the individual one? The Arabs have not yet made up their minds on this. The importance of *history* is growing because man no longer uses God's commandments, God's eternal order and God's Book as criteria of his values. So he turns and asks history: What is man, that being for whom and through whom the World appears to exist?

The Arabs have three attitudes to history, two of them not very fruitful: idealization and denial.

Idealization is the attitude of the great majority of nationalists while one of the temptations which Communism offers to young Arabs is its promise to liquidate a history of which they are ashamed. The third and only fruitful attitude is objective criticism of history. Only this can tell us what and how certain people were at certain times. This true consideration of history, Berque believes, 'is acquiring stronger and stronger characteristics and is developing its possibilities. Yet it cannot be said that it has been definitely achieved.'

Still less can the existence of the Arabs be considered assured. But the fact that this unrest exists, that the 'cry' can be heard, that people are searching and demanding earnestly and urgently, means for the external observer that he would be most unfair to prejudge this world which is akin to his own and yet so different. And the visitor from the West would do well to remember that, in this present day and age, he, too, is a seeker in his own world even though for the moment he perhaps enjoys the advantage of being able to recognize and name here the outline of a peak on the horizon and there a signpost set up by those who have gone before him.

7

Postscript

THE AGREEMENT TO FEDERATE the three Arab states, Egypt, Syria and Iraq, concluded in Cairo on 17 April 1963, seemed fundamentally to change inter-Arab relations. But it had not been concluded before inter-Arab quarrels on the lines of the previous alignments reappeared. The two governing powers, Nasser in Egypt and the Baath Party in Syria and Iraq, saw eye to eye with regard to a future Arab policy; it was to be socialist, pan-Arab and 'democratic'. But 'democracy' was to mean 'Freedom for the people but no freedom for the enemies of the people'. The quarrel came to be about who was 'the people' or their 'real representative' and who was to be permitted to define 'the people'. Nasserites claimed that they represented 'the masses' and in Syria they could in fact mobilize 'the street' in support of their claims. The Baath proclaimed the true 'people' were not just the chaotic and unstable masses in the streets but the 'organized masses of the people in their popular organizations'; in the role of the potential organizer the Baath Party saw principally itself.

The whole quarrel soon boiled down to a power struggle in which ideological issues became secondary. The Baath could not bring itself to trust Nasser unconditionally—understandably so since, on the occasion of the previous union with Syria, the party had been dissolved and driven from power by the Nasserites. This time the Baath wanted some real position of power as a base from which to talk to Nasser as an equal. The *coups* in Syria and Iraq had lifted it to power and it was not ready to relinquish it. The Nasserites, principally in Syria, felt the great majority of the simple people behind them and showed themselves intent upon overcoming power by street demonstrations and conspiracies inside the army. They found themselves thwarted by the army which during the struggle between Nasserite and Baath officers inside its own ranks gradually moved away from Nasser by expelling some Nasserite officers after every unsuccessful attempt and committing itself in this way more and more to the anti-Nasser stand. Eventually the stage was reached when most officers had to fear for their future careers if Nasser should return to wield power over Syria.

In Iraq the Baathists were better entrenched than in Syria. They proceeded to monopolize power and formed their own militia, the National Guards. Nasserite newspapers were closed down and Nasserite political activity was stopped. On 25 May the Baathist government announced the discovery of a major 'conspiracy' which was ascribed to the different Nasserite groups in Iraq, and which was said to have aimed at 'plunging Iraq into a sea of blood'. Arrests were made and the property of the leading Nasserite politicians impounded. The heat of the attacks against the Nasserites was such that a break-down of the planned federation seemed almost inevitable. The Baath neverthe-less maintained their will to implement the agreements, but it seemed improbable that Nasser would agree to federation with countries where his partisans were persecuted and driven from power, even though they had brought such persecution on themselves by their own conspiratorial activities and methods.

With the rise of the Baathist governments in Iraq and in Syria, the position of the Communists in the Arab countries has changed. The Baath, even though ideologically close, are their mortal enemies, principally because of the long clandestine struggle between the two groups under the Qasim régime. Tension between the Soviet Union and the new Iraqi régime soon became visible and even found its expression in press polemics. In May the Iraqi government announced its intention of reverting to buying British armaments instead of Soviet weapons and aircraft.

Nasser, from having been the most anti-communist of the new Arab leaders, became the closest—relatively—to Russia. Iraqi students returned from Russia or became exiles; those who returned will have to learn English and switch over to American universities, their scholarships being financed by American foundations.

It would be wrong obviously to attribute much significance to such slight, purely tactical changes in the Communist position in the Arab Near East. What is much more significant and serious are the strategic advances Com-munist-style thinking and behaviour are making in the same region and at the same time. The absolutist governments, Baathi and Nasserite, aim at a Soviet-style state economy; their concepts of 'freedom' and 'democracy', their parlia-mentary style of pseudo-representation have been taken over from the Soviet political and ideological arsenal. American support, by helping Nasser to overcome the critical years of 1961 and 1962 economically and politically, has done a great deal to foster these developments. The breakdown of the last western-style and—in intention—really democratic government in Syria appears today as the watershed between 'democracy' and 'popular democracy' in the region. The quarrels will go on, but the small available capital of liberal thought and authentic democratic institutions, always scarce commodities in the region, will soon be entirely squandered.

Beirut, 26 May 1963

INDEX